Fodor's

E X P L O R I N G

IRELAND

FODOR'S TRAVEL PUBLICATIONS, INC.
NEW YORK • TORONTO • LONDON • SYDNEY • AUCKLAND

Second Revision 1996
First Edition 1994
Copyright © 1996 by The Automobile Association.
Maps copyright © 1996 by The Automobile Association.

Published in the United States by Fodor's Travel Publications, Inc.
Published in the United Kingdom by AA Publishing.

Fodor's and Fodor's Exploring Guides are registered trademarks of Fodor's Travel Publications, Inc.

ISBN 0-679-03008-5
Second Edition

Fodor's Exploring Ireland

Author: **Lindsay Hunt**
Series Adviser: **Ingrid Morgan**
Joint Series Editor: **Susi Bailey**
Copy Editor: **Hugh Chevallier**
Cartography: **The Automobile Association**
Cover Design: **Louise Fili, Fabrizio La Rocca**
Front Cover Silhouette: **Erick Lars Bakke/Black Star**

Special Sales

MANUFACTURED IN ITALY
10 9 8 7 6 5 4 3 2

Lindsay Hunt turned to travel journalism after a career in publishing and a year spent sampling *tapas* in Spain. She has traveled extensively and researched many destinations for *Holiday Which?* magazine. She has also written, edited and contributed to numerous hotel and travel guides, including books on Spain, France, Germany, Italy, and Florida.

*Glencolumbcille,
County Donegal*

How to use this book

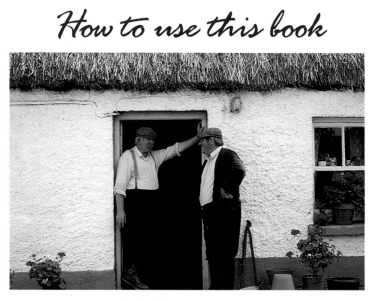

This book is divided into five main sections:

❏ Section 1: *Ireland Is*

Discusses aspects of life and living today, from politics to boglands.

❏ Section 2: *Ireland Was*

Places the country in its historical context, and explores those past events whose influences are felt to this day.

❏ Section 3: *A to Z Section*

Is broken down into regional chapters, and covers places to visit, including walks and drives. Within this section fall the Focus-on articles, which consider a variety of subjects in greater detail.

❏ Section 4: *Travel Facts*

Contains the strictly practical information vital for a successful trip.

❏ Section 5: *Hotels and Restaurants*

Lists recommended establishments throughout Ireland, with a brief description of each.

How to use the rating system

Most of the places described in this book have been given a separate rating:

▶▶▶ **Do not miss**

▶▶ **Highly recommended**

▶ **Worth seeing**

Not essential to see

Map references

To make the location of a particular place easier to find, every main entry in this book has a map reference. This includes a number, followed by a letter, followed by another number, such as *176B3*. The first number (*176*) refers to the page on which the map can be found, the letter (*B*) and the second number (*3*) pinpoint the square in which the main entry is located. The maps on the inside front cover and inside back cover are referred to as IFC and IBC respectively.

Contents

This quick-reference guide highlights the features of the book you will use most often: the maps; the introductory features; the Focus-on articles; the walks and the drives.

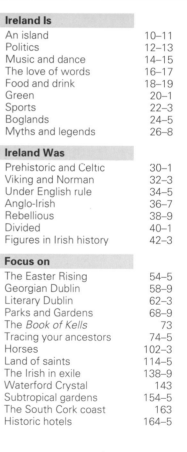

The Print Room, Castletown House, County Kildare

7

Lord Killanin
One of the most widely known Irishmen of his generation, Lord Killanin has had a career embracing journalism, the army, movie-making, business and sports administration. Educated in Britain and in France, he holds honorary degrees from the National University of Ireland and the University of Ulster. He came to international prominence as President of the International Olympic Committee from 1972 to 1980.

My Ireland

by Lord Killanin

The Ireland that most people read about in their papers is riven with sectarian divisions which visitors are (rightly) warned to be careful how they discuss. The Ireland which greets their eyes is a very different place. The soft, glowing beauty of a magical countryside, the stylish architecture and vigorous life of the towns, the charm and wit of a warm-hearted population—these make the first impact. To them add the visual and practical importance of water.

Ireland has some 3,100 miles of main coastline, jagged with indentations, cluttered with coves and rocks, studded with smaller islands, green or bare. The famous Aran sweater was originally designed for the sad purpose of identifying the bodies of drowned fishermen—a different pattern for each family. The waters of springs and rivers play their part in the distillation of Irish whiskey and the making of stout, two other ingredients of Irish life by no means to be disregarded.

My family has been in Galway since the 14th century, so naturally I think first of the sea, but my career has brought me into contact with almost every important facet of Irish life, from racing and the Gaelic games (handball, Irish football, and hurling) to film-making and preserving the national heritage. I have seen changes, not all for the better (like the peculiar form of bungalow bliss spreading across the countryside), but let me end with a reassurance. The Irish, whether from the North or South, and of whatever religion or none, are agreed on one thing: that they are Irish, and nothing else. As such, whoever you are, they will give you a warm welcome.

My Ireland

by Joss Lynam

Can I separate Ireland from the Irish? Perhaps as a walker who loves solitude, I can. Alone from a Connemara summit I can enjoy a near aerial view of pale yellow beaches, surf-fringed islands and cloud shadows stippling the horizon-edged sea; from a nearby summit, I see glistening quartzite peaks, dark lakes and green and brown valleys. There are other landscapes; strangest is the Burren of County Clare, bare gray limestone, concealing in its fissures the most beautiful flowers in Ireland. Wildest perhaps are the rounded coastal hills of North Mayo and Donegal, cut off in great shattered cliffs dropping suddenly to the sea, with remnant stacks to show the angry power of the waves.

But I'm choosy; the Cliffs of Moher are diminished, made almost commonplace by the crowds. *My* Ireland demands solitude, or at most few and congenial companions, if I'm to savor to the full the awe, the fear, the joy, the excitement of the wonderful surface, shape and colors of our island.

But my Ireland is people too. Our hospitality and friendliness is a cliché, its truth only slightly dented by the vandals and thieves which, like every nation, we have to shame us. I've lived in many parts of the world, met many delightful people of many countries, but there is still something uniquely pleasurable in drifting into the welcome of an Irish pub.

Joss Lynam
Born in 1924, Joss Lynam has been climbing and walking all his life. Apart from many expeditions to the Himalayas and other great ranges, he has walked extensively in Ireland. He has written or edited many guidebooks to the Irish mountains, including *Irish Peaks*. Though born in London, his family is also from Galway, and he knows the mountains of Connemara and South Mayo perhaps better than anyone. He has been Chairman of the Cospoir Long-Distance Walking Routes Committee for some years.

IRELAND IS

Many of Ireland's charms are perfectly straightforward. Visitors head there for the spectacular scenery and the warmth of the people—and to find peace of mind, despite the Troubles. Ireland's real fascination, though, is its ability to confound people's preconceptions. The Irish can be as unpredictable as their country's fickle weather, changing in a moment from gregarious to taciturn, or from solemn to profane.

10

One island Is it one place or two? One part evokes all things green and Gaelic; the other is an outpost of the U.K. To enjoy Ireland, you need barely be aware of this division. On both sides of the border are glorious landscapes, friendly people, and plenty of good pubs. On one side the mailboxes are Irish green, on the other red, and for tourists (except in Belfast, perhaps) few other differences are apparent. There is certainly no need to feel anxious about visiting the North. Statistically, Northern Ireland is one of Europe's safest places.

On the edge of the island perches Dunluce Castle, in County Antrim

Landscapes Ignoring the boundary, then, there are 32 counties of Ireland, each with its own distinctive character. Though at a glance Ireland may seem universally damp, mild, and green, with no very high mountains and little variation of climate or landscape, it has more variety in its small confines than many larger countries. The scenery varies from rural pasturelands cut by many rivers, through wild boglands and low-lying hills, to the most spectacular mountain scenery (mostly in the west and north) sweeping down to the sea in high cliffs and craggy promontories. Offshore lie many islands, some of which are inhabited or contain ancient forts and ruined monastic

settlements; several others are bird sanctuaries.

The commonest of Irish rocks, limestone, produces great systems of porous caves, some containing stalactites and stalagmites. Volcanic activity created the highlands of the North, and the extraordinary crystalline formations of the Giant's Causeway in County Antrim. The surface of the land was glaciated during the last Ice Age, leaving classic geological features such as U-shaped valleys, corries (circular hollows), tarns (small lakes), and eskers (long, winding ridges).

Social conditions Recently, great improvements have been made to many of Ireland's roads. Those in the North are financed by U.K. investment; in the Republic vast sums have been acquired in the form of European Union (E.U.) Regional Development Fund grants as part of a scheme to help the poorer countries of the E.U. (of which Ireland is one). Funds have also been allocated to many other projects in the North and South to develop tourism and other industries. One of Ireland's continuing struggles since the 18th century has been against economic depression and unemployment, and

The pace of life is noticeably slower to the west of the Shannon

the resulting departure of many of its most energetic and talented citizens abroad. The population has fluctuated considerably, its fecund Catholic communities producing many large families, even though they often put off marriage until late in life, especially in rural areas. Ireland now has about five million inhabitants, with a higher proportion of young people than virtually any country in Europe.

For visitors, though, Ireland still seems pleasantly old-fashioned, retaining a gentle pace of life and a generous allocation of time for almost anything—something that has been lost in so many places. Not that it is ever boring. The sociable and lively Irish are always ready to strike up a conversation, play some music, or buy the next round of drinks.

If you have little time to spare, the best bet for a trip to Ireland is a short break in Dublin, combined with excursions to the Wicklow Mountains, or perhaps the Boyne Valley and the antiquities of Newgrange. If you have longer, head west for Connemara, Cork, Kerry, or Donegal. Longer still, see the rest of the country, including its great monastic sites and grand houses. For extensive touring, you definitely need your own transportation—a car, possibly a bike or even a horse-drawn caravan. You can also explore much of Ireland from a boat on its huge inland waterways.

"If you think you understand Ireland," some legendary wit once remarked, "you've been sadly misinformed." And indeed almost every aspect of Irish life is full of contradiction. That rule also applies to its politics, which are inextricably entwined with religion.

Paradoxes Certain elements of Irish political history may strike an outsider as somewhat contradictory:
● Anti-English feelings have long been associated with Ireland's Catholic majority, but some of Ireland's greatest nationalists (or at any rate critics of the English as Irish overlords) have been Protestants, some from English backgrounds. Examples of such men include Jonathan Swift, Henry Grattan, Wolfe Tone, Robert Emmet, Charles Stewart Parnell, W. B. Yeats, and even William Gladstone. Two of the Republic's presidents have been Protestants.
● Both the Pope and the King of Spain supported Protestant William III's cause at the Battle of the Boyne, not the Catholic Jacobites (see page 36 for more details of this).
● Only about 2 percent of the Republic's population are

Ministerial buildings next to Leinster House, seat of the Irish Parliament

Protestants, yet many of its most important churches are actually Church of Ireland (Protestant), including both of Dublin's cathedrals.
● Northern Irish Unionists, far from being in line with the U.K., are often in bitter opposition to London. While British politicians have met, talked, and reached amicable agreements with the Republic's leaders, the Unionists, thus far, have adamantly rejected all compromise.

Ireland's constitution The Republic of Ireland's constitution operates under a prime minister (*Taoiseach*), two chambers (senate and assembly), and a president (who is largely a ceremonial figurehead). Its main political parties sprang up during or soon after the struggle for independence in the early 20th century. Since then, parliamentary power has been dominated by Fianna Fáil (Soldiers of Destiny), the party set up by Éamon de Valera in 1926. In 1933 its more liberal and moderate

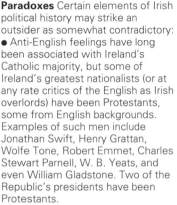

12

Mary Robinson, Ireland's first woman president

(though hardly left-wing) rival, Fine Gael (Tribes of Gaels), appeared. Roughly speaking, these parties mirror the positions taken by pro- and anti-treatyites during the Civil War; in other words, they either accepted (Fine Gael) or rejected (Fianna Fáil) Ireland's partition in 1921. Both parties have found it difficult to achieve majority rule recently, and the latest elections (based on proportional representation) resulted in an uneasy stalemate followed by behind-the-scenes horse-trading with minority socialist parties to form a workable coalition. The wild card is Sinn Fein, the political wing of the I.R.A. Originally founded in 1908 (making it older than any other party), it has achieved massive popular support at certain stages in its history, but now commands only a tiny fraction of Republican Irish

votes. Because its leaders have so far refused to denounce the violence of its paramilitary offshoot, the I.R.A., both Britain and Northern Ireland had been reluctant to negotiate with the party—until the ceasefire of autumn 1994.

A conservative mentality The winds of change are blowing through Irish politics, a notable event being the election in 1991 of a woman president (a possibility absolutely discounted by social historians only a few years before). Mary Robinson is a liberal attorney with known sympathies for certain issues (such as the liberalization of divorce laws) that currently perplex Ireland. The position of women in the Republic is much affected by the power of the Catholic Church and Pope John Paul II's reaffirmation of its doctrines on contraception, abortion, and divorce. Ireland ranks last among the world's developed countries in access to birth control (though the impact of AIDS has had a sharper effect than decades of religious dogma), and is alone in Europe in having no civil divorce. In 1992, the case of a 14-year-old girl made pregnant by rape and refused an abortion, or even permission to travel abroad to obtain one, hit world headlines and caused yet another complex referendum. Again, Ireland voted against liberalization of these laws.

Catholics complain justifiably of their lack of civil rights in Northern Ireland, yet the Republic's Protestants would also have an interesting case in any international court of human rights. Both sides of the border are far from a compromise—a concept still rejected by both staunch Loyalists and extremist Republicans.

13

Ireland's musical traditions date back continuously over many centuries, but the current scene is exceptionally lively, with a new interest in popular folk music encouraged by tourism. Irish musicians figure prominently in rock and country-and-western groups, and some Irish virtuoso performers, such as James Galway, have become world famous.

A Celtic tradition The poems and stories related by Gaelic bards at court were often accompanied by music, most typically played on the harp, Ireland's national emblem. The 12th-century historian, Gerald of Wales, praised the deftness of Irish fingerwork, and the expertise of Irish harpists was recognized as far afield as Renaissance Italy. After the Battle of Kinsale (1601), the great Gaelic clan houses declined, along with their patronage of the arts. Music was perceived by the ruling English as potentially dangerous, arousing nationalist sentiments, and it was suppressed along with other aspects of Irish culture. Musicians became itinerant, traveling from house to house to seek their fortunes at the hands of the new aristocrats; the

The tradition of live folk music lives on in countless Irish pubs

blind harpist, Turlough O'Carolan (1670–1738), was the most celebrated exponent of this tradition. The 18th century witnessed a new flourishing of musical talent in Dublin's Anglo-Irish circles, mostly influenced by European developments; Handel's *Messiah* was performed for the first time in the capital in 1742, conducted by the composer.

Meanwhile, traditional music continued to be played in Gaelic households. The ancient styles were either plaintive melodies with no distinct rhythms (possibly inherited from Spanish or North African cultures), or brisk, lively dance tunes. In 1792 a great harp festival held in Belfast aroused interest in more traditional Irish forms, and folk tunes increased in popularity. The lyric ballad, with words by such poets as Thomas Moore set to music, was sung in elegant drawing rooms throughout

Ireland. Many budding musicians left their native land, as did writers, to seek fame in England. John McCormack, the famous lyric tenor, spent most of his life in the United States (see page 240).

Irish instruments Most distinctive of the instruments used in Irish music, besides the harp, are the *uilleann* (elbow) pipes, a relative of the Scottish bagpipes but with a more elegiac tone particularly suited to reflective Irish tunes. The violin (simply called the fiddle in Ireland) is held casually on the shoulder and played with only a small section of the bow. Expert Irish fiddlers are technically highly skilled, however; Fritz Kreisler is said to have declared that if he practiced for a thousand years he would never be able to play as well as the Sligo fiddler, Michael Coleman. The *bodhrán* is one of the most ancient Irish instruments, a goatskin drum played with a small stick. Wind instruments include the famous tin whistle (no mere toy to a skilled player) and the flute, whose capacities have astounded worldwide audiences in the hands of the modern exponent, James Galway.

The modern scene In the 20th century Irish music has played an important role in the revival of nationalist sentiment and has achieved enormous popularity. The most usual venues to hear it are *ceilis*, where whole communities gather to dance and make music, or pubs, where *seisuns* (sessions) are held all over Ireland. The popularity of Irish music is unquestionably affected by tourism, sometimes losing both its dignity and its authenticity in the process. In the summer, when an audience is guaranteed, every pub seems to offer musical happenings. Out of season, however, they may be quite difficult to find. Doolin in County Clare is a particularly well known mecca for groups of musicians. Other forms of music are

In Ireland, as in the Celtic areas of Britain, dance lives on as an important facet of life

15

encouraged at major festivals—opera at Wexford, light opera at Waterford, and jazz at Cork.

One of the most influential figures in Irish music in modern times was Seán O'Riada, former director of music at the Abbey Theatre, Dublin. Though classically trained, his main interest was folk music, which he greatly popularized. His group, Celtóiri Chualann, was a forerunner of the world-renowned Chieftains. The tradition continued through groups such as the Clancy Brothers and the Dubliners. Other groups took a different line of hard rock, notably Bob Geldof's Boomtown Rats, U2, Hothouse Flowers, and the Pogues. Individual performers have also hit the charts—Van Morrison, Chris de Burgh, Enya, and Sinéad O'Connor.

no one pals *The daylight* *Loiterer bene a* *ith lips of b* *wif* *Oscar*

The Irish are famously articulate. From the loquacious Celts, alleged by the Greek traveler Strabo (writing around the time of the birth of Christ) to be fond of "wordy disputes" and "bombastic self-dramatization," through that master of empty promises, the Earl of Blarney, to today's garrulous stage Irishman, words have been a constant source of delight—sometimes at the expense of action. The peerlessly eloquent Oscar Wilde said, "We are the greatest talkers since the Greeks—but we have done nothing."

A prolific streak The Irish have written much; Ireland's contribution to English literature in all its forms—poetry, drama, novels, essays—is colossal, considering the size of its population. It seems as strong today as ever, with new talents bursting on to the stage and filling bookshop shelves with new novels and poems, while, in more ephemeral media, Irish eloquence commandeers hours of airwave time and reams of newsprint. Three writers have won Nobel prizes (W. B. Yeats, George Bernard Shaw, and Samuel Beckett). Both speech and writings take innumerable forms, but are characterized by a

Jonathan Swift, satirist and cleric

❏ Ogham script was used in Ireland from about the 4th century, but was eventually superseded by the Roman alphabet introduced by Christian missionaries. It continued to be used until after the 8th century. It was written as a series of scratched lines, and most usually appears on commemorative standing stones or monuments. Its uses for practical purposes were very limited. The key to interpreting the characters is the *Book of Ballymote*, written in 1391 in Sligo. Examples of ogham stones can be found in several places; there is a good one in the church at Killaloe (Clare) and another two in the abbey ruins of Ardmore (Waterford). ❏

natural flamboyance, passion, and wit, coupled with idiosyncrasy. Much of the inspiration comes, inevitably, from the tensions generated by persecution and oppression.

The Gaelic heritage Besides Ireland's outpourings in English, it has a rich Gaelic tradition. At various periods during the imposition of English rule, the Gaelic language (now mainly referred to as "Irish") was suppressed. After independence, strenuous attempts were made to revive it; indeed it was declared an official language. Éamon de Valera wanted to use it for political reasons, to assert Ireland's separate identity from Britain. Ireland's first president, Douglas Hyde, was a distinguished Gaelic scholar who

Samuel Beckett

loved the native language for its own sake. Despite compulsory schooling in Gaelic and regular radio and television broadcasts, the use of Gaelic as a first language has dwindled to a few areas largely in the West, and there is now little writing in Gaelic.

Anglo-Irish writers The first flowering of Anglo-Irish literature occurred during the late 17th and 18th centuries. Jonathan Swift (see page 62) was the giant of the age, publishing savage satires to expose the hypocrisy and injustice of life under English rule. In a lighter vein, Oliver Goldsmith, R. B. Sheridan, William Congreve, and George Farquhar entertained English upper classes with their lively comedies of manners. Edmund Burke wrote philosophical and political essays in elegant prose complex enough to win present-day admirers from the whole political spectrum.

Irish writing in the 19th century came thick and fast, from George Moore and Maria Edgeworth's sharply observed novels about the Irish "Big House," such as *Castle Rackrent*, to Shaw, Oscar Wilde and Yeats toward the end of the century, and even Bram Stoker, who introduced the world to Dracula. Anthony Trollope, though born in England, wrote many of his novels while working in Ireland; some, such as *Phineas Finn*, have Irish characters.

The tradition lives on In the 20th century, Irish writing has reflected the turmoil of independence, and a long twilight of censorship. Modern Ireland out-pruded the English Victorians, sending many great writers into self-imposed exile (James Joyce and Beckett are the two outstanding examples); J. M. Synge's and Seán O'Casey's plays caused riots in Dublin. Novelists and poets have proliferated within and without Ireland, however. Patrick Kavanagh, the late Louis Macneice, and Seamus Heaney are among its best-known modern poets; Molly Keane, Edna O'Brien, Brian O'Nolan (Flann O'Brien), Christy Brown and Roddy Doyle are popular novelists. Frank O'Connor, Seán O'Faoláin, Mary Lavin, and Liam O'Flaherty perfected the art of the short story, and talented modern dramatists include Brian Friel, Hugh Leonard, Billy Roche, and Frank McGuinness. The writer Christopher Nolan won great acclaim for his poems, *Damburst of Dreams*, and his novel, *Under the Eye of the Clock*.

The formidable George Bernard Shaw

17

In today's Ireland, it seems almost impossible to imagine the grim days of the 19th century when so many of the population starved, or that, in those days, many poor people had no clue how to prepare any food other than boil a potato. Nowadays, it is quite possible to eat both well and heartily all over the island.

Changing tastes Tourism has made a vast difference to the standards of cuisine in Ireland. Until recently, there was hardly any tradition of eating out in many districts, except perhaps on very rare occasions at a local hotel. Patterns of diet were conservative, based firmly on "meat and two veg" (somewhat overcooked), potatoes (of course), and large quantities of dairy fat. Now things are very different. Tourist demands for predictable, inexpensive fast food are met, as everywhere, with hamburgers and pizzas—a better bet being fish and chips. But more sophisticated tastes have introduced organic foods and vegetarian restaurants (almost unheard of before), and a vast number of new eateries, often French in style, have opened in the main tourist centers. Food "events" such as Kinsale's Gourmet Festival or Galway's Oyster Festival arouse great interest. With V.A.T. at its present rates (as much as 21 percent for luxury goods), eating out in Ireland is expensive, particularly if you like a drink with a meal. Casual (but respectable) dress is the norm just about anywhere.

One of the best meals in Ireland (as in Britain) is breakfast. A "traditional Irish breakfast" (or the "Ulster fry" north of the border) is a brimming plateful of bacon and eggs with soda and potato breads. Accommodation rates are nearly always quoted with a full breakfast included, so you might as well fill up for the day and get your money's worth!

A traditional—and substantial— Irish breakfast

Irish cuisine Whatever Irish cuisine lacks in finesse, it nearly always makes up for in copiousness, and ingredients are of a high quality. Home-grown produce includes rich dairy foods, beef, lamb and pork, a fascinating range of new Irish cheeses, and a great variety of seafood, shelled or finned. One of its great specialties is bread. Traditional Irish soda bread made with buttermilk, eaten fresh and warm, is a banquet in itself, and is automatically proffered at every meal. At midday, a basket of Irish bread, a bowl of seafood chowder, and a glass of Guinness makes a cheap and completely satisfying lunch.

Recently there has been a welcome return to simple, hearty Irish food such as Irish stew and potato dishes. Try colcannon (potatoes with onions and white cabbage), champ (potatoes mashed with butter and chopped chives) or coddle

(potatoes with bacon and onions). Black puddings use up those bits of pig not usually found on the dinner table. At teatime, try barm brack, a delicious sweet tea bread with dried fruit and spices.

Fish can easily be found in most of Ireland, and you don't have to be rich or posh to enjoy oysters here. If you're adventurous, try dulse or carrageen (types of seaweed), used to make various desserts—a change from the usual apple pie and ice cream.

Whiskey and stout All alcohol (especially in the South) is highly taxed and expensive, although measures of spirits are larger than in the U.K. Take

If you wish to order half a pint, ask for a "glass"

advantage of your duty-free allowance if you like a drink. Pubs, though, are more than mere boozing sheds; they are the social heart of many communities and often full of life and atmosphere especially if there is some music. Pub food is rarely very imaginative, but you can usually get snacks at lunchtime, and coffee all day. At some stage every visitor should try Ireland's "nectar," Guinness (see panel on page 56). Some consider it tactless to request Scotch in an Irish pub—try the local Bushmills, Powers, or other Irish brands, straight or with a splash of plain Irish water. It is also delicious in Irish coffee, or in one of those creamy liqueur concoctions. The local lager is Harp (brewed by Guinness). If you prefer something akin to English bitter, ask for Smithwicks Ale.

Not for nothing is Ireland called the Emerald Isle. Its greenness is legendary, the stuff of postcards and purple prose—and of course the national color. As one travels through the island, landscape after landscape seems to scorch the retina with that vivid Kelly green that almost hurts.

❑ "Wearing of the green" takes place on St. Patrick's Day (March 17), when Irishmen and women all over the world join in national celebrations to commemorate their country and their patron saint. The largest festivities and grand parades are held in Dublin. Traditionally, everyone on that day wears a shamrock, Ireland's national emblem. This cloverlike plant is alleged to have been used by St. Patrick to illustrate the nature of the Trinity to King Cormac at Cashel. ❑

In a few remote areas old farming methods are still employed

The color of Ireland In places Ireland is chocolate brown or almost black—the color of stripped bogland, glinting with clear pools that mirror the sky. It is gray with mist or cloud, with the wan limestone of the Burren and the lace of stone walls. It is splashed with yellow furze, scarlet fuchsia, or purple heather. Most of all, though, it is green, a verdancy induced by frequent rain and the tempering effects of the Gulf Stream.

Ireland is still a predominantly rural country, with few mineral resources and little heavy industry. For centuries, the main changes to its land-scapes were brought about by farmers who cleared the primeval oak woods and drained the peat bogs to make pastureland. Sheep, cattle, oats, and barley have been raised on its fertile soils since neolithic times. Later, crops such as potatoes and flax have waxed and waned according to the vagaries of economics, and recently the rate of change has accelerated, particularly since Ireland's membership of the European Union (E.U.). Agricultural grants flood into Irish farmers' pockets, enabling them to introduce more intensive methods of production. The use of artificial herbicides and fertilizers is growing, causing pollution to wash into waterways, threatening wildlife. Compared with some other E.U. countries, however, the problems are minor. Ireland has done its best to attract "clean" industries, such as electronics and financial services, rather than the smoky mills of more industrialized nations.

Green concerns Nearly all of Ireland's original oak forests have long since been felled for fuel and building materials. New forestry is replacing some of these trees, but mainly (until recently) with non-native conifers. Many old Anglo-Irish estates are now in state hands as forest parks, and broad-leaved woodlands are being planted, sometimes on stripped peatlands. The exploitation of the bogs continued unchecked for many years, and large areas are virtually denuded. Boglands, however, are now recognized as a unique and irreplaceable habitat for many rare species.

Other threats to Ireland's wildlife are significant. Increased tourism means more disturbance of Ireland's wild places. The Office of Public Works has recently angered conservationists by proposing to construct visitor centers in sensitive areas such as the Burren, Boyne Valley, and Wicklow Mountains (court cases have forestalled two of these so far). Unfortunately, more places for people inevitably mean fewer places for wildlife.

A gold problem Another threat to the environment is the discovery of gold in Mayo, Galway, and the Sperrin Mountains of Northern Ireland. Gold has always been known in Ireland, of course—prehistoric peoples used gold for their ornaments—

but until recently it was thought to be uneconomic to extract it. The Croagh Patrick site in County Mayo is particularly sensitive, for it is both an area of scenic beauty and a site of great religious importance, where Saint Patrick is said to have banished the snakes from Ireland and where thousands of pilgrims gather annually. Prospecting for minerals disturbs the landscape and can threaten the surrounding area with serious pollution by heavy metals and cyanide.

Pink trout In certain coastal areas, puzzling signs have sprung up by the roadsides, depicting a fish, with the legend "Save the Sea Trout" emblazoned on it. This reflects a growing local concern about the effects of one of Ireland's fastest-burgeoning industries—fish-farming. The farming of salmon and trout in huge hatcheries in Galway and Donegal has affected wild populations in ways not yet fully understood. One theory is that vast numbers of parasitic sea lice among the farmed fish are debilitating the wild species. The fish on your plate is just as likely to have been reared artificially and fed pink-tinted hormones than swum the ocean and leapt waterfalls.

The greenness of Ireland, here seen on Mizen Head, County Cork

21

The passion for competitive sports and athletics of many kinds reaches unprecedented heights all over the Republic. Its specialist games such as hurling and Gaelic football draw capacity crowds and cause vast excitement. Soccer is also popular, thanks largely to the success of the Republic's national team, though Irish hopes were dashed at the 1994 World Cup in the United States.

The big match When there's a big match on, even the least enthusiastic sportsman or woman is condemned to know about it. Flags and banners of the colors of the competing county teams sprout all over the land, on telegraph poles and gateposts, from car windows and roof-tops. Switch on the radio for the news, and you will find nothing of importance has happened in the world—except the match. Needless to say, huge crowds cause boisterous disruption to everyday life (especially on the roads), and plenty of noise in the pub afterwards, but they are rarely the occasions of hooliganism once seen at British soccer matches. Highlights of the year are the All-Ireland hurling and football finals, held at Croke Park, Dublin, in September, where

The distinctly Irish sport of hurling

tickets are prized. In the past, however, Gaelic games were regarded as a focal point for nationalist sentiment, and were alternately discouraged or banned by English authorities and fostered by Republicans. In 1884 the Gaelic Athletics Association (G.A.A.) was formed in Tipperary to halt the spread of anglicized games and promote Irish ones. The organization, like the Gaelic League, was a fertile recruiting ground for political activists.

Rugby enjoys limited popularity, but is remarkable in that the national team represents *all* of Ireland, with southern nationalist playing alongside northern Unionist.

Hurling This fast and furious game has an ancient pedigree, dating back before the Christian era. The Ulster

champion Cuchulainn was renowned for his prowess at hurling, and teams of warriors are supposed to have played it for days on end. It is something like no-holds-barred lacrosse, played with an ash stick or "hurley" and a small leather ball—"sliotar." Players (15 a side) may strike the ball any distance and at any height, or carry it on the hurley. It's most popular in Cork and the west of Ireland, but also played in Antrim, almost exclusively by Catholics.

Gaelic football There are two types of football in Ireland (Gaelic and soccer), with minimal

support for the Gaelic game among Protestants. The ball is smaller than a soccer ball, and teams score one point by hitching the ball over the crossbar, or three by putting it into the goal below the crossbar. The game requires great physical strength and stamina.

Tourist activities As a tourist, you are unlikely to do more than watch these exciting pastimes, but there are splendid opportunities for exercise in many forms, especially golf, equestrian sports, cycling and fishing. There are about 300 golf courses throughout Ireland, some of international class or in wildly beautiful settings, especially in the North. Greens fees vary considerably. Many claim Ireland is an unparalleled fishing destination, both for the quality of the sport and its low costs. Sea fishing for shark is popular in some areas (such as Achill Island). Permits are necessary on privately owned waters (and on public waters in the North), and you need a national license for

rod-fishing for salmon or sea trout.

That other Irish passion shared by the British is racing (horses and greyhounds), and many towns have dogtracks or racecourses. Sailing centers are mostly in the Southwest, between Youghal and Dingle, with lake and river or canal cruising focused on Lough Derg, the River Shannon, the two Loughs Erne, and the Grand Canal. In May 1994 the restored Shannon–Erne waterway opened, enabling boaters to cruise all the way from Upper Lough Erne to the

Gaelic football it may be, but handling of the ball is allowed

mouth of the Shannon. Hiking is increasingly popular in Ireland. Many long-distance footpaths are now in place and more accessible open spaces are planned. In the meantime, take sensible precautions before setting out. Prepare for bad weather, take the best map you can find, and let someone know where you are heading.

Both Bord Fáilte and the Northern Ireland Tourist Board produce plenty of literature on specialist sports.

23

The bogs of Ireland once covered immense tracts of the central lowlands. To former generations, it must have seemed wholly inconceivable that they could ever disappear, or perhaps that it would matter much if they did. However, today's conservationists have recognized them as unique and precious ecosystems, and are racing to ensure that what little is left is preserved before they all vanish.

The formation of the bogs After the Ice Age, the saucerlike bowl that forms the center of Ireland lay awash with lakes. These gradually filled up with compost from lakeside vegetation and, eventually, peat accumulated because the microorganisms that cause decay cannot survive in these wet conditions. There are two main types of bog in Ireland. Blanket bog, composed of dead sedge and grass, develops to a depth of 20 feet in the wettest areas and is found mostly in mountainous parts of the West, or in the Slieve Bloom Mountains. Raised bog, consisting mostly of sphagnum moss, covers wider areas of the central plain, where rainfall is lower. This gradually builds up into a dome above the ground water and can reach depths of 40 feet.

Roundstone Bog, Galway, one of the last untouched bogs in Ireland

A vanishing landscape As a result of massive exploitation, the boglands have shrunk to a fraction of their original size. Ireland has almost no coal or oil reserves, so peat has always been used as fuel. In the past, turf (the Irish term for peat) was cut by hand, using a spade or *sleán*—many people still have "turbary rights" to cut turf on local bogs. The top layers of living plants are removed and replaced on the cut surface to encourage regeneration; as a result, the effects of cutting peat by hand were minimal.

In 1946 Bord na Móna (the Peat Development Authority) began mechanical digging, and now great tracts can be seen laid waste in black, sodden wildernesses, later replanted with coniferous timber. Peat moss from the surface layers is bagged up and distributed to garden centers, while peat from the lower levels is used for fuel—about a quarter of Ireland's electricity comes from peat. It has become obvious that if the present rate of extraction continues there will soon be none left, so some of the best bogs are now protected as nature reserves. About 10 percent of Ireland's land surface is peat bog, proportionally more than any other country save Canada and Finland.

A unique ecosystem Bogland flora is fascinating and very varied indeed. The only plants that can survive are highly specialized—some have roots reaching deep down through water-retentive mosses into a compost of half-rotted vegetation; other, fly-trapping plants supplement their diet with animal protein. Few mammals can survive true boglands, but rare

24

insects, flowers, and birds can be seen. The bogs are also of great interest to archeologists. Their virtually sterile environment preserves animal and vegetable matter—tree stumps, bog butter (see panel on page 239), even corpses have been pulled from the bog, virtually intact, after centuries.

Safety on bogs Walking on peat bogs can be dangerous. Some deep pools may be disguised by soft mats of vegetation. It is easy to get lost as there are few paths or visible landmarks. An insect repellant is useful at some times of year, and rubber boots are essential.

Best bogland attractions:
- **Peatland World** Lullymore, County Kildare (tel: 045 60133).
- **Peatlands Park** near Dungannon, Lough Neagh, County Armagh (tel: 01762 851102).

Re-creation of a bog village at Glenbeigh, County Kerry

- **Ceide Fields** Ballycastle, County Mayo (tel: 096 43325)—neolithic settlements preserved in bog.
- **Corlea Bog Visitor Centre** Kenagh, County Longford (tel: 043 22386)—pre-Christian timber track discovered beneath bog
- **Clonmacnois and West Offaly Railway** Shannonbridge, County Offaly (tel: 0905 74114)—5½ mile tour over bog.
- **Raised bogs**: Mongan and Clara (both County Offaly).
- **Blanket bogs**: Roundstone (County Galway), Owenduff (County Mayo), Slieve Bloom Mountains (County Laois).

For more information, contact the Irish Peatland Conservation Council, Capel Chambers, 119 Capel Street, Dublin 1 (tel: 01 872 2397 or 872 2384); the National Parks and Wildlife Service, Office of Public Works, 51 St. Stephens Green, Dublin 2 (tel: 01 661 3111), or in Northern Ireland, Peatlands Park (see above).

Myths and legends

The Irish tradition of storytelling can be traced back to the Celts, well before Christ, whose sagas of epic battles and great champions, gods, and supernatural events were passed down orally at firelit feasts, then transcribed by early monks in manuscripts such as *The Book of the Dun Cow* or *The Book of Leinster*.

Interwoven traditions Irish mythology is incredibly complex; different accounts of similar stories are often interwoven with other traditions, and echoes of other Indo-European legends can often be found—epic tales of Greeks and Romans, for instance, or biblical stories. At first the stories were not written down, but related orally as evening entertainment, which meant embroiderings in every telling. A trained *file* (Celtic bard) was expected to be able to relate about 350 full-length tales in poetry by

The Children of Lir, see page 236

heart, and would spend years learning his art. The early Christian fathers were the first to record these legends, sometimes interspersing it with their own material and turning Celtic gods into Christian saints (Saint Brigid is an example).

The Celtic revival Although bardic traditions declined under English rule, interest in Celtic legends revived sharply toward the end of the 19th century under the influence of writers such as W. B. Yeats and the rise of Irish nationalism. The leaders of the Easter Rising of 1916 were imbued with ancient myths, seeing themselves as heroes battling against dark forces of evil. Even today, paramilitary groups sometimes use mythological rhetoric to justify their violence.

Celtic mythology remained alive in rural Ireland until the age of television, with a storyteller in every parish; superstitions and tales of fairy folk and monsters still abound. Ireland's leprechaun is the best-known figure of popular lore—the little man in green mending shoes and guarding his crock of gold—while the banshee is a more sinister creature, a female spirit whose wailings are believed to portend a death. Places associated with ancient magic are often treated with great respect by country people, for fear of disturbing whatever spirits or fairies inhabit them.

Groups of sagas Irish sagas are classified in four main groups. The Mythological Cycle deals with pre-Celtic gods and heroes and their long-running and complicated struggles for supremacy; the Children of Lir is one of the best-known stories.

A romanticized depiction of Cuchulainn by E. Wallcousins

The Ulster Cycle contains the epic adventures of the Red Branch Knights of Navan Fort and their champion Cuchulainn, one of the most famous being the Cattle Raid of Cooley. The later Ossianic (or Fenian) Cycle revolves around another hero, Finn MacCool (Fionn mac Cumhaill), builder of the Giant's Causeway and Gráinne's betrothed. The Historical Cycle (or Cycle of Kings) recounts tales from various early Irish kings, and is similar to Malory's tales of Arthur. The Celtic "otherworld," *Tír na n'Og* (the Land of Eternal Youth, believed to lie somewhere on an island in the far West) figures in these sagas—the paradise every culture dreams of for its afterlife, where pain and suffering are no more.

The Cattle Raid of Cooley This was one of the first stories to be written down. Queen Maeve of Connaught became jealous of her husband's possessions, in particular his magnificent white bull. She tried to obtain the mighty brown bull of Cooley to match it, at first peacefully, then by force,

The Flemish cartographer Ortelius chose an east–west orientation for his 16th-century map of Ireland

invading with a great army. The hero of Ulster, Cuchulainn, defended the province alone, and after a huge struggle, defeated Maeve's army. But he was mortally wounded, and died strapped to a stone pillar, facing his enemies.

Gráinne and Diarmuid The beautiful Gráinne was betrothed to the aging hero, Finn MacCool, but fell in love instead with the handsome Diarmuid. They eloped, taking refuge under dolmens. Eventually, Diarmuid was killed by a boar on the slopes of Benbulben Mountain in Sligo. The story has clear parallels with Tristan and Isolde.

Cuchulainn, Hound of Ulster At the age of five, Setanta, nephew of King Conor, set out to join his uncle's court, taking his hurling stick and ball with him to play on the way. At a banquet held in the house of Culainn, he was attacked by a great mastiff guard dog. Setanta hurled the ball down the beast's throat and killed it. Culainn was glad he was safe, but distressed at the death of his dog, asking "Who will guard my house now?" Setanta promised that he would take over the role of protector, and so found his new name— Cuchulainn, the Hound of Culainn, and champion of Ulster.

See panels on pages 215 and 238.

Biblical stories are carved onto 10th-century Muireadach's Cross at Monasterboice, County Louth

IRELAND WAS

Remnants of Ireland's prehistoric and early Christian past lie scattered throughout the island, although many are shrouded in mystery and still a puzzle to archeologists. The megalithic tombs of the Boyne Valley or the ornamental jewelry of early populations show clear evidence of highly sophisticated peoples.

Prehistoric Ireland The earliest inhabitants to have left traces of their existence probably arrived from Scotland in about 6000 BC or 7000 BC. These were hunter-gathering peoples who slowly adopted more settled lifestyles and advanced methods of farming as the Stone Age progressed. They wove cloth, made pottery, fished from coracles (simple boats), raised stock, and cleared trees to plant a few grains. One of the earliest settlements is Glenaan, in the Glens of Antrim, where flint ax heads have been found.

The clearest legacy of the Neolithic Age is burial places. Between 4000 BC and 2000 BC, many megalithic tombs (using large blocks of stone) were built. Most impressive are the passage tombs at Newgrange, but important sites can be found in Sligo and eastern Ireland (the court tombs of Creevykeel; dolmens, like those at Proleek; and wedge tombs, as at Labbacallee in County Cork). From the Bronze Age (1750 BC onward) came stone circles or mysterious single standing stones, such as those at Drombeg in Cork or Lough Gur in Limerick. Little is known of these people, but ancient lore terms them the *Fir Bolg* (Bag Men, because they carried fertile soil to rocky fields in large leather bags), a short, dark race who lived to no more than 30 or so.

The Celts In about 700 BC a new wave of invaders began to arrive on Irish shores; the Celts, a disparate group of tribes whose cousins can be found all over Europe. Driven west by the Romans, who called them *Galli*, they were known as *keltoi* by the Greeks, and became Gaels in Ireland. Their loose clan structures revolved around a leader or chieftain (*Taoiseach*—the word still used for Ireland's prime minister) who was elected rather than dynastic. As time progressed, leadership became more centralized under a single high king, though the idea of "nationhood" never developed fully in Celtic times; clans continued to live in isolated settlements of round huts, protected by sturdy defenses or by lake moats.

Celtic legacies Some aspects of Celtic culture seem to have filtered into the Irish character. The Celts were hospitable folk, who enjoyed feasting, music and storytelling. Their love of adornment is evident in the gorgeous jewelry they made—bands of decorated gold and other metals, of great artistry. Most of all they loved fighting—no mere internecine squabbles, but epic battles between warrior champions epitomized by the legendary heroes, Cuchulainn and Finn MacCool. Elevated into semi-divinities, the myths (perhaps the Celts' greatest legacy) tell of their great deeds, ringing with the clash of sword on shield, dripping with gore.

Drombeg Stone Circle, County Cork

They worshipped many gods, often adopting the sacred sites of past inhabitants for their rituals and royal residences (Tara is one of the most celebrated). Efforts to propitiate these gods were unsparing—vast quantities of treasure were heaped on the altars of the dead, and grisly sacrifices took place. One of the most chilling rituals was the "wicker man," a huge effigy of straw and wood filled with living creatures—men, women, children, animals—and set alight.

Beyond Roman rule Ireland is unusual in western Europe in having no Roman history. The Romans gazed across at the Emerald Isle, and

Tacitus wrote, somewhat airily, "I have often heard Agricola declare that a single legion, with a moderate band of auxiliaries, would be enough to finish the conquest of Ireland," but they never colonized it. (Cynics say that, if they had, the roads might have been better!) As it was, the Celts held sway in their piecemeal fashion through several Christian centuries. Some recolonized west Britain in the first centuries AD, joining with the native Picts to plague the Romans along Hadrian's Wall. These Irish Celts were known as Scots, some of whose descendants are the Protestant occupants of Ulster, now regarded by some extreme Nationalists as aliens.

PREHISTORIC AND CELTIC SITES

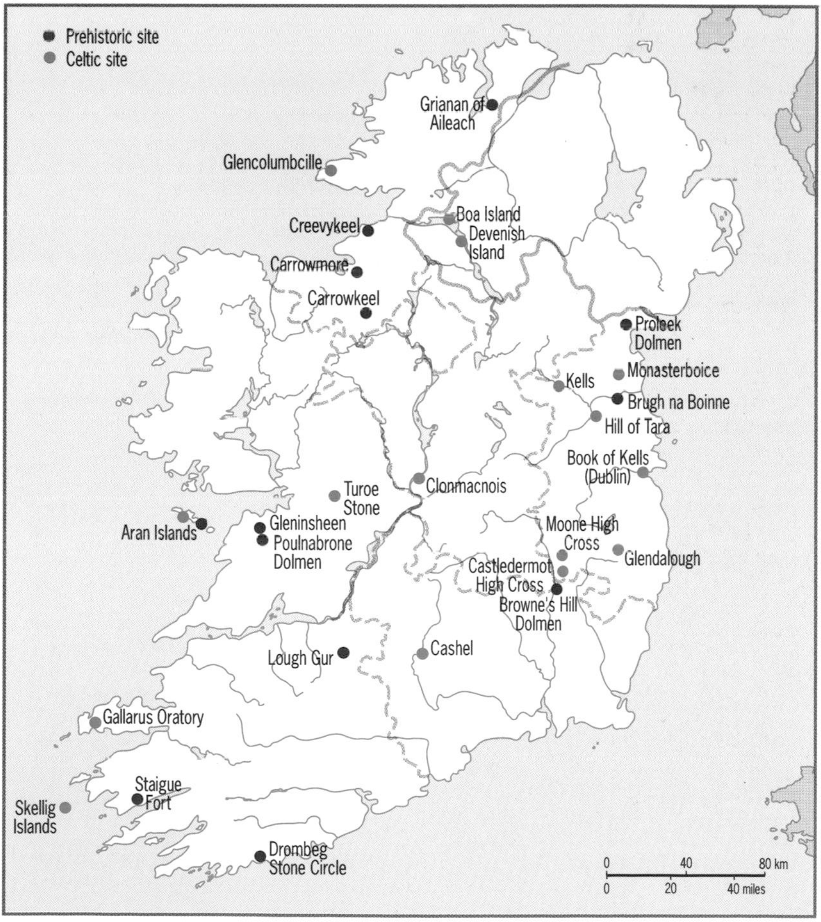

- Prehistoric site
- Celtic site

Grianan of Aileach
Glencolumbcille
Creevykeel
Boa Island
Devenish Island
Carrowmore
Carrowkeel
Proleek Dolmen
Kells
Monasterboice
Brugh na Boinne
Hill of Tara
Book of Kells (Dublin)
Turoe Stone
Clonmacnois
Aran Islands
Gleninsheen
Poulnabrone Dolmen
Moone High Cross
Castledermot High Cross
Glendalough
Browne's Hill Dolmen
Lough Gur
Cashel
Gallarus Oratory
Staigue Fort
Skellig Islands
Drombeg Stone Circle

| 0 | 40 | 80 km |
| 0 | 20 | 40 miles |

After the arrival of Christianity in the 4th century (some time before St. Patrick), Ireland enjoyed a golden age while the rest of Europe languished in the dark aftermath of the fall of the Roman Empire. Monasteries flourished as great cultural centers and Irish missionaries traveled back to mainland Europe to spread the Good Word.

Viking invaders The good times were not to last. From AD 795 pirate raiding parties began to attack Ireland's shores, envious of the riches of the Celtic monasteries. By AD 837 a wholesale Norse invasion was taking place, and this time the interlopers stayed. The native Gaels and monks built Round Towers as lookouts and refuges, and reinforced their simple wood or wattle dwellings and churches with hard stone. The Vikings caused immeasurable destruction and bloodshed as they arrived, but later settled into more peaceable habits, often intermarrying and becoming assimilated with the local population. Though illiterate, they had many skills, and founded sophisticated walled cities to defend the estuaries by which they had entered Ireland (Waterford, Wexford, Cork, Dublin, Limerick). They passed on their great knowledge of seafaring and boat building, established important foreign trade links, and introduced coinage. Some converted to Christianity. The Vikings were eventually routed at the Battle of Clontarf (near Dublin) in 1014 by the famous High King, Brian Ború. Unfortunately, a retreating Viking treacherously dispatched Ború after the battle, and Ireland's chances of becoming united under a strong leader receded again.

MacMurrough and Strongbow In one of the subsequent feuds, Dermot MacMurrough abducted the wife of a rival chieftain, Tiernan O'Rourke. The other clans turned on him. In retreat, with many of his lands and his Leinster throne lost, MacMurrough sought help from abroad. Henry II of England, already considering the conquest of Ireland, and with the support of the Pope (himself an Englishman), allowed MacMurrough to recruit from among his barons. Richard FitzGilbert de Clare, Earl of Pembroke, better known as Strongbow, was rewarded

Fearsome Strongbow now lies peacefully in Dublin's Christ Church Cathedral

The Anglo-Norman keep of Carrick-fergus Castle has walls 8 feet thick

for his timely aid with the hand of MacMurrough's daughter and great parcels of land. The Normans had arrived, and they stayed. In England, Henry II looked anxiously over his shoulder at these powerful adventurers and decided to assert his authority. He came to Ireland with his army and demanded allegiance from Irish leaders who, also fearful of MacMurrough and Strongbow, gave it. From then on, England was Ireland's overlord. Henry granted the province of Meath to his follower, Hugh de Lacy, and empowered him to act as deputy governor. English control radiated from the Dublin area, which later contracted to a small region about 30 miles north, south, and west of the capital, defended by an earth rampart, known as the Pale.

Norman rule Irish sub-kingdoms were established farther afield ("beyond the Pale"), enabling Gaelic rulers to hold sway as long as appropriate tributes were paid to England, and loyal support given in times of war. Needless to say, not all Ireland's inhabitants were content with such meek subjection, and many rebelled. Land was confiscated as punishment, leaving an enduring legacy of resentment among the Gaelic chieftains, and great English estates began to develop, based on the feudal manorial system. All the colonizers remained free; the Irish peasantry were serfs, tied to the land. Nonetheless, their lot in a productive estate under strong leadership may well have been happier than before. In 1177 John de Courcy invaded Ulster and conquered it swiftly. On Strongbow's death without heirs, Henry's son, Prince (later King) John, took over as Lord of Ireland. Anglo-Norman administrative structures of government and law were set up within Ireland, great castles were built and city walls strengthened. Outside the towns, clan chiefs and Norman lords protected themselves with tower houses, sometimes enclosed by a "bawn," a high wall with turreted corners.

Henry and his heirs consolidated their claim on Ireland by invoking heavenly allies and strengthening the position of the Church. The monasteries flourished anew, and many great churches and abbeys were built, emerging gradually from modest Romanesque to lofty Gothic as architecture progressed. The Irish Church was reorganized along Roman lines and continental monastic orders appeared—Augustinians, Cistercians, and Franciscans.

The Normans, like the Vikings, invaded with ferocity, but integrated with the local population surprisingly quickly. English rulers perceived a dilution of their influence as the distinctions between Anglo-Norman and native Gael blurred.

Catholic repression In 1366, one of the most repressive of attempts to subdue Ireland took place. The Statutes of Kilkenny aimed to quell the Anglo-Norman tendency to "go native." Irish citizens were prohibited from intermarrying with Normans, forbidden to enter walled cities, and their dress, language, names, and customs were outlawed. Like all such measures, they were doomed to fail, and Gaelic influence continued to grow until the Pale had dwindled to a small area immediately around Dublin, despite the construction of many more castles across Ireland.

While England was enmeshed in the Wars of the Roses (1455–1485), a powerful Anglo-Norman family, the Fitzgeralds, extended their influence over much of east and southeast Ireland. The Tudor kings, who gained the English throne after the war, saw the Fitzgeralds (warily) as allies. But when Henry VIII renounced the Catholic Church, handing out its land to his Protestant supporters, Lord Offaly of the Fitzgerald house of Kildare (Silken Thomas) staged an insurrection. Thomas was defeated and executed (see page 70), but the precedent was set for future stands against the English Crown. Henry tried to assert his overlordship, demanding that the mutinous lords surrender their property and assume vassal status. When they refused, he took their lands and gave them to the first Protestant "planters" from England and Scotland.

The Flight of the Earls In the latter half of the 16th century, the process

Fourteenth-century English settlers are brought provisions

THE Right Honorable and vndaunted Warrior OLIVER CROMWELL Lo: Governour of IRELAND

Cromwell in Ireland

of plantation continued under Mary I, a Catholic and then Elizabeth I, who fought four wars in Ireland in defense of the Reformation. Her aims were to assert the Protestant religion and to prevent any intrigues against England hatched by Ireland and Spain. The first plantation attempts were failures— more rebellions took place, led by the Desmonds of Munster, and more seriously, by Hugh O'Neill, Earl of Tyrone, a formerly compliant court protégé who had hoped to become Lord of Ulster. When he realized how little autonomy he would have under Elizabeth he joined forces with Red Hugh O'Donnell, Earl of Tyrconnell, and resisted. The final showdown came at the Battle of Kinsale (1601). Spanish reinforcements caved in under siege, O'Donnell fled to Spain where he met his death, and O'Neill was forced to sign the Treaty of Mellifont, unaware that Elizabeth I had died six days earlier. All the lands of the defeated chieftains were handed to planters from Scotland, encouraged to emigrate by James I. The proud O'Neill and Red Hugh's brother and successor, unable to accept their humbled status, left Donegal forever in 1607, in the sad exile known as the Flight of the Earls.

Plantation This cleared the way for more plantation, this time more successful. Ulster's new settlers were hard-working Calvinists, chalk to the Catholic cheese, and they have never integrated. They quickly made great improvements to the land they acquired, introducing advanced methods of agriculture. Many of the settlers were skilled craftsmen, bringing new talents to its workforce.

In 1641 the dispossessed Irish made another attempt to regain their lands, rebelling violently at Portadown and killing many Protestants. Gaelic leaders allied with the "Old English" Catholics to defend their faith, property, and political rights in the Confederation of Kilkenny. Meanwhile, in England, the Civil War began. Rumors of atrocities toward Ulster planters circulated, and in revenge, Cromwell brought over 20,000 Ironsides, storming Drogheda and Wexford, slaughtering thousands and sending many into slavery. Most Catholic landowners were dispossessed and banished west of the Shannon River ("to Hell or to Connaught," in Cromwell's phrase). When he had finished, much of Ireland was devastated and its Catholic population had dwindled to half a million, bitter beyond belief at English injustice.

35

The agony of Cromwellian times was briefly dispelled by the restoration of the Catholic Charles II in 1660, although he was never in a strong enough position to help Irish Catholics significantly. The dangerously pro-Catholic leanings of his successor, James II, precipitated the Glorious Revolution and William of Orange's accession. James II fled to France, from where he invaded Ireland for a last stand.

The Battle of the Boyne James II was initially successful at drumming up support in Ireland, but his ambitions were thwarted when he reached Derry. There the young trade apprentices slammed the gates of the city, and (London)Derry endured the longest siege in British history. The Protestant cause prevailed, but only after much suffering, which further polarized Anglo-Irish attitudes. In 1690 William III won his decisive victory over Jacobite (Catholic) forces at the Battle of the Boyne, and further conflicts took place at Athlone, Aughrim, and finally Limerick, where the Jacobite army eventually surrendered with honor. The Treaty of Limerick granted civil rights to Catholics, but the English reneged on it, to Ireland's everlasting disgust. Measures were taken to consolidate Protestant ownership of land and Catholic subservience.

William III senses victory at the Battle of the Boyne...

Penal laws A series of repressive laws were passed, collectively known as the Penal Code. This forbade Catholics to practice their religion publicly, or educate their children in the Catholic faith. They could not enlist for military service, buy land, or inherit it other than by equal division among all sons. Viable estates became useless divided parcels of land. If one child converted to Protestantism, he (or she—daughters were allowed to inherit in this case) would get everything! Land ownership by Catholics tumbled to about 14 percent by 1700, and Irish language, music, and literature were suppressed. Once again, opposition fanned the flames. "Hedge schools" (where teachers and pupils could hide) were run for Catholic children and Mass was said in secret, with members of the congregation acting as lookouts for English spies.

Georgian Ireland The 18th century in Ireland was peaceful and full of achievements—literary, artistic, and economic. Many of the great country houses of Ireland date from this time (naturally, these were for the Protestant settlers, not the native Irish). Greatest of all the architects of this period was Richard Cassels (anglicized as Castle, or Cassel), from a Protestant family who had settled in Germany (see panel on page 250).

Whole villages and towns were planned, with wide streets, tree-lined malls, and grand civic buildings. Domestic architecture excelled in Dublin, with dignified terraces and squares satisfying the new aspirations of the city-dwelling

middle classes. Comparatively few churches survive from Georgian times (in particular Catholic ones), but they generally followed neoclassical patterns inspired by Greek temples. Michael Stapleton and the Swiss-Italian Francini brothers were masters of stucco work, a popular medium in Ireland in the mid-18th century. Literature and music flourished (see pages 58–9 and 62–3), as did many applied arts, such as silverware and furniture making.

An attempt at reform The surface prosperity and success of the Anglo-Irish Protestant Ascendancy hid tensions seething among the underprivileged peasantry, many of whom lived in appalling conditions. The Catholics were not the only ones to suffer; Presbyterians were also disadvantaged, and during the 18th century many Ulster settlers emigrated

...while the vanquished James II flees from Irish shores

to seek their fortunes across the Atlantic. Protestants were irked by Westminster rule, and gradually a spirit arose in favor of more autonomy. The American War of Independence appealed to both Catholic and Protestant sentiment, and prosperous merchants ceased to equate their interests with those of England.

Henry Grattan, a Protestant barrister, was at the forefront of this movement. He entered parliament in the same year as the American Revolution began, declaring "the Irish Protestant could never be free until the Irish Catholic had ceased to be a slave." Westminster sat up and listened. In 1782, Grattan's Parliament was formed, an assertion of Irish constitutional independence. Some minor measures to alleviate the lot of Catholics were passed. Before any major achievements could be seen, the specter of the French Revolution intervened in 1789, and once again, England battened down the hatches of reform.

Ireland caught the prevailing revolutionary mood from France and, for a while, Dublin's inhabitants went around calling each other "citizen." In the countryside, violence grew as secret societies dedicated to overthrowing their oppressive landlords maimed horses, burned barns, and drove cattle over cliffs.

Religious tensions During the days of the Penal Code Irish Catholics had learned that dissimulation and evasion were necessities for survival. To follow their faith, they had to attend secret meetings and, as they had no redress in law, they took the law into their own hands. As Cecil Woodham-Smith says in *The Great Hunger*, "These were dangerous lessons for any government to compel its subjects to learn, and a dangerous habit of mind for any nation to acquire." After relaxation of the laws that had prevented them from owning land, many Catholics moved to Ulster, forcing up prices. The Ulster planters began to feel threatened, and formed their own ruthless organizations. A vigilante group called the Peep o' Day Boys attacked Catholics, burning them out in dawn raids and, in 1795, the Orange Order was formed to defend Protestant interests.

Emmet prepares for the insurrection which was to cost him his life...

Wolfe Tone and Robert Emmet In 1796, the radical Protestant barrister Wolfe Tone (see page 42) set up the Society of United Irishmen in Belfast. Initially it existed as a middle-class debating society, but after its suppression by Prime Minister William Pitt, it became seditious. Tone rallied support from France and attempted a naval attack on Bantry Bay (see page 151). After its failure, Pitt imposed martial law. United Irishmen were rounded up and publicly tortured to inform on their comrades, but fury at this led to open revolt, and in 1798 thousands took up pikes and rusty swords against the English soldiers. Over 30,000 died, and Tone was captured, later committing suicide in his cell before he could be executed.

All concessions to Catholics were withdrawn, and, on January 1, 1801, the Act of Union was passed, centralizing government in London. Initially the mood was buoyant; triumphant proclamations of equality were made

...and the life of the unfortunate Lord Kilwarden, caught up in the chaos caused by Emmet's uprising

for England, Ireland, Scotland, and Wales within the new legislative structure, but the high hopes were unfounded. English imports swamped the Irish economy and its industries collapsed. Ireland was now hopelessly divided between the impoverished Protestant ruling class and the dispossessed and powerless Catholics. Robert Emmet, a middle class Protestant, staged yet another abortive uprising of United Irishmen, and was hanged. His speech from the dock inspired future generations of freedom fighters.

Daniel O'Connell Twenty years later, a new inspirational force arose in the form of Daniel O'Connell (see page 42), known as the Liberator, who championed the cause of Catholic emancipation and the repeal of the Act of Union. Voting rights were granted to Catholics in 1829, but O'Connell's attempts to change Ireland's fate peacefully failed.

In the midcentury Ireland was struck down by the complete failure of the potato crop in 1845, 1846, and 1848. Terrible famine ensued, but the British did little to help; while Ireland starved for lack of potatoes, vast quantities of beef and grain were being exported to Britain. A million died, and a million emigrated.

Charles Stewart Parnell The next great figure on the political stage was Parnell (see pages 42–3), who campaigned openly for Home Rule and reform of the oppressive land tenancy laws. Gladstone's repeated attempts to introduce a Home Rule Bill were rejected by the House of Lords, despite a groundswell of support for it. More violence took place and in 1882 the British Chief Secretary and Under-Secretary for Ireland were stabbed to death in Phoenix Park. British opinion turned against Home Rule, and, by the turn of the century, the scene was set for the breakup of Ireland. The Sinn Fein party (meaning roughly "We Ourselves") was formed by Arthur Griffith in 1908, advocating secession from Britain. On the brink of war, Britain finally acceded to demands for Home Rule in 1914, but postponed it until hostilities had ceased. The Irish Republican Brotherhood (precursors of the I.R.A.), unable to wait, staged the Easter Rising in Dublin (see pages 54–5) in 1916; meanwhile in Ulster, the Orangemen prepared for battle.

Ireland's history since partition has been as tragic as it was before, at least in the North. At last, however, hopes are rising for a peaceful settlement. The I.R.A. ceasefire in 1994, followed by a wary resumption of negotiations—or at least talks about talks—has given the war weary province a welcome if fragile respite from its exhausting Troubles. Peace has paid a visit to the North, the people of Ireland hope that it has come to stay.

40

The Civil War In 1918 Sinn Fein, led by the Easter Rising veteran Éamon de Valera, won a massive 73 seats at the general election, and independence was declared at a meeting of the first Dáil Éireann (Irish Parliament). The Irish Republicans (now the I.R.A.) attempted to undermine British control, using guerrilla tactics, and British soldiers (the Black and Tans) were brought over to maintain order, which they did ruthlessly. Under the 1920 Government of

British Prime Minister, Lloyd George, left, meets de Valera in 1921

Ireland Act, separate parliaments were created for Northern Ireland (the Six Counties, which remained within the U.K.), and Southern Ireland, which was granted dominion status under Crown authority. The Anglo-Irish Treaty was signed in December 1921 by Michael Collins and Arthur Griffith. De Valera refused to accept its terms and Ireland was plunged into a disastrous and bloody civil war, a conflict between those willing to accept Ireland's partition and the rest. Many politicians, British and Irish, hoped that partition would be temporary, and that eventually the two sectors would unite peacefully when emotions ran less high. They failed to take account of Loyalist feelings in the North. Under Sir Edward Carson (see page 43), Protestant Unionists resolved to fight to the death to prevent being absorbed into the new Irish Free State.

Eire is born The new Ireland suffered badly in interwar depression, made worse by de Valera's poor relations with Britain. A tariff war with Britain made Ireland's stagnant economy virtually moribund. In 1937, political links with Britain were reduced, and the name of Eire was introduced. During World War II Ireland remained officially neutral, although its position was ambivalent. Over 50,000 citizens of the Republic enlisted voluntarily in the British armed services, but anti-British feelings were sufficiently strong to encourage some collaboration with Germany, too. Eire's refusal to order a blackout enabled the strategic target of Belfast to be pinpointed more easily, which caused many civilian losses. (Dublin was also bombed in May 1941.) De Valera, to his everlasting shame, was the only world leader to offer condolences to the Reichstag on the death of Hitler.

After the war, many people emigrated from Ireland, mostly young and talented, and ironically many of them chose Britain for their new home. The election of the forward-looking Sean Lemass in 1959 signaled a welcome break from the politics of Kilmainham Gaol, which de Valera had symbolized. Gradually, economic prosperity increased and Ireland's stifling doldrum of artistic censorship and priest-ridden Victorian morality began to lift. Ireland dropped the name Eire in 1949, and joined the European Community in 1972. After this immediate benefits were felt in agriculture, tourism, and the construction industry.

The Troubles continue The upswing did not improve relations with Britain or the North. In 1968 the civil rights movement began, demanding equality for Catholics. Demonstrations and marches provoked rioting on both sides;

The Irish delegation to the Anglo-Irish Treaty of 1921

Derry was a particular flashpoint. In 1969 British troops were sent to protect the Catholics, who were now barricaded in ghettos, but soon their protective role was perceived as an aggressive one. Just eight days after Ireland joined the E.C., 13 unarmed civil rights demonstrators were shot by British paratroopers (the event became known as "Bloody Sunday"). An angry crowd burned down the British embassy in Dublin, Stormont (the Northern Irish parliament) was suspended and the province came under direct rule from Westminster. The I.R.A. made a disastrously triumphant resurgence in a deadly new "Provisional" guise. The "Provos" differed from the "Official" I.R.A. in having as their only goal the overthrow of British rule in Northern Ireland, by whatever means necessary.

Since 1972, persistent attempts have been made to bring the two sides together. "Power-sharing executives" come and go, at Sunningdale in 1973, and at Hillsborough (the Anglo-Irish Agreement) in 1985. So far, intransigence on both sides has resulted in failure and a resumption of terrorist outrages in Ireland and the U.K. The latest initiatives, begun in 1994, offer renewed hope, but the search for a lasting peace in Northern Ireland remains an elusive, perplexing, and frustrating quest.

41

CHARLES STEWART PARNELL

NO·MAN·HAS·A·RIGHT·THE
BOUNDARY·TO·THE·MARCH·OF·A·NATIO
NO·MAN·HAS·A·RIGHT
SAY·TO·HIS·COUNTRY
US·FAR·SHALT·THOU
·AND·NO·FURTHER·

It is impossible to ignore Irish history as you tour the country. Its central figures (heroes or villains, depending on your point of view) keep cropping up. What follows puts just a few of them in context, and pinpoints one or two places closely associated with them.

Patrick Sarsfield, 1st Earl of Lucan (d. 1693). Hero of the 1691 Siege of Limerick, with 500 troops, he made a daring raid on William III's supply train at Ballyneety, destroying all his munitions. After the Treaty of Limerick was signed, he sailed to France (Flight of the Wild Geese), and died, fighting again, in Belgium. He was married in Portumna Castle (Galway).

Wolfe Tone (1763–1798) The father of Irish republicanism, this middle-class Protestant lawyer founded the United

Sir Edward Carson, as depicted in 1912

Irishmen in Belfast in 1791. After a period in America, he instigated two unsuccessful attacks using French naval support, at Bantry Bay in 1796 (see the Armada Exhibition at Bantry House, page 151), and in Donegal during the Great Rebellion of 1798. After capture at Letterkenny he was sentenced in Dublin to be hanged, drawn, and quartered, but cut his throat before it could be carried out, lingering in agony for seven days.

Robert Emmet (1778–1803) A disciple of Tone, Emmet staged an abortive revolt in 1803, planning to seize Dublin Castle. Emmet was sentenced to the same grisly death as Tone, whereupon he said, "When my country takes her place among the nations of the earth, then and not till then let my epitaph be written." Padraic Pearse, leader of the Easter Rising of 1916, paid tribute to his sacrifice.

Daniel O'Connell (1775–1847) Known as the Liberator, O'Connell was a witty, eloquent, and brilliant lawyer who gave up his career at the Bar to fight for Catholic Emancipation and the repeal of the Act of Union. Elected MP for Clare (1828), he won popular support, greatly alarming British authorities, although he always renounced violence. His house at Derrynane (Kerry) is a museum to his memory.

Charles Stewart Parnell (1846–1891) A political giant, Parnell (a Protestant) was born at Avondale House in Wicklow (see page 92). Elected MP for Meath in 1875, he campaigned tirelessly for Home Rule and agrarian reform. In 1877 he founded the Irish Land League with Michael Davitt.

42

Charles Stewart Parnell

He used peaceful tactics, favoring "filibustering" (disruption of parliamentary debates by long speeches) and "boycotting" (ostracizing oppressive landlords). His career ended in a scandal involving the wife of a fellow MP.

Sir Edward Carson (1854–1935) Champion of the Ulster Unionists and the architect of partition in 1921, Carson was a Dubliner, knowing little of Ulster or its people. A brilliant lawyer (defending Lord Queensbury at Oscar Wilde's trial), he organized resistance to Home Rule and Irish independence, founding the Ulster Volunteers, an armed band of Loyalists. He is buried at St. Anne's Cathedral, Belfast.

Dublin celebrates the release of Daniel O'Connell, September 1844

Michael Collins (1890–1922) Born near Clonakilty in County Cork, Collins was an imposing Republican hero who took part in the Easter Rising. His tactics were ruthless and he was responsible for some brutal killings. He signed the Anglo-Irish Treaty, intended to partition Ireland peacefully. A British signatory, F. E. Smith, said, "I may have signed my political death warrant." Collins replied, "I have signed my death warrant." Anti-treatyites ambushed and killed him near Macroom (Cork) a few months later.

Roger Casement (1864–1916) Born at Ballymena, County Antrim, this career diplomat was knighted by the British in 1911. He was arrested as he landed at Banna Strand near Tralee in 1916 in a German submarine containing arms for the Easter Rising. His case was not helped in those days by the knowledge that he was a practicing homosexual and he was hanged for treason. His grave is in Glasnevin Cemetery, Dublin.

Éamon de Valera (1882–1975) "Dev," the "Long Fellow," was born in New York, but grew up at Bruree (Limerick, small museum). A veteran of the Easter Rising (pardoned because of his dual nationality), he, more than any politician, determined Ireland's course after the formation of the Free State, and was the founder of Fianna Fáil (Soldiers of Destiny). Three times premier, he was president from 1959 to 1973, but did little to heal the divisions between North and South.

DUBLIN

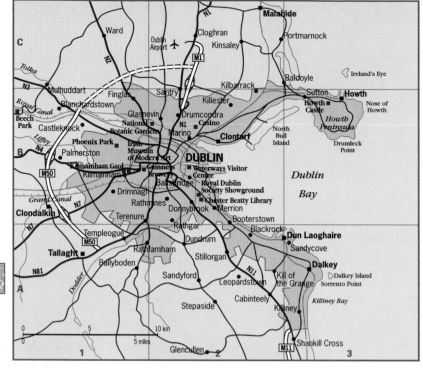

Looking north up O'Connell Street, named after Daniel O'Connell, "the Liberator" (see page 42). It was previously known as Sackville Street.

Dublin The capital's very size and city-like qualities in what is still a largely rural country make it atypical, yet it encapsulates so much that is endearing and exasperating about Ireland that it represents the Emerald Isle better than any other town. Not that the rest of Ireland necessarily thinks so; Dublin is regarded with the same mix of wistful envy and resentment by its provinces as most capital cities, and its inhabitants as a race apart. (To many Dubliners, the rest of Ireland is a rural backwater.) To miss Dublin, though, is to miss a colossally entertaining place, full of paradox and whimsy. It's a city of pubs, churches, grand buildings and fine museums, boozers and talkers, down-to-earth commerce and airy pipe dreams—above all, an intimate place whose pulse must be taken over some time, possibly through a glass of Guinness, apocryphally tasting of the peaty waters of the Liffey.

The fair city? It is indeed a beautiful place, set on a broad river basin fringed by the majestic sweep of Dublin Bay and the tantalizingly close Wicklow Mountains. Yet the "fair city" of song was better described by James Joyce, one of its most famous citizens, as "dear, dirty Dublin."

The best of its Georgian architecture rivals anything that can be seen in Bath or Edinburgh, but much has been destroyed by development or sheer neglect. Some of the demolition is forgivable; those pretty Georgian façades often disguise impossibly friable brickwork and tottering foundations that only total reconstruction would cure. What has replaced those seemly proportions sometimes defies belief, however, especially around gap-toothed

DUBLIN

St. Patrick's Cathedral, Dublin

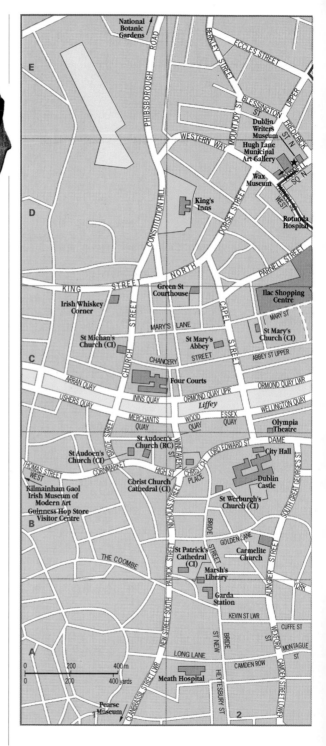

Dubh linn

The *dubh linn* (dark pool) that gave its name to the city was the confluence of the Poddle and the peat-colored waters of the Liffey. From the 9th century it was the harbor, where the original Norse settlers moored their longships on the low-lying banks below their fortress. A grilled opening in the south wall of the quay by Grattan (or Capel Street) Bridge shows the last remains of the River Poddle, which now runs underground for the final 3 miles of its course. This site was the port of Dublin until the 18th century, when a new port was built to the east by the Custom House. The original Gaelic name for Dublin (still its official name in Gaelic) was Baile Átha Cliath (town of the hurdles). This name is visible on the front of some buses, on road signs, and on postmarks.

National Botanic Gardens

BERKLEY STREET
ECCLES STREET

PHIBSBOROUGH ROAD

BLESSINGTON ST

MOUNTJOY ST

UPPER FREDERICK ST N

WESTERN WAY

Dublin Writers Museum

Hugh Lane Municipal Art Gallery

Wax Museum

WEST

SQ N

King's Inns

CONSTITUTION HILL

DORSET STREET

Rotunda Hospital

PARNELL STREET

NORTH

KING STREET

Green St Courthouse

Ilac Shopping Centre

Irish Whiskey Corner

CHURCH STREET

MARY'S LANE

CAPEL STREET

MARY ST

St Michan's Church (CI)

St Mary's Abbey

St Mary's Church (CI)

CHANCERY STREET

ABBEY ST UPPER

ARRAN QUAY

Four Courts

ORMOND QUAY LWR

USHERS QUAY

INNS QUAY

ORMOND QUAY UPR

Liffey

WELLINGTON QUAY

MERCHANTS QUAY

WOOD QUAY

ESSEX QUAY

Olympia Theatre

BRIDE STREET

St Audoen's Church (RC)

WINE TAVERN ST

DAME

St Audoen's Church (CI)

HIGH ST

CHRIST CH PLACE

LORD EDWARD ST

City Hall

SOUTH GREAT GEORGE'S ST

THOMAS STREET WEST

CORNMARKET

Christ Church Cathedral (CI)

NICHOLAS STREET

Dublin Castle

Kilmainham Gaol Irish Museum of Modern Art

St Werburgh's Church (CI)

Guinness Hop Store Visitor Centre

BRIDE STREET

GOLDEN LANE

Carmelite Church

AUNGIER STREET

THE COOMBE

PATRICK STREET

St Patrick's Cathedral (CI)

Marsh's Library

YORK

NEW STREET SOUTH

Garda Station

KEVIN ST LWR

CUFFE ST

CLANBRASSIL STREET LWR

ST NEW

BRIDE ST NEW

CAMDEN ROW

MONTAGUE ST

CAMDEN STREET LOWER

0   200   400 m
0   200   400 yards

LONG LANE

HEYTESBURY ST

Meath Hospital

2

Pearse Museum

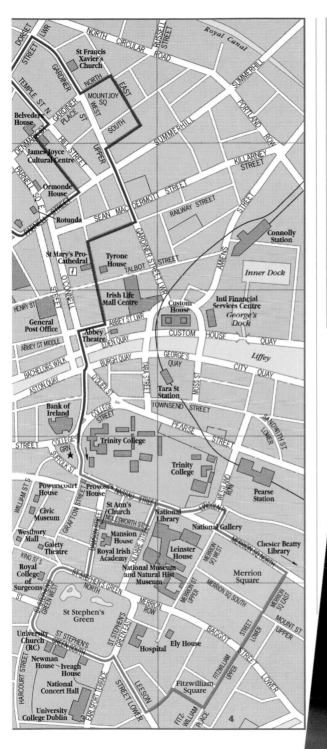

47

IF IT'S ON IT'S IN **in** DUBLIN

24 HOURS A DAY

DUBLIN

The motto means "happy the city whose citizens are obedient"

St. Stephen's Green or mutilated Fitzwilliam Street. The main thoroughfare on the north bank, O'Connell Street, is disappointing, its monumental dimensions and few remaining dignified buildings interspersed with seedy fast-food outlets and dull office buildings. Fortunately, though, Dublin has avoided the high-rises that have ruined the skylines of other cities, and north of the river, the unsightliness is more due to dereliction than deliberate destruction. Now, thankfully, the process is being reversed and Dublin's fanlit doorways glow amid newly restored surroundings.

The social divide To some extent, as in London, the great divide is the river. The Liffey neatly bisects Dublin from east to west, meeting the Poddle near the Grattan Bridge and forming the *dubh linn*, or dark pool, that gives the city its name (see panel on page 46). The respectable classes enjoy elegant architecture, chic restaurants, and fashionable shops now based mostly in the south around St. Stephen's Green and Trinity College. In a few other areas the city's poor inhabit twilight zones of bricked-up windows and dubious backstreets where tourists are recommended not to stray. Street crime, some drug-related, some intensified by chronic unemployment, is more of a problem here than in bomb-torn Belfast, though less than in many capital cities. But in its salubrious quarters Dublin is a distinctly enjoyable and friendly place. A conversation struck up with strangers is not regarded as a sign of impertinence or lunacy, but a simple acknowledgment of fellow humanity. There is a natural friendliness about both its citizens and the whole atmosphere of the city.

Laid out by Sir Arthur Guinness in 1880, St. Stephen's Green is one of the city's favorite meeting places

The capital Although the central areas feel compact, and can be explored on foot, the capital is by far the largest city in Ireland. Currently the Greater Dublin area contains about a million people, almost a third of the Republic's population, many of whom have drifted in from country areas in search of work. A large proportion of Dublin's

The magnificent coffered dome of the City Hall; this building, on Lord Edward Street near Dublin Castle, was designed in 1769–1779 by Thomas Cooley

The magnificent coffered dome of the City Hall; this building, on Lord Edward Street near Dublin Castle, was designed in 1769–1779 by Thomas Cooley

Billy-in-the-bowl
This extraordinary character terrorized the neighborhood of Stoneybatter, near Arbour Hill in northwest Dublin in the mid-18th century. Billy was born without legs, but learned to get about by propelling himself in an iron bowl with his arms. Naturally his upper limbs developed great strength, which he turned to criminal use. He lured passersby to his side by appealing to their sympathy, then seized them and strangled them for their purses. When he was eventually convicted for his multiple felonies, he was sentenced to "as much hard labor as his condition would allow" for the rest of his days.

49

inhabitants are under 25. It is a cosmopolitan city with many different nationalities and social groupings, but there is by no means the same racial mix as in, say, London or Paris.

Dublin has declined somewhat since its 18th-century heyday, when great architecture sprouted all over the city, when the first performance of Handel's *Messiah* was held here, and when it was considered one of the foremost cities of Europe. Things have improved in recent years, however, with Ireland's entry into the E.U. and a vast influx of funds for redevelopment making great changes to the city.

A newfound prosperity and confidence inspires the Dublin scene: Georgian buildings and their contents are cherished and conserved, restaurants buzz with patrons, and many fashionable celebrities have made the city their second home.

Traditional music in Dublin's Brazen Head pub

St. Valentine

St. Valentine was a priest martyred in Rome for helping persecuted Christians. Legend relates that he restored his jailer's blind daughter, but this availed him nothing and he was clubbed to death in about AD 269. The adoption of the saint as the patron of lovers seems to have resulted from the fact that his feast day, February 14, was traditionally associated with various springtime traditions, including the Roman feast of Lupercalia, when birds were believed to mate. Chaucer and Shakespeare both refer to this tradition; "For this was on seynt Valentyne's day / Whan every foul cometh there to chese his make," wrote Chaucer in *The Parliament of Fowls*. Girls would choose their sweethearts then, and gradually a custom of sending presents and cards to loved ones developed. The crocus is St. Valentine's flower.

From the oriental collection at the Chester Beatty Library, Ballsbridge

► **Carmelite Church**   *46B2*

57 Aungier Street

Although the church stands on the foundations of a pre-Reformation Carmelite priory, nothing remains of these older buildings. What you see now dates entirely from the 19th century and is the handiwork of George Papworth, the same architect who designed Dublin's St. Mary's Pro-Cathedral. Inside, it is a highly distinctive church, its spacious, light interior oddly like some municipal assembly hall, full of side chapels and little shrines. Worshipers wander in and out between shopping to light candles to various saints, including St. Valentine (see panel), patron saint of lovers, whose remains were allegedly donated to the church by Pope Gregory XVI from a cemetery in Rome and whose shrine is to the right of the nave. Hopeful couples may well add a bit more candle wax. Others in need pass to St. Albert's Well, where a relic of the Sicilian saint grants physical and spiritual healing. A 15th-century oaken Madonna and Child is also worth a look.

►►► **Chester Beatty Library**   *47B4*

20 Shrewsbury Road

Sir Alfred Chester Beatty (1875–1968) was an American mining engineer of Irish ancestry. By the age of 40 he had acquired a vast fortune, but had also developed incipient silicosis, so turned his prodigious energies to the more sedentary occupation of collecting exotic fine art. He made many trips to the Middle and Far East to add to his hoard and improve his health. He settled in Dublin in 1950, and gave his astonishing collection to the nation in 1956, living to the grand age of 93. Modern low-rise buildings in the salubrious suburbs of Ballsbridge now display his magpie genius—only a tiny fraction at a time because there is so much of it. The vivid showcases contain outstanding examples of mostly oriental and Middle Eastern art—gorgeously decorated Chinese silk robes, Japanese *netsuki* and lacquer boxes, illuminated manuscripts and scrolled Korans, books of jade or ancient papyrus, snuff bottles and rhinoceros-horn cups, woodblock prints and miniature paintings. Apart from its academic importance, the collection is simply beautiful to look at, and should not be missed.

Christ Church Cathedral, known officially as the Cathedral of the Holy Trinity

Dublinia
This entertaining, multimedia presentation of life in medieval Dublin can be seen in the old Synod Hall over the bridge from Christ Church. It features a model of Dublin ca. 1500, a display of items unearthed from Wood Quay and a medieval maze, along with an exciting audiovisual show.

► ► **Christ Church Cathedral** 46B2

Christ Church Place

Oddly for a staunchly Catholic city, both of Dublin's cathedrals are Protestant. Christ Church is the seat of the Anglican Bishop of Dublin and Glendalough. It has been a Protestant church since 1551 and is inevitably closely linked with English rule of the city, though it has some rebellious streaks in its history; in 1487 the Yorkist Pretender, Lambert Simnel, was crowned here by his supporters in a counterclaim to Henry VII's throne. The cathedral stands within the original city walls, and until 1871 it was the official state church. It has a long history stretching back before the Anglo-Norman invasion to 1038 when Sitric Silkenbeard, the first Viking Christian King of Dublin, founded a wooden church on this site. This was replaced by a stone edifice in Norman times. Part of this, the south wall, collapsed in 1562, and the north wall is still half a meter out of line. Today, the buttressed gray early Gothic buildings show evidence of a ruthless 19th-century restoration which time has not yet softened. Inside, though, there is much of interest, including the so-called "tomb of Strongbow" (Richard de Clare, Earl of Pembroke, who commanded the Anglo-Norman invasion in 1169), and the heart of St. Laurence O'Toole, Archbishop and patron saint of Dublin, in the chapel of St. Laud. Some of the original 13th-century tiles are incorporated into the floor, and the eagle lectern is also medieval. The crypt contains an odd jumble of quaint broken statues and the city stocks. Other curiosities include the bodies of a cat and a mouse, which apparently died in full flight when they both got stuck in an organ pipe, and the 1689 tabernacle and candlesticks of James II.

The Fenian Society
This secret, militant group was formed in a Dublin timberyard on St. Patrick's Day 1858, financed by $400 donated by expatriate Irish who had emigrated to the United States during the Famine years. Its members were bound by oath to loyalty to the aim of establishing an Irish Republic. From it the Irish Republican Brotherhood, and later the I.R.A., developed, and it was suspected of many terrorist activities in its efforts to get the British out of Ireland. Parnell's Land League had links with the Fenians, which damaged an otherwise sympathetic hearing in Britain. Its anti-clerical, Republican stance put it at odds with the Catholic Church, and known members faced excommunication. Today, Republican paramilitary groups are allegedly still partially financed by expatriate funds.

The Throne Room of Dublin Castle also contains a brass chandelier weighing more than a ton

►► Dublin Castle   46B2
Dame Street

This is no longer so much a castle as an assembly of courts, offices, and ceremonial accommodations dating from many different periods. Although it stands on high ground that was originally a strategic site at the junction of the Liffey and the Poddle, it is now hemmed in by the surrounding buildings and offers little in the way of a city landmark. Nor does it command significant views; in fact, Queen Victoria is said to have been so disappointed by the rear outlook onto slum tenement buildings that she insisted a wall be built so that she shouldn't be reminded of such indigent neighbors next time she visited. At various stages of its history the castle has been used as fortress, prison, viceregent's residence, and function rooms for important state occasions. It also serves as a useful hotel for high-risk V.I.P.'s (such as British politicians) whenever they visit to discuss Ireland's tangled affairs.

The most castle-like bit of the building still standing is the round Record Tower, dating from the 13th century when King John first ordered its construction. It stood on the site of an earlier Viking fortress, sections of which have been excavated and can be seen in the undercroft (vault), along with the old moat and bits of city wall. After 1684, much of the structure had to be replaced because of fire, and much of what you see now dates from the 18th century. The church next to the Powder Tower is the Church of the Most Holy Trinity, modeled in somewhat prissy neo-Gothic and consecrated in 1814 on the site of the earlier Chapel Royal. The arms of all the viceroys from 1172 to 1922 can be seen inside. Modern buildings around the courtyard house the tax office and conference facilities. One of the most charming bits of the older buildings is the clock-towered inner courtyard.

Visits are by guided tour only, which, though informative, are somewhat impersonal. If you have time to wait, it is a good idea to see the photographic exhibition in the reception building (which also serves good refreshments) to get a clear idea of the layout of the complex. Inside, you see the main state apartments (provided no other functions are going on there), which are sumptuously furnished to provide a suitably opulent setting for the many dignitaries who have made use of the castle. Vast Waterford chandeliers, tapestries, hand-tufted Donegal carpets mirroring the ceiling plasterwork, and Adam fireplaces abound, revealing the palatial lifestyle led by the viceroys acting on behalf of the Crown. St. Patrick's Hall is one of the most impressive rooms, all cluttered with banners and coats of arms, beneath an ornately painted ceiling. It is now used for the inauguration of Ireland's presidents. The throne room contains a massive throne believed to have been brought to Dublin by William of Orange after his victory at the Boyne. During the Easter Rising the castle was briefly threatened by an assault from the roof of the nearby City Hall. After the suppression of the rebellion, the captured rebel, James Connolly, was held (wounded) in one of the state rooms before being taken to Kilmainham to face execution.

► Dublin Civic Museum 47B3

58 South William Street
Housed in what was once the City Assembly House, the civic museum traces the history of Dublin from Viking times in old maps and photographs, prints, items from excavation sites, etc. The city's mercantile past is portrayed in sections devoted to various aspects of Dublin's trade and industry, and there is an interesting section on transportation, including a model of the Howth tram. Temporary exhibitions on city life are held every few months. One curiosity is a sculpted head of Lord Nelson, placed here after his column was blown up in O'Connell Street in 1966 on the 50th anniversary of the Easter Rising.

Limited resources
As the center of English power in Ireland, Dublin Castle was for centuries probably the most heavily guarded fortress in the country. Yet, during the Easter Rising in 1916, insurgents abandoned a scheme to take the Castle —without knowing that, at the time, it was manned only by a corporal's guard.

Dublin Civic Museum has a section devoted to firefighting. In this is a collection of fire-insurance plaques, such as the one below. They were once placed on houses to guide the insurance companies' own firemen to houses insured by them

53

The Easter Rising

The Easter Rising was a curious event, tiny in comparison with the rebellion of 1798, for instance, with only about 2,000 people actively taking part in it. It was disastrously badly organized and commanded very little public support, but its martyred heroes still glow in the imagination of republican Ireland as icons in the struggle against British rule.

Pearse Museum

This little museum is situated in the house once run by Padraic Pearse and his brother William as a boys' school. Their curriculum placed a strong emphasis on Gaelic studies and Irish culture. The United Irishman Robert Emmet courted his bride in the grounds. The house is now devoted to memorabilia connected with Pearse's life and the events that led to his death. It is situated in St. Enda's Park in Rathfarnham, a southern Dublin suburb.

54

The General Post Office soon after the Easter Rising

Irish heroes The leaders were Padraic Pearse and James Connolly. Pearse, a shy schoolmaster, was an unlikely commander, but he was inspired by a kind of mystical belief that bloodshed was necessary to cleanse Ireland. He was an Irish Volunteer, a group pledged to establish Home Rule at all costs. James Connolly was a more practical man, a socialist, born into a poor Irish family in Scotland, and in the British army at 14. He founded the Irish Citizens Army, closely allied to the Irish Volunteers.

The Rising On Easter Monday, April 24, 1916, Pearse, at the head of 150 men armed with ancient rifles and farm tools, took over the General Post Office, where he solemnly read out a stirring document proclaiming the new Irish Republic. Meanwhile, volunteers took over other buildings—a brewery, lunatic asylum, factory, and bakery. Many Dubliners were as bemused as the British forces by the collapse of the city into chaos, and, instead of joining the rebels, they made tea for the British. The fighting lasted for six days, and on the Saturday Pearse surrendered, by which time over 400 people had died. Twice as many police were killed as rebels, and four times as many civilians. Much of central Dublin lay in ruins, and the leaders of the Rising were even less popular than they had been at the start.

The tragic aftermath Then the tide turned. Instead of listening to the advice of moderate Home Rule supporter John Redmond not to execute any of the rebels, the British shot 14 of them, including Pearse and Connolly. From then on, they were heroes in the classic republican tradition. The release of hundreds of Irish internees later that year (among them Arthur Griffith, founder of Sinn Fein, Éamon de Valera, and Michael Collins) did nothing to assuage the bitterness that surrounded the aftermath of the Easter Rising. The fact that thousands of Irishmen died just a few months later on the battlefields of the Somme, fighting in the British Army, was all but eclipsed. A bronze statue in the rebuilt General Post Office, depicting the mythical hero, Cuchulainn, at the moment of death, symbolizes the glorified leaders.

Despite the clear dangers, life continued almost as normal for many Dubliners

Kilmainham Gaol This prison (*Inchicore Road, Kilmainham*), last used as such in 1924, is an excellent museum documenting the Irish struggle for independence. There, many policitical prisoners were held—United Irishmen, Fenians, Land Leaguers. A reorganization of its exhibits has made it a gripping and memorable place, and a fascinating, if partisan, insight into political and prison history. Serpentlike monsters writhe over the entrance gate. The main body of the prison, a classic barnlike shell of metal stairways and chicken-wired galleries, contains numerous display cases of items and documents. The guided tour begins at the scaffold where just one prisoner was hanged, and continues to the west wing where political internees were held in tiny separate dark cells. Passing the much more comfortable room where Parnell was imprisoned for seven months, it leads, finally, to the stonebreakers' yard where 14 leaders of the Easter Rising were executed by firing squad. James Connolly had a gangrenous leg, and was shot in a chair. Another, Joseph Plunkett, was married to Grace Gifford by candlelight in the prison chapel, just two hours before he was shot. They were allowed ten minutes together.

The monument in the General Post Office

The children's corner at Dublin Zoo...

Guinness
Arthur Guinness established his brewery in Dublin in 1759 and soon began experimenting with a London-brewed beverage made with roasted barley, known as "porter" (after its popularity with the porters of Covent Garden). By 1799 he concentrated all his production efforts on this distinctive drink, a rich black liquid topped with that "foamous" creamy head (as James Joyce called it). After the Napoleonic Wars of the early 19th century, an even stronger ("extra stout") beer was produced, and it rapidly reached most parts of the globe, even the South Pole (freezing is not generally recommended!). Though technology is now greatly advanced, the basic recipe of Guinness remains the same—Irish-grown barley, soft water, hops, and the strain of yeast Arthur Guinness used in 1759. A highly successful marketing policy has employed many talented artists in poster campaigns. The profits from Guinness have funded worthy enterprises such as the Wexford Opera Festival and the Georgian Society.

▶ **Dublin Zoo** 44B1
Phoenix Park
Established in 1830, Dublin's zoo is the third oldest in the world. If you are short of time it is not essential viewing, but as zoos go, it is attractive, set in 29 acres of gardens with fauna roaming in pleasant surroundings. Its most celebrated inhabitants are the lions, one of whom achieved undying fame as the beast roaring above the M.G.M. film studios' logo before every cinematic presentation.

▶ **Guinness Brewery** 44B1
James's Gate
Way upstream of most central sights is a Lowryesque skyline of smoking factory chimneys and giant metallic storage vats. This is the largest brewery in Europe, producing what can only be described as Ireland's *vin du pays*, though in fact it was first invented in London. Arthur Guinness's famous "porter" is shrouded in a sort of misty-eyed Celtic mythology which declares it can never be the same drunk outside Dublin, or from a can, or that the art of pulling a pint takes years to learn. This may be nonsense, but the production process is certainly a complex one and conditions of storage are important. You can't visit the brewery itself, but in a nearby back street (*Crane Street*), a visitor center in a handsome 19th-century warehouse called the Hop Store tells you all you could possibly want to know about grist and malt in a well-displayed walk-around exhibition with original brewing equipment, casks, and posters. Thrown in with your tour is a free half-pint or so, straight from the horse's mouth, as it were. The areas immediately surrounding the brewery and the Hop Store are insalubrious and strolling through the back streets as a conspicuous tourist is inadvisable.

▶▶ **Hugh Lane Municipal Gallery** 46D2
Parnell Square
The pictures are displayed in an elegant house designed by Sir William Chambers for the Earl of Charlemont in 1762. Today this north Dublin area is no longer very fashionable, but it was then highly desirable, and the house is a fine example of that early Georgian heyday. Its contents, however, are even more splendid—and in some ways it is more enjoyable and intimate than the National Gallery. Corots, Courbets, and Monets glow on the plain walls, along with some good Jack Yeats—and a portrait of Maud Gonne, who captivated his literary brother. A good coffee shop adds to the gallery's attractions.

▶▶ **Irish Museum of Modern Art** 46B1
Royal Hospital, Military Road, Kilmainham
This museum certainly deserves a visit, though rather more for its glorious setting than the contents themselves. The Royal Hospital is one of the finest 17th-century buildings in Ireland, constructed in 1684 as a home for retired and invalid soldiers. It is based on the style of Les Invalides in Paris, though on a much more appealing scale. It was restored by the government in 1986 at vast cost and now, somewhat bizarrely, houses ultramodern works of variable quality on iceberg walls. There are lively temporary exhibitions, along with educational and community programs of music, theater, and visual arts. Its

...and the children's corner at the Municipal Gallery

Hugh Lane

When Hugh Lane went down with the *Lusitania* in 1915, he bequeathed a problem as well as a magnificent art collection. He had left his estate "to the nation." The difficulty was (in the light of contemporary political events) to decide which nation he meant. Britain naturally claimed he intended the collection to be British, whereas Dublin said it should stay in his native land. Eventually the dispute was settled with a classic British compromise. The collection was simply split in two parts. Half the pictures stayed in Dublin; half in the National Gallery in London, and every five years they changed over. Would that all Anglo-Irish problems could be solved so amicably! (Under a new agreement, most of the bequest is now actually on view in Dublin.)

hearty self-service restaurant is a good reason to visit, particularly after a look at Kilmainham Gaol, just beyond the hospital's gates. Seek out the curious chapel with its remarkable riot of papier-mâché decoration on the ceiling. The museum is closed on Mondays.

▶ Irish Whiskey Corner 46C1
Bow Street
One of the warehouses used to mature whiskey has been converted by Irish Distillers into a museum showing the production process of the "water of life." An audiovisual show and a model of an old distillery illuminate the visitor, who is then regaled with a tasting to establish the difference between Scotch, Irish, and bourbon. If you are touring, there are larger and better whiskey distilling attractions in Northern Ireland (Bushmills) or County Cork (Midleton). Dublin's version is in a sleazy area of the city.

▶▶▶ Kilmainham Gaol 46B1
(See Focus on the Easter Rising, page 55.)

A re-creation of a cooper's workshop at the Guinness Brewery

The period from about 1714 to 1830 was Dublin's apogee, a great flowering of architecture, literature, philosophy, and art. The quality of Irish craftsmanship in silverwork, glassware, and furniture, and in Dublin's superb Georgian buildings, epitomizes the "age of elegance."

Dublin's heyday After the depredations of Cromwell's visits and the turmoil of Williamite battles, the 18th century was a time of comparative peace and prosperity in the English Pale. For the upper classes, life was highly civilized. Aesthetes and businessmen, wealthy gentry and talented artists merged resources to make Dublin one of the foremost cities of Europe. Terraces, parks, squares, imposing monuments, and dignified townhouses burgeoned throughout the central parts of the city, bounded by the Grand and Royal Canals. In 1757 the Wide Streets Commission, Europe's first planning authority, established new guidelines for building development, and in 1773 the Paving Board set up sensible regulations on lighting, cleaning, and drainage, making densely populated residential areas much more salubrious. This

The figure of Hope rests upon her anchor atop the magnificent Custom House

confident assertion of the good life for the Anglo-Irish Ascendancy disguised the wretched lot of the poor; in 1770 even the English viceroy was forced to admit that the Irish peasantry were "amongst the most wretched people on earth."

North of the Liffey In the earlier years of the 18th century, Dublin's fashionable center of gravity lay north of the river, and the first typically Georgian housing appeared around Mountjoy and Parnell (formerly Rutland) squares and Henrietta Street. These have not fared well since conversion to tenement buildings after the Act of Union caused a dramatic fall in property values, and until recently the buildings presented a sad picture of neglect and decay. A few attempts at restoration have been made in some areas, such as North Great George Street, and some gems glimmer in this tarnished setting. Modest examples can be found in **Parnell Square►►** (the Hugh Lane Municipal Gallery, see page 56, is in a splendid town house of the period; **Belvedere House►** on Great Denmark Street, now a Jesuit college, is another). Two grand set pieces north of the river, monumental buildings designed by James Gandon, can be seen to advantage from the opposite bank of the Liffey. The weighty **Custom House►►** of 1791 (see panel) floats on a fragile platform of pine planks on swampy riverside land. Further west is the **Four Courts►** of 1785, the seat of the High Court of Justice for Ireland. The Courts of King's Bench, Exchequer, Common Pleas, and Chancery radiate from a circular central hall, liveliest at lunchtimes when bewigged lawyers hobnob with their clients. Another Gandon building stands away from the river, in Henrietta Street; the **King's Inns►** (1795–1827) were Dublin's Inns of Court, where budding barristers lived, studied, and ate dinners. The **Rotunda Maternity Hospital►►**, the first purpose-built maternity hospital in Europe, has some superb stucco-work in its chapel.

South of the Liffey The best preserved and most enjoyable examples of Dublin's Georgian heritage can be seen south of the river. The shift in popularity occurred around the year 1750, after the construction of the opulent **Leinster House►►** (now Ireland's parliament building) for the Duke of Leinster in 1745. At the time, he was ridiculed for his choice of a green-field site away from the hub of fashionable Dublin, but as he rightly predicted (with that self-effacing modesty typical of the era!), "Wherever I go, they will follow."

Dublin's Georgian heritage was largely spared aerial bombing during the World Wars, but it has fared ill at the hands of 20th-century developers and politicians. After the creation of the Free State in 1922, renovation of buildings reminiscent of English rule was not exactly a high priority. Much thoughtless and irreparable destruction took place. But there is still much to enjoy among the fanlit doorways of its 18th-century squares. A new generation of conservation-minded citizens who do not blame bricks and mortar for Ireland's disastrous history now seem bent on preserving what is left.

See the following two pages for a walk around Dublin's finest Georgian buildings.

Tailor's Hall
Not far from Christ Church (on Back Lane) stands Dublin's only surviving guild hall, quite different architecturally from anything else you will see in the city. It is now the headquarters of *An Taisce*, (broadly speaking the Irish equivalent of the British National Trust, see pages 230–31) which is dedicated to the conservation of historic buildings and scenic landscapes. Tailor's Hall dates from 1706 and has a fine 18th-century interior with tall Queen Anne windows and a minstrel's balcony. Admission is free but donations are welcome.

North George Street: the lantern above the door was lit when the mistress of the house was "at home to visitors"

Inspecting Georgian Dublin
The Custom House, Four Courts, Bank of Ireland, and Leinster House (while Parliament is in session) are not officially open to the public. Nevertheless, it is occasionally possible to visit these buildings. If you are genuinely interested in the interiors you may be able to persuade a friendly official to let you in, or ask at the tourist office, as guided tours are occasionally available.

Walk A walk around Georgian Dublin

See map on pages 46–7.

Within the bounds of 18th-century taste, Irish craftsmen found great scope for personal expression, and the details of buildings are hugely varied and imaginative. Little touches—door-knockers, coal-hole covers, boot-scrapers—are the rewards of a sharp-eyed wander around Georgian Dublin.

College Green is a good starting point for exploring Dublin. This was the center of power during the 18th century until the Act of Union centralized government in Westminster. What is now the **Bank of Ireland**▶▶ was built by Edward Lovett Pearce between 1729 and 1739 to house the Irish Parliament. During banking hours, visitors may see the former House of Lords, sumptuously furnished with a Waterford chandelier, 18th-century tapestries and coffered ceiling. **Trinity College**▶▶▶, on the other side of the Green (see page 72), dates mainly from the 18th century. Its 300-foot façade, attributed to Theodore Jacobsen, was built between 1752 and 1759, and the **Provost's House**▶▶ on the corner of Grafton Street is one of Dublin's grandest Georgian mansions.

Turning down Kildare Street, you find Georgian **Leinster House**▶▶▶ the most imposing of several monumental public buildings (see pages 58–9), while nearby Molesworth Street contains three early Georgian houses built for Huguenot families in 1736–1755. Known as **Dutch Billies**▶, they are a revival of a style popular after William of Orange's conquest, featuring curvy gables and huge chimneys. On Dawson Street, 18th-century buildings include: **St. Ann's**▶▶ of 1720 (see page 70); the **Royal Irish Academy**▶ of 1785 housing a splendid library of Irish manuscripts; and the balustraded façade of the Lord Mayor's residence, **The Mansion House**▶ (1705, actually a Queen Anne building), is sometimes open for exhibitions. **St. Stephen's Green** is one of the landmarks of the Georgian city, although its buildings date from many periods and its park was not laid out until Victorian times (see page 68). The best of the Georgian buildings are: the **Royal College of Surgeons**▶▶ (1806) scarred by the Easter Rising; **Newman House**▶ (Nos. 85 and 86 on the south side), original home of the Catholic university (one of these houses, ironically, was built for a vehement anti-Catholic, Thomas "Burnchapel" Whaley, by the great 18th-century architect Richard Castle); and **Iveagh House**▶▶ (1736), now the Department of Foreign Affairs (not open). Off St. Stephen's Green, are **Harcourt Street, Ely Place** and **Leeson Street,** with many attractive and well-preserved domestic townhouses.

St. Stephen's Green

Leinster House, designed by Castle

Fitzwilliam Street► contained the longest stretch of Georgian buildings in Europe until an astonishing piece of civic vandalism in the 1960s permitted a hideous office building to tear a hole in it. The Electricity Supply Board (whose administrative headquarters it is) has now sheepishly rebuilt one of the houses it tore down. **Number 29►** is open (free) as a little museum, and its elegant rooms re-create something of the atmosphere of late Georgian times. **Fitzwilliam Square►►**, although not the largest or most famous Georgian example, is actually one of the best preserved. Many fan-lit doorways retain original features such as glass recesses for lamps, and anti-burglar spikes set in the walls. A glance down Mount Street reveals the attractive late-Georgian church of **St. Stephen's►►**, known as the Pepperpot from its unusual dome. In the mid-18th century, the **Grand Canal** beside the church would have been a bustling highway of commerce and passenger traffic.

Merrion Square►►► is the final great "set piece" on this walking tour. The blue plaques all around many of the houses commemorate famous former occupants, suggesting how fashionable it once was. Planned in 1762 for Lord Fitzwilliam, it is unquestionably one of the finest of all Dublin's squares. Oscar Wilde's parents lived here, along with Daniel O'Connell, the statesman; W. B. Yeats; and many other respected figures.

Georgian elegance in every detail

Dublin is an emphatically literary city. Most great (and many not-so-great) Irish writers gravitated there at some stage so, to some extent, the literary history of Dublin is the literary history of Ireland. The ghosts of Yeats, Shaw, Synge, Beckett, O'Casey, Wilde, Swift, and others haunt its streets and bookshops. The National Library, near Leinster House, contains a splendid collection of first editions and works of 17th-century Irish authors, as well as later writers, including Swift, Goldsmith, Yeats, Shaw, and Joyce.

62

Top: Oscar Wilde

James Joyce Tower
The 22-year-old Joyce spent only a week or so there in the August of 1904, though he later immortalized it in the first chapter of his masterpiece *Ulysses*. The Martello Tower belonged to Oliver St. John Gogarty, an ebullient surgeon and poet, who invited Joyce to stay with him there. For more details of his eventful stay in the tower, see page 97.

Stella and Vanessa
Jonathan Swift's women friends are immortalized in his letters and other writings under pseudonyms. "Vanessa" was Esther Vanhomrigh, who lived in Celbridge, County Kildare (at Barberstown Castle, see Hotels and Restaurants, page 271). Swift met her in London in 1708 and may even have fathered her child. She followed Swift to Ireland but broke off her friendship with him when he became involved with "Stella." The second great attachment of his life was another Esther (Johnson), with whom he had a deep but apparently platonic relationship. Memorials to Swift and Stella can be seen in St. Patrick's Cathedral (see page 71).

Georgian flowering Along with its architecture, Dublin's literary scene blossomed during the 18th century, a time of great intellectual ferment and scientific discovery. One of the giants of the era was the Dean of St. Patrick's Cathedral, Jonathan Swift. Probably the greatest satirist in the English language, he is most famous for *Gulliver's Travels.* He was a Protestant and obviously part of the Anglo-Irish Ascendancy, but some of his bitterest invective was directed against the cruel and unequal conditions of the Irish poor. In *A Modest Proposal* he attempted to stir up the complacent attitudes of the time by suggesting, deliberately outrageously, that Irish children should be fattened up for English tables.

Swift's contemporaries included William Congreve and George Farquhar, both of whom were educated at Trinity College, Dublin. Like many other Irish writers, however, they soon left for London, as did the later authors, Oliver Goldsmith and Richard Brinsley Sheridan. During the 19th century, dramatists who achieved greatest fame were Oscar Wilde and George Bernard Shaw (who lived on until 1950), both of whom, following the usual pattern, left their native land to dazzle London society.

The Gaelic Revival Meanwhile, however, another strand of writers began to receive attention in Dublin. At the end of the 19th century a renewed interest in all things Irish (the Gaelic Revival) was inspiring artists such as W. B. Yeats and his friend George Russell; Celtic myths interweave their work. The turn of the century saw a great flourishing of theatrical talent, this time a home-grown version using Irish, specifically Gaelic themes. John Millington Synge's works for the Abbey Theatre were among these, followed by the pacifist works of Sean O'Casey. Both these writers were controversial, and aroused much furor when they broke away from the norms of light social comedy.

James Joyce The literary giant most closely associated with Dublin, James Joyce (1882–1941), is surprisingly not among its three Nobel-prize-winners (Beckett, Shaw and Yeats), all of whom have strong links with the capital too. Joyce, however, lived and breathed the place, although he always had a love–hate relationship with it and spent most of his adult life abroad. He referred to his native city as the "center of paralysis": "How sick, sick, sick I am of Dublin. It is a city of failure, of rancour and unhappiness. I long to be out of it," he wrote. The works in which Dublin appears, almost as the central character, are *A Portrait of the Artist as a Young Man, Ulysses, Dubliners,* and *Finnegan's Wake.* Ironically, Joyce, spurned and hounded into exile while he lived, is now fêted by the tourist authorities as one of the city's greatest ambassadors—every step of his Dublin-set masterpiece *Ulysses* carefully documented in self-guided walks and wall plaques. Keen followers of his work can buy a map and follow the route taken by Leopold Bloom on that famous June day. The trail leads well out of the city center to the southeast suburbs of Dalkey and Sandycove, where you can find the James Joyce Tower, which features in the opening chapter of *Ulysses.* Inside is a museum set up in 1962 by Sylvia Beach, original publisher of his great novel, containing Joycean memorabilia and some letters. Next to the tower is the Forty Foot Pool, where Buck Mulligan (based on Gogarty, see panel) swims at the start of *Ulysses.* Nearby Dalkey was the setting for Flann O'Brien's novel *The Dalkey Archive.*

The prolific George Bernard Shaw

Brendan Behan

Of all the characters who trod Dublin's literary stage during the course of this century, few were more rambunctious than Brendan Behan—variously remembered as a lovable rogue or an arrogant sot—whose over-draught of Guinness contributed to his untimely death in 1964 at the ripe young age of 41. During his creative years, the pubs in Dublin were officially closed on St. Patrick's Day, and one of the few places where one could openly get a drink was at the annual dog show in the Royal Dublin Society's premises in Ballsbridge. On repairing there one St. Patrick's Day, Behan is said to have howled "Who the hell brought a ****ing dog into a place like this, anyway?" —or words to that effect.

William Butler Yeats (1865–1939)

Walk A walk around literary Dublin

See map on pages 46–7.

Most of Ireland's great writers spent some of their time in Dublin, and this walk explores some of their haunts.

Start off in Parnell Square, at the Dublin Writers Museum. Housed in a restored 18th-century mansion, this contains a fascinating collection of first editions, portraits, manuscripts, and memorabilia. A couple of doors away is the Hugh Lane Municipal Gallery (see pages 56–7), where you can see works by Jack Yeats and a portrait of Maud Gonne who drove his brother, W. B. Yeats, to heights of romantic distraction. On the corner of Granby Row, the National Wax Museum displays effigies of the writers Joyce, Yeats, Shaw, and O'Casey in a suitably bookish setting. In the center of the square lies the Garden of Remembrance, a park commemo-

It's worth looking up when visiting the Dublin Writers Museum

rating all who have fallen for Irish freedom. Plans for the Easter Rising were made in a house nearby, and the captured rebels were held prisoner in this square overnight. The fountain pool and its swan sculptures by Oisín Kelly evoke the myth of the Children of Lir, turned into birds for 900 years (see page 236). The rest of Parnell Square is taken up by the Rotunda Maternity Hospital (see page 59). Founded in 1745, it has excellent plasterwork and woodcarving. Part of it is now the Gate Theatre, where many Irish and foreign playwrights staged productions from 1929 onward.

Leaving Parnell Square at the southeast corner, head for North Great George's Street, where heartening restoration work of the fine Georgian houses has taken place. One of them (No. 35) contains the James Joyce Centre (library, bookshop, Joycean walks, lectures, etc.; tel: 01 873 1984). Belvedere House in Great Denmark Street is another well-

On the Ulysses *trail along the sidewalks of Dublin*

preserved Georgian mansion, now a Jesuit college (Joyce was a former student). A detour up Temple Street North leads to Eccles Street, site of Leopold Bloom's fictional home in *Ulysses* (No. 7 no longer exists, though you can see the front door in the Bailey pub on Duke Street). Heading northeast, you reach St. Francis Xavier Church (see page 70), an ornate Jesuit building. Mountjoy Square was once home to several writers, this side of town having cheaper rents for impecunious writers than the posher south bank. Sean O'Casey lived at No. 35 and later at 422 North Circular Road, using the area as the setting for *Shadow of a Gunman* and his other plays for the Abbey Theatre. Brendan Behan grew up in 14 Russell Street.

Continuing down Gardiner Street, you follow the same route as Leopold Bloom on that famous day in June 1904. Up Railway Street stood Bella Cohen's Brothel, immortalized in *Ulysses*, typical of many houses of ill repute in this area. Cutting down Waterford Street and Marlborough Street, note the Pro-Cathedral (see page 70), Dublin's most important Catholic church. On Abbey Street is the Abbey Theatre, scene of many significant dramatic productions. The theater was first opened in 1904 under the auspices of Lady Gregory

and W. B. Yeats. One of its most memorable productions was the first staging of John Millington Synge's *Playboy of the Western World*, which caused riots among the Dublin audience because of its depiction of a parricide and its mention of an item of female underwear ("shift"). Sean O'Casey's play, *The Plough and the Stars*, also caused a furor because it bravely refused to idolize the leaders of the Easter Rising. The Abbey was burned down in 1951, and rebuilt in a modern, blockish style. Back on O'Connell Street are more Joycean sites—Prince's Street, by the General Post Office, where Bloom worked at the *Freeman's Journal,* and Graham Lemon's sweetshop.

Finish the walk over the bridge at Trinity College, in the Long Room, where the ghosts of many graduate *literati* stalk, from Swift and Goldsmith to Shaw and Wilde, connecting Ireland's current lively writing scene with those unknown monks who illuminated the Gospels of the *Book of Kells* in the 8th century.

One of many memorials to Joyce

▶▶ **National Gallery** 47B4

Merrion Square West

The National Gallery is a fine collection, though not in the first rank of European art galleries. About 2,000 works are on show at any one time, representing Irish, U.S. and all major European schools of art up to the 19th century. More recent works are on display at the Irish Museum of Modern

The intricate beauty of the Tara Brooch, housed in the Treasury of the National Museum. Despite its name, it has no known connection with Tara in County Meath

Viking foundations
One of the first additions to the National Museum's collections was a Viking sword, which appropriately came to light when the builders were digging the foundations for the museum just over a century ago.

Art housed in the Royal Hospital, Kilmainham, and the Hugh Lane Municipal Gallery (see pages 56–7).

The National Gallery first opened in 1864, with only a tiny fraction of the paintings it now possesses. Much of it was due to the energies of William Dargan, a railway magnate largely responsible for building Ireland's rail network. He was the moving spirit behind the Dublin Exhibition of 1853, using the profits to found the gallery, and his statue stands on the lawns near the entrance gate. The building was designed by Francis Fowke, who also designed the Victoria and Albert Museum in London.

The collection contains a number of works by Jack B. Yeats, brother of the poet, W. B. Yeats, which make a gritty contrast to the sentimental productions of other members of the Irish School. Other highlights include Degas's *Ballet Girls* and Sir Joshua Reynolds's *Earl of Bellamont*. The Impressionists are well represented, as are Italian and Dutch schools and earlier French artists from the 17th century onward. A fascinating collection of Irish portraits lines the grand staircase, culminating in the fiery Countess Markiewicz who was furious at being pardoned for her part in the Easter Rising (see pages 54–5). The gallery has an attractive coffee shop and restaurant. Admission is free, and it is open every day (until 8:30PM on Thursday).

▶▶▶ **National Museum** 47B3

Kildare Street

This museum houses many of the finest masterpieces of Irish Celtic art from the Bronze Age to the Middle Ages. Its greatest treasures (appropriately housed in the Treasury) include the Tara Brooch, the Ardagh Chalice, the Cross of Cong, the Shrine of St. Patrick's Bell, and many other exquisite pieces of gold jewelry and croziers. The Tara Brooch is perhaps the most important and most copied of all Celtic jewels. It dates from the 8th century AD and is made of white bronze, silver-gilt, amber, and glass, and although it measures only about 2 inches across, it is intricately decorated with scrolls and spirals and strange beasts on both sides. The Ardagh Chalice, from about the same period, is inspired by Byzantine art—a shapely wide goblet of gilded bronze, chased with gold filigree and studded with colored glass.

A department called *Ar Thoir na Saoirse* (The Road to Independence) contains mementoes of the Easter Rising and the Civil War, including a fragment of the flag flown over the General Post Office in 1916. Other sections contain superb porcelain of Irish, English, European, and Asian origins, many items from Japan, rare textiles, glass, ceramics, silver, and old musical instruments such as Irish harps and uilleann pipes. A particularly interesting section called 'Viking Age Ireland' shows what life was like for those fierce Norsemen, using exhibits from settlements in and around Dublin. Temporary exhibitions are regularly mounted. A testament to amateur archeologists is the Derrynaflan Hoard, discovered by a group of metal-detecting enthusiasts in County Tipperary. Like the National Gallery, admission is free (closed Monday).

► Natural History Museum 47B3
Merrion Street

This is part of the National Museum (and has the same opening hours), but is housed in a separate building. In a large hall, a crowded display of taxidermy can be seen, including a comprehensive collection of Irish mammals, birds, fish, and insects, together with various mineral exhibits. Upstairs are animals from other parts of the world, while whales once stranded on the Irish coast now hang from the roof.

The gallery of Dublin's Natural History Museum

Weather permitting, it is never difficult to find a place to get away from the traffic noise in Dublin. The Georgian layout of the city naturally produced a system of spacious squares and landscaped gardens around its principal monuments, and Dublin is full of green open spaces, neat and municipal, or wilder and more natural.

Short-term tenancy
The apocryphal story is told of a prominent and somewhat self-opinionated 20th-century Irish politician who went to Glasnevin Cemetery in search of a suitable plot for himself. On being offered one in the poshest part of the grounds, he declined, saying that it was far too good for him. The official then came up with a more medium-priced alternative, which was also spurned—to the growing surprise and frustration of the cemetery office. But all turned to smiles when a much cheaper one was suggested and promptly accepted. "After all," said the politician, "I only need it for three days."

The Three Fates quietly watch life pass by from their vantage point in St. Stephen's Green

Town squares The most famous of the Georgian squares is **St. Stephen's Green**, which was formerly common land. In 1880 Lord Ardilaun (heir to the Guinness fortunes) paid for the present gardens to be laid out, and they now encompass 21 acres of lawns, flower beds, paved walks, shrubberies, and an ornamental lake with wildfowl. Bandstands, statues, and pergolas dot it at intervals; its various monuments include Henry Moore's memorial to Yeats and a statue of Wolfe Tone amid stone slabs ("Tonehenge"). The gardens are open during daylight hours when they become one of Dublin's most popular spots for strolling and having a lunchtime sandwich.

Merrion Square is another attractive open space dating from Georgian times, and has the restored Rutland Fountain inset in its railings. During the Famine years (1845–1848) a soup kitchen was set up in this well-heeled residential square to feed starving refugees who poured in from the devastated country areas. Today you are more likely to find artists selling their wares on weekends.

Phoenix Park At the west end of the city lies the huge open space called **Phoenix Park**. It stretches along the Liffey for about 3 miles, and covers 1,700 acres, about five times the size of London's Hyde Park. The park's name comes from the Gaelic *fionn uisce*, meaning "clear water," referring to the spring in the Furry Glen. In it are lakes, woods, fields, a racecourse, and sports grounds. It also contains Dublin Zoo (see page 56), and the headquarters of the *Garda Siochána*, or Irish police force. Its most striking monuments are the 200-foot obelisk to Wellington and the Phoenix Column, erected in 1747 by Lord Chesterfield, a former lord lieutenant. The parklands once belonged to Kilmainham priory, until seized during the Reformation, and later became a deer park owned by the Duke of Ormonde (deer still roam the park, descended from the original herd). During the 18th and 19th centuries it was a fashionable place with desirable residences, one of which now houses the Irish President. The so-called 15 acres (now playing fields) were well known as a dueling place in the 18th century. Phoenix Park's popularity suffered when in 1882 Lord Cavendish, the Chief Secretary, and Burke, the Under-Secretary, were stabbed here by obscure malcontents called the Invincibles. The assassination caused a great furor at Westminster, where the question of Home Rule for Ireland was at last being seriously debated. The park's main entrance is at the southeast corner, off Parkgate Street.

Other green spaces A little way east lies **Arbour Hill Cemetery**, a quiet memorial garden where the leaders of the Easter Rising are buried, their names carved in stone beside a copy of the stirring proclamation of independence. Dublin's other interesting cemetery is in **Glasnevin**, in the north of the city, where lie the graves of Éamon de Valera, Gerard Manley Hopkins, and Roger Casement (see page 43). Close by are Dublin's **National Botanic Gardens▶▶**, set up in 1795, and containing about 20,000 species of plants and trees, including specialist rose and vegetable gardens. The ornate glasshouses known as the Curvilinear Range were constructed by Richard Turner, a famous 19th-century iron founder also responsible for producing the Palm House in Belfast. Riverside walks lead through bog and peat gardens and the arboretum.

One of Dublin's wilder spaces is **North Bull Island**, a strip of dunes and beaches off the coast, reached from the road to Howth. It is now a nature conservancy area, but visitors can walk out along the causeway to the lighthouse. Many species of birds can be seen there and further information can be gleaned either from the guided tours or at the interpretive center.

The Curvilinear Range of greenhouses at the Botanical Gardens

Poet James Mangan, St. Stephen's Green

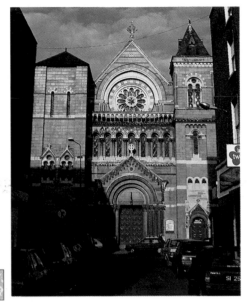

St. Ann's is built from pale granite interspersed with single courses of red brick

Silken Thomas
In 1534 the 10th Earl of Kildare, known as Silken Thomas for his love of fine clothing, mutinied against Henry VIII and declared vengeance on him at St. Mary's Abbey for his apostacy against the Catholic Church and the supposed beheading of his father (a false rumor). Thomas was captured and executed in 1537.

Some believe that one of the mummified bodies in St. Michan's Church is that of a medieval Crusader

▶ **St. Ann's Church** *47B3*
Dawson Street
This church's Italianate façade of 1868 in neo-Romanesque granite disguises an 18th-century interior including polished wood balconies and ornate plasterwork. Wooden shelves beside the altar were constructed to hold loaves of bread for the poor, a bequest left by Lord Theophilus Newtown.

▶ **St. Francis Xavier's Church** *47E3*
Upper Gardiner Street
This classical Jesuit church was constructed as soon as Catholic emancipation was achieved in 1829. It is built in the shape of a Latin cross, and has an Ionic portico. Inside its most striking features are its fine coffered ceiling and the green *faux* marble altarpiece brought from Italy.

▶ **St. Mary's Abbey** *46C2*
off Capel Street
The remains of the Pale's most prominent Cistercian monastery, founded by the Benedictines in 1139, lie here. Much of the stone was removed to build Essex Bridge nearby and only the chapter house still stands.

▶ **St. Mary's Pro-Cathedral** *47D3*
Marlborough Street, east of O'Connell Street
Dublin's most significant Catholic church has never been granted full cathedral status. Originally destined for the site occupied by the General Post Office, it actually

stands in a fairly undistinguished site off O'Connell Street, its dome and Doric façade barely visible among discount shops and street markets. Inside, its 1820s Renaissance interior has some dignity, though few points of major interest. John Newman first avowed his conversion to the Catholic faith there in 1851, and the famous tenor, John McCormack, was a member of the Palestrina choir.

▶ St. Michan's Church 46C1

Church Street
This little church (begun in 1095) in a run-down area at the back of the Four Courts arouses a certain ghoulish excitement for the mummified corpses in its vaults, which are on display to anyone who cares to peer through a hatch. Their remarkable preservation is due to the hygroscopic action of the surrounding magnesian limestone, plus a few whiffs of methane gas from some subterranean disposal site. Handel is supposed to have played the organ here, and at the "penitent's pew" malefactors knelt to make their offenses public.

▶▶ St. Patrick's Cathedral 46B2

Patrick's Close
The precise status of this cathedral is a puzzle. Just a few hundred yards down the road stands another Church of Ireland cathedral, Christ Church. The two have always been great rivals. St. Patrick's is the national cathedral, the home of the first university in Ireland (1320–1520) and is Ireland's largest church. It is legendarily associated with St. Patrick because of a neighboring well, where the saint was believed to have baptized many converts. From 1191 onward the original church was replaced by the present building, much restored in the 1860s on the proceeds of Guinness. The cathedral stands in a desolate wasteland of tenement housing and looming cranes, outside the city walls. By far its most celebrated incumbent was Jonathan Swift, author of *Gulliver's Travels*, who was Dean here for over 30 years (1713–1745) and is buried in the cathedral beside his beloved "Stella," Esther Johnson. A plaque is inscribed with Swift's self-penned epitaph which, translated from the Latin, reads: "Where fierce indignation can no longer rend the heart,/ Go traveler, and imitate, if you can, this earnest and dedicated champion of liberty." Nearby is a memorial verse from Alexander Pope dedicated to Swift, and Swift's death mask, chair, and writing table can be seen in the north pulpit. At the west end of the church is a 17th-century monument to the Boyle family, typical of the period, the demure parents presiding over a multitude of neatly replicated offspring. The young Robert (the scientist who was later to formulate Boyle's Law) is on the lowest tier.

Next to St. Patrick's is **Archbishop Marsh's Library▶▶**, similar to (but smaller than) the Old Library of Trinity College. The barrel-vaulted upper room houses a wonderful collection of ancient leather-bound tomes in dark floor-to-ceiling cases. Several fascinating manuscripts, such as old herbals with beautiful plant illustrations, are separately displayed. Swift's annotated copy of Clarendon's *History of the Great Rebellion* is here among 25,000 other volumes. Cages where readers could be locked to consult valuable books can also be seen.

Chancing your arm
A curious feature in the nave of St. Patrick's Cathedral is a free-standing wooden door with a hole in it. This was formerly the chapter door of the south transept, and is the subject of an intriguing tale. The warring Earls of Kildare and Ormonde confronted each other at the cathedral in 1492, and Ormonde had barricaded himself inside the church for protection. The Earl of Kildare offered to make peace, and cut a hole in the door through which he thrust his arm to shake hands with Ormonde. The phrase "chancing your arm" was born.

St. Patrick's has no crypt because the River Poddle flows directly beneath the cathedral

▶▶▶ Trinity College 47B3

College Green

This single-college university was founded by Elizabeth I in 1592 on confiscated monastery land, ostensibly "to civilise Ireland with both learning and the Protestant religion." Small wonder, then, that it became a source of division in the city. Catholics were always allowed entry to the college, and free education—provided of course they converted; up until 1966, Catholics had to obtain a special dispensation to attend on pain of excommunication. Now, however, the proportion of Catholic students at T.C.D., as it is known, is about 70 percent. The "honor roll" is

impressive; Edmund Burke, Jonathan Swift, Oliver Goldsmith, Bram Stoker, Wolfe Tone, William Congreve, J. M. Synge, and Samuel Beckett have all passed through these hallowed portals.

Today T.C.D. occupies a prime location at the heart of Dublin, in an oasis of gardens and parks. Little remains of the original buildings; the imposing, classical façade and Corinthian columns give it an unmistakably 18th-century feel. Inside, like ancient English universities, its buildings are arranged around quadrangles of lawns and cobbles. The theater, examination hall, chapel, dining hall, and the old brick student accommodations known as the Rubrics can be seen as you pass from the Front Court to the Library Court. The campanile, by Charles Lanyon, marks the site of the original priory. To the right is the Old Library, where the *Book of Kells* is housed.

Since 1801 Trinity College has had the right under copyright law to claim a free copy of all British and Irish publications, and now houses nearly 3 million volumes in eight buildings. About a half-mile of new shelving is needed every year to keep up with all the new publications.

Bus tours roll up to visit Trinity's concession to the tourist industry, a 40-minute video called *The Dublin Experience*, which gives a brief history of the city in the Arts Building behind the library, from late May to October.

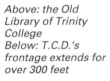

Above: the Old Library of Trinity College
Below: T.C.D.'s frontage extends for over 300 feet

CHAPEL

After over a thousand years, the intricate decoration and bright colors of this Latin text of the Gospels gives a clear proof of the inventive skill and dedication shown by early Irish scholars. The glowing patterns illuminated not merely the pages of the text, but the whole of the Christian world.

The Old Library of Trinity College houses about 2 million volumes, stacked in a double-decker layer of huge floor-to-ceiling shelving in twenty bays of a splendid cathedral-like hall accurately called the Long Room, measuring 210 feet by 39 feet. The building was designed by Thomas Burgh in 1712; its barrel-vaulted ceiling was added in the 19th century in order to provide more much needed shelf space. At the far end of the library are two harps, one of them traditionally associated with the great Irish king Brian Ború, though actually from the 15th century. By far the most famous and precious of all the treasures in The Old Library of Trinity College is the 8th-century illuminated manuscript of the four gospels, known as the *Book of Kells*. Inscribed in Latin on vellum parchment, its pages are magnificently ornamented with patterns and fantastic animals. The designs closely resemble the interlacing patterns found on Celtic metalwork and are obviously influenced by those traditions. Although the manuscript was certainly kept at the monastery of Kells in County Meath, there exists some doubt whether it was actually produced there, some authorities believing it may have been copied in Iona or Lindisfarne. The book's 680 pages were rebound during the 1950s into four separate volumes. Two of these are generally on display in the Old Library, with the pages being turned every so often to give a different view. Conservation of such a priceless document is of the utmost importance and a constant battle; you may have to be content with a facsimile version. The Colonnades is an exhibition area featuring annually changing displays and a well-stocked shop. Besides the *Book of Kells*, there are several similar manuscripts kept at Trinity—the *Book of Durrow*, the *Book of Dimma*, and the less colorful *Book of Armagh*.

The startlingly beautiful and complex Book of Kells

An Ancient theft
The *Book of Kells* was stolen one night from the western sacristy of the great stone church of Kells (Meath) in 1007. The *Annals of Ulster* tell that it was recovered after two months and twenty nights, "its gold having been taken off it and with a sod over it."

Genealogy is now big business in Ireland. Hundreds of visitors from the New World annually attempt to find their roots. Around 60 million people, mostly in North America and the Antipodes, are estimated to be of Irish descent. Of these by far the largest number live in the United States (40 million or so), 5 million live in Canada, and another 5 million in Australia and New Zealand. The rest, hard to assess precisely, are somewhere in Britain or scattered throughout the globe.

Before it became the Heraldic Museum, No. 2 Kildare Street was the home of a gentlemen's club. On one of its columns (and visible from the road) are two monkeys playing the gentlemanly sport of billiards

74

An exhibit at Dublin's Heraldic Museum, showing the Irish harp

Finding your roots Ancestor-tracing is particularly popular in Dublin, where most of the records are held, and in the west of Ireland, which saw vast emigration during the Famine years. Ulster also has strong links with the New World; many "Scotch-Irish" Protestant settlers have made their homes in Canada or the United States. In September 1992, Ireland staged a large cross-border Homecoming Festival. Along with the *ceilis* (evenings of folk music and dancing) and the "crack" (fun) went many more earnest events such as clan rallies and history seminars, and lots of hints on the tracing of forebears.

The great interest in origins is fostered by recent research overseas. Canada, for example, has carried out a detailed survey on Irish settlement of its Atlantic seaboard. For many people, a visit to Ireland is a chance to see the Old Country, to track down the family town or homestead, and perhaps look up a few living relatives.

Irish archives A burgeoning number of organizations and centers throughout Ireland will now help you draw your family tree. Increasingly, family records and databases are being computerized and interlinked, making it much quicker and easier to track down records that would have taken hours of patient poring over documents in the past. Inevitably, there's a cost involved, but unless your roots are particularly elusive, the charges are generally quite modest. You could just pay a few pounds for a five-year search through the births, marriages and deaths certificates, or up to IR£150 for a detailed survey of several generations, neatly documented. Research concentrates mainly on civil and parish records, census forms, wills, papers dealing with land or property transactions, etc.

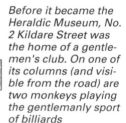

Emigration records Irish data is somewhat patchy. In 1922, at the start of the Civil War, the Public Record Office, then housed at the Four Courts in Dublin, was shelled and many documents were lost (fortunately some copies were kept elsewhere). During the Famine years, scant records were kept of those who emigrated or died on the way—such was the despair and chaos of those times. The best bet is to start at the other end, where detailed immigration papers were completed in most American and Australian ports of entry. Seven volumes of immigrant records list every arrival into New York from 1846 to 1851 (*The Famine Immigrants*, published by the Baltimore Genealogical Publishing Company). Australia's records are also good, particularly of those who left Ireland on "assisted passage" schemes, or who were deported for a criminal offense (often a trivial misdemeanor or political involvement—the chances of unearthing some serial killer in the family archives are small). Contact the National Library in Canberra, or the Mitchell Library in Sydney.

If you want to track down your Irish roots, try to do as much research as you can before you arrive. Living relatives, family papers, and records in your own country are the first sources to tackle. Build up as complete a picture as you can of the ancestors who emigrated—full name, trade, religion, and which town or county they came from. (Many emigrants named their new homes after their former parish or town, which can be a clue). When you arrive, visit one of the organizations or genealogy centers in the county of origin. It is wise to make an appointment in advance, especially during the summer. The Republic's tourist office, Bord Fáilte, produces an information sheet (No. 021) on tracing your ancestors, which contains useful advice, lists of publications and addresses.

Banners in the Heraldic Museum

Northern Ireland addresses
Public Record Office of Northern Ireland, 66 Balmoral Avenue, Belfast BT9 6NY (tel: 01232 661621).
Ulster Historical Foundation, 12 College Square East, Belfast BT1 6DD (tel: 01232 332288).
Irish Genealogy Ltd., 2 Mellon Road, Castletown, Omagh BT78 5QY.
(Please enclose international reply coupons or self-addressed stamped envelope if you write for advice.)

Provincial addresses
Clare Heritage Centre, Corofin, County Clare (tel: 065 37955).
Mayo North Family History Research Centre, Enniscoe, Castlehill, Ballina (tel: 096 31809).
Roscommon Heritage and Genealogy Centre, Strokestown, open only from May to September (tel: 078 33300).
Irish Family History Foundation, 1 Clarinda Park North, Dun Laoghaire, County Dublin.
Irish Family History Society, PO Box 36, Naas, County Kildare.

Dublin addresses
Genealogical Office, 2 Kildare Street, Dublin 2 (tel: 01 6618811).
The Heraldic Museum—full of arms, banners, crests, etc.—is at the same address.
National Library, 2 Kildare Street, Dublin 2 (tel: 01 6618811).
National Archives, Bishop Street, Dublin 8 (tel: 01 4783711).
Births, Deaths and Marriages, Joyce House, 8–11 Lombard Street East, Dublin 2 (tel: 01 6711000).
Registry of Deeds, Henrietta Street, Dublin 1 (tel: 01 8732233).

DUBLIN

Accommodations

The Shelbourne Dublin's grandest hotel is no less than an institution. The 19th-century Shelbourne, on the most fashionable "Beaux Walk" stretch of St. Stephen's Green, is part of the nation's heritage; in the movie of Brian Moore's novel, *The Lonely Passion of Judith Hearne,* it is the ultimate proof of wealth and status. The Irish Free State's constitution was drafted here in an upper room. Despite its lofty pedigree, the Shelbourne is pleasantly unstuffy. Everybody is welcome, at least for a coffee or a drink in the Horseshoe Bar. For the restaurant, you are advised to dress up a little, and remember your wallet.

Cheaper alternatives If you find the Shelbourne's tariffs are a bit steep, there are plenty of other options. The best bet if you want somewhere within reach of most of the sights and shops is to stay south of the river, somewhere around the St. Stephen's Green area, or farther out in the pleasant residential suburbs of Ballsbridge. Many attractive Georgian townhouses have been stylishly converted into guesthouses and small hotels, where you can glimpse something of Dublin's former glory in an appropriate setting. The Georgian House is probably one of the best, and best-located, of these, with a lively seafood restaurant. Others include Longfield's, Stephen's Hall, and The Gray Door. An excellent and refreshingly different style is provided at No. 31 Leeson Close, in an architect's former home.

Farther south, the tariffs will be lower and the buildings more recent, probably Victorian or Edwardian. Be prepared for a bus or taxi ride to the city center. Some of the best are Simmonstown House, Raglan Lodge, Ariel House, and Merrion Hall. Elsewhere in the city, pick your location with care: some areas are not particularly pleasant for walking after dark. The seedier dives around Connolly Station and off upper O'Connell Street are best avoided, and not even particularly cheap. The Gresham Hotel, one of Dublin's best and longest-established, once in a prime location on O'Connell Street, now suffers from run-down surroundings.

ISAAC'S
This popular hostel, also known as the Dublin Tourist Hostel, is located a block or two behind the Custom House on the north bank of the Liffey. It is an agreeable conversion of a wine warehouse dating back to the early 1700s, and as far as possible its architectural features have been kept intact. For simple accommodations at a low price it is hard to beat. The self-service restaurant (open to non-residents) stays open all day from 7:30AM and serves cheap, filling fare with an emphasis on organic and vegetarian dishes. There is music laid on in summer. A similar hostel (with the same name) exists in Cork.

76

The Shelbourne faces St. Stephen's Green

If you want a hotel with all the trimmings, modern business hotels such as the Conrad or the Westbury are well located. Buswell's, a favorite haunt of politicians and journalists, has more character, and a certain 18th-century cachet. Jury's, the Dublin flagship of a well-known Irish hotel chain, or the Burlington can provide all possible facilities, including lively nightlife, in modern box-like premises south of the river.

Farther out If you have a car, consider staying even farther out in the more peaceful suburbs, or on the coast, say in Dalkey or Blackrock. Parking in the city center is always difficult and a car is a constant security risk. Avondale House in Scribblestown is a good out-of-town choice, a former hunting lodge dating from the 1720s with a country-house atmosphere. There are many cheaper B.&B.s in the coastal areas. You will find it difficult to enjoy Dublin's night scene (or its pubs) staying this far out, however.

Hostels and rentals If you are on a tight budget, and want to stay centrally, consider a hostel. You may have to share a room, but an increasing number of decent, privately run hostel-style rooms are now available. ISAAC'S (see panel) is a good bet for young travelers. For slightly more comfort, Avalon House in Aungier Street (near the Carmelite Church) offers simple but stylish accommodation and a pleasant coffee shop.

Apartments and houses can be rented at all price levels, and some even have maid service. If you prefer more independence or perhaps have children, this may be the ideal solution. A number are listed in Bord Fáilte's self-catering (rentals) guide. There are no central campsites in Dublin—the nearest you'll get is somewhere south of Dun Laoghaire or in Donabate to the north of the city. Unofficial camping is not recommended and could also be risky.

Book ahead Accommodations in Dublin are plentiful, but the best are not cheap and can fill up rapidly during special events or conferences. Book ahead if you can. The tourist office provides a booking service and will telephone around (for a fee) if you turn up on the spot. (See also Hotels and Restaurants, pages 269–83).

Number 31
One of Dublin's most surprising guesthouses lies hidden behind a secluding stone wall in a quiet cul-de-sac off Leeson Street. The former home of a leading architect, Sam Stephenson, it is now a coveted, small B.&B. The center of these double townhouses has been gutted to create a large, sunken sitting room with a small bar. Vast breakfasts are served in an upper dining-room overlooking a roof garden billowing with exotic vegetation, while intriguing objects bestrew the house. The rooms are simple, but all have good bathrooms. The atmosphere is civilized, but relaxed.

77

Outside the Shelbourne Hotel

Food and drink

No visitor to Dublin should miss sampling the famous Guinness

Dublin coddle
4 back rashers of bacon
4 large sliced potatoes
4 large sausages
black pepper
2 onions, sliced
cornflour
Place the bacon, sausages, potatoes and onion in a pot and cover with cold water. Bring to a boil and simmer gently for 1–2 hours until the meat is cooked. Thicken with cornflour, season with black pepper and serve immediately with fresh soda bread.

The Powerscourt Townhouse, off Grafton Street, good for cafés

A wider choice The eating scene in Dublin is immeasurably better now than it used to be, with a far wider choice of cuisine, and more emphasis on healthy, high-quality ingredients rather than filling, high-fat dishes (although Ireland cannot claim to be the gastronomic capital of the universe). Needless to say, there is plenty of fast food available, especially in areas north of the river. Most outlets are predictably indifferent, with the exception of a couple of good fish and chip shops (e.g., Burdock's or Beshoff's) and pizza joints (e.g., the Bad Ass Café or Le Pasticcio). For gourmets, the city has plenty of choices in the smart townhouse restaurants around St. Stephen's Green, most of which produce classic French or nouvelle cuisine dishes, but you can expect to pay handsomely for the privilege there. The best of these (Patrick Guilbaud, The Commons, Le Coq Hardi, Les Frères Jacques) have earned their high reputation; others verge on pretension.

For several years now Dublin has been home to a number of very good ethnic restaurants—the Rajdoot and Shalimar produce interesting Indian food, the Imperial and the Sichuan are the best of the Chinese restaurants, while, for Italian food, Kapriol and Caesar's are recommended. Besides foreign cuisine, though, traditional Irish cooking is making a healthy comeback, so you may try a Dublin coddle (sausages, bacon, onions, and potatoes in a thickened sauce) or oysters and Guinness. One of the most unusual restaurants serving Irish food is Gallagher's Boxty House, in the lively Temple Bar quarter. (A "boxty" is a sort of Irish potato pancake with all kinds of savory fillings.) The ambience and decor are agreeable and the prices not at all expensive, hence its popularity.

Pubs Dublin pubs concentrate on the drinking side rather than food, but the demands of tourism have meant that more and more serve snacks at lunchtime, though it is rarely particularly imaginative. A civilized touch, however, is that most will serve coffee at any time of day, including, of course, an Irish coffee. The mystique surrounding the serving of Guinness is less overt here than you might expect, but if you look as though you would appreciate it, a shamrock will be etched deftly into the creamy head.

Two Irish specialties, oysters and Guinness

Brown soda bread
4½ cups wholewheat flour
1 cup white flour
1 teaspoon salt
1 teaspoon bread soda
⅜ cup oatmeal
2½ cups buttermilk
Sieve all the dry ingredients together. Make a well in the center, pour in the buttermilk, and stir until the mixture forms a soft dough. Turn on a floured surface and knead lightly to form a round disc roughly 15 inches in diameter. Cut a deep cross into the dough with a sharp knife. Place on a buttered baking dish and bake in the middle of the oven, 425°F, for 15 minutes, then reduce the temperature to 350°F for a further 25 minutes until rich and crusty. Cool on a wire rack.

Cafés For lunchtime snacks some of the most attractive restaurants are in museums or shopping centers—National Gallery, Hugh Lane Municipal Gallery, Dublin Castle, Kilmainham Hospital, Kilkenny Design Centre, and the Powerscourt Townhouse. One place that cannot be ignored is that great institution known as Bewley's Café. There are four of them in Dublin altogether, set up by a Quaker family of tea and coffee importers over a century ago to enable customers to sample their products. The most famous, Bewley's Oriental Café, is on Grafton Street, a wonderful dark and mysterious emporium of stained glass and mahogany serving good food and staying open late. Upstairs is a quieter café area with a small museum.

Other options If you don't want to spend too much in the evenings, head for Temple Bar, which is young and upbeat, but rather more enticing than the sectors north of the river. Many of the restaurants there come and go with the wind, but some of the more long-lasting ones include the Boxty House (see above), the Elephant and Castle, and the Bad Ass Café.

If you want an excursion, there are several excellent restaurants in some of the coastal resorts; Na Mara in Dun Laoghaire, Ayumi-Ya in Blackrock, or King Sitric in Howth are perhaps some of the best. Seafood is usually excellent. Check what days they close if you plan your excursion visit around them.

On Sundays, Dublin can be a desert as far as eating goes. Many of the good places are closed, and those that stay open are likely to be fully booked. If you are in the city on a weekend, plan your eating well ahead of time and make sure you have a table.

Cuisine more Italian than Irish is advertised on this wall in Cecilia Street

79

Shopping

Markets At the north end of Grafton Street is an eye-catching statue in bronze, affectionately known to Dubliners as "the tart with the cart." The subject, of course, is the famous Molly Malone (see panel), wheeling her wheelbarrow. To find today's Molly Malones, you will need to head for the old-fashioned street markets held in Moore Street (mostly selling fruit and vegetables, off Henry Street near the General Post Office), or alternatively the Liberties in Meath Street beyond Christ Church Cathedral, where dozens of stalls of cheap clothing and household goods are on colorful sale.

Shops for visitors Most tourist shopping, however, is done in rather different surroundings, either in the safe, if highly priced, confines of a modern hotel or in one of the city's specialist shops. The main shopping area in the center of town lies between Grafton Street and O'Connell Street. The big department stores are there—Clery's and Eason's north of the river (along with Marks and Spencer and bargain basement stores such as Dunne's in the Ilac Centre, or Arnotts), and more exclusive Switzers or Brown Thomas in Grafton Street. Many international chain shops such as Benetton, Next, Principles, etc., can also be found around pedestrianized Grafton Street. Smaller side streets contain most specialist craft and fashion shops. Nassau Street is a particularly good area to head for if you are looking for typical Irish craft products such as ceramics, knitwear, tweed, linen, crystal, or Celtic jewelry. The outlets vary considerably in quality, one of the more upscale being the excellent Kilkenny Design Centre, a branch of the enterprise based at Kilkenny Castle. Others worth checking out (also situated in Nassau Street) are the exclusive tweed and clothing store, Kevin and Howlin, the Sweater Shop for Aran knitwear, Blarney Woollen Mills and the Best of Irish. For traditional Irish music, Claddagh Records (at 2 Cecilia Street) is one of the best shops.

Dublin boasts a number of new shopping precincts. One of the best is in the imaginatively reconstructed shell of

Molly Malone
In Dublin's fair city where the girls are so pretty
I first set my eyes on sweet Molly Malone.
She wheeled a wheelbarrow through streets broad and narrow
Crying "Cockles and mussels, alive, alive-O!"

Nassau Street has a fine range of shops, from secondhand bookstores to retail outlets more geared to tourists

an 18th-century building, called the Powerscourt Townhouse, with splendid plasterwork ceilings and exterior façade (just off Grafton Street). This complex houses many individual shops, restaurants, and cafés. Another central shopping mall is on St. Stephen's Green, an unmissable, modern, greenhouse-like structure with yet more shops and cafés. Tierney's has one of the better craft displays here.

Bookstores are legion in this literary city, most of them around St. Stephen's or College Greens or the quaysides. Several of these sell collectable secondhand volumes. Fred Hanna's (27/29 Nassau Street), Greene's (Clare Street), Hodges Figgis (54 Dawson Street), the Winding Stair (40 Lower Ormonde Quay) are some of the best known, besides the larger and more general retailers, Waterstone's and Eason's. For antiques, head for Francis Street in the Liberties (beyond Christ Church Cathedral).

Beyond the center Out of the city center, the suburbs of Blackrock or Dalkey have their own shopping complexes and markets, not necessarily worth a special trip. Closer into town on Pearse Street (take a bus two or three stops from Pearse Station) is the Tower Design Centre, a 19th-century sugar-refining tower now run by the Irish Development Authority and housing about 35 separate craft enterprises producing souvenirs in fashions, stained glass, painted silk, knitwear, jewelry, etc. Visitors are welcome to wander around the complex and watch the artists at work. There is no pressure to buy.

Practicalities Shopping hours in Dublin are generally Monday to Saturday, 9AM–6PM, with some of the smaller shops geared to tourists opening on Sundays as well. For non-E.U. residents, the V.A.T. waiver scheme called Cashback makes high-taxed Irish goods more attractive, although there is a fair bit of red tape involved in claiming this back at Dublin or Shannon Airport. Collect a form as you shop and have it stamped as you leave the country.

Shopping is an enduring pastime for these two Dubliners

A crowd-pulling display in Brown Thomas, Grafton Street, one of Dublin's most famous shops

Nightlife

Decisions, decisions Dublin is famous for its pubs—over 800 of them if you care to count—and for its theater. These therefore form the core of the city's evening entertainments. Like most capital cities, however, it can offer much more—many kinds of music, from rock to classical, around two dozen movie screens, and a host of nightclubs and wine bars. Some larger hotels offer well-advertised cabaret shows, Jury's being the most widely publicized. There is always plenty going on if you know where to look, but most parts of the city can seem pretty quiet after midnight, and a few are unsafe.

The main concentration of nightclubs is in Leeson Street. Most of them are basement bars, so the seemly Georgian façades are not at all rowdy. Generally they don't charge entrance, but drinks are pretty expensive. They are at their liveliest on weekends (Thursday to Sunday) and get going after 10PM.

Pubs Pubs and bars are scattered all over the city and take innumerable forms, some modern and plastic, others ancient and Victorian, most of them somewhere in between—suitably "modernized" for tourists. The "pub of the moment" is difficult to pin down, with fashions changing, although regulars may stick to one or two favorites all the time. Most of the well-known places are very busy at night despite the high cost of alcohol in Ireland. They seem generally good-tempered, but they can be very noisy and boisterous. Some have notable gay scenes; others may be popular with drug users, of which Dublin has many. Though predominantly masculine, Dublin's bars are not unfriendly towards women, who will usually get a civilized welcome.

Some of the best-known and most "characterful" bars on the south side are Doheny and Nesbitt (5 Lower Baggot Street), O'Donoghue's (Merrion Row), Toner's (139 Lower Baggot Street), Neary's (1 Chatham Street); further west, the Stag's Head (1 Dame Court, off Dame Street), and Mother Redcap's (Back Lane, off High

Joycean pubs
In The Bailey (Duke Street) Joyce fans can find the door of No. 7 Eccles Street, the fictional home of Leopold Bloom in *Ulysses*, rescued by the pub's proprietor, John Ryan, from a builder's skip. At Davy Byrne's, you can be served a faithful version of the lunch Bloom enjoyed there on June 16, 1904 (Bloomsday)—a glass of burgundy and a Gorgonzola sandwich.

The capital has a thriving youth culture as Dubliners U2 and Bob Geldof might suggest

The Abbey Theatre
The Abbey is one of Dublin's most classic traditions, yet it has staged some controversial productions. The first performance of J. M. Synge's *The Playboy of the Western World* in 1907 caused riots because an Irishman used the word "shift" (meaning petticoat) on stage. Police had to be called to protect Synge from the outraged audience for over a week. In 1926 O'Casey's play *The Plough and the Stars* caused a similar uproar when the national flag was shown in the presence of a prostitute. After a later production of this play in 1951, the theater burned down (accidentally).

Street). Near the Liffey, upriver from O'Connell Street, the Brazen Head (20 Lower Bridge Street) and Ryan's (28 Parkgate Street) are now in fairly sleazy areas, but still have old-fashioned interiors. Ryan's is a confection of mahogany and brass unchanged since 1896. The Brazen Head claims to be Ireland's oldest, where Wolfe Tone and Robert Emmet dreamed of Irish independence. Davy Byrne's and the Bailey (both in Duke Street) have Joycean associations which keep them eternally popular.

Music and theater Many of the pubs offer evening music sessions, Irish traditional, jazz, etc. One specializing in music is Bad Bob's Backstage Bar, a trendy nightspot in Temple Bar. Dublin, of course, has launched many a rock or pop star on the way to fame and fortune; U2, the Chieftains, the Dubliners, Sinéad O'Connor, and Chris de Burgh have all performed in Dublin's nightspots on many occasions. For more traditional music, head for the National Concert Hall in St. Stephen's Green; the Royal Hospital at Kilmainham also stages a number of concerts and evening events. One of the theaters offers music on weekends—Midnight at the Olympia on Fridays and Saturdays involves disco dancing between aisles of plush red seating. Earlier in the evening (and during the week) it usually offers an assorted range of light entertainment. The Gaiety is similarly popular. For more heavyweight theater, head for the Gate or the Abbey, where Dublin's great theatrical tradition started. The annex to the Abbey, called the Peacock, and the Project Arts Club in Temple Bar, specialize in avant-garde or experimental work.

Film There isn't much of an art film scene in Dublin, although some films may be released earlier in the Republic than in London. Most of the two dozen screens on or near O'Connell Street are fairly run-of-the-mill or downright seedy. For an alternative to commercial movies, head for the Lighthouse, or the Irish Film Centre in Temple Bar. There are very few movie theaters in the suburbs.

To find out what's going on in Dublin, get the *Irish Times*, which has daily listings, or the magazine *In Dublin*, on sale in any newsdealer.

The Brazen Head
Ireland's Oldest Pub
ESTD. 1198

The Rubrics at T.C.D., see page 72

The Rubrics at T.C.D., see page 72

Sightseeing tours
Dublin Bus runs sightseeing coach tours of Dublin using open-top vehicles (covered in wet weather). The heritage tour visits ten locations near city sights, and with an all-day ticket you can hop on or off at any point. Buses run hourly between 10AM and 4PM in high season.

Dublin's coat of arms embellishes this street sign

What's happening Dublin is an exceptionally friendly city and most people will be only too happy to help you out. The main tourist office is at 14 O'Connell Street, open weekdays 9AM to 5PM. It is usually crowded, but there are many leaflets to pick up, not all of which are free. Walking tours around the city are also advertised here, and can be fun and informative. Another useful start to city orientation is the Dublin Experience show at Trinity College, on view during the summer months.

If you are short of time, plan carefully and cut out extraneous attractions. Some of the big sights close for part of the weekend or on Monday, and Dublin Castle is occasionally shut altogether. Ask before you set off. Things not to miss are the Castle, Trinity College, and the National Museum and Gallery. Try to catch some of the Georgian architecture around Merrion Square and St. Stephen's Green, and the two cathedrals to the west of the city. If you can, visit Kilmainham Gaol and Hospital, and walk in Phoenix Park. Art lovers will want to find Hugh Lane's Gallery, and, if the lighter side of culture appeals, head for the Guinness Brewery Hop Store Museum. Choose a promising-looking day for excursions to Howth or Dalkey; the best beaches lie around Killiney Bay or Sandymount (some dangerous currents). There is also a magnificent stretch of sand on North Bull Island, a peaceful nature reserve.

If you happen to be in Dublin during a big match, you'll certainly be aware of it. Gaelic games are played at Croke Park, north of the city center. The All-Ireland Hurling and Football Finals take place in September. St. Patrick's Day (March 17) is a fine time to be here, with parades and other happenings, although celebrations are smaller than in New York and Boston, for example. To find out what's going on, get a listings magazines (the best is *In Dublin*).

City transportation A bus map is worth getting. Although the central areas are reasonably compact,

Dublin can make you footsore, and hopping on a bus occasionally may be welcome. The routes, if not always the schedules, are more or less adhered to. Most of them start from Busáras, the main station, just north of the river near the Custom House, or from the streets near College Green. If you plan to do much exploring, it is worth getting a pass lasting one or several days. The words *An Lár* on the front of a bus indicate it is going to the city center. For longer trips, contact Bus Eireann's offices just across O'Connell Street from the tourist office. A branch of Thomas Cook (118 Grafton Street, tel: 677 1721) can answer general travel inquiries. For youth travel, student discounts, etc., contact the U.S.I.T. office on Aston Quay.

For travel to the nearest coast, the D.A.R.T. (Dublin Area Rapid Transit) route, a single rail line between Bray and Howth, is an entertaining excursion with fine coastal views. You can catch the D.A.R.T. trains at Connolly, Tara Street, or Pearse stations. For train services farther afield (between Dundalk and Arklow) you should head for the main station, Connolly. Heuston Station serves the western and southern regions.

Taxis are not generally hailed in transit, but stand in lines in some of the main streets, and are fairly expensive. Parking is always difficult and costly in the city center. Always park in official places, not in quiet backstreets, where the incidence of vandalism and theft is very high. Never leave anything remotely valuable inside.

Crime The problems of urban life have caused a sharp rise in street crime generally, exacerbated by economic depression and drug and alcohol abuse. Conspicuous tourists are easy prey. Don't carry too much money and don't stray into unknown areas off the main tourist trail. The streets west of St. Patrick's Cathedral, or many north of the river, are not advisable for unscheduled sauntering.

Rock 'n' Stroll
Self-guided walks round Dublin inevitably focus on its Georgian architecture or literary associations, or perhaps pub crawls for the thirsty. An alternative themed walk is the Rock 'n' Stroll Guide, which leads its followers to the principal places in Dublin associated with the contemporary music scene. Revisit The Chieftains' first gig at the Gresham Hotel, Mary Black's stamping ground at the Olympia, or U2's launch pad in Mount Temple Comprehensive School! Pick up the tour guide in any tourist office.

85

O'Connell Bridge, at the heart of the city

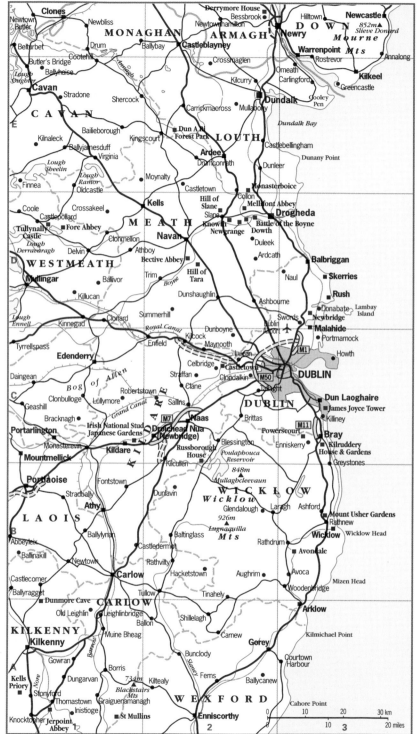

The gentler aspect of the Wicklow Mountains

Eastern Counties The counties immediately around Dublin constitute the Pale, the area most strongly influenced by English rule from Norman times onward. What lay beyond the Pale was less easily subjugated and often perceived (accurately) as a threat to English interests. The pull of the capital ensures these eastern counties still receive a steady flow of visitors, though scenically (with the exception of Wicklow) they are not Ireland's most exciting regions. There are, though, a good many reasons to spend time there. They are enormously rich in history, layer upon layer of it from prehistoric to recent times. The famous passage graves at Newgrange are Ireland's best-known neolithic site. Then there are Celtic High Crosses, the evocative monastic settlement of Glendalough, many later abbeys and churches, castles and several of Ireland's grandest houses and gardens. Horse lovers will want to visit the Curragh at Kildare and the nearby National Stud. For walkers, the heather moors and wooded glens of the Wicklow Mountains bristle with opportunities. If you are thinking of a beach holiday in Ireland, the drier sunnier climate of the southeast makes a seaside stay a reasonable gamble instead of a long shot. The best beaches in this region are in County Wicklow.

County Louth is the smallest of the 32 counties of Ireland. Inland, it echoes the drumlin country of those other border counties, Cavan and Monaghan—a gentle, placid landscape of little hills and lakes. Its easterly section is more dramatic, a precursor of the Mountains of Mourne that loom enticingly across Carlingford Lough. The Cooley Peninsula, setting for one of Ireland's greatest epics (*Táin Bo Cuailgne*—the Cattle Raid of Cooley) makes a fine excursion, where the lakeshore village of Carlingford is one of the most delightful low-key holiday bases, managing to avoid (for the most part) the strains of other border towns such as Dundalk or Monaghan. Drogheda, Louth's other main town, seems to have weathered its Cromwellian torments more resiliently than most and amply repays a stop, or even a stay. All around

The little gentleman in black velvet
This favorite Jacobite toast during the reign of Queen Anne is still drunk in certain nationalist and Catholic circles. The little gentleman is the mole that is alleged to have killed William III when his horse Sorrel stumbled on a molehill and threw him on February 21, 1702, badly fracturing his collarbone. The king died in London two weeks later. If this sounds a heartless tradition, the anti-Catholic toasts of the Orange Order are much more savage. The 19th-century British Prime Minister, Sir Robert Peel, apparently drank to these in his early life, and became nicknamed "Orange Peel" by the Irish.

The lonely Vale of Glenmacnass in the Wicklow Mountains just south of Dublin. Glenmacnass means "the valley of the sons of Neasa"

it, stretching into County Meath, is a rich cluster of prehistoric and Celtic sites, great abbeys and castles, the Hills of Slane and Tara suffused with legends and national symbolism. The River Boyne is a place of pilgrimage for many tracing the progress of that famous battle of 1690 along alternate banks, although this was only one of numerous skirmishes between Jacobite and Williamite troops in those troubled years.

Dublin's hinterlands Closer to Dublin, the coast is studded with small fishing ports, most fairly dull. Howth and Malahide are the ones to visit—the first for its breezy headland views and castle gardens, the second for an interestingly furnished castle and art collection. The capital's immediate hinterland is County Kildare, where the rolling springy grassland provides pasture and an exercise track for dozens of fine-boned thoroughbreds. This is the heart of Ireland's bloodstock industry, one of the more solid mainstays of Ireland's shaky economy. Keen followers of horse racing may want to time their arrival carefully to coincide with one of the big annual races. Naas (the county seat) holds its big race meeting in April, at Punchestown Racecourse. The Curragh, famed for horse racing since time immemorial, hosts all of Ireland's classic events—the Oaks, the Derby, and the St. Leger.

Naas is near enough to all this to benefit from horse-borne prosperity and far enough from Dublin's suburban tentacles to have a spirit of its own. It makes one of the best places to pause and plan a route. If horses aren't your scene, you can search for Round Towers and Celtic High Crosses, follow the great canal routes that crisscross the county or investigate the mournful Bog of Allen, where there is an interesting interpretative center explaining the significance of bogland ecology, Peatland World, Lullymore, near Rathangan (tel: 045 60133). Kildare's most important stately home is Castletown, one of Ireland's largest Palladian houses.

South of Dublin lies County Wicklow, one of the capital's favorite "lungs." A glance at its topography soon indicates why—the Wicklow Mountains reach a significant altitude by Irish standards (Lugnaquilla is Ireland's

third-highest peak at 3,039 feet) and contain some very beautiful and unpopulated scenery. The coastline, too, has attractions—breezy headlands and great sweeps of sand stretching from Bray southwards, the best being Brittas Bay south of Wicklow Head. A trip over the central heights is most rewarding; choose one of the routes around the Sally Gap and take in the awe-inspiring views around Glencree and Glenmacnass, or seek out the hidden lakes of Tay and Dan. Powerscourt Gardens and Russborough House shouldn't be missed; ensure you time your visit to find them open. The other "unmissable" is Glendalough, a collection of ancient monastic buildings in a gorgeous setting. Wicklow's impressive range of sights also includes the great gardens of Kilruddery and Mount Usher, and Charles Stewart Parnell's house at Avondale, now a forest park and museum to his memory. There is no shortage of excellent accommodations or restaurants in County Wicklow; its nearness to Dublin ensures a steady year-round trade and it has a quietly prosperous air.

The most famous bits of the Boyne valley and the holiday resorts of the east coast are also pretty well equipped, and County Kildare has a number of good places to stay or eat. The less popular regions of Louth and Meath, however, offer rather patchy choices and it needs some planning to stay anywhere pleasant. If you have time, it's worth reaching Carlingford.

The tower of Trim Abbey, as seen from the town's castle

Leinster taboos
In ancient Ireland, the lives of kings and other notabilities were hedged in by taboos, doubtless going back into the mists of prehistory. Death was the inexorable outcome of these being violated one by one, a subject beloved of the dramatic storytellers of medieval Ireland. Five taboos recorded for the king of the Leinstermen included those forbidding him from:
● traveling widdershins (counterclockwise) around the Wicklow Hills on a Wednesday;
● sleeping between Dublin and the Dodder River with his head facing to one side;
● setting up camp for nine days on the plains of Cualu (Bray);
● traveling alone on the road to Dublin on a Monday;
● riding on a dirty, black-hooved horse over the plain of Mullaghmast (County Kildare).

The meaning of the interwoven spirals, found on several stones at Newgrange, remains unclear

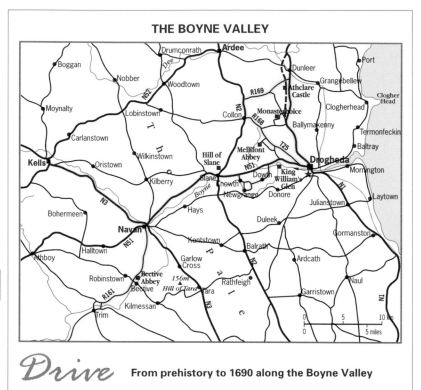

THE BOYNE VALLEY

Drive **From prehistory to 1690 along the Boyne Valley**

A drive through the past from prehistoric times to Ireland's most significant battle site whose divisive echoes reverberate more than 300 years later in the streets of Belfast and London. (It is recommended that you follow the precise route of this drive on a detailed, large-scale map.)

Head north from Drogheda on N1. Clearly signed to the west are the High Crosses and Round Tower of **Monasterboice** (see page 105). Looping back south again by the Mattock valley, watch for signs to the remains of **Mellifont Abbey**, in a maze of quiet lanes (see page 106). About 4 miles west of **Drogheda** (well signed off the N51 from the town) is the historic **King William's Glen**, site of the famous Battle of the Boyne in 1690. An orange and green sign by the river marks the main site of conflict. A marked trail from the Townley Hall Estate (the extensive grounds of a Georgian mansion) leads to a viewing place above the battle-

ground showing where the opposing armies camped, and where William's army crossed the river from the north at two separate points, taking the forces of James II on the southern banks by surprise. An explanatory diagram and display board outlines the battle maneuvers. It is worth getting a leaflet or map (from local tourist offices) showing the battle sites if you want to explore in detail, since dodging back and forth across the river can be disorienting. The battle route passes the Boyne Navigation Canal, part of a grand scheme to connect Ireland's major waterways.

The battle was a historical landmark for many reasons, a minor point of interest being that it was the last conflict in Europe in which opposing monarchs played an active military role; William III himself narrowly escaped death from a sniper's bullet on the morning of the battle. William's soldiers used sprigs of leaves to distinguish themselves from the Jacobite forces, since they wore

A mural on a cottage near Droghcda celebrates the famous battle

no clearly recognizable uniforms. As they crossed the river they played the Orange marching tune *Lillebulero*. Gradually, James's forces were pushed back south toward **Duleek**, where one of Ireland's oldest stone churches once stood. St. Ciarán's was built in the 5th century soon after Christianity first reached Ireland. The remains now visible date from later centuries. The final skirmish of the Battle of the Boyne took place at Duleek, and William is thought to have spent the night after the battle near there. Buried in the churchyard is Lord John Bellew, a Catholic who died at the subsequent Battle of Aughrim. He was shot in the stomach, and is said to have died bravely, facing his enemies.

Farther west lie some of Ireland's most important neolithic remains, including the passage graves of Dowth, Knowth, and Newgrange, collectively known as **Brugh na Boinne** (see pages 108–9). Besides the main tombs, at least 40 other burial places are believed to lie in and around this fertile farmland within a strategic bend of the River Boyne. Some of these sites have not yet been excavated, although from the Newgrange tomb several strange humps and mounds are clearly visible in the surrounding landscape.

Kells (formerly known as **Ceanannus Mór**), up the Blackwater valley, is best known for the *Book of Kells*, a splendid illuminated manuscript now housed in Trinity College Dublin (see page 73). Many other antiquities and sacred sites are clustered along the Boyne valley around **Slane**, **Navan**, **Tara**, seat of the High Kings of Ireland, and **Trim** (see their respective entries throughout this chapter; the Hill of Tara is on page 107). Castles dating from more recent times are scattered throughout the region. Trim itself has an enormous fortress—the largest dating from Norman times. The evocative ruins of **Bective Abbey** are also worth looking out for on the peaceful meadows by the river between Trim and Navan.

This simple church at Kells dates from the first millennium

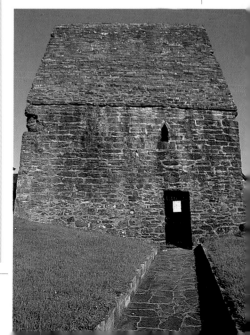

Avoca Handweavers give daily demonstrations of their craft

Parnell and Kitty O'Shea
Parnell fell in love with Kitty, wife of Captain Willy O'Shea, by whom she had three children. It was not a successful marriage, however, and the two spent long periods apart, constantly impecunious. She first met Parnell outside the House of Commons in London, and the attraction was instant. Within a short time the two were secretly living together, and Parnell fathered her remaining children. O'Shea put up with the situation at first, hoping for the inheritance from Kitty's wealthy aunt. When his chances were dashed, he sued for divorce. (See also pages 42–3.)

► **Avoca** *86B3*

Avoca, a pretty hamlet of neat white cottages in a wooded setting by the meeting of the Avonbeg and Avonmore rivers, is the home of Avoca Handweavers, who produce some of Ireland's most energetically marketed craft products from a group of whitewashed buildings containing the oldest surviving handweaving mill in Ireland, dating from 1723. The business was built up over 40 years by the Wynne sisters, who claim to have invented the car blanket! Bright tweeds of natural fibers are manufactured (mostly on modern machinery) and made into hats, suits, and voluminous cloaks. High-quality Avoca products can be found all over the country. Bus tours converge to watch weaving demonstrations, enjoy good lunches or teas in the café, and (perhaps) take something home with them.

►► **Avondale** *86B3*

Deep in one of County Wicklow's most beautifully wooded areas is the Georgian birthplace and home of the 19th-century politician Charles Stewart Parnell, now a museum dedicated to his memory. Parnell was one of Ireland's greatest campaigners for democracy and land reform. Though at first regarded by the English as a dangerous revolutionary because of his association with the Irish Land League, he eventually won Gladstone's abiding respect and persuaded many people that Home Rule was a viable option for Ireland. His career foundered abruptly after his long-standing liaison with the wife of a fellow Member of Parliament became public knowledge (see panel). Soon after divorce proceedings were instituted, Parnell was ousted from his political position and died of strain and ill-health. A film relates the background to Parnell's life story and the history of the house, which is interestingly furnished and contains many touching mementoes and political cartoons. Some of his eloquent love letters to Kitty O'Shea are framed on the walls, as is the extensive Parnell family tree, many of whose members died tragically of madness, vaccination, fevers, or grief.

The grounds were taken over by the state in 1904 as a forestry school. Much research on arboriculture is conducted there and the forest park is full of fine and flourishing trees of many different species. Walks lead through the 500-acre park by the riverside.

Bray 86C3

Bray is a convenient place for Dublin's citizens to gain a breath of sea air, though it cannot be described as the most exciting bit of Ireland's coastline. It is the southerly terminus of the D.A.R.T. suburban railroad line from Dublin, so is easily reached without a car. The best views are from Bray Head, the final projection of the Wicklow range, from where the Great and Little Sugar Loaf Mountains can be seen. North of Bray is the long sandy beach of Killiney Bay.

Bray has literary associations with James Joyce, who lived briefly at 1 Martello Terrace, which featured in *A Portrait of the Artist as a Young Man*. It is now privately owned and not generally open to the public. A more accessible place of interest is **Kilruddery House and Gardens▶** to the south of the resort, a rare example of 17th-century landscaping. Ponds, avenues, parterres, and hedges are laid out with mathematical precision. The house dates from the 1650s (extensively remodeled in the 1820s) and contains many interesting features— Grinling Gibbons carving, Chippendale furniture, and a water-powered stable clock (open May, June, and September, afternoons only).

93

▶▶ Carlingford 86E3

The most enjoyable place on the Cooley peninsula (see page 96) is Carlingford, between the green slopes of Slieve Foye and the blue waters of the lake, with the Mourne Mountains beyond. This delightful village is by far the best base in the area, with several excellent, inexpensive pubs and guesthouses. For its modest size, it has some imposing monuments, indicating that it was a place of some significance during the Middle Ages. King John's Castle stands on the north side of the harbor, a massive D-shaped fortress dating from the 13th century. Its opposite number is Greencastle, on the Northern Irish side of the lake. In the village itself are Taafe's Castle and the Mint, both fortified houses, and the old town hall, or Tholsel, an arched gateway.

Avondale House is famous as the birth-place of Charles Stewart Parnell. In the surrounding Forest Park you may be fortunate enough to catch sight of an otter

The banner of a local fishermen's guild now in the Millmount Museum, Drogheda

▶▶ Castletown House 86C2

This huge stately home is rated as one of the finest examples of Palladian (classical) architecture in the Republic. It has many intriguing features, and has been extensively restored by the Irish Georgian Society. It was built in 1722 for William Connolly, Speaker of the Irish House of Commons, who made a colossal fortune from forfeited estates after the Battle of the Boyne—it is hardly surprising that local attitudes to the house have been somewhat ambivalent. Designed by Alessandro Galilei in the style of an Italian villa, it contains wonderful plasterwork by the Francini brothers, and a sumptuous Pompeiian Long Gallery with splendidly hideous Murano chandeliers. The extensive grounds feature clipped yew trees and a folly obelisk. Though it is no longer lived in, its contents clearly reveal the character and tastes of its former owners. Lady Louisa Connolly, who married in 1758 at the age of 15, was one of its most influential collectors and decorators. An extravagant woman in some ways, she appears more compassionate and socially aware than many of her class, declaring when faced with the gargantuan banquet menus of the time, "It can never be right or useful that one set of people should be gorged with food and the other part in want."

▶▶ Drogheda 86D2

This was originally a Viking town, later expanded into one of Hugh de Lacy's principal Norman strongholds, although little remains of the old town walls. In 1412 the two parts of the town on either side of the Boyne were united by charter to become the largest English town in Ireland; something of this ancient medieval pattern can still be seen in the hilly streets. The Millmount to the south side is topped by an 18th-century military barracks and fort, with a fine view of the northern part of the town and the railway viaduct spanning the river.

Drogheda stands at the lowest bridging point of the River Boyne, just a few miles from the site of the famous battle of 1690. Wartime violence was nothing new; in 1649 Drogheda saw one of Cromwell's bloodiest assaults. Women and children who took refuge in one of its churches were burned alive and the defending garrison, driven south of the river to the hilltop Millmount Fort, were ruthlessly massacred after their surrender. The garrison commander, an English royalist, was battered to death with his

own wooden leg. "I think that we put to the sword altogether about 2,000 men," Cromwell wrote smugly, "It is right that God alone should have all the glory." Today the Millmount Fort houses a strangely peaceful collection of items in the excellent, privately run **Millmount Museum►►**—medieval guild banners, old trade machinery and tools, and a coracle made of willow and leather. Other sections of this garrison have been converted into craft studios and a restaurant.

Over the river again, several buildings in the densely packed main town catch the eye: the 1224 Magdalene Tower, last remnants of a Dominican friary; the fine 13th-century St. Laurence Gate, surmounted by two drum towers; the little chapel of the Siena Convent; and the Tholsel, an 18th-century town hall now used as a bank. The two churches of St. Peter's are also worth a look, the Protestant one for its grim "cadaver" gravestone, the Catholic one for the famous shrine of St. Oliver Plunkett (see panel on page 114), Primate of all Ireland, whose blackened head was rescued from the flames after his execution at Tyburn (London) for high treason (his crime was simply unrepentant Catholicism)

Despite these somewhat grisly memories, Drogheda is an attractive place, with some good music pubs (notably Carbery's on North Strand and McHugh's on Lawrence Street) and a lively, purposeful air. It makes a convenient and pleasant base for exploring the rich heritage of the Royne valley, which contains some of Ireland's most impressive antiquities.

Drogheda and Cromwell
The atrocities committed by Cromwell's troops are well documented in many sources, although the precise number of casualties is hard to establish. Yet the municipal records of Drogheda on both the day before *and the day after* the alleged massacre in 1649 deal with the vexatious topic of street lighting, and make no mention of Cromwell's frightful conduct—even in cowed acquiescence. It is indeed an odd omission. There is no doubt that some of Cromwell's actions have been exaggerated for propaganda purposes, though he amply earned his hated reputation in Ireland.

Castletown House, considered by some to be the finest 18th-century mansion in the Republic

The Long Woman's Grave

Near the Windy Gap on the Cooley peninsula a plaque relates the strange tale of the Long Woman's Grave. A man courted a tall Spanish beauty, telling her he owned all the lands that could be seen from a high place. She married him and came to Ireland, then asked him to show her his inheritance. He brought her to the Windy Gap, where the views are closely obstructed by cliffs. She died of shock and is buried in the Long Woman's Grave.

Dundalk 86E2

Dundalk is a border town, uncomfortably close to the most sensitive section of the Northern Ireland frontier. However, it is able to boast a few features of interest, the most noteworthy building being its **Cathedral of St. Patrick►**, a pastiche of King's College Chapel, Cambridge, which has rich mosaics inside. A museum and interpretative center, which are housed in an old 18th-century distillery, relate the history of County Louth.

Just outside of the town, there is a huge bird reserve at **Dundalk Bay►**, where thousands of wading birds can be found searching for food and shelter among the mudflats. North of the town, a few minutes' drive takes you into the lovely scenery of the hilly, granite **Cooley peninsula►►**, attractive in its own right, but also overlooking tempting views of the Mountains of Mourne across the lough which divides the Republic from Northern Ireland. Cooley is associated with one of Ireland's best-known myths, the Cattle Raid of Cooley, in which Queen Maeve, who is jealous of her husband's prize white bull, attempts to take the brown bull of Cooley by force. Cuchulainn, the Hound of Ulster, becomes the hero of the hour, but is mortally wounded during the battle (see pages 27–8). Curiosities on the Cooley peninsula include the giant Proleek Dolmen, accessible via a footpath from the Ballymascanlon House Hotel, and the Windy Gap, a mountain pass closely hemmed in by cliffs and crags, and scene of an incident in the Cattle Raid epic.

Colimore Harbour in Dalkey, not far south of Dun Laoghaire

JOHN POWER & SON
IRISH WHISKEY
SMITHFIELD, DUBLIN 7
ESTD. 1791
DISTILLED AND BOTTLED IN BOND BY
John Power Son
DUBLIN
PRODUCT OF IRELAND
40% vol
750 ml
e

97

▶ Dun Laoghaire   86C3

Weary ferry travelers from Britain usually have difficulty either spelling or pronouncing the name ("Dun Leary") of this major entry port into the Republic. Its former name (Kingstown) commemorated the English George IV, who visited in 1821. Its Irish name refers to an earlier monarch, the 5th century High King of Tara, Laoghaire, who allowed St. Patrick to set up his mission in Ireland. When the harbor was constructed by the Scot, John Rennie, in the early 19th century, its vast granite piers were the largest in the world. Besides its commercial traffic, Dun Laoghaire is a prestigious yachting center. Apart from catching ferries, visitors stray to this Victorian town of brightly painted houses to look at the **National Maritime Museum▶**, in the former Mariners Church on Haigh Terrace, which houses a French longboat captured at Bantry, County Cork, in 1796, and the old optic from the Baily Lighthouse on Howth Head.

The **James Joyce Martello Tower▶** at Sandycove is another place of interest. Joyce spent a brief and disturbing time here with the poet-surgeon, Oliver St. John Gogarty, who later appeared as Buck Mulligan in *Ulysses*. Apparently, one of the guests had a nightmare and fired several shots into the fireplace of the room where they were sleeping. Gogarty then shot at a row of saucepans above Joyce's head, shouting "Leave him to me!" Joyce, tempering valor with discretion, left the next morning. The Martello Tower houses a small museum set up by Sylvia Beach, with Joycean memorabilia, including a tie given by Joyce to Samuel Beckett. The gunpowder magazine now houses the Joyce Library and Joyce's death mask, made on January 13, 1941 (open April–October). Close by is the Forty Foot Pool mentioned in *Ulysses,* a natural seawater swimming hole where nude bathing was once permitted, for men only. Women are now allowed, but togs are required—by law! Nearby Dalkey▶ (pronounced Dawkey) is an attractive resort with ancient fortified mansions and summer boat trips to Dalkey Island, a bird sanctuary and home to a herd of wild goats.

A detail from the Christ in Majesty sculpture, in Dun Laoghaire

The vanishing stone

The antiquarian, W. F. Wakeman, noted in 1893 that a "celebrated inscribed stone, which was supposed to mark the grave of an Irish monarch, gradually disappeared from the *Rightfert*, or 'King's Cemetery,' at Glendalough. Bit by bit it was sold to tourists by the lying 'guides' (so called) who infest that time-hallowed spot."

Traditional fare

An unsubstantiated story tells how Grace O'Malley, the famous 16th-century pirate queen from the west of Ireland, came on a visit to Howth and found the gates of the castle barred against her. She then abducted the young heir, and promised to return him only on condition that a place should always be laid at the family table for any unexpected guests—a practice still scrupulously followed to this day.

▶▶ **Glendalough** 86B2

This collection of monastic remains is one of the most important in Ireland. Bus tours visit it from Dublin, and the crowds have brought about a tawdry rash of souvenir shops, pubs, and cafés in the local villages, along with plenty of guesthouses and hotels. Once away from this, however, the utter peace and beauty of the location are captivating, perhaps more than the ruins themselves. It is easy to see why St. Kevin (see page 115) sought solitude there in the 6th century, but his plans were somewhat thwarted. Beset by acolytes and lovelorn women (whom he treated brusquely by thrusting into nettles or pushing in the lake), he eventually set up a large religious settlement there, which held great sway until it was attacked by Vikings in later centuries and was at last overrun by English forces in 1398, after which its influence declined. Restoration work took place during the 19th century.

The ruins stand around two lakes in a beautiful wooded valley sheltered by great spurs of the Wicklow Mountains. The main concentration can be seen near the Lower Lake, by the visitor center, where traffic converges. This modern building contains an exhibition of religious antiquities and an audiovisual presentation of monastic life in Ireland—giving an intriguing overview of this aspect of Celtic history. From there you can take a guided tour or make your own way around the remains. The famous sites are the well-preserved 100-foot Round Tower and the intact church often called St. Kevin's Kitchen because of its chimney-like bell tower. Against the backdrop of the wooded slopes, this assembly of quaint stone rooflines and pencil spires is unforgettable. Also visible are the

One of the most famous—and most visited—of Ireland's Round Towers is to be found in the beautiful wooded setting of Glendalough

shells of the roofless cathedral and the Priests' House, and many crosses and gravestones. Farther up the valley (a pleasant walk or short drive) near the more spectacular and peaceful Upper Lake are various minor sights—a bee-hive cell, an early fort and another ruined church. St. Kevin's Bed is a suitably masochistic rocky ledge high on a cliff face (safely accessible only by boat) where the saint used to sleep. Keen walkers have an excellent choice of routes in this area (a national park information point is open in summer, and there are several local hostels).

Howth remains a working fishing port, and has a good range of fish restaurants

►► Howth 86C3

This is now little more than a suburb of Dublin, but its attractions are still easily appreciated, particularly at the coast. Howth (it rhymes with "both") Head gives fine views of Dublin Bay and the Wicklow Mountains or Boyne valley beyond. In the bay is the rocky bird sanctuary and monastic island of Ireland's Eye, to which boat trips may be taken in summer. Cliff paths lead around the coastline, through Howth village and its ruined abbey, and past Baily Lighthouse. The 15th-century Howth Castle is inland near the Deer Park Hotel, partly ruinous, but with fine rhodo-dendron gardens. A small transport museum can be visited near the D.A.R.T. railway station, featuring Howth's famous open-topped tram. Howth's pubs, hotels and fish restaurants make it a pleasant outing from Dublin.

Both this High Cross and the Round Tower have lost their sum-mits, but Kells's small oratory remains intact, see page 91

► Kells 86D1

North of the Boyne lie several fine monastic buildings. Kells (formerly known as Ceanannus Mór), up the Black-water valley, is best known for the *Book of Kells* (see page 73). A facsimile copy is in the modern Church of Ireland occupying the site of St. Columba's 6th-century monastery. A Round Tower, five High Crosses (the best is the South Cross, carved with biblical scenes) and a simple two-story church all date from the first millennium.

EASTERN COUNTIES

*Kildare, popular with
canal enthusiasts*

High Crosses

South Kildare contains several well-preserved High Crosses. The best are at Moone and Castledermot. The Moone example stands over 16 feet and depicts biblical scenes (lane signposted near post office). There are two crosses at Castledermot, again carved with scriptural themes. Both sites stand in the ruins of ancient monasteries.

Canal trips

County Kildare is traversed by two great canal systems, the Royal and Grand Canals, which connect Dublin with the interior lakelands and the Rivers Shannon and Barrow. They were major arteries of trade during the Industrial Revolution until the 1801 Act of Union stifled Ireland's economic development. The place to find out more about the canals is Robertstown. There, trips run from the restored Old Canal Hotel (exhibition), which was built in 1803 to serve canal-borne passengers; candlelit dinners with music are sometimes held in summer.

*A range of shoes is
on offer to Kildare's
four-footed residents*

►► Kildare   86C1

The county town, Naas, has a village-like air; gaily painted shop-fronts, old pubs, and of course a betting shop cluster around its market square by the sturdy tower of **St. Brigid's Cathedral►**, dating from the 13th century, but much altered since. Stained-glass windows depict Ireland's great saints—Brigid, Patrick, and Columba. During the 5th century Kildare was one of the few religious houses in Ireland exclusively for women. The cathedral is flanked by a tall **Round Tower►**, which you can climb in summer for extensive views of this rolling horse country. Immediately outside town is the wide, springy, gorse-speckled plain called the Curragh, which will stir the heart of any racing *aficionado*. The Curragh is Ireland's largest military camp, where the armored vehicle that carried Michael Collins to his fatal ambush in 1922 is on display.

If you are at all interested in horses, one place you will certainly want to see is the **Irish National Stud►►**, based at Tully just outside the town. Visitors can tour the neat buildings and see the horses being exercised and groomed, or at ease in carefully fenced paddocks. These valuable animals enjoy a standard of living many humans would envy, and their occupation may appeal, too. The stallions stay hard at work from January to July; the rest of the year is their "vacation." They have to perform as stalwartly in the covering sheds as they ever did on the racecourse.

The stud was set up in 1902 by the British, and transferred to the Irish state in 1943. Its eccentric founder was Colonel William Hall Walker, who believed that the stars influenced the horses' form. The stallion boxes are built with lantern roofs to allow heavenly bodies their full effect on the horses. Every time a mare foaled, Colonel Walker would cast its horoscope, and race or sell the progeny accordingly. The system, it is said, was uncannily successful.

Spring and early summer are the most interesting times to visit, when you will see new foals with the mares. The foaling area contains a special unit in which orphan foals can be safely fostered. Later in the year the Sun Chariot Yard holds promising yearlings whose paces are just about to be tested. Veterinary research is carried out at the stud, along with all aspects of the complex and rarified science of horse breeding. The animals are not pets and should not be approached; apart from their extreme value, they can be fierce and may bite or kick, and mares with foals can be particularly savage.

The ornamental lake near the stable units provides mineral-rich drinking water for the horses, said to encourage good bone structure. Also in the grounds are the ruins of the Black Abbey, dating from the 12th century, along with the **Irish National Stud Horse Museum►**, dedicated to all aspects of the equine species. The skeleton of the legendary steeplechaser Arkle is on display, as well as Pat Taafe's whip and the Duchess of Westminster's racing colors.

Next to the Stud is a completely different attraction, although it can be visited on a joint ticket. The **Japanese Gardens►►** symbolically depict man's progress from birth to eternity, via a series of landmarks representing disappointments and failures on the road to enlightenment and final happiness. On the way, visitors pass such features as the Marriage Bridge, the Hill of Ambition, and the Tunnel of Ignorance. The intricate landscaping makes the gardens seem much bigger than they really are. They were created by the Japanese gardener Eida and his son between 1906 and 1910. A garden center offers bonsai trees for sale, and tea rooms provide sustenance. Open daily in season.

Two bodies
A saint's relics were of huge importance to the economy of a monastery because of the pilgrims who came to venerate them, and strife between monasteries for the possession of such relics was by no means uncommon. One recorded instance concerned the relics of St. Abban, a south Leinster saint. His medieval *Life* tells of a struggle between the monks of Killabban (his County Kildare birthplace) and those of his monastery at Maganey, for the possession of his body. The former claimed it because they were his first followers, while the latter based their claim to it on the fact that the saint had lived and died among them. Divine Providence, however, stepped in and settled the matter satisfactorily by bestowing an identical body of the saint on each of the communities!

The elegant Japanese Gardens are a surprising find next to the National Stud

The English and the Irish probably come closer to understanding each other through their mutual love of horses than in any other way. Ireland is currently estimated to have about 55,000 horses, including 15,000 racehorses.

Laytown Races

The much loved and highly unusual Laytown Races are held just once a year in either July or August. The course is a gently shelving beach of soft sand in a little coastal resort in County Meath, near Drogheda. As soon as the tide goes out the six-furlong track is quickly marked and the horses thunder across the strand, amid a lively seaside atmosphere of cotton candy stalls and paddling children. The competitors race not only each other, but the advancing tide! Sadly, a serious accident in 1994 has cast a shadow over Laytown's future.

A focal point of Ireland's racing country is Punchestown racecourse, County Kildare

A land of horses Ireland is the heart of the racehorse industry, where many of the world's best thoroughbreds are reared and trained. It also has facilities for every type of equestrian sport: flat-racing, steeplechasing, show jumping, eventing, or trekking. Equestrian centers abound, and fox hunting is alive and well. For other aspects of the horse world, turn up at the jolly Connemara Pony Show (Clifden, August), the fashionable Dublin Horse Show (August), or the horse fairs in Buttevant (County Cork, July 12) and Ballinasloe (County Galway, October), where all classes of horseflesh change hands amid an arcane code of palm-slapping and luck money (IR£5 or so that the seller gives so the horse's new owner will have "good luck" betting on his purchase).

Irish breeding Horses thrive in Ireland's mild climate and lush, unpolluted pastureland. The grass overlies a base of limestone, which produces the calcium needed for healthy bones. The native Irish horses are Connemaras, those cheerful animals that survive on saltmarsh grasses and seaweed in the far West. Romantic legends tell how Spanish Arab horses escaped from Armada vessels shipwrecked off the Galway coast in the 16th century and intermingled with the native stock, producing a taller, faster and more elegant breed. The two other distinctively Irish equines are the powerful draft horses, used to plow fields and draw carts, and the charismatic creature of the turf, the long-limbed thoroughbred. Crossbreeding between draught and thoroughbred produces the sturdier but athletic animals used for hunting or show jumping.

Horses

The lure of the turf Horse racing is more than a mere sport in Ireland; it is a passion, consuming and generating vast sums of money. In-course betting turnover amounts to about IR£90 million a year, and thousands are avid studiers of form. The breeding industry turns over staggering amounts, aided by favorable government tax breaks. Many British breeders, trainers, and owners now base their operations in Ireland. Racing, however, was known in Ireland many centuries ago. The legendary Red Branch knights of Ulster raced, as did later Gaelic warriors, although it was then mainly a sport of kings. The Normans and Elizabethans loved it; Cromwell, with his characteristic lack of *joie de vivre*, tried to ban it as the work of the devil —possibly one of his least popular moves in Ireland. During the 18th century racing was all the rage, and two neighbors in County Cork coined a new phrase with their epic cross-country dash between the spires of Buttevant and Doneraile churches—"steeplechasing."

Today, racing "over the sticks" still has a great following, although not nearly as much money is involved as in flat-racing. Jumpers are usually gelded, so when their sporting days are over they cannot retire gracefully to sire lucrative strings of winning progeny, as flat-racers do. Nonetheless, the courage and stamina needed of both horse and rider in steeplechasing make it an exciting and highly respected sport.

Ireland has nearly 30 racecourses, and meetings are held somewhere on about 245 days of the year, including Sundays. They vary enormously from state-of-the-art Leopardstown, just outside Dublin, to the quaint Laytown Races (see panel). Ireland's most celebrated flat-racing venue is the Curragh in County Kildare, 5,700 acres of gorsy plain where visitors will see strings of racehorses testing their paces on the springy turf. The great national hunt (steeplechasing) courses are at Fairyhouse (where the Irish Grand National is held), Punchestown, Navan and Galway. You can find full details of the racing calendar in any Irish paper, or from the tourist board. The most valuable race is the Irish Derby; the winner, whose progeny will be closely watched for hereditary swiftness, commands a guaranteed place in the annals of racing history.

The tack room at one of Ireland's many riding schools; this is at Donacomper, near Celbridge in—almost inevitably—County Kildare

National Stud
Tully, near Kildare, is home to the Irish National Stud (see pages 100–1). Set up by the British in 1902, it passed to the Irish in 1943, and now welcomes visitors to look round the palatial quarters inhabited by the resident stallions and their precious offspring. The Irish National Stud Horse Museum is also there, exhibiting the skeleton of the peerless Arkle, three times winner of the Cheltenham Gold Cup in Britain.

Inside Malahide Castle highlights include the Oak Room, full of intricate paneling from the 16th and 17th centuries

Newbridge
Beyond Malahide, in Donabate, lies the former home of the Cobbe family. Designed by George Semple, Newbridge is an 18th-century house set in wooded parkland. Guided tours are available; the drawing room is an authentic example of Georgian décor, and the areas "below stairs" contain original utensils and equipment. More unusually, the much-traveled Cobbes built up a charming little museum of curiosities from many foreign places. Craft workshops and period transport displays are on show in the courtyard.

▶▶ Malahide Castle 86D3

With the exception of a brief spell under Cromwell, this romantic-looking building was the seat of the Talbot family for nearly 800 years before it was bought by Dublin County Council in 1976. The Talbots were Jacobite supporters and fared badly in the Battle of the Boyne. It is said that the 14 cousins who sat down to breakfast at Malahide on the morning of the battle were all dead by nightfall. The tour of the building enables you to see its transition from a simple fortification to a charmingly domestic country house in elaborate Gothic style; the present turrets and battlements are entirely ornamental. It contains many original furnishings, mostly 18th-century, and a fine collection of portraits which now form Ireland's National Portrait Gallery. The structure of the house dates from several periods, the oldest section being its 14th-century tower. The Great Hall is especially noteworthy, the only one in Ireland to be preserved in its original form.

The beautiful gardens around the castle contain a remarkable botanical collection; beyond lie many acres of well-kept parkland. In the castle yard is the **Fry Model Railway Museum▶**, with engines and rolling stock handmade by a Dublin railway engineer, Cyril Fry. The O gauge railroad is an amazing scale model with stations, bridges, streetcars, buses, barges, the River Liffey, and the Hill of Howth. There are also perfect models of Cork and Heuston Stations, O'Connell Bridge, the Halfpenny Bridge and the Guinness loading wharf.

▶ Marino Casino 86C3

If you are on your way to Malahide or Howth, this little Georgian gem is worth tracking down in Dublin's northern suburbs, although it is perhaps a long trek from the center to see this one building. The Casino has nothing to do with gambling, but was built for Lord Charlemont (who lived in what is now the Hugh Lane Municipal Gallery, see page 56). It was simply an exuberant bit of neoclassical frivolity, a skittish aside to a villa in which he planned to house some of the works of art he brought home from a grand tour. The villa no longer exists, but the restored Casino survives, flamboyantly decorated with urns concealing chimneystacks. Nearby Marino Crescent (also known as Ffolliot's Revenge) was built by a painter out of spite to block Lord Charlemont's view of the sea. The backs of the houses were made particularly hideous with ill-proportioned windows and scruffy sheds.

Maynooth 86C2

If you are touring west of Dublin you will probably drive through Maynooth at some point, a pleasant Georgian town with a ruined castle and, nearby, the famous seminary and lay university of St. Patrick's College, where many of Ireland's priests are trained. During the Reformation it was suppressed, but reopened in 1795 after the repeal of the harsh Penal Laws against Catholics. It can be visited free of charge by appointment (tel: 01 628 5222) and contains an ecclesiastical museum. The town's main square is in Victorian Gothic style and was designed by Augustus Pugin. Close to the town is the large estate of Carton House, a fine Georgian mansion built for the dukes of Leinster in 1740.

▶▶ Mellifont Abbey 86D2

Remains of the first Cistercian church in Ireland, founded in 1142, stand in a maze of quiet lanes by the River Mattock. Built by St. Malachy, Archbishop of Armagh, it was heavily influenced by the French Cistercian monastery at Clairvaux, where St. Malachy had stayed and befriended the abbot, St. Bernard. There's a fairly good overview of the ruins from the parking lot, but a modest entrance fee is charged if you wish to take a closer look. The most striking section of the ruins is the Romanesque octagonal lavabo, or washing place, about half of which is still standing.

A Tasmanian connection
The late Lord Talbot de Malahide was also the owner of another Malahide —in Tasmania, where his relatives still live. Inspired by his family's interests there, and by his own fascination for botany, he wrote the definitive multi-volume work on the plants of Tasmania. He also introduced to the Irish Malahide garden plants from his antipodean property, as well as others from Africa, North and South America, China, Australia, and Mexico—which makes it a plantsman's paradise.

105

Portraits from the National Gallery in Dublin now hang in the imposing setting of Malahide Castle

Mount Usher Gardens make the most of their position on the River Vartry

The Hill of Tara, once a site of pagan importance, is one of many such places to have been "Christianized"

►► Monasterboice 86E2

North of Drogheda, off N1, is one of the best examples in Ireland of a carved High Cross. This is the 10th-century Cross of Muiredach, nearly 20 feet high, which bears numerous biblical scenes in deep relief, such as Cain slaying Abel, David and Goliath, and the Last Judgment. The west face is devoted to the life of Christ, including the arrest in the Garden of Gethsemane, and the risen Christ returning to meet St. Peter and St. Paul. At the bottom of the cross is an inscription in Gaelic saying "A prayer for Muiredach by whom this cross was made." Two other more eroded High Crosses can be seen on the site, along with a fine Round Tower and a pre-Gothic sundial. Two ruined 13th-century churches stand within the enclosure.

►► Mount Usher Gardens 86B3

These lovely gardens stand in 20 acres of well-watered land on the banks of the River Vartry. Water forms an essential part of the scenery, with cascades and bridges visible in just about every section. It is quite possible to get utterly lost if you forget which way the water is flowing. They were laid out by Edward Walpole, a Dublin businessman, and his sons, from 1868, as a wild garden, and contain about 5,000 species, including many rhododendrons and eucalypti. The gardens offer fine displays of color throughout the summer opening period. The maples in late September and October are especially striking. Several craft and clothing shops stand by the entrance, where there is a tearoom.

► Navan 86D2

Navan occupies a strategic site on the Boyne. Not compelling in itself, it makes a good base for seeing several places in the area. Within the town, the most interesting sight is **Athlumney Castle►**, over the bridge. This 15th-century tower house was apparently burned down by its

last owner, Sir Lancelot Dowdall, a devout Catholic who refused to let it fall into William's hands after the Battle of the Boyne. He is said to have watched his home blaze all night from the opposite banks, then set off into exile.

Eight miles south of the town is one of Ireland's most famous antiquities, the **Hill of Tara►►**. This shows evidence of occupation from many different periods, and was the symbolic seat of the High Kings until the 11th century. Its history is steeped in legends, but archaeological evidence suggests that some grim events must have taken place there. Various ring forts can be seen, although some were damaged in recent years by British Israelites searching for the Ark of the Covenant (see panel). The site has probably always been associated with religious cults of some kind, but its influence waned after the arrival of Christianity. It was from this hill that King Laoghaire and the Druids first noticed St. Patrick's defiant fire on the nearby Hill of Slane.

The Hill of Tara is now just a grassy flat-topped hill grazed by sheep, reached by a field path from the parking place. It rises only 300 feet or so from the surrounding land, but the views over the plains are very extensive. Various inconclusive mounds and earthworks indicate the locations of the old palaces, banquet hall, and Bronze Age burial sites, and many artifacts have been unearthed. A visitor center in a nearby church explains the site. Tara's most significant event in recent times was a mass meeting called by the nationalist leader Daniel O'Connell (see page 42), which is said to have attracted over a million people. This alarmed the British government, which suppressed O'Connell's activities and thus put one more nail in the coffin of a peaceful Anglo-Irish settlement.

South of Tara is **Dunsany Castle►**, a private residence originally built in the 12th century by Hugh de Lacy to defend Anglo-Norman territory. It contains a fine collection of art and some unusual Jacobite relics (the Lords of Dunsany are the Plunkett family to which the famous Saint Oliver belonged). The castle is open in high season (tel: 046 25198 for more details).

Today, visitors to the Hill of Tara are more inclined to appreciate the views than dig vainly for the Ark of the Covenant

The Ark of the Covenant
In 1899, the purchase of a book on Charing Cross Road in London led a group known as the British Israelites to the belief that the Ark of the Covenant lay buried on the Hill of Tara. One of their number, a Mr. Groome, went to Ireland to excavate in furtherance of his biblical quest. When he found nothing, some locals took pity on his disappointment and placed some Roman coins where he would dig on the morrow and where, inevitably and to his own delight, he duly discovered them the next day. But after a singular lack of success in locating what he had set out to find, he packed his bags and returned to England. The Ark still remains undiscovered on the Hill of Tara—or anywhere else.

The entrance to the passage-grave, with the roof-box above the lintel

The sparkling white of the quartzite lends added drama to Newgrange

▶▶▶ Newgrange   86D2

Newgrange is unquestionably one of Ireland's most important archeological sites, and is perhaps the most spectacular passage-grave (the tomb takes the form of a long passage covered by a vast mound) in Western Europe. Dating from ca. 3000 BC, it is possibly 1,000 years older than Stonehenge. The tumulus stands in a sloping field above the road, overlooking the glittering snake of the Boyne and a vast sweep of quiet farmland. It is easily spotted because the front retaining walls of the grass-covered mound are faced with brilliant white stones of quartzite. The nearest source for these stones is the Wicklow Mountains, south of Dublin, so thousands of tons of material must have been dragged huge distances. Egg-shaped gray stones are studded at intervals among the white ones, though the original pattern of these (if there was one) is a matter of speculation. The mound itself measures about 330 feet across, and is about 35 feet high at its central point. Over the years it had collapsed and was reconstructed during the 1960s, using careful measurements to determine its precise dimensions. In the front of the mound is a low entrance formed by slabs of rock, and above it another rectangular opening, the roof-box. This sophisticated device is constructed with a narrow slit in the stone so that, once a year, for about 15 minutes on the morning of the winter solstice, the rays of the sun illuminate the interior of the tomb. All around the edge of the tomb is a low wall of large boulders, some carved with spiral shapes. The significance of these is unknown; they may have been purely decorative.

You can walk all around the mound (the white wall does not go all the way) to see what remains of a circle of standing stones. A guided tour takes you into the inner

stone chamber of the tomb, from which three recesses lead. The magnificent dovetailed structure of the vaulted roof still keeps the water out. Other mysterious patterns are carved on the inner stones, some invisible from outside and presumably for some cult purpose. Stone basins contained the bones of the cremated dead with offerings of beads and pins. At the end of the tour a light is switched on to re-create an approximation of the solstice phenomenon.

Newgrange is open all year and is besieged by school groups and visitors in high season. During the winter solstice (December 21 and several days around that date), access is virtually impossible; places are booked many years in advance to see the phenomenon within the tomb. Tourism at this sensitive site is carefully managed, but even so, erosion is occurring. The Office of Public Works has constructed an interpretative center near the site with a model of the tomb to reduce the pressure of visitor numbers.

Newgrange is by no means the only local antiquity. The nearby mounds of Dowth and Knowth also contain passage tombs. As you look from Newgrange, over the lush pastureland enclosed by this sheltered bend of the Boyne, the shapes of numerous strange humps and tumuli are visible—these are other burial sites, about 40 in all, some of which have not yet been explored. The Irish name for this giant graveyard is *Brugh na Boinne*, the palace of the Boyne. Its builders were a farming community who were apparently fairly settled and peaceful, clearing forests and raising stock. The looping River Boyne furnished them with a useful artery of communication and a natural defense barrier.

Many aspects of the tombs are puzzling and myths and theories abound. The fatally wounded Diarmuid, lover of Gráinne, is alleged to have been brought here "to put aerial life into him." Other legends declare these tombs (inaccurately) to be the burial places of the Kings of Tara, while the sun-cult rituals echo those discovered in ancient Egyptian tombs, although these graves probably predate the pyramids by several hundred years.

There are several inscribed stones at Newgrange; this one is at the back of the mound

Tomorrow never comes
In early Irish mythology, Newgrange was associated with the Dagda, the good god of the Celts, his wife Bóann (the divinized River Boyne) and his son Oengus—all supernatural beings belonging to the Tuatha Dé Danann (peoples of the goddess Danu), who had defeated the *Fir Bolg* people (see page 30) and had occupied Ireland before the Celts. The 12th-century *Book of Leinster* tells the tale of how Oengus used a verbal trick to get possession of the great mound at Newgrange from his father. The Dagda, it seems, was persuaded to let his son have it for a day and a night, and when he asked his son to return it the next day, Oengus replied that a day and a night meant forever—so he kept it. He had probably argued, with impeccable Irish logic, that tomorrow never comes as every day is today.

Daniel Robertson
The terraces of Powerscourt Gardens were indelibly stamped by the unsteady hand of this gouty and eccentric architect who, in 1840, was commissioned by the 6th Viscount Powerscourt to draw up new plans for the garden. Apparently Robertson's *modus operandi* was to be trundled around the gardens in a wheelbarrow, directing staff while swigging intermittently at a bottle of sherry. Once the bottle was empty he ran out of ideas and all useful work for the day ground to a halt. Robertson's habits were expensive, and he was constantly in debt. Whenever the sheriff called, he used to hide in the copper dome of the house.

The Great Sugar Loaf Mountain forms a memorable backdrop to the gardens at Powerscourt

► ►   **Powerscourt**   86C3

The pretty village of Enniskerry and the dramatic backdrop of the Wicklow Mountains add to the appeal of this great estate, which covers about 13,000 acres. Even the entrance drive is impressive—almost a mile long. James I granted the land to the 1st Viscount Powerscourt, Sir Richard Wingfield, in 1609. A magnificent house was designed by Richard Castle, whose Palladian handiwork can be seen all over Ireland. Unfortunately the great edifice burned to a shell in a disastrous accident in 1974 just after a long program of restoration. There are plans to re-create the house, but the phenomenal cost of the exercise has so far daunted enthusiasts. All that can be seen now are the splendid gardens, laid out on the south-facing slopes in front of the house which overlook the Great Sugar Loaf Mountain. They were first created in the mid-18th century soon after the completion of the house, but redesigned in the 19th century by the redoubtable Daniel Robertson (see panel) with classical parterres and Italianate statuary. They contain glorious lakes with spouting fountains and winged horses, and magnificent specimen trees which grow to a prodigious height in this mild climate. Unusual touches include a Japanese garden (1908) on reclaimed bogland sporting little scarlet bridges, a pet cemetery dedicated to many faithful friends (Jack, Sting, and Taffy), mosaic terraces made of beach pebbles from Bray, and neat, homey kitchen gardens. A garden center, pleasant tearoom, and a gift shop maximize tourist revenue.

An additional attraction about 3 miles away (separate entrance charge) is the **Powerscourt Waterfall**►►, which plunges about 400 feet in a mare's-tail plume down a jagged rock face. There are excellent local walks around the valley below and, to make the most of the entrance fee, take a picnic and make an outing of it. Refreshments and picnic tables are provided.

▶▶ Russborough House 86C2

Like nearby Powerscourt, this grand Palladian mansion shows the Anglo-Irish ascendancy in the Pale at its most confident and powerful. It was designed by the ubiquitous Richard Castle (and, after his death, Francis Bindon) for the 1st Earl of Milltown, a wealthy Dublin brewer. The structure is palatial; two huge semicircular wings stretch from the main body of the building to two side pavilions. Inside, the grandeur continues in magnificent plasterwork by the Francini brothers. Some of it, like elegant cake icing, swirls around exquisite oval sea scenes by Claude Vernet, commissioned specially for the house.

Today the house is owned by the nephew of Alfred Beit, the German cofounder (with Cecil Rhodes) of the De Beer Diamond Mining Company. Besides a multitude of antiques, tapestries, and valuable porcelain, his fabulous collection of art (strong on Spanish, Dutch, and Flemish schools) is now held at Russborough. At least, some of it is, for Russborough has suffered two major burglaries. The first was in 1974 when, in a *cause célèbre* that hit all the headlines, Dr. Bridget Rose Dugdale stole 16 paintings for her I.R.A. lover (the haul was recovered, undamaged, later). In May 1986 another break-in occurred and this time the owners were not so lucky. Now the house is under a fair degree of surveillance and some important works have been donated to the National Gallery in Dublin. There is, however, still plenty that makes the house well worth a special visit. The grounds consist of woodland and a large artificial lake (actually a reservoir), with views of the Wicklow Mountains beyond.

Nearby **Blessington▶** is one of the most charming villages in the Wicklow Mountains, and makes a popular base for exploring the area. Its wide street is flanked by tall trees and dignified Georgian buildings. Blessington was once a stop on the coach route from Dublin to Carlow. Dame Ninette de Valois, founder of the Sadler's Wells Ballet Company, was born nearby.

Apart from a wonderful collection of paintings, Russborough House is also the home of some unusual dolls

A dramatic display
When King George IV announced his intention of visiting Powerscourt in 1821, a path was hurriedly laid out from the great house to the waterfall in the grounds, and an artificial lake with sluice gates created at the top of the fall to make a more dramatic cascade for the King to admire. But the delights of the luncheon table in the mansion gave His Majesty insufficient time to visit the waterfall, and when the sluice gates were subsequently opened, the great onrush of water destroyed the wooden platform on which the King should have been standing. So the English monarchy has reason to be thankful to Powerscourt—and a good lunch!

Skerries is so-called because of the islands lying just off the coast; the name means "sea rocks" in Gaelic

The road to Slane
The reason, it is said, why the road from Dublin to Slane was made so straight (unlike most in Ireland) was to minimize the time it would take King George IV to reach his mistress in Slane Castle when he visited Ireland in 1821.

A shield set into the walls of Slane Abbey

 Skerries   86D3

This is one of the biggest resorts on the northeast coast, mostly visited by Dubliners. The strange indentations at Red Island are claimed to be the footprints of St. Patrick. Boat trips to St. Patrick's Island enable visitors to explore a ruined church where a national synod was held in 1148. Just south is the pretty fishing village of Loughshinny.

► **Slane**   86D2

The town was built on the instructions of Viscount Conyngham in the 18th century, around a crossroads. For its modest size it has considerable historic interest, and is a pleasant gray-stone place of agreeable Georgian proportions. The estate of Slane Castle, former home of the Conynghams, lies behind firmly locked gates, although it can be glimpsed occasionally from nearby roads. Open-air rock concerts have been held in the castle grounds, but it is not generally open to the public. It is currently being restored since it was damaged by fire. The Marchioness Conyngham was rumored to have been George IV's last mistress, and he apparently spent a good deal of time there. Near the riverside is a mill. The four identical Georgian houses set at equal angles to the crossroads in the village center have given rise to one of those appealing Irish tales that are almost certainly untrue.

The houses were supposedly built for four quarrelsome spinster sisters whose exasperated brother became so fed up with their wranglings under one roof that he insisted they live separately. Whether or not the story is true, the houses are fine examples and deserve a close look.

A humble laborer's cottage (now a museum) a short distance from the center of Slane was the birthplace of the lyric poet Francis Ledwidge. A plaque outside displays one of his most haunting verses, written after his friend Thomas MacDonagh was executed for his part in the Easter Rising of 1916:

"He shall not hear the bittern cry
In the wild sky, where he is lain,
Nor voices of the sweeter birds
Above the wailing of the rain."

Ledwidge himself was killed soon after this—at Flanders, fighting on the British side. He was only 30 and is now lamented as a great loss to literature, though his work

was not widely read at a time of such political upheaval.

Outside the village is the **Hill of Slane▶**, on which the ruins of a monastery stand. The site is famous as the place where St. Patrick lit Easter fires to challenge the pagan king, Laoghaire, who had forbidden flames to be kindled within sight of his palace at Tara (see page 107).

▶ Straffan   86C2

This village on the banks of the Liffey has two tourist attractions, although both are open only in high season. The **Butterfly Farm▶** is the only one of its type in Ireland, with tropical species fluttering about in a hothouse full of exotic plants. The **Steam Museum▶** documents the history of the steam age in Ireland, showing how it revolutionized industrial as well as agricultural practices such as butter churning and corn threshing. Working steam engines are on display, including Richard Trevithick's prototype steam-powered road vehicle. The engines stand in the courtyard of an 18th-century house. Phone in advance to attend a "live steam day" (tel: 01 627 3155).

Swords   86D3

This is now a bustling modern town where new housing takes some of the commuting overspill from central Dublin. But it has an ancient pedigree, and was formerly the site of a monastery founded by St. Columba in the 6th century. Swords Castle stands at the north end of town, a fortified manor built in about 1200 by the Archbishop of Dublin. Two towers can be seen in the grounds of the Protestant church—a Round Tower from the 11th century, and the last vestiges of a 15th-century church.

Garrick Castle
Sited near the Boyne a few miles upriver from Slane is the ruined castle of Garrick. Close by was a weir and, so the story goes, fish caught in a net there touched a wire connected to the castle kitchen, so that the cook would know when to serve up the freshest of salmon on the menu.

113

Slane Abbey was founded in 1512 for four priests, four clerks, and four choristers

Land of saints

Christianity reached Irish shores during the late 4th century, not with Roman fire and sword, but through the persuasive urgings of an extraordinary band of missionary monks who brought the glad tidings to the pagan Gaels. Many of these early Christian teachers and founders of monasteries are now Irish saints.

St. Oliver Plunkett (1629–1681)
One of the most interesting of Ireland's saints was canonized as recently as 1976. St. Oliver Plunkett, Archbishop of Armagh and Primate of All Ireland, had the misfortune to live during the troubled years of the 17th century, when Catholicism was rigorously suppressed by English authorities. He was on friendly terms with the Protestant clergy of Ulster, who had a high regard for his sincerity and achievements, but false allegations by Titus Oates in 1678 over a "popish plot" to bring French soldiers into Ireland resulted in his arrest, although the charges were blatantly absurd. On July 1, 1681, he was executed in London for "treason," his offense being simply that he was an unrepentant Catholic. At his trial the Lord Chief Justice declared, "The bottom of your treason was your setting up your false religion, than which there is not anything more displeasing to God." Plunkett's severed head was rescued from the flames and brought back to Ireland. It lies in a shrine in the Catholic Church of St. Peter, Drogheda.

114

Saintly lives Innumerable saints are encountered on any visit to Ireland. Most of them are obscure (who now remembers St. Gobnet or St. Lurach?) and the patterns of their lives are often very similar—they renounced the world, founded monasteries, and did good works. The achievements of these early monks, however, are hard to overestimate. The trials they endured, the distances they traveled in uncharted terrain and their dazzling artistic talents are truly staggering. Christianity was indeed a faith that moved mountains. The Christian message was mainly interpreted by men, just as it is now, and attitudes to women were extremely misogynistic. Just a few intrepid women saints braved this exclusive and hostile masculine preserve, among them St. Brigid, who founded one of the earliest of Ireland's nunneries at Kildare.

In today's Ireland, the saints still play an active role in the lives of many devout Catholics. You will find candles burning at every shrine, votive offerings in sacred places, and eager pilgrims praying for their intercession in everyday affairs or for the perpetual forgiveness of sins. Factual evidence about most of the early saints is sparse. Their lives are but shadowy, and wreathed in legends or miraculous tales. Some of them are composite figures or even Christian incarnations of pagan Celtic gods. The most famous Irish saint, of course, is St. Patrick, the most effective of all the early missionaries (see page 226 for more details of his life, and of places associated with him).

St. Columba (ca. 521–597) Also known as Columcille (meaning "dove of the church") St. Columba was born at Lough Gartan in Donegal. He was a high-ranking member of the O'Neill clan, a scholar, poet, and natural leader. After training as a monk at Moville and Clonard, he founded the monasteries of Derry and Durrow, possibly also Kells. In 563 he left Ireland with 12 companions to found a monastery in Iona, an island off the Scottish coast, but retained his links with Ireland. He was a charismatic figure, tall and striking, well educated, persuasive and ardently committed to his cause. Some of his actions seemed less than saintly. This endearingly human paragon was, by all accounts, a thief and a cheat—stealing a ceremonial cross from a neighboring church and secretly copying a psalter he borrowed from a friend. This resulted in the deaths of thousands at the Battle of the Books (see page 210).

St. Ciarán (ca. 512–545) The founder of the great monastery of Clonmacnois, St. Ciarán had an auspicious pedigree as a Christian leader—he was the son of a carpenter. His first monkish years were spent on the Aran Islands with Enda, the islands' most famous saint. Later he went to Scattery Island, in the mouth of the Shannon, and finally to Clonmacnois farther upstream, where he died soon afterward. Apparently he aroused such jealousy among his fellow clerics that they prayed he would die young—and he did! But his good works lived on, and the influence of Clonmacnois spread far and wide, surviving until 1522, despite many Viking raids.

St. Brendan the Navigator (ca. 486–575) This famous Irish saint was the founder of a monastery at Clonfert in County Galway, and also Ardfert in Kerry. His missions took place mostly in western Ireland, but he is best remembered as a great traveler. His epic voyage is chronicled in the 10th-century account, *The Navigation of St. Brendan*, in which he set sail with 12 disciples in search of an earthly paradise in the Atlantic Ocean. The journey lasted over seven years, and it has been suggested that his account of "crystal columns" (icebergs?) and "curdled seas" (the Sargasso?) may pinpoint him as the first to cross the Atlantic. St. Brendan's supposed voyage was imaginatively re-created in similar conditions by the modern explorer Tim Severin, and the wood-and-leather boat he sailed across the Atlantic in 1976 can be seen in the history theme park of Craggaunowen, County Clare (see page 183).

Clonmacnois, founded by St. Ciarán, was for centuries the intellectual capital of Ireland

This little church at Glendalough is familiarly known as St. Kevin's Kitchen as the small bell tower resembles a chimney

St. Kevin (died ca. 618)

Founder of the great monastery at Glendalough, County Wicklow, St. Kevin came from a noble Leinster family and was educated by monks from childhood. After his ordination he adopted a hermit's existence at Glendalough. His quest for solitude was in vain, however, for crowds of disciples soon gathered around him and he became the leader of a great and influential community. He is alleged to have murdered a woman who attempted to seduce him, shoving her from his rock-ledge cave into the lake below. The tale conveniently bolsters the early fathers' belief that women were the source of all corruption.

The stark silhouette of the Yellow Steeple; nearby stands a section of Trim's town walls

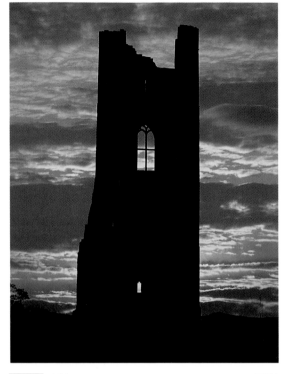

Michael Dwyer's escape
The year 1798 witnessed great upheavals against English rule, especially in the southeast. During the harsh winter of 1798–1799 the Wicklow-born rebel Michael Dwyer took refuge in a cottage in Derrynamuck, in the Glen of Imaal. More than 100 English soldiers surrounded it, but he declined to surrender, although he requested that the owners of the house be freed. The army allowed this, then battle commenced. A fellow rebel, Sam McAllister, sustained a broken arm and could fight no longer, so offered to sacrifice himself to give Dwyer a chance to escape. He showed himself at the door and drew the English fire. He was immediately killed, but while the soldiers were reloading their muskets, Dwyer was able to slip away. The cottage is now a museum.

116

Captain Robert Halpin
Robert Halpin (1836–1894) was one of Wicklow Town's most prominent citizens. His main achievement was as commander of the *Great Eastern*, the iron steamship that laid the first transatlantic telegraph cable. A granite obelisk commemorates him in the town, and a plaque at the church of St. Lavinius, but for further insights, head for his former home, Tinakilly House, 2 miles north of town, now a luxury hotel and restaurant.

► **Trim**   *86D2*

Trim Castle is one of the most imposing Anglo-Norman fortresses in Ireland, and as it stands in the center of the town by the River Boyne it is easy to get a good idea of its size and layout. The ruins cover about 2½ acres and include a vast keep flanked by rectangular towers. Sections of curtain wall are interspersed with battle gates. The original castle was built by Hugh de Lacy in 1172, although the present structure dates from a later period. After recent restoration the ruins are freely accessible. Nearby are the ruins of the Royal Mint and a gaunt skeleton called the Yellow Steeple, dating from the 14th century, the last remnants of an Augustinian abbey, destroyed in 1649.

Bective Abbey►►, between Navan and Trim, is one of the earliest examples of a Cistercian foundation in Ireland. Hugh de Lacy was buried here in 1195, and it was obviously a place of some significance (its abbot sat in the English House of Lords). Most of the surviving ruins date from the 15th century and stand in a gloriously peaceful setting in a field by the Knightsbrook River.

► **Wicklow**   *86B3*

The county town of this much-visited area is small and unassuming, but it makes a pleasantly unstressful base, as its name, meaning "Viking meadow" suggests. Its history, however, has been far from untroubled. In AD 432 St. Patrick had an unfriendly reception when he landed at Travilahawk Strand. One of his entourage had his teeth knocked out and became known as Mantan (the toothless one). Irish clans (O'Byrnes and O'Tooles) slugged it out with the Anglo-Norman Fitzgeralds for centuries and after the rebellion of 1798 many of the participants were tried in the town's courthouse; those who evaded capture took to the hills. Wicklow's main features of interest are the scanty remains of the Black Castle by the road above the harbor, a fine headland for coastal walks, a ruined 13th-century friary, and a heritage center in the town jail (local history and genealogical research). The Protestant **Church of St. Lavinius▶**, topped by a Byzantine dome, has several unusual details, including a Romanesque doorway and a fine roof. In Norman times the slopes to the River Vartry were planted with vines, a testimony to Wicklow's comparatively sunny climate. The harbor area is oddly severed from the main town; beyond it stretches a long, shingly beach trapping a brackish lagoon (Broad Lough), which makes a sheltered habitat for wildfowl.

▶▶▶ The Wicklow Mountains 86B2

These wild hills on Dublin's doorstep are a great boon to city dwellers. From the southern suburbs you can gaze at them on clear days; by public transportation or a car they take just half an hour to reach. If you have time enough you can even walk there on the 82-mile Wicklow Way, starting just outside Dublin in Marlay Park. The route is not very clear in places, and the mountains can be dangerous in misty conditions. The rounded hills of ice-eroded schist and granite enfold a strange mixture of bleak, awesome glens and boggy plateaus, interspersed with welcoming Shangri-La valleys like Glendalough or the Vale of Avoca. The improbable cones of the Great and Little Sugar Loaf Mountains protrude suddenly from the surrounding contours, their granite caps more resilient than the rest. The wildness and emptiness of the mountains made them good hiding places after the 1798 rebellion and during those troubled times they were full of insurgents. One of the main arteries through the region, the military road linking Rathfarnham and the garrison at Aghavannagh, was constructed by English forces in yet another attempt to impose control on recalcitrant Ireland.

The Duke of Wellington
A monument in Emmet Street, Trim, commemorates Arthur Wellesley who lived as a boy here before being, as the Duke of Wellington, the victor at Waterloo. He had been born in Dublin in the same year as his great adversary, Napoleon. But he seems to have had very low regard for the capital city of his birth, if we can judge by the answer he gave when asked what he thought of Dublin, "If a man is born in a stable, that does not make him a horse."

Wicklow was one of the bases used by the Vikings on the east coast of Ireland

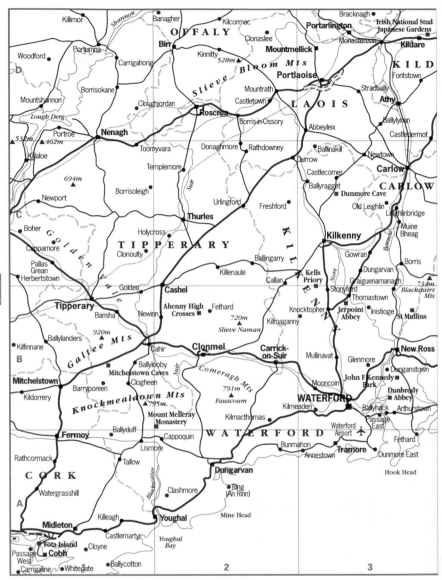

Killimor
Banagher
Kilcormac
Bracknagh
Portarlington
Irish National Stud
Japanese Gardens
OFFALY
Clonaslee
Monasterevin
Kildare
Woodford
Portumna
Birr
Kinnitty
528m
Mountmellick
KILD
Carrigahorig
Portlaoise
Fontstown
Mountshannon
Borrisokane
Cloughjordan
Mountrath
Stradbally
Athy
Lough Derg
Roscrea
Castletown
LAOIS
Ballylynan
Portroe
Borris-in-Ossory
Abbeyleix
Castledermot
532m 462m
Nenagh
Toomyvara
Donaghmore
Rathdowney
Ballinakill
Newtown
Carlow
694m
Templemore
Durrow
Castlecomer
CARLOW
Newport
Borrisoleigh
Urlingford
Freshford
Ballyragget
Dunmore Cave
Old Leighlin
Leighlinbridge
Boher
Thurles
Holycross
Muine Bheag
Cappamore
Clonoulty
TIPPERARY
Kilkenny
Gowran
Dungarvan
Borris
Pallas Green
Herbertstown
Ballingarry
Golden
Killenaule
Callan
Kells Priory
Stonyford
Graiguenamanagh
734m
Blackstairs Mts
Tipperary
Bansha
Cashel
Ahenny High Crosses
Fethard
720m
Slieve Naman
Kilmaganny
Knocktopher
Jerpoint Abbey
Inistioge
St Mullins
Kilfinnane
Ballylanders
920m
Galtee Mts
Newinn
Clonmel
Carrick-on-Suir
Mullinavat
Glenmore
New Ross
Mitchelstown
Barryporeen
Ballylooby
Mitchelstown Caves
Cloghleen
Comeragh Mts
791m
Fauscoum
Mooncoin
John F Kennedy Park
Dunganstown
Kildorrery
Knockmealdown Mts
795m
Mount Melleray Monastery
Kilmacthomas
WATERFORD
Kilmeaden
Dunbrody Abbey
Ballyhack
Arthurstown
Fermoy
Ballyduff
Cappoquin
Waterford Airport
Passage East
Fethard
Rathcormack
Lismore
WATERFORD
Bunmahon
Annestown
Tramore
Dunmore East
CORK
Tallow
Dungarvan
Hook Head
Watergrasshill
Clashmore
Ring (An Rinn)
Killeagh
Youghal
Mine Head
Midleton
Castlemartyr
Youghal Bay
Fota Island
Cobh
Cloyne
Passage West
Carrigaline
Whitegate
Ballycotton

118

An attractive thatched cottage at Kilmore Quay; traveling around modern Ireland, you are more likely to see whitewash than thatch

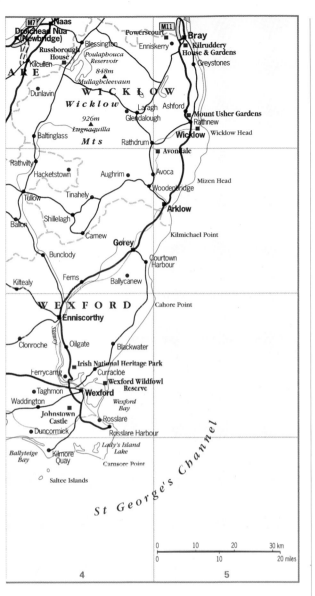

119

Southeastern counties In contrast to the scenic wildness of western Ireland, the landscape of the Southeast
is mostly low-lying and docile. Rich pastureland watered
by brimming rivers extends gently to a quiet coastline of
long sandy beaches, estuarial mudflats of wading birds
and low cliffs fringing deep bays. Ireland's most fertile
farmland lies in the Golden Vale, making Tipperary one of
the most prosperous inland counties. There is a great deal
to see and do, although to reach all its scattered attractions you will need a car. The sunny, drier climate of the
Southeast attracts both Irish and foreign visitors for summer holidays, and there is an excellent choice of beaches.

Tacumshane, near Kilmore Quay, has the rarity of a thatched windmill in working order

Town and cultural attractions Development here remains low-key; Tramore is the only significantly built-up resort, offering amusement parks and a costly multimedia attraction themed on the Celts. If this atypical brashness doesn't appeal, it is easily avoided. The Southeast's other resorts are all small and village-like, even the county town of Wexford. Waterford is the only "towny" place, a thriving port and commercial center where derricks unload cargoes on the wharves and industrial complexes hum. Most famous is the crystal factory about a mile out of town. This is the largest of its kind in the world, and its annual turnover is boggling—although recession and competition from other production plants have dented Waterford's trade badly. Nevertheless, there is no shortage of visitors on the free guided tours, even if few leave clutching a chandelier (see page 143).

The other sizable towns of the area are medieval Kilkenny, an upscale tourist town with enough attractions to act as an excellent base, and Tipperary's prosperous county town, Clonmel, where Georgian influences are more noticeable. Carlow, however, is disappointing: neither the town nor the county have much to detain you.

County Tipperary's great tourist honeypot is the Rock of Cashel. Bus tours flock to this atmospheric outcrop of limestone in the middle of lush plains to admire the majestic ruins clustered on its summit. If abbeys and monasteries interest you, this is a good area to explore— the great settlements at Holy Cross (County Tipperary), Duiske, Jerpoint (both County Kilkenny), Dunbrody and Tintern (both County Wexford) are some of the finest. Castles, too, stud the bridging points in these great river valleys—no significant town is without some bristling fortress or other. Cahir, Kilkenny, Lismore, Nenagh, and Enniscorthy are among the most impressive.

Sports and fitness breaks As well as for conventional touring or seaside breaks, the Southeast is a splendid area for exercise. The flatter coastal terrain makes walking and biking vacations less strenuous than in some parts of the country, though inland the hill ranges of the Comeragh, Blackstairs, or the splendidly named Knockmealdown Mountains have plenty of visual drama. The South Leinster Way through Carlow and Kilkenny takes in some of the most beautiful scenery around the Nore and Barrow rivers. The Munster Way meanders along the borderland of Tipperary and Waterford over the spectacular high point known as the Vee Gap, and the lovely valley of the Nire. You can link the two routes (they meet at Carrick-on-Suir), or pick up the Kildare Way along the River Barrow towpath from Graiguenamanagh. Bird watchers should head for the reclaimed Wexford Slobs, Hook Head peninsula or the Saltee Islands.

For fishing vacations the region is excellent; the rivers teem with brown trout, salmon and all kinds of other fish, particularly the Blackwater River. Dungarvan and Dunmore East are the best centers for deep-sea fishing. Lough Derg in the far northwest of County Tipperary is another good location for water sports, including cruising, though the main centers are in Clare or Galway (Killaloe, Mountshannon and Portumna). Equestrian sports are popular in this horsy country; hacking (renting horses) and

Traveling people
There are about 3,000 itinerant families in the whole of Ireland, amounting to a population of around 20,000. Many live in illegal roadside camps in conditions of great squalor. Notices discouraging "travellers" can be seen as you approach many towns and villages. The origins of the true "traveller" may date back to the 18th century, when many families were dispossessed by the harsh Penal Code, and took to the roads as tinsmiths (hence the old term "tinker") and dealers. They ranged far and wide, gathering together at events such as the Ballinasloe Horse Fair, where their "king" was elected. Recently, economic decline has resulted in a sharp increase in homeless families, and today's travelers represent a considerable social problem, for large groups of disruptive itinerants prove unpopular even among a race as tolerant as the Irish.

fox hunting can be arranged. Tipperary breeds some of Ireland's finest racehorses, and the interest in racing is evident from no fewer than four racecourses, while greyhound racing centers on Clonmel. Competitive sport is a passionate preoccupation throughout Ireland, but the traditional games of Gaelic football and hurling are played in Tipperary with special enthusiasm. It is no surprise to discover the Gaelic Athletic Association (G.A.A.) was founded here by the sportsmanlike Archbishop of Cashel.

Irish Horse Racing

A turbulent history The Vikings held sway over this region for many years, finding those broad estuaries and inviting harbors easy landings from which to torment the native Celts with pillage and nose taxes ("Pay up or we'll cut your nose off!"). Following their example, Strongbow invaded Ireland for the Anglo-Normans via Waterford in 1169, ostensibly to aid Dermot MacMurrough in regaining his Leinster throne. In return, Strongbow received the hand of Dermot's daughter, the first dynastic alliance between Irish and Norman. But the Normans stayed on and their power grew. The Gaelic MacMurrough Kavanaghs resented the curtailment of their influence, and remained a thorn in the English side, rebelling every so often with unexpected ferocity. Cromwell finally broke their resistance, and is unaffectionately remembered in this part of Ireland for his slaughter of hundreds of unarmed citizens at Wexford. The Southeast was relatively peaceful through the 18th century, but the surface calm disguised many ill feelings. When a confrontation with the yeomanry fanned smoldering passions in 1798, the people of Carlow and Wexford erupted in fury, wielding pikes in a brave but hopeless stand against English cannon fire at the decisive battle of Vinegar Hill, Enniscorthy.

121

The Vee Gap, near Mitchelstown in County Tipperary, looks especially dramatic in "Irish weather"

Ardmore's 100-foot Round Tower; it is one of the finest (and latest) in Ireland

Ardmore's Round Tower
"The tower… is said to have been built by St. Declan in one night; that when it had arrived at its present height, a woman coming to gather herbs, looking up, asked the Saint what he was doing, upon which he threw down his trowel and killed her, and coming down he threw her upon the top of the tower, where a part of her remained till a few years ago. It is certain, however, that the tower was never raised higher than it is, which it is said it would have been, had not the woman interrupted the Saint in his pious work."
P. D. Hardy: *The Holy Wells of Ireland* (1836)

▶ **Ardmore**   *118A2*

Ardmore is an attractive little resort at the foot of high cliffs, where simple hotels and a guesthouse or two command awesome views over the bay. A blue-flag award for its clean beach and a "tidy town" commendation indicate a sense of local pride. One of its best-known residents is the popular novelist Molly Keane. An ancient place, Ardmore saw the foundation of Ireland's earliest Christian settlement when St. Declan arrived here from Wales, some 30 years before St. Patrick. His bell and vestments were miraculously borne across the water by a glacial boulder, now tilted on a little spur of rock on the beach. It promises wondrous healing powers for all agile enough to creep beneath it.

Excellent views can be seen from the monastery. Most of the remains date from after Declan's time; a well-preserved Round Tower and cathedral are largely 12th century. The cathedral displays clear and vigorous carvings of biblical scenes, such as the Judgment of Solomon and the Weighing of Souls. Inside are several ogham stones (see page 16). St. Declan's Oratory is an older structure which may contain the saint's remains, the surrounding earth much pillaged for its restorative properties. St. Declan's Well and another ruined church where the saint spent his final years can be found along the cliff walk leading from the village.

▶▶ **Cahir**   *118B1*

The fortress in the center of this small town on the Suir River is in fine condition after recent restoration work. **Cahir Castle**▶▶ dates mainly from the 15th century with many later alterations, and was formerly a stronghold of the powerful local Anglo-Norman Butler family, Dukes and Earls of Ormonde. Queen Elizabeth I's favorite, the Earl of Essex, rammed a few cannonballs into its masonry in 1599, but it survived Cromwellian times little scathed. The huge walls enclose three separate "wards," outer, middle and inner, the inner one guarded by a gate with a portcullis. Rooms in the keep are whitewashed and contain armor displays and period furnishings from the 16th and 17th centuries. The hammer-beamed great hall dates only from the 19th century. An audiovisual presentation fills in some local background.

Cahir's fortunes waxed and waned through the centuries, but in peace time it developed an important milling industry introduced by local Quakers. The town is something of a time warp, and some of its shops and houses appear little changed for decades. One of them, Keating's Draper's Shop, traded in pre-decimal currency until it closed down a few years ago. Another agreeable feature of the town is its evident lack of religious or political bigotry. Protestants and Catholics used to worship simultaneously in its ruined church, separated only by a curtain wall. Somewhat unusually, in the main square is a war memorial dedicated to the many local men who joined Irish regiments and fell in the Great War. Throughout most of the Republic, the World Wars seem unmarked, and the people who gave their lives in these conflicts are forgotten.

The other curiosity in Cahir is the **Swiss Cottage►**, lying just outside the town on the Clonmel road. This quaint thatched building with its eyebrow windows and corkscrew timbering looks like something out of Hansel and Gretel rather than the Swiss Alps. It was designed in about 1810 by the royal architect, John Nash, for a scion of the Butler family, in a then-fashionable genre known as a "cottage orné," a sort of rustic summerhouse or hunting lodge in which the wealthy gentry relaxed and amused themselves in what they imagined to be rural simplicity. The cottage was rescued from dereliction by various enthusiastic conservationists and extensively restored recently; the original hand-painted French wallpapers and fabrics have been faithfully copied, and it is now elegantly furnished with many fascinating period details. It stands in pretty woodland gardens by the riverside.

Cahir Castle was once thought to be impregnable, but Cromwell took the castle in 1650

At around 100 tons, the capstone of Browne's Hill Dolmen weighs heavy upon its supporting stones

An intriguing shop front in Carrick-on-Suir

Carlow
118C3

Though a county town, Carlow is disappointingly lackluster apart from a few nice old shop fronts (Cigar Divan on Dublin Street is a fine example of authentic Victoriana). It lies on the east bank of the Barrow in the once tempestuous borderland at the edge of the Pale, old warehouses lining its former quays. Its castle, standing in the grounds of a mineral-water bottling plant, is perilously ruinous after the misguided attempts of a Dr. Middleton in 1814 to reduce the thickness of the walls in order to convert the castle into a lunatic asylum. Unfortunately he understood little of the explosives he was using for the purpose, and the walls were well and truly modified, becoming so unsafe that some parts later had to be demolished. Also worth a brief look in the town is the county museum with various reconstructed farm interiors. The 19th-century Gothic cathedral is easily spotted by its unusual lantern spire, looking like a crown of thorns. It contains an elaborate pulpit and a finely sculpted marble **monument to Bishop Doyle►**, or J.K.L. (James of Kildare and Leighlin). The story goes that the artist, John Hogan, forgot to include the bishop's ring, and was so mortified by this omission that he committed suicide.

Three kilometers east is the impressive **Browne's Hill Dolmen►**, clearly visible across a field, though it stands some way from the road. The tilted granite capstone is enormous, weighing around 100 tons, and is thought to be the largest of its type in Europe. It poises on its supporting stones as delicately as a ballerina. A fenced path leads from the parking place round the edge of the field.

► Carrick-on-Suir
118B2

A border town straddling the counties of Tipperary and Waterford, Carrick is noteworthy for its beautiful Tudor mansion. This is all the more remarkable because such buildings are a rarity in Ireland, in comparison with literally hundreds of fortresses and abbeys. Despite its name,

Ormonde Castle▶, the house is completely unfortified, perhaps in misplaced expectations of less turbulent times. The building was commissioned by "Black Tom," a swarthy-faced 10th Earl of Ormonde, in anticipation of a visit by his cousin Queen Elizabeth I (who never turned up). Tom was a great favorite of the Queen's, a potent reason for an attempted poisoning by his rival the Earl of Leicester, which he survived. Tom remained an ardent royalist and contributed greatly to the maintenance of English rule in Ireland during this troubled period, though his Anglo-Norman Fitzgerald relations were in disagreement with the English by this stage.

Behind the gray-stone, gabled exterior pierced with many mullioned windows lies lovely stucco work, particularly fine in the 100-foot Long Gallery where royal coats of arms surmount the fireplace. The timber roof contains no bolts, only carpentry joints. Marks can be seen in the attic-room beams, where garrisoned soldiers would stick their knives before retiring for the night.

There is probably no truth in the legend that Anne Boleyn (Queen Elizabeth's mother) was born at Carrick. Today the town is much prouder of a more recent hero, Sean Kelly, the bicycle racer, who was ranked number one in the world for five consecutive years. He won many of the sport's major events. A square in the town is named after him.

Just outside Carrick (on N24) a well-signed thatched roadside showroom indicates the factory of **Tipperary Crystal**▶. Visitors are welcome to look around the production plant and of course buy the hand-decorated glassware. The founders of this enterprise learned their trade at the much more prestigious Waterford factory, but were laid off during hard times and used their severance pay to set up a rival company, using similar techniques. Prices are slightly lower, and Tipperary Crystal has been successfully competing with Waterford—a gratifying piece of vengeance for those laid-off workers.

Ormonde Castle, one of the finest examples of an Irish manor house

A literary ransom
The Butler family of Carrick Castle had many notable warriors, but it also included men of letters, notably one Émonn mac Risderd Butler. He employed scribes to write for him, and one of their manuscripts, dating from the middle of the 15th century, is now preserved in the British Library in London. So highly prized were his manuscripts that two were given to the Earl of Desmond in ransom for Émonn's life after he had been defeated in the Battle of Pottlerath in 1462.

Gaelic Athletic Association
This largely rural movement was first founded in 1884 in Thurles, 10 miles north of Cashel, under the sponsorship of the Archbishop of Cashel, Thomas William Croke (1824–1902). The G.A.A.'s purpose was ostensibly to popularize traditional Irish pastimes such as hurling, handball, and Gaelic football, and today it remains Ireland's most important sporting association. Though not party political, it has proved a fertile recruiting ground for Republican activists, and in the past has been suspected of I.R.A. sympathies. Most of the hunger-strikers of 1981 were G.A.A. members

The Rock of Cashel rears up from the fertile plains of County Tipperary

▶▶▶ Cashel   118C2

Stories tell how the devil bit a huge chunk out of the Slieve Bloom Mountains, then spat it out in disgust here in the Golden Vale when he saw St. Patrick preparing to build a great church. This erratic outcrop of limestone among the patchwork plains of rich cattle pasture looks almost freakish enough to justify such a tale. The Rock of Cashel is a mere 200 feet high, but approached from below, the craggy outline of towers and gables crowning the hilltop looks most ethereal, especially in certain conditions of light or weather. Close up, the romantic image fades a little under the pressure of tourism. It is one of Ireland's most popular sights and is always besieged by visitors in high season. The little town of Cashel has managed to avoid the worst excesses of commercialized religiosity, however, and remains a pleasant country town of tastefully restored shop fronts and pubs and several additional minor sights to complement the Rock itself.

Cashel has long been a place of great significance, and rivaled Tara as a royal seat for the kings of Munster from the 4th century AD. St. Patrick arrived in about AD 432 and converted King Aengus, who became Ireland's first Christian ruler. Among many legends associated with this event, St. Patrick is alleged to have used a shamrock leaf to illustrate the nature of the Holy Trinity. During Aengus's baptism, St. Patrick accidentally drove his sharp crozier through the king's foot, but he did not complain and his wound was discovered only after the

ceremony. A shocked St. Patrick asked why he had said nothing, and the king replied that he had assumed the suffering was some sort of initiation rite, emulating the pain of Christ.

The buildings now visible on Cashel date mainly from the 12th and 13th centuries. Earliest of these structures is probably the **Round Tower►**, remarkably preserved, with an entrance doorway 12 feet above ground level. **Cormac's Chapel►►**, ornately carved with beasts and human figures, begun in 1127, is in excellent condition and displays the Irish Romanesque style clearly. A sarcophagus in the Chapel is said to be the tomb of Cormac, the bishop-king of Munster, who presided during Cashel's great time of influence in the 12th century. The roofless 13th-century **cathedral►►**, the largest building on the Rock, with tall lancet and quatrefoil windows and a later central tower on Gothic arches, witnessed a particularly unpleasant act of Cromwellian barbarism when Lord Inchiquin besieged the town in 1647. The citizens fled to sanctuary in the cathedral, whereupon turf was piled up around the walls and set on fire, roasting hundreds of unfortunate townspeople to death. Various attempts were made to repair the building, but it gradually declined and in 1749 Cashel's main place of worship was moved down to the town. The **Hall of the Vicars►**, a 15th-century residence for privileged members of the choir, at the foot of the Rock, contains a museum with St. Patrick's Cross and Coronation Stone. The Brú Ború heritage center promotes Celtic studies and performing arts.

In the town, a small **folk village►** attracts many tourists. It features reconstructions of 18th-century buildings and displays artifacts of the period. The **G.P.A.-Bolton Library►►** in the grounds of the Protestant Cathedral is an unusually gripping collection of old tomes; it contains over 12,000 volumes, including part of Chaucer's *Book of Fame*, printed by Caxton, and a collection of church silver. Not to be missed at a glance at **Cashel Palace►**, a splendid brick edifice, former home of the Archbishop of Cashel, and now a luxury hotel (see Hotels and Restaurants, page 275). Visitors can take advantage of the basement Buttery Restaurant, one of the coziest places in town for a hearty meal or quick snack. A path leads from the hotel gardens up to the Rock.

St. Patrick's Cross

Miler Magrath
Buried in the cathedral at Cashel is Archbishop Magrath, a noted pluralist who enjoyed the best of both worlds. Born around 1523, he began his religious life a Franciscan friar, soon becoming Catholic Bishop of Down and Connor, an office he later combined with being Protestant Archbishop of Cashel. At his death (1622) he had amassed 70 parishes, four bishoprics, two wives, and numerous offspring.

Inside the museum at the Rock of Cashel

Charles Bianconi
This adopted citizen of Clonmel was born at Tregolo in northern Italy on September 24, 1786. He was dispatched to Ireland by his father to avoid a scandal at the age of 16 after he had fallen in love with a neighbor's daughter who was destined for a marriage with the nobility. On July 6, 1815, he began a one-horse cart service between Clonmel and Cahir, which rapidly grew into a thriving mail-coach business and reputedly the world's first public transportation system. His vehicles were known as "bians" (after Bianconi) and ran thousands of miles each day all over Ireland, despite competition from the railroads. His headquarters were in Hearn's Hotel on Parnell Street (recently restored) and he became Mayor of Clonmel twice.

The attractive harbor at Dunmore East continues...

▶▶ Clonmel   118B2

Clonmel is Tipperary's county town, a prosperous and pretty place with plenty of life and, if home-grown novelist Laurence Sterne's writings are anything to go by, some whimsical goings-on. Sterne lived during the 18th century and is best known for his novel, *Tristram Shandy*. Other novelists have connections with the town; Anthony Trollope worked for a while in the local post office, and George Borrow, the 19th-century traveler and writer, was at school here. There are no outstanding sights in the town, but it has lots of pleasant shops and eating places, and stands on the edge of some extremely picturesque touring country. The **circular drive▶▶** to the south, along the Nire and Suir valleys, is well worth taking on a fine day. So are trips into the unspoiled Comeragh Mountains.

The town was once an important stronghold of the powerful Butler family. Its Main Guard replaced the courthouse destroyed in the Cromwellian siege. The West Gate dates from 1831 and stands on the site of an earlier medieval gateway. Near St. Mary's Protestant church are sections of the old 14th-century walls which defended the town against Cromwell for longer than any other Irish town. Several churches have eye-catching, 19th-century, "streaky bacon" colored brickwork.

Clonmel is famed for its field sports, notably fox-hunting and hare-coursing (sending dogs after hares). It is a great center of the greyhound world, and the slim animals can often be seen being exercised along the road, much as racehorses are in Kildare.

▶ Dungarvan   118A2

A bustling fishing port and resort on the Colligan estuary, Dungarvan is surrounded by low cliffs and gentle hills. The setting is rather more appealing than the town itself, but it caters well for simple family stays with an excellent beach at Clonea Strand. The center of the town is Grattan Square, flanked by stately buildings. Down by the harbor a maze of tiny alleyways laces between warehouses towards the quayside, where several attractive old inns serve good seafood. Old Market House contains a museum of local history, where the sad tale of the *Moresby*, shipwrecked in Dungarvan Bay, is recounted. Close to the town the remains of Dungarvan's Castle, built by King John, can be seen, and on the east bank of the Colligan is an Augustinian abbey overlooking attractive **Helvick Head▶▶**. The drive around the bay to this headland leads through the tiny Gaelic-speaking village of **Ring▶**, with fine coastal views on the way.

▶▶ Dunmore East   118A3

This substantial village at the seaward end of Waterford Harbor is now a popular resort and sailing center, but tourism is a secondary interest. Dunmore has its own raison d'être dating from 1813, when it was chosen as Waterford's mail packet station.

Bright fishing boats crowd the pretty harbor of what is obviously still a well-used port. Visitors are warned that they approach the waterside at their own risk; ropes and steel hawsers bestrew the workmanlike quays. The setting is lovely—red sandstone cliffs, topped with vivid emerald turf and golden gorse catch the sun, while beneath lie sheltered coves of soft sand. A lighthouse guards the headland. The picturesqueness has encouraged an influx of well-heeled visitors and the village has been used more than once as a film location. Waterford residents retire or escape here in spacious architect-designed bungalows, and more transient vacationers stay in thatched homes. The core of the old community is still visible closer to the harbor, in a pleasing assembly of well-kept Georgian and Victorian cottages. The village boasts an exceptionally good range of reasonably priced accommodations, and unpretentious eating places, and is an excellent place to stay to explore Waterford City or any of this attractive coast.

Master McGrath

At a fork in the road 3 miles northwest of Dungarvan stands a splendid commemorative monument —to a greyhound. It was erected by local sportsmen to Master McGrath, winner of the Waterloo Cup three times (1868, 1869, and 1871) and victor in all but one of the 37 courses he ran. Doubtless they were keen to honor both his triumphs and the bets he won for his backers.

...to be the mainstay of the local economy

From the County Wexford Museum in Enniscorthy

► ▶ Enniscorthy 119B4

The market town of Enniscorthy on the banks of the River Slaney is remembered for a terrible battle in the troubled year of 1798. On June 21 about 20,000 rebels, including many women and children, armed with agricultural implements and metal bayonets or swords, gathered on Vinegar Hill just outside the town. They had held it for nearly a month, but English troops under General Lake, finally losing patience, strafed the insurgents with continuous cannon-fire. Exactly how many were killed is not known (many slipped quietly down the far side of the hill), but the massacre remains vivid in the minds of Irish people. The Battle of Vinegar Hill effectively marked the end of the 1798 uprising, but Enniscorthy played an active anti-British role in the Easter Rising of 1916. A fascinating collection of items connected with the battle can be seen in the **County Wexford Museum►**, housed in the sturdy square-towered castle. This impressive Anglo-Norman

An impostor
The Round Tower which dominates the Irish National Heritage Park at Ferrycarrig gives the impression that the hill on which it stands was the site of an early Irish monastery, to which Round Towers normally belonged. However, a plaque in the wall gives the game away; the tower is a 19th-century copy commemorating the men of Wexford who died in the Crimean War (1853–1856).

In its heyday, Jerpoint Abbey was surrounded by a small town, but few, if any, traces of this now survive

building was briefly leased to the Elizabethan poet and politician, Edmund Spenser, during his inglorious period of office in Ireland. From the castle you can see the slopes of Vinegar Hill, golden with gorse most of the year, and crowned with the stump of an old windmill which served as the rebels' H.Q. The town is the center of the Southeast's soft-fruit industry, and every July a Strawberry Fair is held. Enniscorthy's other noteworthy building is its Gothic cathedral of St. Aidan's, designed by Pugin, architect of the Houses of Parliament in London.

A few miles up the road lies **Ferns▶**, now just a village but formerly the capital of Leinster. Its eye-catching ruins are the remains of a fine 13th-century castle and an Augustinian abbey.

▶▶   Ferrycarrig   119B4

Just where the River Slaney broadens into tidal mudflats west of Wexford, a popular new attraction draws the crowds. The **Irish National Heritage Park▶▶** re-creates many aspects of daily life in Ireland through about 9,000 years of history up to the Anglo-Norman period. Full-scale models of lake settlements, ring-forts, burial places, and a complete Norman castle lie hidden among hazel groves and reed beds in a large park. This is "theme-park Ireland," but of its kind it is well done, informative, and naturalistic, helping to put into context many of the scattered antiquities you will find as you travel around Ireland. An audio-visual presentation is available at the visitor center, along with a wide selection of guidebooks, good snacks, and teas. It rewards a visit, particularly if you have children to amuse.

▶   Holy Cross Abbey   118C2

Holy Cross Abbey, about 5 miles south of Thurles, is set in peaceful water meadows by the River Suir. It was founded in 1169 and restored in the 15th century. After that it fell into decay until 1971, when much rebuilding and interior whitewashing made it usable again as a parish church. The abbey's great treasure which attracts thousands of pilgrims to its wall shrine is an alleged splinter of the True Cross, thought to have been given to Murtagh O'Brien, King of Munster, by a 12th-century pope—yet another fragment of that ubiquitous piece of carpentry! The Ulster clan chiefs O'Donnell and O'Neill stopped off to pray here on their way to Kinsale, but the True Cross was apparently not on their side (see page 162). The interior contains a rare wall painting of a Norman hunting scene and some fine stonework.

▶▶   Jerpoint Abbey   118B3

These evocative Cistercian ruins seem to have a much more authentically medieval ring about them than somewhat commercialized Holy Cross, the stone tower and battlements erupting suddenly on a quiet bend south of Thomastown. Quite a lot can be seen by peering through the gaps in the walls, but if the visitor center is open it is worth the modest entrance charge to wander around the cloisters and chancel for a close-up of the vivacious carvings of medieval figures and strange beasts on capitals and tombs. The **glassworks▶** at Jerpoint produce a plainer style than most Irish crystal factories.

Near Enniscorthy
"Before dinner had a most delicious walk by myself along the banks of the River Slaney, which, for two or three miles out of the town, are full of beauty, and this sunny evening was quite worthy of them. It was likewise delightful to me to be alone in such a scene, for it is only alone that I can enjoy Nature thoroughly; men and women disturb such scenes dreadfully."
Thomas Moore: *Diary*, August 25, 1835.

131

Characterful figures adorn the tombs at Jerpoint Abbey

The Long Gallery in Kilkenny Castle includes portraits by Van Dyck and Lely

Dunmore Cave

These caverns are located just north of Kilkenny town in craggy limestone farmland, with an entrance lying down a long flight of steps. One has a thick stalagmite pillar and lots of tiny ceiling straws like icicles. A collection of items and geological material is on display at the visitor center by the ticket office. One grisly find included the bones of more than 40 people, many of them women and children, who are believed to have taken refuge in the caves, perhaps to elude the Vikings. Their undamaged bones suggests they died of starvation, or may have been suffocated by smoke.

▶▶▶ **Kilkenny**   *118C3*

One of Ireland's most delightful towns, Kilkenny stands on a bend in the River Nore. It is packed with history (in summer, with tourist traffic, too) and its medieval heritage is particularly well preserved. Discerning visitors will find a number of high-quality craft studios and good restaurants. One of the most popular times to visit is during the Arts Week festival in the last two weeks of August. The beautiful countryside around Kilkenny makes it an excellent touring base. The most striking building is the castle▶▶, a stronghold of the Butler family until this century, which began life as a Norman fortress and gradually became more domesticated through the centuries. It saw conflict recently, however, when anti-Treatyites occupied it briefly during the Civil War in 1922. After massive restoration, the castle is once again on show. The hammer-beamed picture gallery, lined with portraits and elaborate ceiling decorations, is the most memorable room. The well-proportioned 18th-century buildings opposite the castle have now been converted into an imaginative enterprise called the Kilkenny Design Center, where local artists produce high-quality crafts. A large retail outlet fronting the street supplies some of the best goods on sale in Ireland and is an attractive place to do some shopping, though prices are pitched at a well-heeled market.

Kilkenny's historical importance formerly rivaled Dublin's, and several significant political events took place there. The Statutes of Kilkenny, passed in 1366, were a notorious and crude attempt to assert English authority in Ireland by what was essentially a form of apartheid. The Anglo-Norman settlers were prevented from intermarriage or social intercourse with the native Celtic Irish, on pain of death. Gaelic names were banned, the language was suppressed, and the native population was forced to live outside the city walls. Understandably, the Irish grew restless at this repressive regime. After the Reformation had suppressed even their religious beliefs, the "Old English" and Gaelic aristocrats (both Catholic factions) formed an uneasy alliance called the Confederation of Kilkenny, a parliamentary assembly which aimed to resist the ferociously unjust anti-Catholic laws imposed by Protestant England. Cromwell's invasion brutally put a stop to this and thus drove an iron stake through the heart of Anglo-Irish integration, which, if left to itself, would, over time, probably have resulted in a harmonious community.

Many other interesting buildings are scattered through the old town. **St. Canice's Cathedral►►** is its most notable church and one of the finest 13th-century buildings in Ireland, despite Cromwell's use of it to stable his horses in 1650. The monuments of the black limestone known as Kilkenny marble are particularly impressive—one female statue wears a traditional Irish cloak. Next to the cathedral are a **Round Tower►**, which can be climbed for splendid town views, and the valuable **St. Canice's Library►** containing many rare early volumes. St. Mary's Cathedral is the Catholic counterpart built in 1849. Other medieval churches include the Black Abbey, the ruined St. John's Priory, and St. Francis's Abbey.

One of several Tudor buildings is **Rothe House►**. This stone mansion belonged to the merchant John Rothe and his growing family of 12 children, which necessitated the addition of several wings rambling around cobbled courtyards. The restored building has now become a museum run by Kilkenny Archeological Society. The Tourist Information Center is housed in a **Tudor almshouse►** built by the lawyer, Sir Richard Shee, in 1594. A *son-et-lumière* presentation about the town is held upstairs. The Tholsel (town hall) and the courthouse date from the 18th century.

Alice Kyteler

The medieval home of Dame Alice Kyteler is now a popular old tavern in Kilkenny. In 1324 she was charged with witchcraft and the poisoning of her four husbands, all of whom had died painfully in quick succession, leaving Alice somewhat wealthy. Whether there was any truth in the accusation is unknown, but Alice was a fly character, and she fled to Scotland, leaving her poor maid, Petronella, to take her place at the stake.

Kells Priory

The countryside south and east of Kilkenny is pretty. If you head south you will find the romantic remains of Kells Priory, a walled monastery looking like some medieval city standing in a sloping field. A short way south of the tiny medieval village are a Round Tower and a High Cross.

133

St. Canice's Cathedral

THE VEE GAP

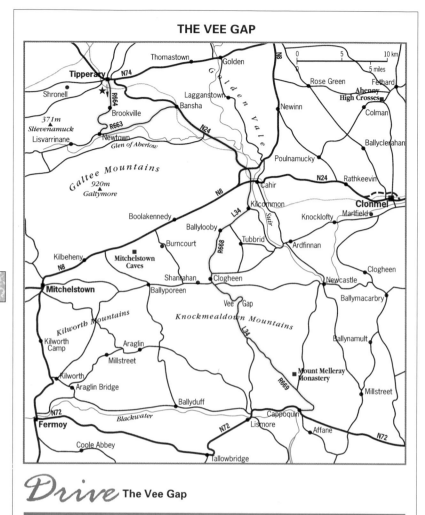

Drive **The Vee Gap**

A roller-coaster drive between southern Tipperary's two ranges of hills, with panoramic views of fertile plains.

From the mundane agricultural town of **Tipperary**, an important dairy farming center, a scenic route is marked via the **Glen of Aherlow►►**. A road through dappled woodland meanders up to a sharp hairpin bend giving a breathtaking vista down the Aherlow Valley. This beautiful glen is about 10 miles long, following the course of the Aherlow River. Shortly afterwards it joins the Glen of Aherlow road with grand glimpses of the Slievenamuck Hills to the north, and the shallow-pitched ridge of the Galtee Mountains on the southerly side. The highest summit is Galtymore Mountain, at 3,018 feet. The Cahir Way and numerous forest trails lead through the hills, past ancient cairns and glacial tarns. The region is noted for its traditional farmhouse cheeses, Galtee bacon and sausages, hams, and even venison. **Mitchelstown** is a good place to buy these products.

From **Bansha** a good main road (N24) leads southeast to the town of **Cahir** (described on pages 122–3). At Cahir the minor R668 runs down toward the old market town of **Clogheen►**, where you can join the spectacular **Vee Gap Drive**▶▶ through the Knockmealdown Mountains. The Vee road winds steeply up through larch and rhododendron, and at its most dramatic loop several safe parking bays offer irresistibly photogenic views. Far below, the Suir Valley and the Golden Vale of emerald fields lie as flat and placid as an embroidered quilt beneath vast skies. Black-and-white cattle graze amid a sprinkling of farmsteads. Just south of these viewpoints the road climbs over heather-, bracken-, and gorse-covered slopes to the V-shaped pass which forms the boundary between Tipperary and Waterford counties. A tarn is visible below the road, and a couple of stone shepherds' shelters. Beyond the pass, the road descends past **Mount Melleray Monastery** (see page 136) to **Cappoquin**.

▶   **Kilmore Quay**   *119A4*

Just offshore lie the Saltee Islands, Ireland's largest bird sanctuary. Boats run from the harbor from May until mid-July, the nesting season for thousands of seabirds. The pretty village of thatched and whitewashed cottages vies with Kinsale by hosting a seafood festival in July—the Wooden House pub is one of the better bars offering traditional music. An old lightship moored in the harbor contains a small maritime museum. The westerly sandspit of Ballyteigue is another important nature reserve, with rare plants.

▶▶   **Lismore**   *118A1*

The **castle**▶▶, looming above the dense woodland of the Blackwater Valley, is one of Ireland's most evocative fortresses. Built by Prince John in 1185, it was extensively remodeled in the 19th century, when Joseph Paxton (designer of the Crystal Palace in south London) was commissioned to re-create a Tudor-style residence for the 6th Duke of Devonshire from the medieval ruins. It was planned on an opulent scale; the gorgeous **gardens** are open to the public during the summer (although you can't see inside the castle). Sir Walter Ralegh lived there for a time, selling it to Richard Boyle, father of the famous chemist who was born in the castle. It also functioned as an archbishop's palace, eventually passing in 1753 to the Cavendish family, the Dukes of Devonshire, whose Irish seat it remains to this day. For many years Lismore Castle was the home of Fred Astaire's sister, Adele, who married a Cavendish.

The other main buildings of interest in Lismore are the two cathedrals. **St. Carthage's**▶, the Anglican one, is mostly 17th century, its notable features including the splendidly carved MacGrath tomb dating from 1548, and two bright lancet windows by the pre-Raphaelite artist, Sir Edward Burne-Jones. The Catholic Cathedral, built in 1881, contains many ornate decorations in Italian Romanesque style.

An award-winning **heritage center**▶▶ has appeared in Lismore's stone courthouse. An excellent audio-visual production on the history of the town and the local area dwells particularly on its importance as a monastic settlement and university in the 7th century. Today Lismore is proud of another local celebrity, the travel writer Dervla Murphy, who acquired her wanderlust by cycling around this beautiful wooded valley where she was born.

Surprising Lismore
Lismore Castle is a place of surprises. James II, on looking out of the window over the River Blackwater in 1689, was so amazed at the drop that he started with a fright; the spot is pointed out to this day. In 1814, when workmen were repairing the castle, they found a crozier of ca.1100 in a wall, along with a later medieval manuscript containing the lives of early Irish saints. Both were probably hidden when the castle was besieged and burned in 1645. They are now in the National Museum, Dublin.

135

A figurehead at the Maritime Museum, Kilmore Quay

▶▶ Mitchelstown Caves 118B1

This cave system is believed to be the largest system of river-formed limestone caverns in Ireland. Though privately owned, they remain pleasantly uncommercialized. You buy your ticket at a simple roadside farmhouse, and the 2-mile tour around a small section of the caves is conducted on an amateur family basis, with many references to fancifully named formations ("Is it an old man, a pig, an elephant?"). Minerals in the rocks have caused spectacular colorations. The caves served as a hiding place for the Earl of Desmond during the 16th century. Today, occasional special events take advantage of the acoustics.

▶ Mount Melleray Monastery 118B2

This austere, gray monastery was founded in 1832 by the Cistercian order, who have industriously turned a barren hillside into fertile and productive land. The community (which consisted mostly of Irish monks) was expelled from its original home in France and granted 575 acres here. Visitors are welcome in the main church and can stay in the guest lodge by prior arrangement. Just south of the monastery is a grotto shrine where miraculous visions of the Virgin have been seen, plaster statues weep and rock, and the faithful gather to light candles and pray.

▶ New Ross 118B3

There are few reasons to visit New Ross specifically, but it has such a strategic location that you will almost certainly find yourself driving through it if you are in the Southeast. It commands the lowest bridging point on the River Barrow so you must either take the car ferry between Passage East and Ballyhack or pass through New Ross to travel between Counties Wexford and Waterford. Views of the town from either of the stepped

136

Mitchelstown Caves lie in a limestone trough between the Knockmealdown and Galtee mountains, and are the unexpected home of a very rare spider, Porrhoma Myops

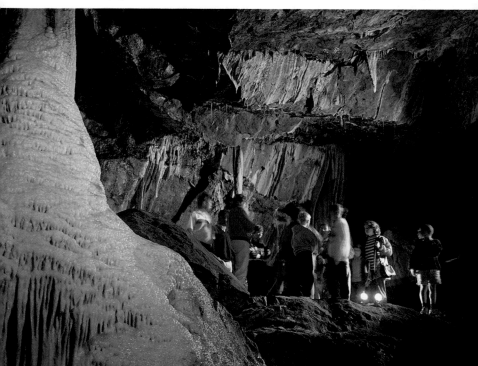

hills rising sharply from the waterfront overlook its busy wharves. It is a very old settlement, founded in the 13th century by Strongbow's son-in-law, William le Marshall, on an ancient monastic site. A few bits of the ancient city gates remain. The waterfront can be pleasantly explored from a boat deck; river cruises up the Barrow are organized in summer on the Galley Cruising Restaurant. Failing that, going in almost any direction from New Ross will provide a rewarding excursion, particularly north, toward Inistioge and St. Mullin's. Flower-dappled lanes wander through ancient villages studded with crumbling castles and abbeys. Sparkling rivers snake through the meadows, and the gentle contours of the Blackstairs Mountains, brown, green, or heather-colored, rise in the background.

The drive northwest through the beautiful Nore valley leads past **Inistioge►** to **Thomastown►►** and **Jerpoint Abbey** (see page 131). Inistioge is a picturesque little town, with linden trees planted in its main square beside the bridge, a pretty riverfront and a jumble of 18th- and 19th-century houses on the lane twisting up from the town center. There are ruins of a Norman castle and an Augustinian monastery. Thomastown, once a medieval walled town of importance, is now a lovely place with mellowed gray-stone buildings and a few ruins. The **Kilfane Glen and Waterfall►** is an 18th-century woodland garden. Return to New Ross via Graiguenamanagh and St. Mullin's (see page 141). Graiguenamanagh, in a spectacular position beside the river, is a little market town, famous for **Duiske Abbey►**, a much-restored 13th-century Cistercian foundation, once the largest in Ireland. The effigy of a knight stands beside the abbey's entrance, and a magnificent Romanesque processional door may be found down the steps from the south transept.

South of New Ross lies the **J. F. Kennedy Park►►**, a vast arboretum occupying over 580 acres of forest and landscaped gardens with about 5,000 types of carefully grouped and documented specimen trees and shrubs. Nature trails lead through the grounds and visitors can drive to a viewpoint on the summit of Slieve Coillte. Much botanical and arboreal research is carried out there.

The J. F. Kennedy Park, near New Ross

Irish-American Presidents
Two recent U.S. presidents have roots in southeast Ireland. President John F. Kennedy's great-grandfather was born in a cottage in Dunganstown, just south of New Ross in County Waterford, and descendants of the family still live there. A memorial arboretum to President Kennedy has been planted close by. President Ronald Reagan's folk probably hailed from the tiny, one-horse town of Ballyporeen, near Mitchelstown in County Tipperary. President Reagan visited Ballyporeen in 1984 and brought great fame to it.

The Irish in exile

"As long as Ireland produces men with sense enough to leave her, she does not exist in vain." George Bernard Shaw's remark is unkind, but apt. Irish-born people or, more broadly, people of Irish descent, have had a most disproportionate influence in many fields, particularly in the arts, media, sports, and politics. But they have often shown this after they have left the island.

Top: a stylized depiction of Ireland's most famous 20th-century exile—James Joyce

The Flight of the Wild Geese
After the final victory of William III's forces at the Battle of Limerick in 1691, many Jacobite officers accepted the terms of surrender at the Treaty of Limerick and sailed away down the Shannon to join the armies of Catholic Europe (perhaps with the hope one day of returning to defeat the old enemy). Among these aristocratic mercenaries was the hero of the Battle of Limerick, Patrick Sarsfield, Earl of Lucan. Like the earlier Flight of the Earls in 1607, this exile of leaders dealt a great blow to Gaelic power in Ireland. Their estates and castles were quickly snatched by Protestant settlers.

A constraining influence Somehow, Ireland seems to breed a listlessness and apathy at home which often crystallizes into formidable energy, talent, and purposefulness abroad. Of course, people with the most get-up-and-go are often the ones likely to leave any country to better their lot, and the Irish who stay at home are by no means devoid of talent. Nevertheless, many periods in Ireland's history have worked against pioneering spirits; the long doldrum since the Irish Free State was formed in 1922 is one of the most noticeable of these in recent times. After English shackles were shaken off, Ireland had everything to play for—high ideals, a young and vigorous population, and a new nation to form. Under de Valera's rule and the constricting influence of a peculiarly oppressive form of Catholicism, Ireland remained fossilized in a twilight zone of romantic mythology, social divisiveness, and economic gloom. Many people have left Ireland since, ironically for the land whose rule they have so roundly rejected.

Artists and Ireland Artists and writers have deserted Ireland for centuries in search of havens where their work would receive a better reception than in the reactionary climate of their birthplace. Since World War II, the Irish government has tried to stem the tide by offering artists (including writers) tax-free status in the Republic. The hugely successful novelist Frederick Forsyth was one of the most notable acceptors of this bribe, though other writers found it odd that a government should encourage literary enterprise with fiscal measures and then censor it on religious or moral grounds. A vast number of Irish writers have made their homes abroad. One, Cecil Day-Lewis, even became an English poet laureate. The novelist Edna O'Brien, herself an exile in London from Tuamgraney, County Clare, described the claustrophobia of Irish provincial life. "Hour after hour I can think of Ireland, I can imagine without going too far wrong what is happening in any one of the little towns by day or by night." For a visit, for a vacation, the pace of Ireland is refreshing, endearing, delightful. For a lifetime, many have found it stultifying.

Enforced emigration Reasons for the steady departure of Irishmen abroad range from general "grass is greener" aspirations to the most dire and desperate emergencies. Most drastically, the Famine years of the late 1840s resulted in massive emigration, mostly from the West. Whole communities were decimated and many have never

recovered. In earlier times, religious persecution was often the spur, famously in the exile of leading Catholic families after the confiscation of their lands (The Flight of the Earls in 1607, see pages 34–5), or after defeat in battle ("The Wild Geese," after the Battle of Limerick in 1691, see panel). The Ulster Presbyterians emigrated in great numbers in the late 18th and early 19th centuries to seek their fortunes in the New World. The best place to learn about this phase of Irish history is at the Ulster-American Folk Park in County Tyrone (see page 234).

Influential exiles To see evidence of Ireland's influence abroad, you need look no further than the list of U.S. presidents. Over a quarter of them are of Irish descent—mostly of Ulster Protestant stock. More recently, John F. Kennedy and Ronald Reagan have partly redressed the balance with their origins in Counties Waterford and Tipperary. Canada, too, has had Brian Mulroney as prime minister. Today more than 40 million U.S. citizens can claim Irish ancestry.

Irish representatives overseas can be found in just about any field you care to name: John Field the composer; John Philip Holland, inventor of the submarine; James Hoban, architect of the White House; the writers F. Scott Fitzgerald and Eugene O'Neill; Sir Hans Sloane, founder of the British Museum; John McEnroe, the tennis star—and a host of others.

The Kennedy homestead in the J. F. Kennedy Park near New Ross shows what early American homesteads looked like

The excellent Ulster-American Folk Park near Omagh, County Tyrone, Northern Ireland

Old Leighlin
118C3

A few minor sights make this village worth a brief stop. One is the squat crenellated tower of the 13th-century Anglican church known grandiosely as St. Lazerian's Cathedral, with, nearby, a 7th-century monastery and Lazerian's well which attracts many pilgrims. The simple cathedral has a Gothic door and two fonts. Leighlinbridge to the east, as its name suggests, is a bridging point over the Barrow (the original bridge here dates from 1320). The scanty remains of the Black Castle can be seen on the east bank, one of the earliest Norman defenses in Ireland.

►► Ring of Hook
118A3

The quiet peninsula on the east side of Waterford Harbor is a strange low-lying place full of deserted villages and migrant birds. The straight, empty roads lead through Ballyhack, where a small shuttle ferry cuts out the long trek inland via New Ross, then through **Duncannon**, a peaceful small seaside resort with a sandy beach and a reputation for fine sea fishing. Military remains indicate its former strategic importance; a fortress built by the Anglo-Normans stands by the waterfront, strengthened to guard against the Spanish Armada in the late 16th century, and during Napoleonic times the British built three Martello Towers to deter the French. The big house here, Loftus Hall, was built by the 4th Marquis of Ely for his bride-to-be, Victoria, the Princess Royal, who called off her engagement for mysterious reasons. It later became a hotel, capitalizing on a ghostly legend that the Devil once escaped through the roof here after a game of cards, leaving cracks that are impossible to repair (a good excuse for leaving them alone, anyway!).

At the craggy, desolate tip of the peninsula stands an ancient lighthouse, the oldest in Ireland. Warning lights for shipping have been kept here for some 1,400 years, but the present, zebra-striped version dates from Norman times. Even earlier than that, a Welsh monk called Dubhand is thought to have kept a form of lighthouse by hoisting a cauldron of burning pitch to a high platform. On stormy days the sea sends dramatic columns of spray through blow holes in the rocks. During high season some enterprising families seek out

---

By Hook or by Crook
The origin of this phrase is much disputed, but Cromwell is alleged to have used it when he was planning his assault on Waterford, declaring he would take the city "by Hook …" (on the eastern side) "… or by Crook" (just below Passage East on the west side of the harbor).

The lighthouse on Hook Head has ancient origins; it was built by one Raymond le Gros in 1172. The sea at Hook Head is also noted for the beauty of the corals found growing on the limestone

these quiet beaches around Fethard and Booley Strand; at other times of year you can enjoy them almost unchallenged. The village of Slade is especially charming and is a well-known scuba-diving center. The remains of some 18th-century salthouses can be seen on the pier (where salt was extracted from seawater by evaporation).

Rosslare   119B4

Well known as a ferry terminal for traffic from Normandy and Wales, Rosslare is actually 5 miles north of its harbor. Rosslare is a popular seaside resort capitalizing on its long, sandy beach and relatively sunny climate. However, there is little of interest in the place, except perhaps for golfers (it has an excellent links course).

Just south of Rosslare is Our Lady's Island, connected to the mainland by a causeway, where the ruins of an Augustinian priory and a Round Tower can be seen (the tower leans more precariously than that at Pisa). There is an annual pilgrimage to the Marian shrine from August 15 to September 8. Some pilgrims crawl around its 12 acres on their knees; others walk with one foot in the water.

► St. Mullin's   118B3

A monastery was founded here in the 7th century by St. Moling, a monk of high birth and apparently artistic talents. The watercourse that he dug with his own hands to power a mill is still there, but the monastery buildings have since disappeared and the remains visible now date from medieval times. In the churchyard are a penal altar, used surreptitiously when Catholic services were banned, and the graves of several Leinster kings, including the fearsome warrior Art MacMurrough, scourge of the Anglo-Normans. St. Mullin's is scarcely worth visiting for its remains alone, which are minimal and hard to track down, but the village itself is at a most beautiful spot by a stream with the Blackstairs Mountains rising behind. Many places around here, or in **Graiguenamanagh►►** upstream where the more impressive monastery of **Duiske Abbey►** stands, are ideal for walks and picnics.

A cannon still guards the busy port of Rosslare

Captain Myles Keogh
Captain Keogh, from Leighlinbridge, was an adventurous soul. He fought for the Pope in the 1860s when Garibaldi was uniting Italy, then joined the American Civil War on the Union side. His third military adventure was with Colonel Custer's 7th Cavalry, where he fought gallantly at the Battle of Little Big Horn against the Sioux Indians in 1876. He was apparently one of the last to die, and as a mark of respect was not scalped after the battle. His horse Comanche was the only survivor on the army's side.

Waterford City has been a bustling center since the Vikings settled there in the middle of the 9th century

Waterford Mutiny

The citizens of Waterford were a fairly pugnacious lot, it seems. Mayor Briver had to be rescued by his wife in 1641 when a riot took place. Mrs. Briver wrote that when she heard swords being drawn against her husband, "I ran oute into the streete without hatt or mantle and laid my handes about his necke and brought hem in whether he wud or no." Later this same mayor lost three fingers from his hand —bitten off by an angry mutineer.

▶▶ **Waterford**   *118B3*

Waterford is by far the largest town in the Southeast and one of the few prospering industrial centers in the Republic. It too has suffered badly from world recession, however, and signs of depression are evident even in its famous glassworks. Other industries include light engineering, electronics, paper manufacture, and brewing. Some visitors find the overtly workmanlike quaysides a turnoff after rural towns in Ireland, but Waterford has a grand history and plenty to explore.

Waterford is essentially a Viking city, with many reminders of this period of its history among the buildings lying immediately behind the waterfront. **Reginald's Tower**▶ was built in 1003 as part of the old city walls by a certain Reginald (an unlikely sounding name for a Danish city governor), and served subsequently as royal residence, fortress, mint, prison, and air-raid shelter. It is now the Civic and Maritime Museum, containing many municipal documents and regalia.

The most interesting churches are St. Patrick's Catholic church of 1750, well restored in terra-cotta and white after being used as a corn store during penal days, and the Protestant Christ Church Cathedral, built in 1770 and containing a weighty colonnade of Corinthian columns and fine stucco ceiling decorations. A grim memorial to James Rice, a mayor who died in 1490, depicts the process of posthumous decomposition in graphic detail. The Catholic Holy Trinity Cathedral also has a remarkably sumptuous interior.

Later civic buildings worth a glance are the 1849 courthouse, with a massive classical portico, the **city hall**▶ of 1788 with magnificent Waterford crystal glittering in the public assembly rooms and the **Chamber of Commerce**▶, a town house of 1795 with a spectacularly beautiful stairwell. You can glance at all this free of charge.

One of Waterford's most interesting recent developments is the **heritage center**▶▶ housed in the disused church of St. Peter's in Grayfriars Street, where the best finds from Waterford's Viking and medieval past (excavated during preparations for a new shopping center) are excellently displayed.

A visit to the crystal factory on the N25 Cork road, less than a mile from the city center, is the most popular tourist activity Waterford has to offer. Free factory tours take place every weekday during the mornings. At busy times of year you should reserve a place.

The tours are indeed interesting, and take about 40 minutes (a good plan for a wet day: to reserve a place contact the tourist office on 051 73311; no children under 5). You are taken around each stage of manufacture. Basic ingredients of glass are silica and potash; lead crystal also requires a significant quantity of lead oxide in powder form (safety regulations must be strictly adhered to with this toxic substance). The lead gives the glass its particular qualities of brilliance and capacity to refract light, and also makes it very heavy. The ingredients are heated to about 1,200°C over many hours, then hand-blown and skillfully shaped before cooling. Finally the glass is cut with deep grid-like patterns, the air filling with minute particles and the screech of carborundum and diamond wheels. You will see Waterford Crystal in grand houses throughout Ireland; today, a modern version of one of those glittering droplet chandeliers costs several thousand pounds.

The plant now covers a site of about 38 acres, and worldwide sales top IR£100 million. By far the largest market for Waterford Crystal is the United States, and American tastes are therefore strongly reflected in the ornate designs. Waterford now has many home-grown rivals throughout Ireland, although Waterford still claims the edge for its high quality (no inferior produce is ever sold; it is simply smashed and melted down again), its purity of color, and its deep cut. Certainly, if you want to find out about crystal, this is the place to do it. Prices start at around IR£22 for a tiny liqueur glass.

The history of Waterford Crystal
The history of Waterford glass started in the late 18th century, when George and William Penrose set up a factory there in 1783. It flourished for 68 years, before the disastrous economic conditions of 1851 caused its closure. A century later, Waterford once again became home for a glassworks, modest at first, but expanding to prodigious dimensions within only 40 years.

A master cutter concentrates on his task

Wexford's Main Street is typical of many of Ireland's shopping thoroughfares

Wexford Opera Festival
This event has been held during October at the Theatre Royal for over 40 years, now attracting opera buffs from far and wide, as well as many international stars. It tends to favor rare or neglected works, and so has a pleasantly off-beat, avant-garde tinge. If you manage to get tickets, you may of course discover why some of these works are rare and neglected! For all that, it's the social event of the year in Wexford, festive but unsnobby, where local people dress up and drink champagne. Book well ahead for seats; they are gold dust (box office tel: 053 22144). If you can't get a ticket, many other events will be going on too—concerts, revues, recitals, jazz in pubs, etc. Many travel companies offer package tours to the festival.

▶▶ **Wexford** *119B4*

For all its bloody history, Wexford has a peaceful air. First glances may suggest it is all too dull, basking in its muddy estuary like some somnolent reptile. But it is by no means moribund. Present traces of a proud past are admittedly vestigial, but a bustling small-town charm and sense of life outweigh any initial disappointment. If you catch it during October when the acclaimed opera festival is in full swing, you will be left with no doubt that Wexford rates itself pretty highly, and why not, achieving full-page write-ups as it does in all the national papers?

The Viking name *Waesfjord* (harbor of the mudflats) is appropriate. The River Slaney and several tributaries empty their silt-laden waters into the sea there, and Wexford's practicality as a deepwater port has long since been overtaken by its rival in the next county, Waterford. But the mud is not all bad. North and south of the town, large areas on either side of the estuary provide a habitat for many thousands of wading birds. The **Wexford Wildfowl Reserve▶▶** is a must for ornithologists. The "Slobs," as the mudflats are known locally, are *polders*, or reclaimed land lying lower than sea level. Follow the signs for the reserve from Wexford's coastal exit roads and you will reach a research station with a visitor center, a lookout tower, identification charts, and hides (like hunting blinds). Entrance is free. The neighboring dunes around Raven Point are also an important nature reserve with rare plants and insects, as well as birds.

The town itself straggles along the waterfront, several blocks deep. The helpful tourist office can be found right in the center of the seafront, where Crescent Quay takes a bite from the shore. The bronze statue outside commemorates Commodore John Barry, the brilliant naval officer who avenged his Irish ancestors by emigrating to Philadelphia and trouncing the English during the Revolutionary War. Wexford is best explored on foot (historic walking tours are advertised) when narrow alleys and one-way streets provide no obstacle. The old center of town is a cheerful mix of agreeable pubs, old-fashioned shops, and plenty of decent down-to-earth eating places. The main historic monuments are the **Westgate▶**, dating from 1300 (*The Wexford Experience*, a short film, is shown inside), and the remains of **Selskar Abbey▶**, where the Anglo-Irish treaty was signed after the Norman invasion, and where Henry II spent many Lenten hours atoning for the murder of St. Thomas à Becket. A couple of modern Gothic churches can be seen, interesting only because they are virtually identical. In the Bull Ring Cromwellian troops slaughtered 300 hapless citizens as they prayed for mercy. Many others were put to the sword in one of the most appalling massacres of the Ironside invasion. When Ireland rebelled again in 1798, Wexford's inhabitants were among the most vigorous pike-wielders, as the statue in the Bull Ring indicates.

Two other sights are well worth a visit if you are in the vicinity of Wexford. The Irish National Heritage Park is described above (see Ferrycarrig, page 131). Toward Rosslare is another museum, in the massive Gothic-revival building called Johnstown Castle, constructed as a private residence around the core of a 15th century tower-house. This contains the **Irish Agricultural Museum▶▶** (the rest of the building serves as an agricultural college). It is the largest collection of its kind in Ireland, full of attractive displays of intriguing implements like furze rooters, barley hummlers, and turnip knives. The veterinary section displays fearsome horse gags and drenching horns. Little workshops have been re-created showing how the tools would have been arranged and used by wheelwrights, coopers, etc. There are also displays of ancient domestic appliances and butter-making equipment. The grounds around this imposing castellated and mullioned gray-stone building are beautifully landscaped and open to the public.

145

The Irish National Heritage Park

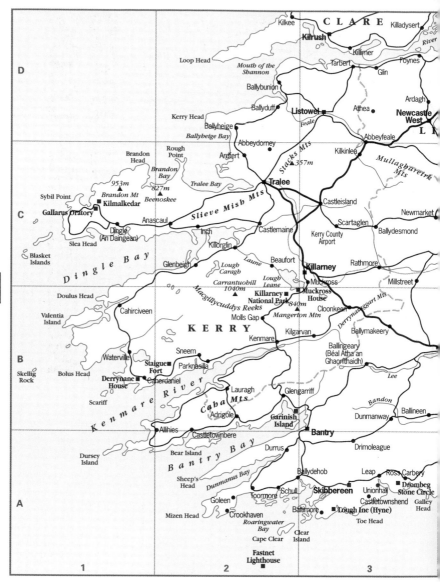

Rain in the West?
"When the glass is up to thirty
Cork and Kerry will be dirty;
When the glass is high O very
There'll be rain in Cork and
  Kerry;
When the glass is low, O Lork!
There'll be rain in Kerry and
  Cork."
"Thirty" refers to high baro-
metric pressure, normally
assuring dry weather!

Slea Head, Dingle

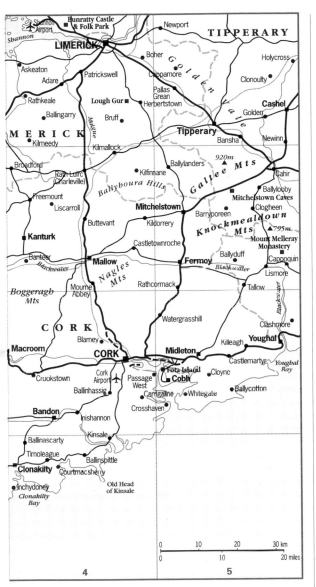

SOUTHWESTERN COUNTIES

147

Southwestern counties Ireland's southwestern corner ranks high with most tourists, and for many people the counties of Cork and Kerry represent the best that Ireland can offer the vacationer, with striking scenery, charming towns, a mild climate, and many places of interest. There is a huge variety of things to do and see for just about anyone, young or old, active or sedentary. To see much of it, you will need your own transportation, as elsewhere in Ireland. If you prefer to see things slowly and in more detail, that could mean a bike—or a Romany caravan! If you can afford to pamper yourself, the region has a fine collection of country house hotels (including a few stately homes) and a high proportion of excellent restaurants.

Fungi the dolphin

This half-tame creature has captured the hearts of thousands in the past few years. His behavior suggests he may have escaped or been released from a marine park at some stage. He cavorts in Dingle Bay to the delight of all onlookers and the great pleasure of the tourist authorities, and has apparently no fear of humans or their boats. He will frolic beside wetsuited swimmers, jump over boats and really gives the impression that he enjoys company. Fungi seems to have become completely fixated by his human visitors and will chase off any rival dolphin who encroaches on his territory. Boat trips from Dingle harbor virtually guarantee a sighting during the summer.

148

The predictable, but pleasant, face of tourism on the Muckross Estate near Killarney

Events such as Kinsale's annual gourmet festival raise both standards of cuisine and the region's popularity with international visitors. The high quality of local ingredients helps; seafood, good beef, and rich dairy products now available everywhere belie the terrible sufferings of the Southwest during the Famine years.

The massive emigration from these counties to the New World results in a backwash of third- or fourth-generation visitors migrating back to the land of their forebears searching for roots. Shannon Airport welcomes transatlantic visitors, who converge on Limerick and Killarney. Many foreigners from continental Europe approach via Cork and some have settled there permanently, adding new influences to the area's restaurants and bringing fresh artistic talents with them.

A warm welcome English attempts to subjugate this old Irish province of Munster produced a mass of fortifications all along the coast, ever-watchful for Catholic plots from Spain and France using Catholic Ireland as an unlocked back door from which to invade Britain. Today, however, the tricky Anglo-Irish interface leaves little mark here.

The Southwest has two of Ireland's largest cities, Cork and Limerick. These are certainly worth seeing, but the rural areas are far more appealing. The coastline is, in places, particularly beautiful, and generally more exciting than the lush inland scenery, cut by its great easterly flowing rivers. An exception is Killarney's National Park, a high spot in any itinerary. Less well known, but also worth exploring, is the forest park of Gougane Barra, on the remote inland borders of Cork and Kerry. It is a place of wildlife, of tumbling streams, and the hermitage of St. Fin Barre. Founded probably in the 6th or 7th century— although the ruins beside the modern church date from

Youghal beach, Cork

the 18th century—the hermitage of Cork City's patron saint is set on an islet in the beautiful Gougane Barra Lake, the source of the Lee, which eventually reaches the sea at Cork. The county of Limerick is the Cinderella of the three, with little to lift its flattish landscapes from mediocrity. Killarney and Blarney are perhaps the only blatant examples of mass tourism in the region. Elsewhere, the tourist scene is low-profile. Kinsale, Kenmare, Dingle, Youghal, and Bantry all make charming and much classier bases for exploring the coast.

A mild and verdant land Few would argue that the islet-strewn peninsulas that trail westward to the Atlantic are the places to visit for the best scenery, where the blue water of never-distant sea sets off the brilliant rain-washed emerald of fields and mountains. There the pace of life is slow and gentle, and the ambience profoundly Irish, perhaps most noticeably in the Dingle peninsula, one of the largest Gaeltacht (Irish-speaking) regions. Traditional Irish music can be heard all over the region, particularly in Dingle and some of the villages of south Cork, such as Leap and Clonakilty.

The influence of the Gulf Stream keeps frost permanently at bay and, although Atlantic storms can be severe, sheltered regions lend themselves to superb subtropical gardens and a great range of flora and fauna. Even the least botanically minded can scarcely fail to be impressed by the lush fuchsia hedges, dripping scarlet all summer the rhododendrons in profusion, or the arbutus trees that grow wild in the valleys of Iveragh. Water lilies and rare bog plants colonize the reedy pools of Cork's quieter peninsulas. The Southwest is a good place for bird watchers, too—the region is first landfall for the myriad of exhausted migrants in spring and autumn on Clear Island or the wild Skellig Islands, the moors, mountains, and lakes of Kerry and the sheltered, muddy estuaries around Timoleague on the south Cork coast.

Rose of Tralee Festival
This is held in the last week of August and is a great tourist attraction for the region. Six days and nights of solid merriment take place, including pipe bands and parades. The main event is a beauty contest which any woman of Irish origins can enter. Visitors from around the world compete for the honor of being crowned Rose; details from the Festival Office in Lower Castle Street, Tralee (tel: 066 21322).

The Spaniard, a pub in Kinsale, Ireland's gourmet capital

The enormous, conical, whitewashed beacon near Baltimore acts as a marker for boats

An enterprising bar in Bantry has erected this elaborate and informative advertisement for its wares

► **Baltimore** 146A3

Baltimore combines salty fishing-village charm with a sturdy castle and several good restaurants. Trips are also available to Sherkin Island, where there is a 15th-century friary, and to the Fastnet Lighthouse on the outermost scrap of Irish territory. In June 1631 Baltimore witnessed a curious and tragic incident, when Algerian pirates stole into the harbor and attacked the village, killing a number of residents and abducting about 200 as slaves to North Africa. Some believe the raid may have been orchestrated by the fierce O'Driscoll clan to frighten off English settlers. If so, it worked; many of them moved upstream where they felt less threatened. The poet, Thomas Davis, wrote a rollicking poem about the raid in 1844:

"The yell of 'Allah' breaks above the prayer and shriek and roar,

Oh Blessed God! The Algerine is Lord of Baltimore."

► **Bantry** 146B3

Most people who tour south Cork pass through this fishing and market center on the main coastal road. The town stands at the head of the long haven of Bantry Bay, sheltered by two of the hilly peninsulas that trail southwest from Cork's mainland. A statue of St. Brendan gazes seaward from its square by the harbor. Bantry was twice an unsuccessful target for French invaders hoping to establish a base in a friendly Catholic enclave from which to overthrow the English. In 1689 a French fleet sailed in, offering support for James II, only to be rebuffed by Williamites. In 1796 the revolutionary Wolfe Tone arrived with another French fleet (see panel), but was driven back by fierce storms. An alert local landowner, Richard White, sent urgent warnings to the English forces and was rewarded for his loyalty by a peerage. His descendants still live in the splendid mansion of **Bantry House►►**, one of the most beautifully located houses in Ireland. The terraced Italianate gardens overlook a gorgeous sweep of Bantry Bay. The house amply repays a visit, its sumptuous rooms full of fascinating contents. The hospitable present owners offer a classy brand of B. & B. (alas no longer inexpensive) in a separate wing of the house (see Hotels and restaurants, page 273), and another recent attraction is the **Bantry 1796 French Armada Exhibition Center►►** in a renovated side courtyard. This lively museum recounts the history of Wolfe Tone's failed rebellion and displays articles recovered from the wreck of the frigate *La Surveillante*, which sank during the storms and was excavated in 1982.

Minor diversions in the town itself are a museum of local history, and the **Kilnaruane Pillar Stone►**, carved with mysterious early Christian symbols of four men rowing, and a cross.

Wolfe Tone's invasion
On December 16, 1796, a French Armada of 43 ships set sail from Brest, bound for Ireland. The French intended to aid Wolfe Tone's rebellion and to deal a blow to the British. From the start, it was a disaster, storms disrupting communications between the fleet. Only 16 battered crews reached Bantry Bay with Wolfe Tone. On Christmas Eve he was ready to attack, but decided to wait for Hoche, the French commander. By the next day his chance of a landing had gone; savage gales had blown the ships out of the bay. Tone wrote in his journal, "We were close enough to throw a biscuit ashore ... The elements fight against us."

►► Blarney   147B4

Everyone has heard of Blarney and, when bus tours clog the village, it seems as if everyone has come to see it, too. Tourists arrive for two reasons—to kiss that stone in Blarney Castle and to visit the large gift and craft centers that have sprung up nearby. Why the Blarney Stone exercises such fascination is hard to fathom, but the superstition that kissing it endows you with Irish eloquence or "blarney" is certainly appealing. The stone is an oblong block of limestone located high among the battlements of a fine 15th-century tower house, once a stronghold of the MacCarthys, former kings of Munster and Lords of Blarney. A Cormac MacCarthy supposedly strung Queen Elizabeth I along with honey-tongued promises and prevarications, until she exclaimed in exasperation, "Blarney, Blarney! What he says he does not mean," and thus the word entered the language. To reach the stone, visitors must clamber up the tower steps (more than 120 of them), join the inevitable line (in high season, at least), and then lie down and lean backward over a sheer drop. It looks awkward but is actually quite safe, even without the two strong-armed retainers there to grab your ankles. The stone is swabbed down regularly enough to prevent transmission of any nasty ailments. Some local will offer to take your photograph while you are kissing the stone, but be warned, it isn't a flattering angle (see above)!

The lush water gardens by the River Lee and the 19th-century Rock Close (a rock garden with fanciful wishing

Whatever one gains from kissing the Blarney Stone, one loses one's dignity

Fastnet Lighthouse
This perches like a fairy-tale castle on its rocky bastion to warn shipping off the treacherous coast. Recreational sailors use it as their westerly target during the biennial Fastnet Yacht Race, starting from Cowes on the Isle of Wight.

*There's more to
Blarney than the stone*

The sinking of the *Lusitania*
Recent speculation about
this has made disturbing
reading. In World War I the
ship, sailing from New York
to Liverpool , was sunk, off
Cobh, by the Germans, who
claimed that she was car-
rying arms, as well as civilians. This was denied, but
evidence now suggests
that it was true. More disturbing is the theory that
the Allies contrived the
episode to hasten U.S.
entry into the war. The
German government had
placed advertisements in
New York papers warning
passengers not to take the
sailing, implying that the
vessel was not a random
wartime target. Both suspi-
cion and casualties were
increased by the unusual
absence of patrolling
British warships. She sank
in 20 minutes, leaving passengers floundering in the
water. Some survived by
clutching floating debris,
one sitting in a cane chair.
The submarine that had
sunk the ship did nothing to
save passengers, although
knowing many were U.S.
civilians, and not a re-
motely legitimate target.

steps and druidical associations) make an attractive foil
for the romantic ruin, and behind the castle is an elaborate
Scottish baronial mansion called Blarney Castle House
(visitable on a joint ticket), furnished in Victorian style.

In the village, craft and knitwear shops catch the purse
strings, the most advertised being Blarney Woollen Mills,
now a colossal hypermarket with a restaurant, hotel, and
large parking lot. The smaller shops are rather more enjoyable than this bargain basement, but there's certainly a
wide range of merchandise from all over Ireland.

► **Castletownshend**   *146A3*
The literary cousins, Edith Somerville and Violet Martin,
lived in Drishane House and are both buried in the gray-
stone church of St. Barrahane, where Edith was organist.
They are better known as Somerville and Ross, authors of
the *Irish R.M.* stories. The village is most pretty, its main
street sloping steeply up from the quayside. If you careen
down it too fast you are in danger of hitting a tree carefully
preserved in the middle of the road. Nearby is an excellent quaint old pub called Mary Ann's. The Townshend
family still live in the local castle, where an idiosyncratic
B. & B. evokes the atmosphere of the *R.M.* books.

►► **Clear Island**   *146A2*
The frayed coastline at Ireland's bottom left-hand corner
disintegrates into a scattering of islets around Baltimore.
From there, or from Schull further along the coast, you
can take a boat to Ireland's most southerly community,
Clear Island, where the Irish-speaking population of fewer
than 200 is greatly outnumbered by the birds. An obser-
vatory enables visitors to delight in the multitude of
streaming migrants—all kinds of gulls, shearwaters,
storm petrels, and rare songbirds, even an occasional dis-
oriented albatross. Other sights pale beside the bird-life:
the well and church dedicated to St. Ciarán, born there in
the 6th century; a wind-driven electricity generator
financed by the E.U. and a small heritage center. It is possible to stay on the island, although amenities are spartan.

►► Cobh   147B5

For many hundreds, probably thousands, of Famine emigrants, the scenic panorama of **Cork Harbour►►** and the colorful houses of Cobh must have been their last glimpse of the Emerald Isle. Many perished *en route* in the dreaded "coffin ships", others never had a chance to return from the New World where they made their homes. The name Cobh (pronounced "cove") means "haven" in Irish. Besides emigrant ships, Cobh berthed some of the great transatlantic liners, including the ill-fated *Titanic* and the *Lusitania*, torpedoed offshore on May 7, 1915, with the loss of 1,198 lives (see panel). Many victims are buried in the local cemetery, and the story of the sinking is told in a heritage center. Today Cobh is a fishing port, seaside resort, and sailing center, its well-restored buildings and slightly raffish air giving it great character. **St. Colman's Cathedral►►** is the most striking landmark, set high on the hilltop, its spire honed to an impossibly slender point. It was designed by Pugin in 1868, and is an exuberant masterpiece of Victorian high Gothic, decorated with intricate marble and mosaics, and full of atmosphere. Harbor trips are available in summer.

Situated in the estuary at the mouth of Cork harbor and connected by bridges to the mainland, **Fota Island►** may be reached via the Cork–Cobh railroad line. This huge estate includes a wildlife park where cheetahs and wallabies breed and an important arboretum with many rare specimen trees.

Built to last?
A 16th-century tower-house at Castlehaven near Castletownshend was built by the O'Driscolls, who gave it to the Spaniards before the Battle of Kinsale in 1601. When the Spanish were defeated, they yielded the castle to the English. Before *they* could occupy it, the O'Driscolls retook it and were about to blow it up when in turn they were surprised by the English, who prevented the destruction. It survived until 1926, when Edith Somerville, one of the literary combination of Somerville and Ross, was out for a walk; she heard a rumble, and found that the castle had collapsed into a heap of rubble behind her.

153

St. Colman's Cathedral sits perkily on top of the Georgian seafront

The Venerable Bede was one of the first to remark on Ireland's favorable weather: "Ireland is far more favored than Britain by latitude, and by its mild and healthy climate ... there is no need to store hay in winter ... and no lack of vines." The typical Irish "soft day" of gentle drizzle and sunshine is ideal for plants—Ireland contains a fine collection of gardens of all types in which many rare species flourish. Many of these are open to the general public in summer, or can be visited by arrangement with the owners.

Strawberry tree
This plant is most closely identified with Killarney and the lush countryside of south Kerry, where it grows to prodigious heights. It is also known as the arbutus tree, *Arbutus unedo*, and has waxy white flowers and dark green glossy leaves. It flowers in the autumn and is then hung with slow-ripening strawberry-like fruits. A song of 1890 commemorates the tree:

My love's an arbutus
By the borders of Lene,
So slender and shapely
In her girdle of green.

Ilnacullin Gardens
Annan Bryce, a Belfast-born MP, purchased Ilnacullin from the British War Office in 1910. His dream to build a mansion and lay out gardens on this bare island off Glengarriff in County Cork was ambitious: the soil was shallow and infertile, the terrain exposed. To realize his project he enlisted the help of Harold Peto, an advocate of the Italian style of garden design and architecture in an age when less formal wild gardens were all the rage. Ilnacullin is a blend of both styles, containing a wide range of oriental and southern hemisphere plants, and many architectural features complementing the splendid natural setting.

A long tradition In early Christian times a major activity of any monastery was gardening—mostly for food or medicines, but also for decorating churches. With the arrival of the Normans horticulture became much more complex and widespread, with new and varied foodstuffs. Sir Walter Ralegh's foreign travels introduced important plants from the New World—tobacco, cherries, and, of course, the potato. His friend, the Earl of Cork, laid out one of Ireland's first Renaissance pleasure gardens in the estates of Youghal. During the latter part of the 17th century gardening was on a grand scale, influenced by the gardens of Versailles, designed by Le Nôtre. Exotic plants began to arrive from abroad, and Dutch immigrants brought innovative botanical techniques. The 18th century was a great age for gardening, as for most aspects of civilized living, passing from baroque formality to the naturalistic landscapes of "Capability" Brown. The Royal Horticultural Society of Ireland was founded in 1816.

During Victorian times botanical tastes diversified, many gardeners concentrating less on design and more on accumulating specimens; several important botanic gardens were planted at this time. Two great gardeners of the age were Daniel Robertson (see page 110) and William Robinson, who introduced a new style of "natural" gardening based on a close observation of landscape. Many smaller, intimate gardens appeared too, some influenced by the English style of Gertrude Jekyll—two gorgeous creations are Heywood (County Laois) and Butterstream (County Meath). During the early 20th century a passion for oriental gardens developed; the Japanese Gardens at Tully, Kildare, are one such example (see page 101).

Period landscapes One of Ireland's most interesting gardens, historically, is Kilruddery, outside Bray (see page 93), which retains its 17th-century canals, parterres, and statuary. Representing an earlier era, the lovely gardens around Lismore Castle were laid out in Jacobean times. Greatest of the Georgian gardens surround houses such as Florence Court, County Fermanagh (see page 230) and Castletown, County Kildare (see page 94). A fascinating late-18th-century example is Emo Court, County Laois, where lawns dotted with neat, clipped yews, and statues provide a foil for James Gandon's neoclassical mansion.

Spectacular gardens Despite its latitude, Ireland has some celebrated gardens in the North, several in the care of the National Trust, among them Mount Stewart and Rowallane (see page 231). In the Southwest, Anne's Grove near Castletownroche represents some of the best work of William Robinson—shrubs, magnolias, rare mallows, and water plants flourish in hedged compartments and walled gardens. The Italianate gardens of Bantry House, set by the sea, are a must for keen gardeners, too, as are the castle gardens of Timoleague and the grounds of Muckross House in Killarney's National Park, where vast rhododendrons and exotic trees (including the strawberry tree, see panel) grow against a mountain backdrop. Derreen Gardens, on the road between Kenmare and Castletownbere, luxuriate in woodland with many subtropical species, tree-ferns mingling with bamboo and eucalyptus. Nearby are the gardens of Dunloe Castle, with more rare trees (Chinese swamp cypresses and the pungent "headache tree," *Umbellularia californica*). One of the most enjoyable of all the Southwest's gardens is Harold Peto's masterpiece, Illnacullin, on an island reached by boat trips from Glengarriff, in County Cork (a landing charge). On a fine day in May or June this Italian garden of Grecian temples and an orderly jungle of flowering shrubs makes a marvelous excursion (see panel).

Bord Fáilte produces a useful leaflet containing information about Ireland's best gardens.

Illnacullin Gardens on Garinish Island

The glorious colors of Rowallane Gardens

St. Fin Barre's Cathedral looks down over the southern branch of Cork's River Lee

The *Cork Examiner*
Cork's daily newspaper seems to epitomize the independent spirit of the city. The *Cork Examiner* (just called "the paper" locally) is a distinguished and dignified piece of journalism. The first edition appeared in August 1841, shortly before the potato famine. Many of the population were illiterate and certainly too poor to afford newspapers, so it was a brave venture. The first edition proclaimed it devoted "to the welfare and interests of the whole community," and that it seems to be, read by all classes of society. It survived attacks by anti-Treaty demonstrators in 1922 when all the machinery was smashed, and has never lost a single day's printing through strikes, wars, or technical problems.

▶▶   **Cork**   *147B4*

Cork has no compelling sights, nor is it especially beautiful, and an initial reaction to the Republic's second city may be one of disappointment. Nonetheless, visitors generally go away well pleased with the place, perhaps infected by the vehement enthusiasm of its inhabitants for their city. The way *not* to enjoy Cork is to drive through panicking about the check-in time at the airport or harbor. A map shows why the city, the first bridging point on the Lee estuary, is a bottleneck. Traffic is invariably congested during working hours, and parking is regulated: leave the car in one of the official parking lots and walk.

Cork takes pride in being the cultural and economic center of the Southwest, constantly challenging Dublin's supremacy. It has always favored ousting British rule, becoming known as "rebel Cork" after supporting Perkin Warbeck (a Flemish impostor who in 1492 claimed to be Duke of York), and was a base for the Nationalist Fenian movement in the 19th century. Its prosperity was based on trade in hides, textiles, butter, and wine. Industries such as ship building and engine manufacture are no more, replaced by skills such as the computer business. The center's streets reveal Cork's mercantile past—tall 18th-century bow-fronted houses and fine warehouses. Those that survive are steadily being restored.

The center is built on reclaimed marshes ("Cork" comes from the Irish meaning "marshy place") and the older part of the city is on an island embraced by two arms of the River Lee. The land rises steeply towards the heights of Shandon; several imposing church spires pierce the skyline, Victorian Gothic being the prevailing style. **St. Fin**

Barre's► was designed by William Burges in a flourish of white limestone steeples. Inside it is richly decorated—angels gazing down from a starry apse. On the Shandon side of town is **St. Anne's Church►**, which soars to a red and white pepper-pot tower surmounted by a golden weather-vane in the shape of a salmon. It houses the famous eight-bell carillon immortalized in the corny ballad known as "The Bells of Shandon." You can climb the tower and, for a fee, "play" the bells. The nearby neoclassical **Butter Exchange►** contains several stylish craft studios, making jewelry, ceramics and traditional porcelain dolls.

On the island, Cork's commercial heart beats along the main thoroughfares of Grand Parade and St. Patrick's Street. Old-fashioned department stores flank trendy clothes boutiques, but the newer and most chic shops are around the pedestrianized area near St. Paul's Street, where you can find interesting bookshops (one, Mainly Murder, is devoted exclusively to thrillers and detective fiction) and good crafts shops. Classy Donegal rainwear and equestrian clothing are also sold in these side streets. To the west lie elegant Georgian malls and the university. The **City Museum►►**—Republican history features prominently—is in the grounds of Fitzgerald Park by the Mardyke Walk, an attractive riverside breathing space.

Cork has plenty of nightlife, from raucous pub discos to avant garde theater. Its opera house (not a pretty sight) is a 1960s addition to municipal culture; other arts venues are the **Triskel Arts Center►** and the **Crawford Art Gallery►** (worth a visit just for its restaurant—see Hotels and Restaurants, page 281). At the end of October, the city is thronged for its acclaimed international jazz festival. Eating in Cork is a pleasure, with plenty of choice, from imaginative, cheap organic foods to gourmet French cuisine. Accommodations in Cork range from civilized Georgian townhouses to well-run, good-value hostels.

► ► ► **Dingle Peninsula**   146C1
See pages 158–9

Elizabeth Aldworth
This young lady from County Cork achieved fame as the only woman ever to be accepted into the bizarre and secretive world of Freemasonry. The local lodge met at her family home in Doneraile (her father was a Mason), but naturally she was always banished during the proceedings. One day in 1712 curiosity got the better of her and she hid in a clock-case to find out what went on, but she was discovered. Once the Masons got over their anger, they decided the only way to keep her quiet was to enroll her, and so she became the order's one and only female member. Her grave is in St. Fin Barre's Cathedral.

Better things to come
"Limerick was, Dublin is, and Cork shall be
The finest city of the three."
Recorded in 1859 as "the old prophecy."

The Coal Quay open market in Cork City

THE DINGLE PENINSULA

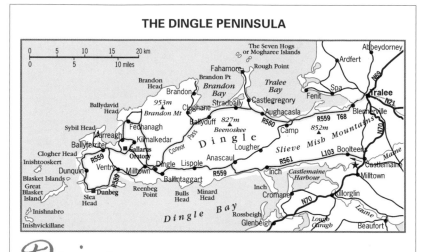

Drive **The grandeur of the Dingle peninsula**

A tour around this remote, Irish-speaking westerly extremity offers many things: superb coastal scenery with peaceful beaches and scattered islands; grand mountains and lush, fuchsia-splashed countryside; a fascinating assortment of antiquities; and a lively scene of music and excellent seafood restaurants based on the charming fishing port of Dingle.

Starting points for this drive are Castlemaine (north of Killorglin) or

The shrine at Slea Head

Tralee. For scenic drama go clockwise (although the scenery at first is quiet and undramatic) with good dune beaches at Inch and small hamlets like **Anascaul**; the strange, secretive tarn (small mountain lake) to the north, **Anascaul Lake►**, is worth a brief detour. **Dingle►►** is the peninsula's main tourist center, constantly lively during the summer. It is by no means undiscovered, as anyone arriving during its festival season (July–August) will note, but it never seems as overcrowded or touristy as Killarney, and it's a great deal classier. Off-season, though, many of its good restaurants, craft shops, and hotels are closed, and no boat trips run. The town is extremely well kept, with restored shop fronts and colorful inn signs. The harbor is particularly appealing—bright fishing vessels moored in a lovely natural haven. In former centuries smuggling was a major source of income.

Beyond Dingle is **Ventry**, where you may see upturned *currachs* (canvas-covered canoes) on the beach. Follow the road marked Slea Head Drive around Ireland's most westerly point. The whole area is riddled with forts, souterrains, standing stones, and crosses; you need a good detailed map to explore them all. On the hillsides you will pass a number of strange little stone huts known as beehives or *clochans*. There are more than 400 in the area altogether. Some farmers may charge you to visit these, and the more perfect specimens may have been reconstructed from the original stones as storage places (or for their more recent value as tourist attractions). **Dunbeg▶**, near Ventry, is one of the best sites (an Iron Age clifftop fort with beehive huts nearby).

If archeology does not thrill you, the scenery certainly will, especially when the wild **Blasket Islands▶▶** appear as you round the **Slea Head** promontory. The Blaskets are uninhabited now, though one belongs to the former Irish Prime Minister Charles Haughey and is used as a vacation home. The last inhabitants moved to the mainland in 1953, the local women no longer willing to confine their marriage prospects within this tiny community. The Blaskets have inspired a thriving literary tradition: Maurice O'Sullivan's *Twenty Years a'Growing* and Tomás Ó Crohan's *The Islandman* are two of the best-known accounts of island life. Summer boat trips visit the islands from **Dunquin▶**, where the film *Ryan's Daughter* was made. The Blasket Centre at Dunquin (Dun Chaoin in Irish) contains an exhibition on island life and literature.

Toward the ragged northwest of the peninsula are two interesting historic monuments. One is the **Gallarus Oratory▶▶**, a tiny but perfectly preserved church built of neatly packed unmortared stones. It dates from between AD 800 and AD 1200 and still keeps the rain out, although its roof-line is sagging slightly. About a mile up the road is **Kilmalkedar▶**, another early church from about the 12th century, roofless but bearing fine Romanesque carvings in purplish stone. By returning to Dingle again, you can start the final dramatic leg of this drive, over the **Connor Pass▶▶** (best on a clear day), past the 3,127-foot summit of Mount Brandon. Once over the pass, you see **Brandon Bay▶** opening in a fantastic geological model of lakes, rivers, and rock-strewn contours. The seafaring monk St. Brendan set sail from these shores in the 5th century. In 1976 Tim Severin re-created this voyage in a similar craft of wood and leather to discover whether St. Brendan could have reached America before Columbus (see the Craggaunowen Project, page 183). The northern coastal strip, back at sea level, is a quiet and easy drive past long beaches and humdrum farmland.

Dunbeg promontory fort, Ventry, dates from between 400 BC and 50 BC

Ross Castle

Ross Castle is a fine ruin dating from the 15th century; a tower house and later dwelling house still remain containing 16th- and 17th-century furnishings. Home of the local chieftains, the O'Donoghues, Ross Castle was the last place in Munster to fall to Cromwellian forces in 1652. The story goes that General Ludlow, hearing of a superstition that Ross Castle would never be taken by land, bought ships to sail up the lake, whereupon the defenders, hitherto defiant, immediately gave up their arms.

From Ross Castle, it is possible to take boat tours of the lake (these are non-stopping) or, alternatively, to rent a rowing boat for a landing on Innisfallen Island. Here, against a landscape of gentle valleys and dark woods, are the ruins of Innisfallen Abbey dating from AD 600.

Kate Kearney

A well-known pub on the way up to the Gap of Dunloe, Kate Kearney's Cottage is named after the colorful local beauty who dispensed illegal *poteen* (home-brewed liquor) to travelers passing through the gap during the mid-19th century. She was apparently in constant trouble with the law, but was finally vanquished by the potato blight which made *poteen* distilling impossible. One night, she simply vanished.

KILLARNEY ENVIRONS

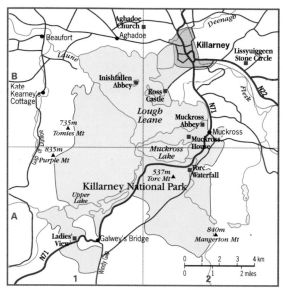

▶▶   **Killarney**   *146C3*

Every visitor to the Southwest has to see Killarney. The town itself, however, is disappointing. Once a seemly little place with a soul of its own, it is now given over wholly to tourism. It becomes hopelessly congested in summer, is very commercialized and, apart from the tall-spired Catholic **cathedral of St. Mary's▶**, designed in flamboyant high Gothic, has no outstanding features of interest. However, the immediate surroundings of the **Killarney National Park▶▶▶** are not to be missed and, if you can evade the milling tour buses and wheedling "jarvey-men" (pony-trap drivers), it takes on the grandeur of genuine wilderness. Macgillycuddy's Reeks, Ireland's highest mountains, lie just outside the National Park, but are clearly visible on fine days. Killarney is the usual starting and finishing point for the popular excursion drive known as the Ring of Kerry (see pages 170–1) although if you have your own transportation you can just about avoid the town center. The tourist office (right in the middle!), however, is very helpful with maps and detailed local information. The Kerry Way is a 35-mile footpath leading through the mountains from the National Park toward Glenbeigh on the Iveragh peninsula.

Once out of the town, the choices for exploration are bewildering. To the south (the east shore of Lough Leane) lie the Muckross estate and various well-known beauty spots on the Kenmare road up to the pass called Moll's Gap. On the way, you may be diverted by the 15th-century **Ross Castle▶** (see panel) by the lakeshore, and **Muckross Abbey▶**, a 15th-century ruin surprisingly well preserved after a Cromwellian visit in 1652. The main attraction, however, is **Muckross House▶▶** and the surrounding gardens and parkland. No cars are allowed within the estate, but you can park by the house. To explore the extensive grounds, you can either accept a ride from one of the jarvey-men (negotiate the fare carefully before you set off) or rent a bike. Muckross House is a furnished 19th-century neo-Tudor mansion designed by William Burn. Attached to it is a folk museum, where craftsmen demonstrate their trades, and several reconstructed farmhouses. The lakeside gardens have wonderful rhododendrons and azaleas, best in early summer. The Meeting of the Waters is a popular spot between the Upper Lake and Lough Leane, where arbutus trees flourish in the mild climate. Lake boats "shoot the rapids" there, and close by is the **Torc Waterfall**▶, plunging 66 feet down a mountainside. All these make excellent picnic sites if you can avoid the crowds. There is also a good tea shop at Muckross House.

Beyond Muckross House the road winds on through woods, heather moors and mountains, becoming ever more beautiful but you'll need to be careful at hairpin bends and tunnels. **Ladies' View**▶▶ is a place to pause for an unforgettable vista across the lakes of the National Park toward the Gap of Dunloe. (The "ladies" were Queen Victoria and her ladies-in-waiting, who presumably caught this view on a fine day and were duly impressed.)

The **Gap of Dunloe**▶▶ is Killarney's other great tourist attraction, a rugged glacial pass between the mountains, providing magnificent views of tarns and cliffs. It lies on the west side of the lake and is reached by heading north from the center of Killarney. Once again, the jarvey-men will be only too happy to stir their bored nags into action from the center of town, but you will save time and money by driving at least as far as touristy Kate Kearney's Cottage (see panel). From there vehicular traffic is banned, so you must walk or rent a pony or jaunting car. Most of the tourists head no farther than the Gap itself, but if you want more seclusion you can continue on foot through the lonely Black Valley down past Lord Brandon's Cottage (a tea shop) to the lakeshore and pick up a boat past the caves of Middle Lake and over to Ross Castle.

Killarney wildlife
Ireland's last wolf was killed near Lough Leane in 1700 and the wild mountain landscape of the National Park, backed by Macgillycuddy's Reeks, has always been home to many species of wildlife, some quite rare. Ireland's only herd of red deer may be found there, together with wild goats, Japanese sika deer, otters, badgers, foxes, hares, and hawks. The remote Black Valley attracts many birds. Whooper swans, with their shiny black legs, yellow-and-black bills, and whooping, bugle-like call, visit every winter; hooded crows and the rare chough can also be seen.

161

Ladies' View, near Killarney, justly one of Ireland's most famous panoramas

Kinsale Gourmet Festival
During the first week in October, Kinsale is even more packed than usual, although its visitors may look more sleek and well-heeled than at other times of year. Kinsale's Gourmet Festival extends the normal tourist season nicely and is well publicized throughout Ireland, attracting a good many discerning foreign palates, too. This is a time for eating, when the town's excellent pubs and restaurants vie with each other to produce gastronomic delights. The emphasis is on local seafood, and the places to look for are clearly advertised, displaying the Kinsale Good Food Circle sign. See Hotels and Restaurants (pages 269–83) for some suggestions of where to go.

Kinsale fishermen tend their nets

►►► Kinsale
147A4

Kinsale has attractions out of proportion to its modest size and so is very popular, though it has managed to maintain a more exclusive image than Killarney. Its setting is seductive—tall slate-roofed houses sprinkled among the steeply wooded estuary slopes of the River Bandon. Its historic interest and fishing-village charm make it an appealing place both to stay (it has excellent accommodations) and to eat (see panel). From Kinsale you can easily explore both Cork City and the glorious coastal or inland scenery of south Cork. It is also a notable sailing and fishing center.

During 1601–1602 a Spanish force occupied Kinsale and was besieged by English troops. Irish allies of the Spaniards were routed, a significant step toward the establishment of the English order (and the decline of Gaelic power) in 17th-century Ireland. Soon afterward the main players in this struggle, the O'Neill and O'Donnell clan chieftains, fled to Europe and abandoned their lands to English settlers. The town was spared a Cromwellian hammering, wisely backing the right side. Later that century James II landed at Kinsale with French forces in an attempt to regain his throne, and from here he finally left Ireland, defeated. Kinsale became an important English naval base, and Desmond Castle (now a heritage center) held many French prisoners in Napoleonic times. The town is evidently proud of its history, which is well recorded in the local **museum►**, a Dutch-style 17th-century town hall in the center of town. Some of its most interesting exhibits relate to the sinking of the *Lusitania* (see page 152). The courtroom in which the inquest was held is a memorial to the 1,198 victims of the disaster.

Of Kinsale's two fortresses the more interesting is **Charles Fort►►** on the east side of the estuary, built in the late 17th century to guard the harbor entrance. One of the best-preserved examples of a star fort in Europe, it remained garrisoned until 1921. You can clamber over the ramparts (keep an eye on children) and visit a military exhibition. The views of Kinsale from this headland are superb; the parking area makes a good picnic spot.

The South Cork coast

From **Kinsale** to **Mizen Head** is by no means undiscovered, but seems far less obligatory and overdone than excursions such as the **Ring of Kerry**, when you take your place in a convoy of tour buses. Meandering along tiny coastal roads through small villages, and undoubtedly getting lost amid Irish signposting, is one of the most delightful ways to enjoy the Emerald Isle.

The Old Head of Kinsale is a lonely headland on which stands a ruined fortress; offshore is the wreck of the *Lusitania* (see page 152). From Timoleague to Clonakilty—the Seven Heads peninsula—is a massively convoluted shoreline. Hidden away down these lanes from all passing trade is a fine restaurant, the Dunworley Cottage (see Hotels and Restaurants, page 281). **Timoleague►**, known for its gardens, is also remarkable for its skeletal Franciscan abbey. There the coast is utterly peaceful, but beautiful. Wading birds paddle in the estuary, and the shores are full of unusual plants. **Clonakilty►** is an engaging place. There's little to see, but it has a lively feel, the main street lined with painted shop fronts and old-fashioned bars. Traditional music, street theater, festivals, and crafts add to its attractions. Outside town is the birthplace of Michael Collins (see page 43), whose exploits are recounted in O'Donovan's Hotel. Seemingly endless, unspoiled sand graces the vast beach at **Inchydoney►**

The drive through the fuchsia-splashed villages of Ross Carbery, Glandore, and Unionhall is glorious; creeks and lagoons mirror wooded slopes and fishing cottages with sandy coves tucked bib-like under their chins. Leap is famous for Irish music, which is based at Connolly's Bar. Beyond lie the pretty village of **Castletownshend►** (see page 152), tidal Lough Hyne, and a scatter of islands in Roaring Water Bay. After **Skibbereen** are the colorful villages of **Ballydehob**, **Schull►**, **Goleen** and the spectacular 722-foot cliffs of **Mizen Head►►**, which is guarded by an O'Mahoney stronghold. Barleycove is a fine beach. To the north, Sheep's Head peninsula is a lovely tour if time permits. The Beara peninsula, is unfairly neglected in favor of the Ring of Kerry, but is as rewarding and less crowded. Some of the highlights include the rugged copper-mining country around **Allihies**, and the **Healy Pass**.

A modern shrine
Between Glandore and Ross Carbery, and not too difficult to search out, is the Drombeg Stone Circle, a good example from the early Bronze Age. Charred bones were buried in the middle of this stone circle. Nearby is a *fulacht fiadh*, or cooking trough, heated with stones from a fire.

The lighthouse at the Old Head of Kinsale

Many of Ireland's historic houses fell into decay or were destroyed during the 20th century, but a heartening number have survived, and those too large to make comfortable family homes have been sympathetically converted for other purposes. Some of them are now splendid hotels, giving many visitors a chance to experience a grandeur granted at one time to only a handful of privileged folk.

A cricketing prince in Ireland
Set in glorious countryside beneath the Twelve Bens in Connemara, but far, far away from any cricket pitch is Ballynahinch Castle, now a comfortable hotel. At the beginning of this century, when still a private residence, it was owned by Prince Ranjitsinhji, a characterful Indian nobleman who played cricket for England on many occasions. See Hotels and Restaurants, page 275, for more details.

Top: Bantry House
Below: Ashford
Castle, County Mayo

A taste of the past These hotels are all highly individual, but fall into several types. The ultra-wealthy favor the great baronial castles (mostly more or less latter-day fakes, but nonetheless with some interesting history and contents, and palatial comfort). Then there is the legacy of the Georgian era, spanning 170 of Ireland's most prosperous years. These may be mansions in rolling parkland, or pleasingly modest rectories. Then there are Victorian properties with famous family histories. Just a few examples can be mentioned; for further suggestions see Interesting Places to Stay (pages 242–3) and Hotels and Restaurants (pages 269–3).

Grand castles Shannon Airport attracts many well-heeled transatlantic visitors who desire nothing more than to stay in a real Irish castle. This need is satisfied by several large, expensive, luxury hotels within easy reach. Nearest, 8 miles from the airport, is **Dromoland Castle**, a vast mock-Gothic mansion on a 370–acre estate. The estate dates back to the 16th century, when it was the seat of the O Brien family, descendants of the great High King, Brian Ború, but the original house was replaced in the 1820s and the interior has recently been given a New York-style face-lift by decorator Carlton Varney. **Ashford Castle** is another Hollywood dream also under American ownership, this time on Lough Corrib, predictably furnished in sheer luxury, and with superb grounds. Once the home of the Guinness family, it incorporates a 13th-

century castle and a later French-style château in its opulent 19th-century shell. Also within reach of Shannon is **Adare Manor**, past seat of the Earls of Dunraven. Again it is Victorian and grandiose with vast mullions and fireplaces and colossal state rooms. On a somewhat smaller scale is **Markree Castle** in Sligo, home of the Cooper family since 1640, and last altered substantially in 1802. Its hotelier owner is a member of the original family, and an accomplished restaurateur. The castle has welcomed literary lights such as Lady Gregory and W. B. Yeats. **Waterford Castle** has a special brand of seclusion. It is set on an island in Waterford harbor, and reached only by private car ferry. The core is a genuine 17th-century castle, with oak paneling, antique furniture, and tapestries.

Elegant country houses One of the earliest period houses in Ireland now open as a hotel is **Assolas Country House** in Kanturk, County Cork. This peaceful place was built about 1590, but is now largely 17th-century in style and has gorgeous gardens and fishing rights. If Georgian elegance is to your taste, one fine example is **Enniscoe House**, near Crossmolina (Mayo), a mid-18th-century mansion with fascinating period features. The perfectly proportioned façade conceals an earlier structure with a different layout of floor levels and room sizes. Its owner, Susan Kellett, is a descendant of the original family. **Carnelly House** (Clare) is also Georgian but was built in Queen Anne style by Francis Bindon. The tall windows, Francini ceilings and Corinthian pillars give a gracious air to this creeper-covered brick house. **Cashel Palace** is an exceptional building of the same period (1730) and for 200 years was a bishop's palace. It stands beneath the Rock of Cashel, and has an ancient mulberry tree on the lawn. **Coopershill** in County Sligo dates from 1774, but echoes earlier times in its utterly relaxing rooms. Regency-period **Marlfield House** (1820) is in Gorey, Wexford. This formed part of the Courtown Estate, later the seat of the Earl of Courtown and a great focus of social life. It retains the tradition of lavish hospitality amid elegant and sumptuous furnishings.

Adare Manor, County Limerick

Tinakilly House, Wicklow
This is one of the most interesting Victorian houses in Ireland. It was built in the 1870s for Captain Robert Halpin, Commander of the *Great Eastern* steamship which laid the first telegraph cable linking Europe and America. Halpin was granted a substantial pension by a grateful government, and retired here to this grand mansion in 7 acres of sheltered gardens by the sea. Unfortunately he barely lived long enough to enjoy it. After a dangerous life of shipwrecks and dubious escapades in the American Civil War he succumbed to blood poisoning at 58, after cutting his toenails! A splendid staircase, mahogany inlaid doors, Italian fireplaces, oil paintings and seafaring memorabilia preserve something of the atmosphere of this flamboyant house, and its larger-than-life owner.

Lough Gur

Limerick's countryside is not especially noteworthy, but there is one little jewel tucked away in the southeast. Lough Gur is a beautiful crescent-shaped lake around which evidence of early civilizations has been found. Antiquities include a wedge-tomb and a large stone circle at Grange. Cartloads of remains were discovered after the partial draining of the lake in the 19th century. An interpretative center has been set up overlooking the reedy lake, with a visitor center and museum in two replica thatched *crannóg* huts of the neolithic era.

King John's Castle is unusual in that it has no keep

▶ **Limerick** *147D4*

Limerick is a significant city in terms of industry and population, currently vying with Galway for third place in the Republic. It has a rich historical background and plenty of interesting sights, and, as a result of its strategic location at the lowest bridging point on the Shannon, most visitors to the Southwest wind up using its traffic systems at some point during their stay. But few visitors choose to stay long here. Somehow, modern Limerick isn't attractive to travelers and, with rather dull scenery on its doorstep, its attractions as a base are limited. Much of the city seems run-down and unemployment is a problem. It has a higher crime rate than most Irish provincial cities, and there are places where you can't leave your car for long, or wander at night. Appealing accommodations are scarce, good restaurants few and far between. Its sad history seems to have left a legacy of bitterness and apathy that dies hard, despite energetic attempts to revitalize the center with new development of its wharves and warehouses, careful conservation of its Norman and Georgian heritage, and an upbeat marketing profile.

For all that, it is certainly worth half a day of anyone's time, more if you are interested in Irish history. Limerick was originally a Viking settlement, due to its strategic location at the mouth of the Shannon. Brian Ború, High King of Ireland, eventually conquered the Danes, many of whom settled down quite happily in Ireland and intermarried with native Gaels. The Norman era was important for Limerick. The Normans expanded the town and built huge fortifications with curtain walls, King John's Castle being one of the most impressive. In Cromwellian times it suffered terribly under the onslaughts of General Ireton, Cromwell's son-in-law and commander of Ireland, who besieged the city walls for over six months. Later that century Limerick was one of the last Jacobite bastions after the Battle of the Boyne, the hero of the period being

Patrick Sarsfield, who made a daring raid on William's ammunition wagons and supply trains.

Eventually, however, Limerick capitulated, and the infamous Treaty of Limerick was signed in 1691. Few incidents in Ireland's history illustrate the role of "perfidious Albion" more clearly than this. Within two months the English reneged on their promises to grant the Catholic population religious and property rights and instituted draconian measures against them. The **Treaty Stone▶**, on which the agreement was signed, became a symbol of all that was hateful about English rule. It can still be seen at the west end of Thomond Bridge, now sandblasted clean in an attempt to erase the memories. Today Limerick is a vehemently Catholic and nationalist city, still locked in its unhappy past.

Within the town center the most notable monument is **King John's Castle▶▶**, near Thomond Bridge. First built in 1200, it still looks the part of a medieval Norman fortress, though much restored after its 17th-century battering during the Siege of Limerick and subsequent alterations. The tower is the oldest section, and housed a British garrison until the birth of the Irish Free State in 1922. An excellent and imaginative visitor center now reconstructs the story of Limerick and its castle, while outside in the castle yard lie re-creations of various curious engines used in medieval siege warfare—find out what the magnonel and trebuchet were and how they worked.

For more history, Limerick's **City Museum▶** in two restored 18th-century houses documents the city's prosperity in Georgian times, when it produced fine silverware and lace. Even more worthwhile is the **Hunt Museum▶▶**, outside the center in the university campus area at Plassey. The art historian and antiquarian, John Hunt, donated a magnificent collection of Celtic and medieval art, including the Antrim Cross and a Bronze Age shield. **St. Mary's Cathedral▶**, in the center, is the city's most appealing religious building, and its oldest, founded in 1168 but dating mainly from the 15th century. Unexpectedly in this strongly Catholic city, it is a Protestant church. Its most interesting features include black oak choir stalls with carved 15th-century misericords (see photograph and caption, above right).

An ornately carved misericord from St. Mary's Cathedral. They were so-called (misericordia is Latin for pity) because they afforded clerics some form of rest when standing through lengthy services. They perched on these small seats, rather than standing unsupported

Inside St. Mary's

The Midleton Distillery even had its own fire engine

The mouth of the Shannon
W. M. Thackeray thought the undulating grounds which border the Shannon estuary enjoyable, if not beautiful; "though the view is by no means a fine one, I know few that are pleasanter than the sight of these rich, golden, peaceful plains, with the full harvest waving on them and just ready for the sickle."

Whiskey
Whiskey (*uisce beatha*— the water of life) has an interesting pedigree. It was probably invented by Irish missionary monks with their arcane knowledge of the Middle Eastern alembic, a still used for making perfumes. Thirteenth-century soldiers were fortified with a dose of the stuff before battle and Queen Elizabeth I herself is said to have been partial to a drop—probably a taste acquired from Sir Walter Ralegh, who was presented with a handsome 32-gallon cask of whiskey by the Earl of Cork. In introducing tobacco and possibly whiskey, it seems Ralegh was responsible for popularizing more than one addictive substance!

►   **Midleton Whiskey Distillery**   *147B5*

In the pleasant little town of Midleton, an impressive 18th-century industrial complex of stone mills and warehouses has been restored to enlighten visitors about the fine art of whiskey distilling. The Jameson Heritage Center is an entrepreneurial venture by Irish Distillers, emulating the successful Northern Irish attraction at Bushmills. For a fee (which includes a tasting) you can tour the modern distillery together with the Old Midleton Distillery, in use for 150 years from 1825 to 1975. The world's largest pot still, with a capacity of more than 40,000 gallons, stands by the reception building. Despite the heritage center's name, it was the brand known as Paddy, rather than Jameson's, that was distilled in Midleton from the 19th century; John Jameson's whiskey was always produced in Dublin.

►   **Rathkeale and environs**   *147D4*

Castle Matrix►, just outside Rathkeale, is a 15th-century tower house containing an important collection of documents connected with the Flight of the Wild Geese (the exodus after the Battle of Limerick). Now occupied by the Irish Heraldry Society, it can still be visited (tel: 069 64284). The farmland of west Limerick and the Shannon estuary is tame compared with the grandeur of Cork or Kerry, but if you have been around the Dingle peninsula you could well find yourself driving through it. A few sights are worth a detour. Ardfert►, north of Tralee, has some roofless monastic remains, recently restored. The beach nearby is Banna Strand, where Roger Casement's abortive adventure took place (see page 43). Hugging the Shannon coast is **Glin Castle►**, seat of the Knights of Glin and a fine 18th-century house with Victorian Gothic additions. The interior contains delicate plasterwork and mahogany furniture. Official hours are restricted (May only), but you can visit by appointment at other times (tel: 068 34173), or even stay there if you are wealthy enough. Further along, and probably the most worthwhile stop of all, is **Foynes Flying Boat Museum►►** in the terminal of the original Shannon Airport. During the 1930s and 1940s, Foynes was the operational headquarters for seaplanes traveling to and from the United States, and for any aviation buff, the museum, with its fascinating collection of film footage, instruments, photos, logs, etc., is a must. Foynes claims to be the original home of Irish coffee, and you can sample a reviving glass of it in the café. **Adare▶**, a notably pretty village of thatched cottages on the main Limerick road, contains the ruins of three ancient abbeys and of 12th-century Desmond Castle. Adare Manor, a lavish Gothic mansion, is now a country house hotel (see Hotels and Restaurants, page 275).

▶▶   Youghal   147B5

Youghal stands by the winding Blackwater estuary, right on the border between Counties Waterford and Cork. Pronounced "yawl," this ancient walled seaport has a rich history and several interesting buildings. Its resilient, salty character is striking, and in 1956 it impressed the director, John Huston, sufficiently to use it as a film location for *Moby Dick*. Its most illustrious resident was Sir Walter Ralegh, once mayor of the town. The 15th-century college warden's house known as Myrtle Grove was Ralegh's house and, though there is little evidence that he spent much time here, the town has enthusiastically adopted him as its standard-bearer. A Potato Festival is intermittently held to comme-morate Ralegh's supposed introduction of the Virginian tuber to Irish shores. A citizen with a more genuine claim to the town's attention was Richard Boyle, father of the famous scientist who formulated Boyle's Law, and builder of the almshouses in the town. **St. Mary's Collegiate Church▶** is Youghal's most impressive build-ing, containing many tombs and effigies, including one to the fantastically wealthy Earl of Cork and his 16 children (by three wives). Other buildings to look for are: the Georgian **clock tower▶** bridging the main street; the dilapidated tower house, **Tynte's Castle▶**; and the **Red House▶**, a Dutch-style merchant's house. The **town walls▶▶** are some of the best examples in Ireland, with large sections still in fairly good condition. Another good reason to pause for a while in Youghal is to visit its excellent seafood restaurant, Ahernes (see Hotels and Restaurants, page 281).

Rose of Tralee
The pale moon was rising
   above the green mountain,
The sun was declining
   beneath the blue sea;
When I strayed with my love
   by the pure crystal fountain,
That stands in the beautiful
   Vale of Tralee.

She was lovely and fair as
   the rose of the summer;
Yet 'twas not her beauty
   alone that won me;
Oh no, 'twas the truth in her
   eyes ever dawning,
That made me love Mary,
   the Rose of Tralee.

William Mulchinock

169

The lighthouse at Youghal

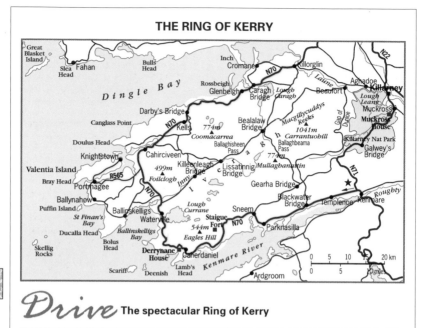

THE RING OF KERRY

Map labels: Great Blasket Island, Slea Head, Fahan, Bulls Head, Inch, Cromane, Killorglin, N22, N70, Rossbeigh, Glenbeigh, Caragh Bridge, Lough Caragh, Beaufort, Aghadoe, Killarney, Dingle Bay, Darby's Bridge, Canglass Point, N70, Kells, 774m, Coomacarrea, Bealalaw Bridge, Macgillycuddys Reeks, 1041m, Carrantuohill, Lough Leane, Muckross, Muckross House, Doulus Head, Ballaghisheen Pass, Ballaghbeama Pass, Gap of Dunloe, Killarney Nat Park, Knightstown, Cahirciveen, 499m, Killeenleagh Bridge, Lissatinnig Bridge, Mullaghanattin, 774m, Galwey's Bridge, Valentia Island, R565, Foilclogh, Inny, Iveragh, Gearha Bridge, N71, Bray Head, Portmagee, Ballinskelligs, Lough Currane, Sneem, Blackwater Bridge, Templenoe, Kenmare, Roughty, Ballynahow, Puffin Island, St Finan's Bay, Waterville, Staigue Fort, 544m, N70, Parknasilla, Ducalla Head, Ballinskelligs Bay, Eagles Hill, Skellig Rocks, Bolus Head, Derrynane House, Caherdaniel, Kenmare River, Scariff, Deenish, Lamb's Head, Ardgroom, 0 5 10 20 km, 0 5 10 miles

Drive The spectacular Ring of Kerry

Perhaps the most popular of all tourist routes in Ireland, this drive offers a mix of dramatic scenery, sights, and eating places—some geared towards the bus-tour trade. Allow a full day to see everything.

Many of the tour buses that ply this route start from Killarney, so if you have your own transportation you stand less chance of being held up in

Sneem caters well for tourists

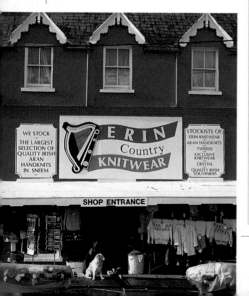

WE STOCK THE LARGEST SELECTION OF QUALITY IRISH ARAN HANDKNITS IN SNEEM

ERIN Country KNITWEAR

STOCKISTS OF: ERIN KNITWEAR ARAN HANDKNITS TWEEDS EXCLUSIVE KNITWEAR CRYSTAL QUALITY IRISH SOUVENIERS

SHOP ENTRANCE

traffic convoys if you do the Ring clockwise, starting in **Kenmare▶**. There are advantages either way; if you prefer to save the best till last, follow the bus route. As a variation, you could take the high mountain road that runs down the spine of the Iveragh peninsula through Macgillycuddy's Reeks. Several roads connect this with the coastal route. From Kenmare, the coastal road begins pleasantly enough through Templenoe and Blackwater Bridge, with peaceful estuary views to the south. At Parknasilla the lush gardens of the Great Southern Hotel give some idea of how mild the climate is, with palms and tender shrubs growing profusely. **Sneem▶** is a pretty village of color-washed houses clustered around village greens. Further on, don't miss **Staigue Fort▶ ▶**, perhaps the best example of a stone *cashel*, or ring fort. It probably dates from about 1000 BC and its stout walls must have been a sturdy defense for the inhabitants huddled within. Now all you will find are a startled sheep or two perched on the walls. An honesty box requests a small fee to compensate the farmer for "trespass." On the southwest tip of the Ring is the Derrynane Estate at **Caherdaniel**, where the Irish states-man Daniel O'Connell lived. The wooded grounds are now part of a national park▶, and encompass lovely rock-and-sand beaches and dunes. The house is now an attractive muse-um commemorating O'Connell, with memorabilia and personal effects.

Waterville▶ faces the Atlantic gales bravely, its short holiday season attracting many visitors to a long sandy beach. Golf and fishing are additional attractions. As you approach Waterville you may spy a brief but unforgettable glimpse of the jagged **Skellig Rocks**, some way out to sea. These inhospitable islets pro-vided a penitential home for Celtic monks who founded St. Finian's Abbey there in AD 560. Oratories, crosses, and beehive huts are among the ruins visible on Skellig Michael, the larger island. Little Skellig is a notable haven for seabirds, especially gannets. Boat trips run in summer from various points along this coast, but landings on the islands are now very limited because of erosion and damage to the sites, not to mention bad weather. Choose a calm day in these waters! The **Skellig**

Experience▶, a new interpretative center near the modern bridge at **Portmagee** linking mainland Kerry with Valentia Island, provides lots of multimedia information about the hardy Skellig monks, the local seabirds, and various aspects of coastal life.

Valentia Island▶ is a strange place of tame hills and a domesticated patchwork of walled fields and fuchsia hedges. The first transatlantic telegraph cable to the United States was laid from there in 1866. Knightstown is the main village, with fishing and tourism its principal concerns. If you decide to stay over-night, you can enjoy some excellent traditional music and dancing there. **Cahirciveen**▶, on the mainland, was the birthplace of Daniel O'Connell. From here the north coast road leads past grand mountain slopes and sea vistas to the tourist town of **Glenbeigh**. A detour inland past the lushly wooded slopes of Lough Caragh makes an interesting variation to the coast road, which is fairly unexciting from here as far as **Killorglin**.

Looking across Valentia Harbour

Red Mary
Máire Rua (Red Mary) O'Brien, who lived in the 17th century, was apparently a perfectly harmless person, although one tale described her as a woman of great lust who had many suitors. Before giving her hand, she would demand that a suitor should prove his worth by riding her fierce stallion—which then promptly raced out over the Cliffs of Moher and deposited his rider in the Atlantic below. All perished except one, who succeeded in bringing the stallion back to Máire Rua whereupon she closed the gates of her castle. In trying to leap over the gateway the horse died, thus explaining the name of her castle—Leamaneagh (*Léim an Eich*, or horse's leap), though neither history nor legend records that she married the brave horseman.

172

A Celtic cross is silhouetted against the darkening sky on Inishmore, the largest of the Aran Islands

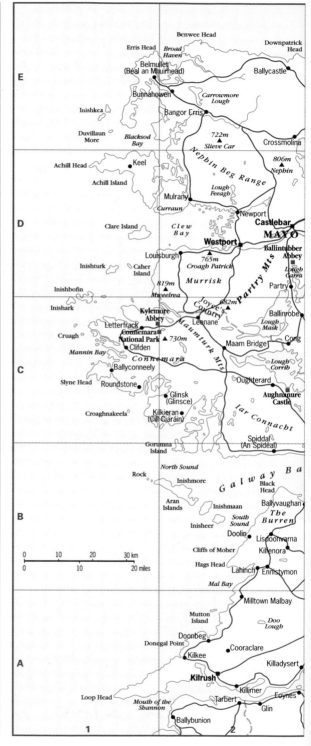

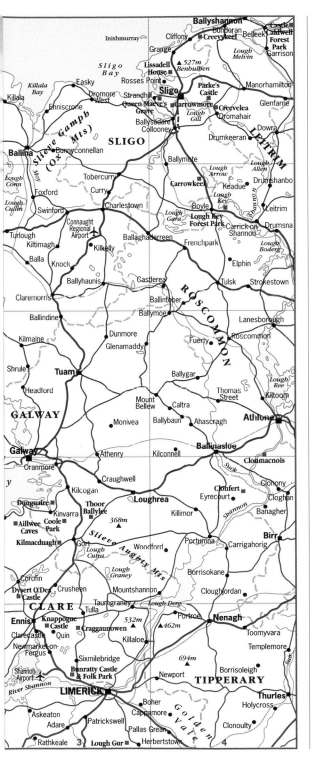

Ballyshannon
Bundoran
Cliffony Creevykeel Belleek Castle
Grange Caldwell
Inishmurray Forest
Lough Park
Melvin Garrison
Lissadell ▲527m
House Benbulben Manorhamilton
Sligo
Bay Rosses Point Parke's
Easky Castle
Killala Sligo
Bay Dromore Strandhill Sligo Creevelea Glenfarne
Killala West Queen Maeve's Carrowmore Dromahair
Enniscrone Grave Lough Dowra
Gill Drumkeeran
Ballysadare
Colloney
SLIGO Drumshanbo
Ballina Bunnyconnellan Ballymote Lough
Arrow Lough
Lough Tobercurry Keadue Allen Drumshanbo
Conn Curry Carrowkeel Lough
Foxford Key Leitrim
Lough Swinford Charlestown Boyle
Cullin Lough Lough Key
Connaught Gara Forest Park Carrick-on- Drumsna
Regional Shannon
Airport Ballaghaderreen Frenchpark Lough
Turlough Boderg
Kiltimagh Kilkelly
Balla Knock Elphin
Ballyhaunis Castlerea Tulsk Strokestown
Claremorris ROSCOMMON
Ballintober
Ballindine Ballymoe Lanesborough
Kilmaine Dunmore Roscommon
Glenamaddy Fuerty
Shrule Lough
Tuam Ballygar Ree
Headford Thomas Kiltoom
Mount Street
GALWAY Bellew Caltra Athlone
Monivea Ballybaun Ahascragh
Galway Ballinasloe
Oranmore Athenry Kilconnell
y Clonmacnois
Craughwell Suck Clonony
Kilcogan Clonfert Cloghan
Dunguaire Thoor Loughrea Eyrecourt Banagher
Kinvarra Ballylee Killimor
Aillwee Coole 368m Shannon
Caves Park Birr
Kilmacduagh Gort Portumna Carrigahorig
Lough Woodford
Cutra Borrisokane
Corofin Lough
Dysert O'Dea Crusheen Graney Mountshannon Cloughjordan
Castle
CLARE Taumgraney
Ennis Knappogue Tulla 532m Portroe Nenagh
Castle 462m
Claracastle Quin Craggaunowen Toomyvara
Newmarket-on- Killaloe Templemore
Fergus 694m
Sixmilebridge Borrisoleigh
Shannon Bunratty Castle Newport
Airport & Folk Park TIPPERARY
River Shannon LIMERICK Thurles
Boher Holycross
Askeaton Cappamore Golden
Adare Patrickswell Clonoulty
Rathkeale Pallas Grean Vale
Lough Gur Herbertstown

Connemara ponies

The qualities of this versatile breed make it popular with horse-lovers all over Britain and Ireland. At most times of year they can be seen roaming the harsh terrain of Connemara, surviving on a diet of brackish grass and seaweed. In August many are brought to Clifden for the Connemara Pony Show to be examined by local dealers. Resilience is an obvious characteristic, but these ponies are also good-tempered and easily taught. A subtle admixture of Arab blood lends style to the sturdy native stock and, when well groomed and smartened up, they are handsome, elegant creatures in any show ring.

Western counties Oliver Cromwell's famous declaration that Irish rebels could go "to Hell or to Connaught" suggests he didn't think much of this western region. In times when soil fertility and accessibility were important considerations, these rain-swept, isolated outposts of barren limestone or waterlogged bog must have held few attractions. Famine struck western Ireland particularly hard and emigration from Counties Galway, Clare, and Mayo has been high. Until the 18th century, British influence was minimal, and the area is still firmly Gaelic in outlook, its population in tiny scattered rural communities rather than towns and villages. The traditional Irish spirit is evident in local speech, music, crafts, and sports. Now, it is the West's very distinctiveness that many visitors find so appealing, and, above all, its scenery. These three counties encompass a colossal variety of landscapes and sights. Scenic highlights are unquestionably the ghostly gray-white expanses of bare limestone in the Burren, and the wild coast and mountains of Connemara, where the Twelve Bens loom over flattering mirrors of water amid moorland and blanket bog. Mayo, to the north, is quieter and less popular, although its peaceful scenery has always appealed to a discerning minority. Achill Island is one of its loveliest (and most visited) spots. Céide Fields, a recent Ballycastle attraction, is an imaginatively displayed neolithic settlement long preserved in peatland.

Tourist attractions Tourism, low-key at first, has boomed and become much more commercialized since

Dún Aengus, on Inishmore, the most imposing ruin in the Aran Islands

Irish cabins

During the early 19th century standards of living in Connaught were extremely poor due to overpopulation and the oppressive land laws of the time. A description in 1823 gives an idea of how many people lived: "a room fifteen feet by nine, no window, no chimney, not even the sign of a fireplace, a mud floor sunk considerably below the level of the road by the side of which it stands, originally ill made and in this wet season covered by almost one foot of water, in one corner are a few lighted sods of turf which, while they afford but little warmth to the wretched group around them, fill the room with volumes of smoke."

the opening of Shannon Airport, near Limerick. This is still an important, though no longer mandatory stop for all transatlantic passenger aircraft flying into Ireland. Worryingly, the importance of tourism to the region's economy may threaten some of its most sensitive sites. Recently, the Office of Public Works planned to build a new visitor center in one of the most remote parts of the fragile Burren. This plan, at least, was rejected by the Irish Supreme Court, but there will doubtless be others.

Off-season (October–April) most of the West is quiet, with everything except the busiest attractions being closed and less choice of accommodations available. In order to tour the area in any depth, it is essential to have a car. If you are unable to drive, the best base is Galway City, which offers plenty to do all year round and opportunities for nearby excursions. One of the most interesting trips is to the Aran Islands— it is advisable to stay a day or two, if you can, and see them all. The West provides ample opportunities for golf, riding, fishing, and relaxing.

The ideal time to visit the Burren is May or June when its fantastic variety of flowers are at their best. For bird watching, however, spring and autumn are good times, particularly on the Cliffs of Moher and Downpatrick Head. Inland, huge expanses of water also attract thousands of wildfowl. Pontoon, between Loughs Conn and Cullin, is an especially good place to watch them. So too are the lonely bogland and mountains of the Connemara National Park and the strange turlough lakes of Galway and Clare— one month, a sheet of water, the next, just an emerald patch of freshly watered vegetation, brilliant with flowers, as the giant underground aquifers steadily fill.

Knappogue Castle in County Clare runs medieval banquets in season; see below for more details

Medieval banquets
These are a popular tourist attraction in the Shannonside region of Counties Clare and Limerick. Three castles are highly promoted for medieval entertainments of various kinds, with costumes, music, feasting, and fun: Bunratty, Knappogue and Dunguaire (see Hotels and Restaurants, pages 269–83). Don't expect anything authentic or highbrow, but they are greatly enjoyed by many visitors, especially those using Shannon Airport. Ask at any tourist office for information—leaflets are widely available explaining how to book a place.

Currachs

These traditional rowboats, with no keels, are made of tarred canvas stretched over a light wooden frame (originally made of hazel rods and cowhide). The stern is flat, the prow high, so the boats ride high in the water and are extremely buoyant in the roughest seas, though very fragile. Most carry three oarsmen. They are carried to and from the water's edge upside-down over the crew's heads to avoid damage by rocks, which gives a most curious insect-like impression to a spectator. They are still used for inshore lobster-fishing and collecting sea-weed, but the popular sport of *curragh*-racing on the west coast of Ireland also helps to keep these unusual craft afloat. (See photograph on page 194.)

Typical Aran cottages, with the ubiquitous dry-stone walls marking the field boundaries

▶▶ Achill Island   172D1

Mayo's western seaboard seems on the verge of disintegration, its straggling peninsulas anchored to the mainland only by a thread. Achill is the largest of these semi-islands, a rough triangle with sides about 15 miles long, linked to Curraun (itself a peninsula) by a modern road bridge over Achill Sound. Its quiet beaches and spectacular mountain scenery make it an appealing destination; touring, by car or bike, surfing and fishing are the main activities and in summer boats make trips to coastal caves or in pursuit of the harmless basking sharks that haunt this coast. Keel is the main village, boasting shops, simple accommodations, and a splendid sandy beach, with some dramatic formations known as the Cathedral Rocks at its farthest end. The most scenic parts of the island can be seen from the Atlantic Drive (signed from the main road near the bridge) which leads past awesome cliffs, heather and gorse moors, and white cottages sprinkled against dark rocks. Beyond Keel, the road stretches toward Achill Head, rearing toward the Atlantic like a sea monster.

▶▶▶ Aran Islands   172B2

The cracked limestone terrain of the Aran Islands, lying about 30 miles out in Galway Bay, links them geologically with the Burren, in County Clare. The islands are flattish, but tilt toward massive sea cliffs in places. Making a living on these bleak rock platforms, virtually treeless and exposed to the full brunt of Atlantic storms, has always been a struggle. Large areas have no natural depth of soil and the islanders have painstakingly created fields from a mixture of sand and seaweed compost, protecting them with an intricate network of dry-stone walls.

Today's dwindling population of islanders (about 1,500) subsist on their age-old livelihoods of fishing and farming, and, increasingly, on tourism. Many speak Gaelic and a very few still wear traditional Aran dress. The canvas fishing boats called *currachs* are used, although now they often have outboard motors. The Arans have always inspired a strong tradition of literature and oral storytelling; J. M. Synge set his play *Riders to the Sea* here,

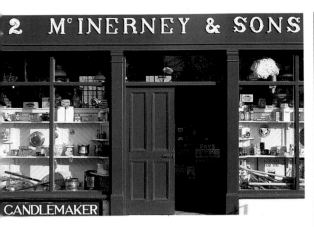

Castles and abbeys
The Shannon region has many ancient buildings, often carefully restored to achieve full tourist potential. Besides well-known Bunratty, there are tower-houses at Knappogue, a MacNamara stronghold, and Dunguaire, near Kinvarra. Less touristy are Aughnanure, on Lough Corrib, and Portumna, on Lough Derg. Some of the best monastic sites include: the Franciscan friaries of Quin and Ennis; Clonfert, which has a lovely Romanesque doorway; Ballintubber, founded by a Connaught king; Ross, near Headford; and the remains at Kilmacduagh, with its leaning Round Tower and cathedral. Cong Abbey, in Mayo, housed the great processional Cross of Cong, now in Dublin.

and the classic film, *Man of Aran*, made by the Irish-American director, Robert Flaherty, in 1934, depicted the harsh life on the island.

Most visitors, on a day-trip to one island, only get a faint whiff of Aran's cultural background; by staying in the islands' simple accommodations, you will absorb far more. Several ferry companies serve the Aran Islands from Galway City, Rossaveal, and Doolin (County Clare). Aer Arann flies tiny aircraft to all three islands from Galway. All transportation services may be affected by weather and you should check schedules carefully.

Inishmore►►► is the largest and most visited island. You can explore by bike, on foot, take a mini-bus, or hire a pony-trap ride along its 7-mile spinal road. Inishmore has a wealth of ancient monuments, notably one of Ireland's outstanding prehistoric sites, the remarkable cliff fort of Dún Aengu. Three concentric horseshoe rings of stone perched atop mighty cliffs seem an odd place of refuge, so exposed to the elements and with a sheer drop to the roaring sea below. Its precise age and purpose are still a mystery. The smaller islands are Inishmaan►► and Inisheer►►, both of which have small fortresses, churches and folk museums to visit.

►► Bunratty Castle and Folk Park   173A3

Bunratty, on the main tourist route from the west coast to Shannon Airport, is now a highly commercialized venture, dragging in bus tours by the thousand for "medieval" banquets and "traditional Irish nights" of fiddle music and Irish stew. For all that, the 15th-century castle is genuine enough and well worth seeing.

Set in the castle grounds, the Folk Park re-creates rural Irish life at the turn of the century by means of a series of "typical" village buildings of the sort you will rarely see in Ireland outside folk theme parks. Chickens cluck around the cottages and costumed staff demonstrate traditional skills. Extraneous attractions include exhibitions, gift- and tearooms, and the famous tourist pub, **Durty Nelly's**, obligatory viewing for any tour. There's a good (stylish) restaurant above it called MacCloskey's.

Stone gates
Despite there being a high density of fields and walls on the Aran Islands, wooden gates are very rare, since trees are scarce. The islanders' answer is to use small gaps in the wall, filled with stones. When access is needed the "gate" is dismantled and then reassembled. Some gates are topped with a branch of thorn to dissuade the occupant of the field from pushing the gate over. See above for an example.

177

THE BURREN

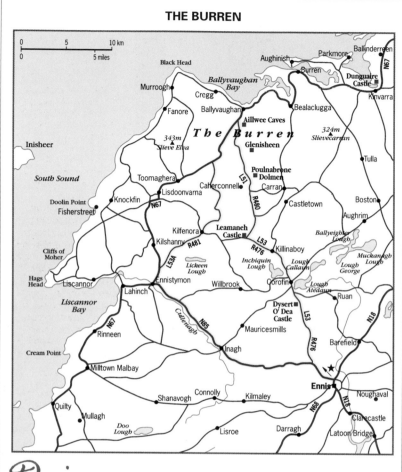

Drive **The eerie beauty of the Burren**

A moon buggy may seem more appropriate for this eerie landscape than a conventional car. Geologists, botanists and antiquity-hunters will be in their element.

From a distance, parts of this treeless limestone plateau in north Clare look bleak, but a closer exploration reveals that the area is astonishingly rich in plant life, playing host to more than 1,100 of the 1,400 species found in Ireland. Although the stone surfaces have been scraped clean by the elements, every crack and hollow contains some fragile vegetation, absorbing moisture and nutrients from minimal resources. Alpine species flourish next to those from Mediterranean shores: rare saxifrages, gentians, maidenhair ferns, and orchids. The best time to visit the Burren for flowers is undoubtedly in May or June.

Within a couple of hours you can drive across the Burren on the major road from Ennis to Ballyvaughan—and get an idea of the landscape of ancient domed hills and gray-white "flagstones." But this moonscape reveals its real charms only to the sharp-eyed observer on foot, so take a picnic, and leave your vehicle at some stage. Walkers on the Burren

Bloody cranesbill, which grows commonly all over the Burren

should wear sensible footwear and take great care. A 20-mile marked trail, the Burren Way, runs from Ballyvaughan toward Doolin.

Ballyvaughan► is an attractive center from which to explore the Burren; other bases with accommodations are **Killinaboy, Corofin** or **Ennistymon.** The southern section of the Burren is characterized by seasonal lakes called *turloughs,* which ebb and fill as the region's water table changes. Gradually, rainwater falling on this limestone plateau finds its way underground into a maze of caves and subterranean channels. Most are too dangerous for novice investigations, but one has been opened and is worth a visit: the **Aillwee Cave►►,** south of Ballyvaughan, is a commercial opera-

tion, but the cavern itself is left reasonably natural apart from pathways and illumination. Near the cave entrance a shop sells local cheeses and other produce.

Parts of the Burren are reasonably fertile, supporting some farming and herds of feral goats. Other areas seem inhospitably bare, a shock after the lushness of most of Ireland. For centuries before the advent of tourism, the sparse population of the Burren lived in grim poverty.

The best way to find out more about the Burren's unique flora and geology is to visit the **Burren Display Centre►►** at Kilfenora, by the partly ruined church known as **St. Fachtnan's Cathedral►►.** Other sights to look for as you cross the central spine of the Burren are ancient tombs, such as the 4,500-year-old **Poulnabrone Dolmen►,** or the **Gleninsheen wedge-tomb►,** easily spotted beside R480 near Caherconnell. The ruins of **Leamaneh,** a 17th-century mansion owned by the O Briens, are a prominent landmark near Kilfenora. Another curiosity is a weatherworn *sheila-na-gig* on the ruined church at **Killinaboy.** These carvings of female figures in indelicate poses were perhaps an ancient fertility symbol, or a dire warning of the sins of the flesh.

Glen Inagh, where the Burren meets the sea

179

There are no snakes in Ireland, as every Irish schoolchild knows. But its five national parks, 71 national nature reserves (plus 44 in Northern Ireland), 68 bird sanctuaries, and 12 forest parks provide a remarkably rich and varied collection of habitats for a vast number of other species, including creatures that are now very rare in Britain, such as corncrakes or otters.

180

The Burren
This unusual terrain soaks up the rays of the sun and releases it gently throughout the winter, keeping temperatures a vital fraction higher than the surrounding area. It supports an amazing variety of plants, including many fragile, low-growing types that would be swamped in the average meadow. Species to look for include the deceptive fly orchid (resembling an insect), gentians, and alpine saxifrages. Mountain avens and wild thyme grow everywhere on the Burren, forming colorful sheets in early summer. Needless to say, visitors are requested not to pick or uproot any plants.

Fly orchid

An unspoiled land Ireland is a predominantly rural country, but like everywhere else, is steadily becoming more built up. Land use is changing, usually to the disadvantage of native flora and fauna, but there are still huge tracts of unspoiled countryside where ancient farming patterns prevail. Migrant birds return year after year to safe haunts, rare orchids and obscure insectivorous plants flourish in specialized niches, and lichen grows thick on walls or tree trunks in unpolluted air. Bird watchers and botanists, or anyone who appreciates country life, will much enjoy a break in Ireland. Remember your binoculars, and a reference book for identifying unusual species. If you plan to walk any of the long-distance footpaths of Ireland, or visit specialist regions like the Burren, check what to look for at an information or visitor center before you set off. Bord Fáilte's leaflet, *Ireland Naturally*, outlines the main nature reserves and places of interest.

Abundant wildlife Practically any part of Ireland offers the keen-eyed naturalist a good selection of species, but a number of locations are especially noted for unusual wildlife. Ireland has fewer mammals than Britain (no moles, for instance), but those that are there can often be found more abundantly. Otters colonize many rivers and streams, even quite near towns. Pine martens, red deer, and red squirrels can be found in the newly designated forest parks. The last remaining native woodlands can be seen in the national parks of Killarney and Glenveagh.

Exotic plants If you are interested in plants, the best region to head for is the mysterious limestone wilderness of the Burren in County Clare (see panel, and pages 178–9). Other areas special for plants are the sand-dune habitats, such as the Raven National Nature Reserve in County Wexford (wild asparagus, round-leafed wintergreen, and lesser centaury), and the lush, subtropical oceanic lands of Kerry and Cork, where wild fuchsias bloom and the strawberry tree grows to unusual size. Mosses and ferns thrive in the moist, mild air. Ireland's boglands support a unique ecosystem of wetland plants, including sundews and butterworts (see pages 24–5).

Rare birds Bird watchers have an immense choice of habitats. There are many exciting coastal reserves, first landfall for rare migrants which cross the ocean to breed or winter in Ireland. Spring nesting seasons begin early for native birds, followed by an influx of species from Africa.

Wildlife

The Irish yew
Every example of this tree ultimately comes from cuttings taken from the mutant discovered in the gardens of Florence Court in County Fermanagh. The branches have an unusual upright habit instead of the normal spreading growth. The original tree was identified and first propagated in 1767, and the Irish yew is now planted widely in graveyards and formal gardens.

Marine reserves
For marine habitats, head for Strangford Lough near Belfast, or Lough Hyne in south Cork, where sheltered sea inlets have fostered unique colonies of creatures usually found in more tropical waters. Giant skate and basking shark glide through the narrow straits, carpeted with bright corals and sponges.

There are pine martens in the forest parks, but you will be lucky to see one

Corncrake

In autumn rare American waders appear in ones and twos, and in winter great numbers of waterfowl fly in from Northern Europe and the Arctic or Canada. Manx shearwaters glide close to Belfast toward dusk, with an eerie cry that once unnerved the Vikings, and nest on Light House Island. Greenland white-fronted geese arrive in huge flocks on the "slobs" (reclaimed *polder* mudflats) of Wexford. Puffins nest in a few rocky places on the west and southwest coast (the Cliffs of Moher, Clear Island, or Puffin Island). Terns colonize the sheltered inland sea of Strangford Lough. Several of the most famous bird reserves are islands; Ireland's Eye, just off Howth near Dublin, the Copelands near Belfast and the wild Skellig Rocks off the southwest tip of Cork. Clear Island and the Saltees are both accessible by boat at the most interesting times of year. Other good birdwatching locations are the quiet estuarial coast of Waterford and Wexford (particularly around Hook Head, Kinsale Old Head, or Kilmore Quay), the muddy flats of Timoleague, and the wild rocky fastnesses of Clare, Mayo, Rathlin Island, and Donegal, where seabirds gather in vast numbers on cliff ledges, at spots such as Horn Head (Donegal), the Cliffs of Moher (Clare), or Downpatrick Head (Mayo). Inland, many of the larger lakes and river systems support huge colonies of waterbirds—godwits, avocets, and swans. Birds of prey can be seen wheeling in lonely circuits around the Wicklow Mountains, the Slieve Blooms, the Sperrins (in the North) or Macgillycuddy's Reeks.

Edward Synge
During the dreadful Famine days, some Protestant landlords attempted to lure their starving tenants away from the Catholic church with offers of soup, education, and other blandishments if they would convert. In Clare, Edward Synge was one such individual; he aroused such passionate antipathy that an attempt was made on his life. A stoutly bound leather Bible in his breast pocket diverted the bullet aimed at his heart, thus finally convincing many of his skeptical flock that God was very definitely on his side! The Bible (complete with hole) is displayed at the Clare Heritage Centre in Corofin.

A justifiably famous Irish viewpoint shows Clifden in its glorious setting by the Twelve Bens, most of which are visible below. Leaving Clifden on the Sky Road (on a clear day) and looking back after about a mile reveals the full panorama

►► Clifden   172C1

The "capital of Connemara" occupies a glorious position at the head of Clifden Bay, with the Twelve Bens mountain range a dramatic backdrop (see photograph below). Clifden is little more than a large village with a population of 1,400 or so, but its location makes it a popular base. It is also an agricultural and market town, but much of the land around it is too poor to farm, and the region's income derives mainly from tourism. It has a range of affordable accommodation, lively bars and fine sandy beaches. An arts festival is held in late September, though a more traditional event is the August Connemara Pony Show.

Cottages and bungalows have sprung up all around the 19th-century core of the town, founded in 1812 by the local landowner, John d'Arcy, descendant of an Anglo-Norman family who converted from Roman Catholicism to avoid dispossession under the Penal Laws. He built the ruined Gothic castle visible from the Sky Road. The town consists of two main streets of attractively restored colorful shop fronts displaying the names of Connemara families, notably Joyce. Main landmarks include two gray-spired churches, one Catholic, one Protestant.

The best views of the town and the surrounding landscape are seen from the Sky Road, a narrow circuit around the Kingstown peninsula to the northwest. This scenic corniche skirts the hillsides, overlooking plunging vistas of white farms, emerald fields and sapphire sea.

►►► Cliffs of Moher   172B2

Sheer, dark walls of rock stretch dramatically for 5 miles along the coast of Clare, an even-topped curtain, in places as much as 700 feet high. These remarkable cliffs are home to a great variety of seabirds, including a colony of puffins, and on clear days there are splendid views of the Aran Islands and the mountains of Connemara. A cliff path leads to the southerly extremity of Hag's Head, fenced as the cliffs are so friable. The rocks are basically

limestone of the same sort as the Burren, but shale and sandstone have formed on top, and are subject to rainfall erosion and the pressure of many feet; keep back from the edge. You can park near the highly commercialized visitor center. Not far away is a folly viewpoint built by the 19th-century M.P., Sir Cornelius O Brien, where a telescope gives a close-up of the huge rock-faces and sea stacks, standing in the lazily moving waves which, from this height, are almost inaudible.

▶ Corofin 173B3

This village amid the pretty lakes of the southern Burren is a fine base for exploring the area. Accommodations consist mainly of B. & B.s, with one good private hostel in the center. Even if you don't stay, visit the **Clare Heritage Centre**▶▶ housed in the former Protestant church. It has a moving exhibition connected with the Famine period, when this part of Ireland suffered particularly badly. In a building close by, a genealogical center has been set up, containing half a million baptismal records of more than 2,500 families. Descendants of émigré families come to find their roots (see pages 74–5).

▶▶ Craggaunowen Project 173A3

This historic reconstruction vividly brings to life Ireland's pre-Christian past and remains one of the best of its kind, very well explained with a good visitor center, coffee shop, and picnic area. The art historian and archaeologist, John Hunt (see page 167), restored the 16th-century tower-house of Craggaunowen Castle during the 1960s, then turned the grounds to imaginative use. A Bronze-Age *crannóg* (island dwelling) stands in a reedy lake; other exhibits include a ring-fort and a stretch of Iron-Age timber road. Also on display is the leather-covered boat called the *Brendan*, in which Tim Severin and his crew sailed the Atlantic in 1976–1977, in a putative repetition of St. Brendan's 6th-century voyage to the Americas (see page 115).

Fun on Judgment Day
When two imaginative girls were growing up in Chile in the early 1900s, each wrote a poetic epitaph for the other, agreeing that whoever lived longer would place her poem on the other's tombstone. Subsequently both came to live near Corofin. When Audrey Douglas (née Sharman) died in 1968, she was buried in the grounds of the Church of Ireland church in the village (now the Clare Heritage Centre). Faithful to her pact, Vanda Cutler inscribed the following on the tombstone, visible for all to read:

Here, as ever, sleeping
 sound,
Lies our Audrey in the
 ground.
If she wakes, as wake she
 may,
There'll be fun on
 Judgement Day.

CONNEMARA

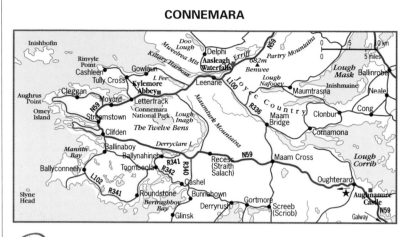

Drive **Mountains, beaches, untouched bogland, and a fjord**

If you're lucky with the weather, this magnificent drive offers superb coastal and mountain scenery, a 5,000-acre national park, and one of the best areas of blanket bog in Ireland.

Connemara is the westernmost section of County Galway, beyond Lough Corrib. Inland are moors and looming hills, lakes and streams fringed by vivid green vegetation, and a massively indented but placid coastline. One main road, N59, leads through the center of Connemara and around the northern area, but though it is scenic enough, it's best to deviate from this for at least part of the way to take in some of the coast. If you start at Galway you take the main road for the first section (via Oughterard).

Oughterard▶ is some way inland, but is surprisingly a great fishing center, serving the resort area of Lough Corrib, Ireland's second largest lake (25 miles long) which virtually splits the county in half. If you have time, a detour along the lush lakeshore toward Curraun is a pleasant option. From Oughterard it's a straightforward and beautiful trip past mirror-

Roundstone, a quiet village on the peaceful Connemara coast

like pools to **Maam Cross**, where the monthly cattle fair is about the only sign of life. There you have a choice between exploring the mass of islets along the coastal peninsulas, or pressing on to the small, unremarkable settlement of Recess. Further on, stop at **Ballynahinch Castle►** (now a luxury hotel, see panel on page 164), in fine parkland by a lake. A detour via the peaceful coastline of **Cashel Bay►►** is a recommended alternative here. Sheltered from Atlantic gales and storms, this quiet bay sprouts luxuriant subtropical vegetation at every turn.

Roundstone► has a particularly attractive setting at the foot of Errisbeg with wonderful views of the Twelve Bens; its tourist industry is taking over from fishing. If you cut across the peninsula instead of following the coast you will see at close quarters one of the best remaining stretches of Irish blanket bog, now at last recognized as an important ecosystem, rather than something to be dried and burned. It's a lonely road with some bad potholes, so drive carefully, especially toward nightfall. The bog is haunted by the ghost of a traveler murdered by two old women who offered him shelter—no advertisement for the local B. & B. trade!

Clifden►► is the "capital" of Connemara. There's not much to the town, but it has magnificent scenery all around, best seen from the immensely scenic Sky Road►►, signed

Kylemore Abbey; there can be few more dramatically sited schools

to the northwest. Just past the seemly Quaker village of **Letterfrack** is the entrance to the **Connemara National Park►►**, containing some of the West's finest mountain scenery. There's a visitor center with an exhibition on local natural history and bogland. Staff can suggest short hikes through the park; guided walks are organized in summer. For more challenging walking, follow one of the routes given in *The Mountains of Connemara; a Hill-walker's Guide*, on sale, about a mile further on, at the shop at **Kylemore Abbey►►** whose fairy-tale towers are reflected in a clear lake. Kylemore, a 19th-century folly, now houses a girls' boarding school, but welcomes visitors to its craft shops and tea rooms. The road to **Leenane►** is especially scenic, running past the long inlet called Killary harbor, where controversial fish-farming is taking place. Leenane recently achieved cinematic fame as the setting for the film, *The Field*. A brief drive over the bridge to **Aasleagh** gives a view of a series of waterfalls, a salmon leap, and the gateway to County Mayo. If you want to return toward Galway from Leenane a couple of routes wind through Joyce Country (so named because nearly everyone there has the surname Joyce) around Lough Corrib.

Oysters and Guinness at the International Galway Oyster Festival, held in late September each year

The Lynch Memorial
This marble plaque over a Gothic doorway can be found near the Collegiate Church of St. Nicholas in Market Street. It commemorates a poignant, though almost certainly fictional, legend that a former city mayor, James Lynch FitzStephen, tried and convicted his own son, Walter, of killing a Spanish rival for the affections of his beloved. The boy confessed to the crime and Judge Lynch felt morally obliged to condemn his son to death as he would any other citizen guilty of murder. But no one would carry out the sentence, so he was forced to hang his son himself. After the execution the mayor retired into seclusion, a broken man.

Claddagh rings
These ornaments of silver or gold originated in The Claddagh, once a close-knit fishing community just outside Galway's old city walls, now a neat suburb. Claddagh rings depict two hands holding a heart surmounted by a crown, symbolizing a promise, or a hope, of eternal love and friendship. The precious heirlooms were handed down the female line and, depending which way the ring was worn, showed whether a girl was engaged, or still on the marriage market.

▶▶   **Galway**   *173C3*

During the 1980s, Galway, one of the fastest growing metropolitan areas in Europe, was rivaling Limerick as the Republic's third city, but in 1993 a major employer, I.B.M., closed its factory. Despite its size, it has an intimate, village-like atmosphere and everyone seems to know everyone else, although this may be an illusion, as much of its population consists of temporary visitors (tourists or students). Besides its prestigious 19th-century university, where students can take their degrees in Gaelic, Galway has several Irish-language schools. None of its sights is essential viewing, but the city seems to add up to more than the sum of its parts, and is a good center for entertainment and shopping (especially secondhand books and classy crafts).

There is always plenty going on, both low- and highbrow—a festival just about every month, an innovative theater, concerts, lively pubs and restaurants. In short, it is perhaps Ireland's most enjoyable and upbeat city, full of vivacity and character and increasingly frequented by younger visitors in search of "good crack" (fun). It hosts high-caliber Irish folk groups and its sporting prowess is a source of pride, particularly in traditional games such as Gaelic football and hurling. The Galway Races (a six-day meeting in July) and its Regatta Festivals are some of the oldest regular events. Beside its own attractions, Galway is a good base for exploring local areas—Connemara, Lough Corrib, the Aran Islands, and the Burren.

Galway's prosperity was founded on its strategic location at the lowest bridging point of the River Corrib, a waterway once used by many vessels, now mainly by the spring salmon that leap the falls by the **Salmon Weir Bridge**▶. Founded by the Anglo-Normans in the 13th century, Galway became known as the City of the Tribes, a reference to the 14 leading families who held sway quarrelsomely in its early history. In its heyday, Galway was a significant port and European trading center; its traditional vessels, the elegant lateen-rigged Galway hookers, traded food and fuel for livestock from the Aran Islands, or smuggled contraband from France and the Channel Isles. By the western mouth of the river are the remains of a Gaelic-speaking fishing community known as **The Claddagh▶** (see panel). The cottages have now been replaced by tidier municipal housing, but old photographs and artifacts displayed in the city's **museum▶** show how it looked. The museum is in a stone structure called the **Spanish Arch▶**, erected by the harbor to protect ships unloading Iberian cargoes of wine and brandy.

Up towards the center of town the most striking monument is the unattractive **Roman Catholic Cathedral of Our Lady Assumed into Heaven and St. Nicholas▶**, a vast limestone structure in neo-Renaissance style, all seeping copper and flashy marble. The amorous behavior of its former bishop (Eamonn Casey), which raised eyebrows in 1992, has apparently failed to dent local faith. More seemly buildings lie in the medieval quarter of the city, where wandering through its delightful streets of well-restored shop fronts and stone townhouses is recommended. Sixteenth century **Lynch's Castle▶**, now an Allied Irish Bank building, was once the seat of the Lynch family and its mullioned façade is decorated with exotic escutcheons and gargoyles. The dignified **Collegiate Church of St. Nicholas▶** has seafaring associations, including a legend that Christopher Columbus prayed there. Eyre Square is a welcome space after the confinement of the tiny old lanes. Dedicated to President Kennedy, it contains several monuments, the most interesting being the crested Browne Doorway, a disembodied portal dating from 1627, removed from a grand mansion in 1905. Bits of the city walls are incorporated into the new Eyre Square shopping center. Nora Barnacle, James Joyce's wife, hailed from Galway, and her tiny house (now a shop) can be visited in the Bowling Green.

Oysters and ale
Galway's native oysters raised in the calm tidal waters around Clarinbridge are world-famous, and it is an ideal place to acquire an expensive taste—whenever there's an "r" in the month. In fact, most Galway oysters are perfectly affordable, being farmed ones from Portuguese stock which, unlike the native oysters, can be eaten in any month. Though carefully prepared, these are served with no pretentious ritual. Wash them down with a pint of Guinness if you like. Each year in early September the Clarinbridge Oyster Festival is held. The best places to try them are Paddy Burke's pub in Clarinbridge, or the quaint waterside restaurant called Moran's Oyster Cottage. You can walk downstream to see the beds when the tide is right. They take about four years to reach maturity.

The beach at Salthill, west of Galway, looks south toward the Burren

Mystic visions
Shrines and grottoes throughout Ireland, most still in constant use, declare the absolute faith many Irish people have in miracles, that is in supernatural religious experiences. To the visitor it may seem extraordinary that so many apparently rational 20th-century people can convince themselves that they have seen visions, or that modern plaster statues move, weep, or bleed, but their testimony is weirdly unshakeable, even under rigorous cross-questioning. Grotto shrines can be seen at Ballinspittle, near Kinsale, and Mount Melleray, County Waterford, among others.

Knock's position on the world pilgrimage trail was confirmed by the visit of Pope John Paul II in 1979

Croagh Patrick
The brooding, conical outline of this mountain dominates the skyline all around southwest Mayo. It is associated with St. Patrick, the site of his Lenten fast and legendary "Pied Piper" act with the snakes. Each year, on the last Sunday in July, pilgrims make an arduous ascent, some barefoot. On clear days, the summit gives magnificent views over Clew Bay to the Partry Mountains and Connemara. If you have sensible shoes, you can climb Croagh Patrick in a couple of hours. (See also page 226.)

Knock
173D3

Knock's pedigree dates back over a century, when it was suddenly transformed from a humdrum little bog village into one of the most revered Marian shrines in Christendom. It is now the "Lourdes of Ireland," with a vast new basilica, constantly thronged by pilgrims. Its present high profile in the Catholic world is due in large part to the energies of a local priest, Monsignor James Horan. He battled with the authorities for an airport which, despite early descriptions as "a foggy, boggy white elephant," has greatly opened up the northwest region to tourist traffic since its eventual inauguration in 1986, seven years after Pope John Paul II made a celebrated visit to Knock. The commercialized religiosity of innumerable souvenir stalls may offend the purist, but today Knock attracts more pilgrims than ever, around 1½ million a year.

On a dark and stormy night in 1879, two village women saw an apparition of the Virgin Mary, with St. Joseph and St. John, on the gable of the parish church. Scarcely able to believe their eyes, they called other villagers, who also saw the vision. It lasted a couple of hours, then faded away gradually. All 15 witnesses were interviewed and cross-examined by a commission of inquiry. Some 50 years later, three surviving witnesses were again independently interviewed, and firmly maintained every detail of what they had seen, giving an unnerving veracity to their story.

The original church still exists, the gable where the vision had appeared now preserved behind a glazed oratory. It has fine features inside, notably stained glass by the ubiquitous Harry Clarke (1889–1931). The new church, designed to hold a congregation of many thousands, was completed in 1976. Though fairly hideous to an unpartisan eye, the hexagonal building contains inter-

This Lisdoonvarna house has turned a few heads

esting examples of modern art and architecture. Its 32 ambulatory pillars each contain stone from a different Irish county, and the windows represent each of the four provinces: Connaught, Leinster, Munster, and Ulster.

Knock's religious significance dwarfs any other reason to come here, but there is a good little **folk museum►** in the village illustrating life in the west of Ireland and giving some background on the shrine.

Lisdoonvarna   172B2

Ireland's only spa stands in this curious village on the edge of the Burren, emitting sulphurous and radioactive iodine-filled springs alleged to cure numerous ills. The bathhouse facilities will seem primitive if you frequent swanky health clubs, but the old-fashioned bathtubs and massage rooms have a certain historic fascination. Needless to say, the water tastes terrible.

Grandiose spa hotels and villas indicate the spa's one-time popularity, but today the village is more renowned for its Matchmaking Festival, held annually in September after harvest time. The festival has an honorable history; wealthy farming families used to pair off their eligible sons and daughters via a "matchmaker" for appropriate dowries of cattle or horses. Later the festival became a dating agency for the famously shy and sexually repressed bachelor farmers of rural Ireland, who often had few social outlets and little opportunity to meet potential brides. Many failed to marry until very late in life, if at all. These days, however, the festival has become a tawdry and depressing event, at which lonely singles turn up for a drunken grope and a one-night stand rather than a soulmate. Unusually in organized dating circles, the proportion of men is far higher than women (about three to one). There's plenty of good "crack" (fun), though, and it's certainly worth a visit as a social curiosity. If you're on the lookout, who knows, you may get lucky!

At the **Lisdoonvarna Smoke House►**, signed from the village center, fish is smoked, amid a choking salty fug of charring wood chippings. Women deftly fillet and trim massive sides of salmon (wild and farmed). You can buy some of the products here, or try them in the Roadside Tavern next door.

Monsignor James Horan
The guiding light behind Knock International Airport may ultimately be super-natural, but its earthly inspiration took the shape of Mgr. James Horan, an indefatigable local priest. He it was who first raised the idea of upgrading the grass airstrip to jumbo-jet capacity. After the Pope's visit to Knock in 1979, Mgr. Horan was convinced the shrine would draw vast numbers of pilgrims. Decried by skeptics as a foggy, boggy white elephant, the airport nevertheless opened in 1986, soon proving popular with both tourists and pilgrims. Indeed the Lourdes–Knock run is used by many French visitors wishing to fish in the lakes of the West!

189

Captain Charles Boycott
The man whose surname has entered the English language as a word meaning to ostracize was land agent for Lord Erne in County Mayo in the late 19th century. He lived at Loughmask House, on the lough's eastern shore. During the 1879–1882 Land War (Parnell's campaign to reduce land rents by 25 percent) he was isolated by the local community "as if he were a leper" for his refusal to cooperate. No one would work for him, or even speak to him, and eventually he was forced to leave Ireland.

Thoor Ballylee, Yeats's retreat from the frantic events of 1920s Ireland

Coole Park
Yeats's patron lived there—the redoubtable Lady Augusta Gregory (1859–1932), a wealthy widow who encouraged many writers and artists at the turn of the century. The house fell into neglect after her death and was demolished during World War II, but the splendid grounds are now open to the public as a national park and are a marvelous place for walks and picnics. The "autograph tree," a copper beech on which many famous visitors carved their initials, can be seen behind railings in the peaceful walled garden. In the park is the lake that inspired Yeats's poem *The Wild Swans at Coole*.

Setting the world to rights in Westport

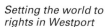

►► **Thoor Ballylee**   *173B3*

An ancient bridge and a more ancient tower,
A farmhouse that is sheltered by its wall,
An acre of stony ground,
Where the symbolic rose can break in flower.
(Meditations in Time of Civil War)

In 1917 W.B. Yeats found this evocative "ivy-covered tower," conveniently close to his friend and patron Lady Gregory, who lived at Coole Park. Thoor Ballylee was a fortified residence built by the Anglo-Norman de Burgo family during the 14th century. Then in his 50s and newly married to his young bride George Hyde-Lees, Yeats purchased the derelict towerhouse for IR£35 and spent intermittent periods of the next decade there with his new family, converting the interior into simple, but stylish living and sleeping quarters. The "winding stair" image which repeatedly appears in his poetry refers to the stone steps leading up the tower. From the battlemented rooftop, views extend over the placid meadows by the nearby millstream to the Slieve Aughty Mountains. Many of Yeats's more mystical writings were produced there, notably *The Tower* and *The Winding Stair* (not generally his most admired work); by this stage his disillusion with the Irish political scene was taking effect and he sought relief in seclusion and mythology. By 1928, Yeats had abandoned the damp tower for warmer climes; he died in France in 1939. The Kiltartan Society took over the decaying tower in 1961 and fully restored it in Yeatsian style, putting many documents, first editions, and manuscripts on display. The audiovisual show gives a good background to the poet, the house, and the turmoil of the times.

►► **Westport**   *172D2*

One of the most charming towns in Ireland's western region, Westport shows its Georgian origins clearly in its broad streets and river, which flows in tidy canals along a lime-fringed avenue called The Mall. It is set on an inlet of Clew Bay, where the Carrowbeg River flows into the sea.

Many of its fine buildings remain, some carefully restored. The Protestant church is late Victorian (about 1880) and has charming art-nouveau influences.

Westport was originally laid out as part of a great estate and, at the turn of the 18th century, prospered greatly from its textile industry. In 1801, though, the Act of Union made local businesses collapse as cheaper products flooded in from England. By 1825 Westport's linen industry was virtually finished. Today, Westport is a market town and fishing center, with a few good beaches nearby. Many visitors pass through, stopping at its main sight on the way.

Westport House►► stands in fine parkland about 2 miles outside the town, near Westport Quay. Designed by those great architects of the 1730s, James Wyatt and Richard Castle, it is the seat of the Brownes, Marquesses of Sligo, and is County Mayo's only stately home open to the public. Though highly commercialized in an attempt to meet the colossal running costs, it is still a remarkable house, beautifully furnished inside with Irish Georgian and Victorian silver and antiques, Waterford crystal, Chinese wallpapers, and a fine collection of paintings, including a *Holy Family* by Rubens. The doors are made with Jamaican mahogany (the 1st Marquess spent time as a governor there, apparently one of its more benevolent rulers, freeing many slaves). The dungeons beneath the house date from an earlier dwelling, allegedly a castle belonging to the pirate queen, Grace O'Malley. These now provide but one of the many attractions and sideshows set up in the park and grounds, which include a zoo, gift shops, boating lake, a model railroad, and horse-drawn caravans. The Browne family has lived in Westport House for over 400 years.

Westport Quay, just outside the main entrance gates to the house, has several good restaurants, and there is a range of accommodations in the town. A couple of summer festivals (arts in October and a street festival in July) and good music pubs are other reasons to head here. The Wyatt Theatre (in season) puts on some amateur productions of Irish drama.

"My wife George"
W. B. Yeats was something of a pessimistic visionary at times, foreseeing the places he lived in going to rack and ruin after he left. On a plaque set into the wall of the tower at Thoor Ballylee, he inscribed the following verse:

I, the poet William Yeats,
With old mill boards and
  sea-green slates
And smithy work from the
  Gort forge,
Restored this tower for my
  wife George;
And may these characters
  remain
When all is ruin once
  again.

191

Westport House also has an attractive modern church in its grounds

Any glance at Ireland's antiquities—its great churches, the jewelry worn by the Celts, the intricacies of illuminated manuscripts like the *Book of Kells*—will show what a long tradition of sheer artistry exists there, what a delight in pattern, shape, and texture. This continues today, encouraged strongly by tourism.

192

Bog-wood carvings

An artist with a highly individual product is Michael Casey, who works at Barley Harbour in County Longford and has achieved an international reputation. He has made a specialty of carving bog wood (blackened timber preserved for thousands of years beneath boglands) into imaginative sculptures of figures or animals. It is a long process. First the wood has to dry out—taking almost two years. Then it is carved, and finished carefully with sandpaper and beeswax to a remarkable sheen. The wood used is mostly yew, pine, or oak.

The labor-intensive and highly skilled craft of lacemaking, here practiced in Monaghan

Souvenir hunting Ireland's craft industries are a major source of revenue. They vary from huge enterprises employing hundreds of workers, like Waterford Crystal, to tiny artisan studios where one person practices woodcarving or jewelry making. Some crafts are still cottage industries—much knitting or lacemaking, for example, is still done at home. Most visitors will want to take at least one reminder of Ireland home, and there is now a wide and attractive choice of souvenirs to suit all purses; shop around for price and quality. Prices can be high in Ireland with V.A.T. at its currently high rates. If you live outside the E.U., consider reclaiming this tax on anything valuable.

Many craft centers and even factories now welcome tourists, and free tours are provided at several large enterprises, such as Waterford Crystal, Tyrone Crystal, Belleek Parian ware, Foxford Woollen Mills in County Mayo, Donegal Parian China, and Magee's tweed factory in Donegal Town. These are often elaborately set up with guided tours, audiovisual shows, refreshments, and showrooms where you can inspect, and of course buy, the product. Packing and shipment arrangements can also be made if you live abroad.

Kilkenny is an attractive place to buy crafts. The Kilkenny Design Center, set up in old stables opposite the castle, provides a high-quality outlet for many of Ireland's best producers. There is also a branch in Dublin (see page 80).

Craft villages Smaller studios have developed (mainly in the west of Ireland, notably in Donegal, Connemara, and Dingle) where economic conditions have justified a special focus of attention on employment opportunities. Artists can rent small workshops in these "craft villages" to produce jewelry, knitwear, pottery, woodwork, handweaving, etc. Connemara marble, a greenish stone, is fashioned into innumerable souvenirs near Moycullen. Several potters in Cork and Kerry have been particularly successful; Stephen Pearce's modern pottery in terracotta colors with abstract stripes of white is a typical example. Produced at Shanagarry, east of Cork City, it is now available in fashionable stores in Dublin or the West End of London. Robin and Jane Forrester's Bandon pottery is also very popular—in blue with a fruit pattern.

Glass and crystal Few visitors will be able to take a stained-glass window home, but in many of the churches of Ireland you will see the work of artists Harry Clarke or Evie Hone, who brought about a revival of this craft in the earlier part of the century. There are good examples at

Crafts

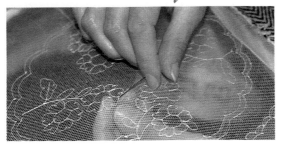

Carrickmacross in Monaghan, Ardara in Donegal, and at Kingscourt, Cavan. Ireland's brand of deep-etched, brilliant lead crystal is most famously produced at Waterford, but now has many competitors—in Tipperary, Cavan, Athlone, Donegal, Tyrone, and Galway. Jerpoint Glass, made in County Kilkenny, is plainer.

Linen and wool Textiles have always been a staple of Ireland's craft industry, linen and wool being the two main fibers used. Today's flax production is quite limited, but high quality dish-towels and tablecloths are available all over the island, subtly woven in damask patterns or more crudely stamped with shamrock motifs. Lisburn has linen trails and a linen museum. Centers of the lace industry are Carrickmacross and Clones in the border counties of Cavan and Monaghan (see panel on page 246) and Limerick. Both produce "mixed lace," which is sewn on to cotton net. Genuine handmade lace is expensive. Knitwear is ubiquitous. The classic Aran sweater is now produced all over Ireland in many different designs.

One of Ireland's most famous products is tweed. Manufacture still centers on Donegal, where those classic, hard-wearing fibers in soft peaty colors are woven in factories such as Magee's. Other natural fabrics are woven by Avoca Handweavers (see page 92). They are one of the most high-profile of Ireland's craft enterprises, producing soft worsteds and mohairs in bright, jewel-like colors of blues and pinks, mostly for women's fashions.

Limerick, too, is renowned for its lace

Stephen Pearce
Stephen Pearce's pottery is at Shanagarry, near Cork, and is open to visitors. Only three designs are made, each in a simple, yet sophisticated style, from local clay. One is a black-and-white glazed earthenware range called Shanagarry, another a terracotta range, and the third a blue-and-white design. There may be only three ranges of pottery, but in all these contain over 400 separate items.

Glass factories
Many of Ireland's lead-crystal manufacturers welcome visitors to look around and watch the glass being blown and cut by hand. Most famous is Waterford (see page 143), but other companies such as Tipperary Crystal, Tyrone, Galway, and Cavan will also allow visitors (contact local tourist offices for details). If you prefer a more modern, plain form of glass, one of the most interesting studios to visit is Jerpoint Glass, at Stoneyford in Kilkenny (tel: 056 24350).

Belleek pottery dates back to 1857

193

Lough Derg

This lake, set in desolate bog and moorland east of Donegal, is a popular destination for pilgrims who converge in droves on a tiny island, ostensibly for inner peace and solitude, although Station Island now is virtually covered by buildings—an octagonal basilica and several hostels. St. Patrick is said to have spent 40 days praying and fasting there, and now the island receives up to 15,000 visitors a year. During a three-day summer vigil of prayer and contemplation only black tea and dry toast may be consumed; no sleep is allowed on the first night. Pilgrims walk barefoot around the island's shrines. If this sounds like an interesting weekend break, be warned that penitents come here from all over the world. Book early to avoid disappointment!

Traditional currachs are still widely used on the west coast

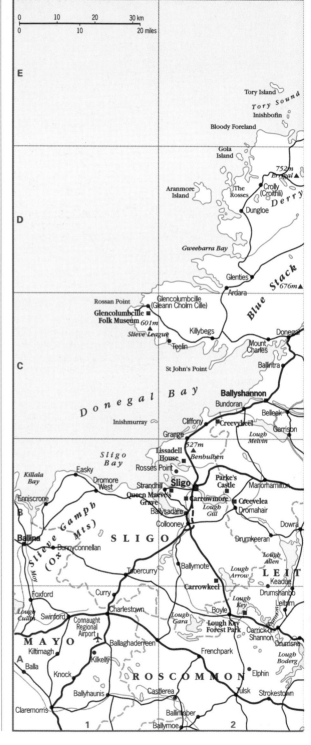

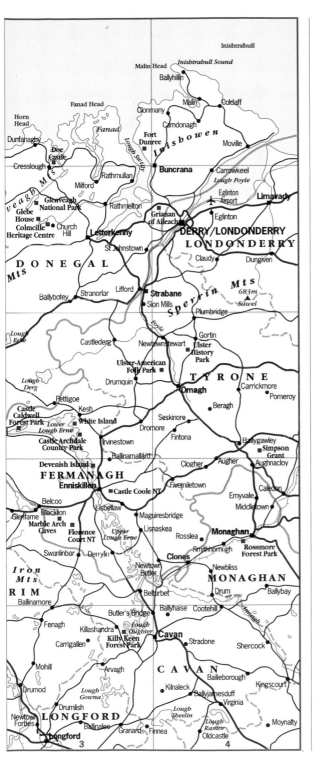

Inishtrahull
Malin Head
Ballyhillin
Inishtrahull Sound
Malin
Culdaff
Clonmany
Carndonagh
Moville
Fanad Head
Horn Head
Dunfanaghy
Fanad
Doe Castle
Cresslough
Lough Swilly
Inishowen
Fort Dunree
Buncrana
Carrowkeel
Lough Foyle
Rathmullan
Milford
veagh Mts
Glenveagh National Park
Glebe House
Colmcille Heritage Centre
Church Hill
Rathmelton
Letterkenny
Grianan of Aileach
St Johnstown
Eglinton Airport
Eglinton
Limavady
DERRY/LONDONDERRY
LONDONDERRY
Claudy
Dungiven
D O N E G A L
Mts
Ballybofey
Stranorlar
Lifford
Strabane
Sion Mills
Foyle
Sperrin **Mts**
683m
Sawel
Plumbridge
Lough Eske
Castlederg
Newtownstewart
Gortin
Ulster History Park
Ulster-American Folk Park
Drumquin
T Y R O N E
Carrickmore
Pomeroy
Lough Derg
Pettigoe
Kesh
Omagh
Beragh
Castle Caldwell Forest Park
White Island
Lower Lough Erne
Seskinore
Dromore
Fintona
Ballygawley
Simpson Grant
Aughnacloy
Castle Archdale Country Park
Irvinestown
Ballinamallard
Clogher
Augher
Devenish Island
F E R M A N A G H
Enniskillen
Castle Coole NT
Fivemiletown
Emyvale
Caledon
Belcoo
Lisbellaw
Middletown
Blacklion
Glenfarne
Maguiresbridge
Marble Arch Caves
Florence Court NT
Upper Lough Erne
Lishaskea
Rosslea
Monaghan
Swanlinbar
Derrylin
Smithborough
Rossmore Forest Park
Iron Mts
Newtown Butler
Clones
Newbliss
R I M
Belturbet
M O N A G H A N
Ballinamore
Drum
Ballybay
Butler's Bridge
Ballyhaise
Cootehill
Fenagh
Killashandra
Lough Oughter
Killy Keen Forest Park
Cavan
Stradone
Shercock
Carrigallen
Mohill
Arvagh
C A V A N
Bailieborough
Kingscourt
Drumod
Kilnaleck
Ballyjamesduff
Lough Gowna
Drumlish
Virginia
Newtown Forbes
L O N G F O R D
Ballinalee
Lough Sheelin
Lough Ramor
Moynalty
Longford
Granard
Finnea
Oldcastle

3

4

The Stolen Child
"Where the wave of moonlight glosses
The dim gray sands with light
Far off by furthest Rosses
We foot it all the night,
Weaving olden dances,
Mingling hands and mingling glances
Till the moon has taken flight;
To and fro we leap
And chase the frothy bubbles,
While the world is full of troubles
And is anxious in its sleep.
Come away, O human child!
To the waters and the wild
With a faery, hand in hand,
For the world's more full of weeping than you can understand."

W. B. Yeats (1865–1939).
(See page 201 for The Rosses.)

Northwestern counties Donegal's spectacular scenery is often considered the best in Ireland, although its location keeps it remote. Outside a brief, intense summer season, when tourists flit through like butterflies, these northern regions (Counties Sligo, Donegal, and Leitrim) can seem forlorn and windswept. All through the year clouds scud rapidly in from the Atlantic, bringing lashing horizontal squalls or drizzling sea mists. Just as suddenly these are followed by shafts of sunlight and vivid rainbows, which transform its glens, cliffs, mountains, and beaches into the landscapes of Irish travel brochures. There, in these far-flung peninsulas, you will find that elusive rural idyll—softly domed ricks of hand-turned hay and whitewashed thatched cottages with scarlet doors. The postcard scene disguises a history of constant struggle against the elements and economic deprivation. In many of these areas emigration is chronic and the population aging. There is little industry other than the old cottage-based crafts of knitting and weaving, although these are now organized to catch the tourist's eye in village-like studio complexes or factories such as Magee's of Donegal Town. Most of the region's income comes from tourism and not all the side-effects are beneficial. On some sections of coastline, insensitive development has resulted in a garish outbreak of modern white bungalows, which bear little relation to their surroundings. Numerous seaside resorts amuse those hardy enough to chance the weather. Bundoran's tawdry image evokes a socially conservative era. Today, some of these splendid unpolluted beaches have achieved a new cachet as Ireland's most outstanding surfing spots.

Northern extremities Tenuously attached to the Republic by a thin isthmus of land between the coast and its severed Ulster neighbors, Donegal waves its tattered banner even farther northward than the Six Counties, constituting Ireland's northernmost extremity. Its cliffs at Slieve League are the highest in Europe and several

The sturdy Irish Draught is especially useful where vehicles cannot venture

wild promontories make important habitats for sea birds. It scores not only with incomparable coastal scenery, but also with inland Glenveagh National Park, where massive glacial valleys carve grandly through moors and blanket bog. Offshore lie several inhabited islands: Tory Island, where the locals fish for lobster and paint naïve art; and Aranmore, more prosperous and biddable, welcoming tourists with vacation cottages.

Third largest county after Cork and Galway, Donegal has the biggest Gaeltacht (Irish-speaking community) in Ireland and nationalist sentiments run high. This is the ancient Gaelic territory of Tir Chonaill—land of Conal. Even after the Flight of the Earls (see pages 34–5), the English never quite got their hands on Donegal's wilder regions, and after partition, though technically part of Ulster, they let it stay with the Republic. Road signs in rural areas may appear only in Irish. A significant proportion of the population on the eastern side of the county are Protestants, however, who look across the border from their prosaic farmland for their spiritual home.

Leitrim and Sligo Farther south is Leitrim, which has a much lower tourist profile than Donegal, and few foreign visitors could pinpoint it on a map. It has pretty enough, but unspectacular, countryside, mostly mixed farmland, lakes and moors on undulating low hills, with just a few dramatic limestone ridges near Manorhamilton. Lough Allen, the first lake on the Shannon, virtually bisects the county, and provides most of its recreational attractions in the form of boating and fishing. Carrick-on-Shannon, the county town, is now a well-established cruise-boat center. Leitrim has few significant historic sights.

Sligo, on the other hand, is rich in history, prehistory, and mythology, with ancient burial places and cairns. The distinctive shapes of Benbulben and Knocknarea loom above the town, redolent of antique Celtic legends. The poet W. B. Yeats has strong links with the county, the scene of his childhood and his last resting place. The landscapes and myths of Sligo weave throughout his best work.

The very Irish Errigal Mountain looms above the white marble church of Dunlewy, County Donegal

The Annals of the Four Masters
During the troubled 17th century a Franciscan monk, Michael O'Cleary, and three lay Gaelic scholars wrote these chronicles of Irish history and mythology. The Annals cover the period from before the Flood to the year 1616, and are an important record of Ireland's Celtic heritage. They are now housed in the National Library in Dublin, where facsimiles of the originals are on display.

► **Ardara**   *194D2*

Knitwear and tweed are the main concerns of this small town at the head of a deep sea-lough (saltwater lake). Outlets vie with each other in the main street, but visitors can, if they prefer, head for any one of half a dozen or so factory shops where you can watch the manufacturing process in action and probably visit a bar or tea shop at the same time. Prices are generally cheaper there than in most retailers. The annual Weavers' Fair in midsummer is a popular local festival with plenty of traditional music and good "crack" (fun). A heritage center has recently been set up in the old law courts. The Church of the Holy Family has a fine stained-glass rose window by the well-known artist Evie Hone.

►► **Carrowkeel, Carrowmore, and Creevykeel**   *194B2*

These confusingly named places are three of the most interesting and important prehistoric sites in the northwestern region. **Carrowkeel►**, in the Bricklieve hills, is an ancient cemetery of circular mounds dating from the late Stone Age (2500 BC–2000 BC). There are some splendid views from the exposed hilltop site. **Carrowmore►►** near Sligo is the largest group of megalithic monuments in the whole of the British Isles, containing about 60 tombs, stone circles, dolmens, and other antiquities, the earliest of which are alleged to predate the famous passage-grave at Newgrange (see pages 108–9) by about 700 years. Many have been damaged or removed, and incredibly, in 1983, plans were drawn up— and luckily abandoned—to turn the site into a dump. **Creevykeel►**, near Mullaghmore, is a fine example of a neolithic court-tomb dating from about 3000 BC, with a double burial chamber surrounded by a wedge-shaped mound of stone. Polished stone axes, worked flints and some bronze Celtic artifacts found there are now in the National Museum in Dublin.

One of the crafts demonstrated at the Donegal Craft Village is the production of tweed

► **Donegal**   *194C2*

Surprisingly, Donegal is not the county town of County Donegal (an honor granted to the somewhat unprepossessing town of Letterkenny), but it is neverthless an attractive and strategic base for exploring the Northwest and, more especially, for shopping. Its main store, Magee's (see panel), is one of the best-known places to buy the regional specialty, Donegal tweed. A short way out of town, on the southern side, are a collection of workshops producing a variety of high-quality crafts—jewelry, handweaving, ceramics, batik, and crystal (look for signs indicating the

*The Diamond,
Donegal Town*

Donegal Craft Village on N15, the main road from Ballyshannon). Several other factory shops can be visited in the area, including those at Ardara (see page 198). **Ballyshannon**, a garrison town to the south, specializes in the region's brand of china, known as Parian ware (because it resembles the clear, white Greek marble from the island of Paros). The **Donegal Parian China Factory►** and visitor center are on the Sligo road. On the Ballyshannon–Belleek road is Celtic Weave China, producing basketware rather similar to the traditional Belleek Parian china produced over the border in Northern Ireland (tours of the factory are free).

Donegal (*Dún na nGall*) means "fort of the foreigners," a reference to its history as a Viking stronghold. After the Vikings left, the town became the headquarters of Tír Chonaill, the territory of the O'Donnell clan. "Red Hugh" O'Donnell built a fortress and a Dominican abbey there in the 15th century. Early in the 17th century the Gaelic chieftains left Ireland in the exodus known as the Flight of the Earls (see pages 34–5), and their lands and castles were appropriated by English and Scottish settlers. Sir Basil Brooke took over Donegal Castle in 1610 and, in the style of the time, enlarged it to a comfortable, if well-defended, Jacobean home with mullioned windows and imposing fireplaces. Today the castle remains are Donegal's most interesting sight. Sir Basil set about making his mark on the town in other ways too, and Donegal displays typical characteristics of Ulster planning, including a classic Diamond (actually a triangular "square") in the city center, where a monument stands to the Four Masters. To the south of town is a lovely stretch of coastline where several rivers flow into Donegal Bay. There the sun sets amid a maze of tranquil islets and sheltered creeks. St. Ernan's Island, reached by a causeway and with an excellent hotel, is one of the best places to enjoy this scenery.

Magee's
This large department store on the north side of the Diamond is an Irish legend, still run by the family who established it in 1866 (the firm has passed to cousins of the original Magees, the Temples). In the late 19th century, handwoven Donegal tweed was produced on wooden looms, some of which are still in use. Magee's is the only company still weaving and tailoring handwoven tweed in Donegal. High-quality men's clothing and suit fabrics are produced under the Magee's label for worldwide export, in light worsteds as well as the hard-wearing, traditional tweed in the soft colors of the Donegal landscape. More than 600 work in two factories using advanced technology, and visitors are welcome for a short, free tour during opening hours. The upstairs café makes a good place for a coffee or light lunch.

THE ATLANTIC COAST

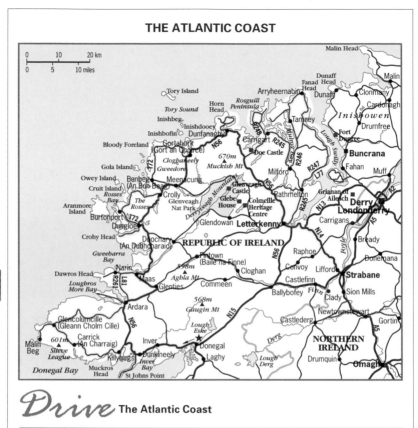

Malin Head, Dunaff, Fanad Head, Dunaff Head, Malin, Clonmany, Cardonagh, Arryheernabin, Tamney, Drumfree, Tory Island, Horn Head, Rosguill Peninsula, Inishbeg, Tory Sound, Inishdooey, Carrigart, R245, R246, Inishowen, Fort Dunree, Buncrana, Inishbofin, Dunfanaghy, Doe Castle, Milford, Fahan, Muff, Bloody Foreland, Gortahork (Gort an Choirce), 670m, Muckish Mt, Lough Swilly, Cloghaneely, Gweedore, Owey Island, Benbeg (An Bun Beag), Meenacung, Glenveagh Castle, Rathmelton, Grianan of Aileach, Derry/Londonderry, Gola Island, Cruit Island, Rosses Bay, The Rosses, Glenveagh, Nat Park, Glebe House, Colmcille Heritage Centre, Carrigans, Aranmore Island, Burtonport, Dungloe, Glendowan, Letterkenny, Bready, Crohy Head, Doochary (An Dubhcharaid), REPUBLIC OF IRELAND, Raphoe, Donemana, Gweebarra Bay, Fintown (Baile na Finne), Convoy, Lifford, Strabane, Narin, 598m, Cloghan, Castlefinn, Dawros Head, Maas, Agbla Mt, Commeen, Ballybofey, Fin, Clady, Sion Mills, Loughros More Bay, Glenties, 568m, Gaugin Mt, Castlederg, Newtownstewart, Gortin, Ardara, Lough Eske, NORTHERN IRELAND, Glencolumcille (Gleann Cholm Cille), Carrick (An Charraig), Inver, Donegal, Derg, Malin Beg, 601m, Slieve League, Killybegs, Dunkineely, Laghy, Lough Derg, Drumquin, Omagh, Donegal Bay, Muckros Head, Inver Bay, St Johns Point

Drive The Atlantic Coast

So complex is north Donegal's coast-line that any tour can take many variations depending how much time you have. Best views are from minor roads rather than N56, but skirting the peninsulas is time-consuming, and roads may be poorly surfaced.

The highlights of the journey are the sculpted rocks at **Crohy Head**►► near Dungloe, the fiery headland known as **Bloody Foreland**►► and the panoramic seascapes around **Horn Head**►► and **Rosguill**►►. If you still have time and a taste for this gorgeous scenery, **Fanad Head**► by the calm fjord of Lough Swilly, or the pastoral **Inishowen Peninsula**►, from which Malin Head relays weather reports, are diverse and unspoiled. Inland, the beautiful and lonely routes through the **Glenveagh National Park**►► are well worth exploring (see page 203).

The weather in this part of Ireland is always uncertain, but its very unpredictability is exhilarating, and compen-

sations include amazing sunsets and glorious rainbows. Facilities for tourists along the Donegal coast are limited but steadily increasing.

The section between Dungloe and Crolly is known as **The Rosses►** (*Na Rosa* means "the headlands"), a bleak, rocky, and fragmented coastline, sometimes worn into stacks and arches. Inland, the terrain is poor, consisting of boulder-strewn bogland waterlogged by myriad tiny lakes and streams. If you have time, you may be able to take a summer boat excursion to **Aran Island►** (also known as Aranmore, but not to be confused with the Aran Islands off Galway Bay) —a 25-minute trip from Burtonport. There's not much to see except bog and lakes, but there are beaches and quiet walks. **Tory Island►** to the north is much less accessible, a treeless wilderness with 150 or so inhabitants who eke out their income from fishing with a school of naïve art. Boat trips leave from several local ports (Bunbeg, Falcarragh, etc.), but you may be marooned in bad weather. Balor, Celtic god of darkness, is said to have lived there on the eastern cliffs.

Gweedore►, the next peninsula, is scenically austere but densely populated, with new cottages springing up along the coast. The most scenic stretch is **Bloody Foreland►►**, a mass of red granite that glows a brilliant color at sunset. The sheer, quartzite cliffs of **Horn Head►►** provide terrific views and a windy ledge for thousands of seabirds. Sheep Haven is particularly attractive, and several roads lead to popular tourist resorts. Marble Hill Strand has a fine beach. **Dunfanaghy** is the main resort, a gentle seaside village near an excellent sandy beach offering windsurfing and canoeing, and a blowhole called **McSwyne's Gun** which "explodes" periodically in rough weather. Beyond Dunfanaghy look out for **Doe Castle►**, a 15th-century fortress rebuilt in Victorian times. Views from the battlements overlook a wide expanse of Sheephaven Bay. Lackagh Bridge provides another vantage point. Inland, the barren, rocky landscape is scattered with lakes. The next outcrop is **Rosguill**, where a 7-mile circular tour called the **Atlantic Drive** is signed past dunes and beaches. Highlights of the **Fanad Peninsula** include the neat plantation villages of **Rathmelton** and **Rathmullan**, where Red Hugh O'Donnell, Earl of Tyrconnell, was treacherously lured onto an English merchant ship for a drink, whereupon he was seized and taken to Dublin prison. On the **Inishowen peninsula►►**, don't miss the stone fort called **Grianán of Aileach**, **Fort Dunree** and **Malin Head** (see pages 206–7 for more details of all these).

The splendor of the Donegal coast

Derek Hill gave Glebe House to the nation in 1980. It makes a short but worthwhile detour from the Glenveagh National Park

Arthur Kingsley Porter
The castle of Glenveagh was once owned by the American art historian Arthur Kingsley Porter, a specialist in medieval sculpture. One day in 1939, he set off on a fishing trip in Donegal; later his boat was found abandoned on an island without a trace of its former occupant. Wagging tongues said he feigned his disappearance to escape an unhappy domestic life; claims that he had been spotted subsequently in the French port of Marseilles and as a Buddhist monk in the Himalayas have never been substantiated, and his real fate remains tantalizingly unknown.

One of the early-Christian standing stones in or near Glencolumbcille

►► Glebe House   195D3

This Regency building on Lough Gartan, a rectory dating from 1828, was for 30 years the home of the landscape and portrait artist, Derek Hill, who hailed originally from England. He furnished the house with immense taste and care, using a great mix of styles and art from all over the world, including oriental and Middle Eastern tapestries and ceramics, Victoriana and original William Morris papers and textiles. Donegal folk art is also well represented and in the adjacent gallery are works by Picasso, Bonnard, Kokoschka, Renoir, Augustus John, and other leading 19th- and 20th-century artists. A particularly interesting part of the collection contains works by the naïve school of painters on Tory Island, notably James Dixon. Temporary exhibitions are held during the summer opening period (end of May–early October).

► Glencolumbcille   194C1

The scenery is the great draw here; the drive along the north shore of Donegal Bay beyond the fishing port of Killybegs past the grand cliffs of Slieve League is thoroughly spectacular, through sheep-strewn moorland, heather, and turf-cut bog to a boiling mass of rocks and sea stacks by the shore. A detour by the coast, for example to the picturesque Gaelic-speaking estuary village of Teelin, is especially recommended. Glencolumbcille, as its name suggests, has many associations with St. Columba (Columbcille), the 6th-century saint from Lough Gartan who lived there for a time. On the saint's day (June 9) pilgrims conduct a barefoot procession around the area, pausing to pray at various antiquities such as early Christian cross-slabs.

A more recent benefactor, as yet uncanonized, was the energetic priest, Father James MacDyer, who made strenuous efforts to alleviate the area's chronic poverty and unemployment. He was responsible for setting up a number of collective enterprises to provide work. The most high-profile of these is the **Folk Village►**, on the edge of town, clearly signed. It is a small project using reconstructed cottages to simulate life in bygone Ireland. Three small dwellings are replicas of those typical in the area during the 1720s, 1820s, and 1920s, furnished with items of the period. The reception building sells craft souvenirs from all over Ireland, and the Shebeen café offers a variety of curious beverages, including some made from fuchsia or seaweed. A "famine pot," filled daily with an unenticing brew of the type of corn porridge during the hungry years, stands in the yard.

►► Glenveagh National Park   195D3

Twenty-five thousand acres of wild scenery make up this park of glaciated valleys and open moorland around Lough Beagh. Parts of the park are wooded with native oak and birch or imported rhododendron and spruce. The approach via Dunlewy at the foot of Mount Errigal gives some of the most spectacular views. Off the main road, an expedition to the Poisoned Glen is worth taking (so called because of a toxic variety of spurge, a shrub that grows by the waterside). Beside Lough Beagh stands the estate of Glenveagh Castle, created during the mid-19th century by John George Adair who built the castellated mansion in about 1870. He is remembered mostly for the harsh eviction of all his tenants after the murder of one of his estate managers in 1861. He later emigrated to the United States. His wife, however, is remembered more fondly. She returned to Glenveagh after her husband's death and created the 27 acres of glorious gardens around the castle.

During the Civil War the castle was occupied by the I.R.A. and the Free State Army, then restored by a benevolent American owner who later transferred the land to the Irish National Parks Service. The estate contains the largest herd of red deer in Ireland, believed to number about 600 at present. A visitor center is unobtrusively located on the estate (free minibus service to the castle in summer) with nature trails and an audiovisual show.

Tory Island
A story about the Tory islanders claims that in 1884 a British gunboat, *The Wasp*, was dispatched to reprimand the inhabitants and to collect unpaid taxes. The islanders apparently called upon the forces of Balor, the one-eyed Celtic god of darkness, by circling the wishing stones in the center of the island, and the gunboat promptly sank with all but six hands.

Glenveagh Castle and gardens

Irish cinema, like that in the U.K., is in a fairly parlous state, and funding is always difficult. But it has a great stock of talent, Ireland's theatrical traditions raising many fine actors and some noteworthy directors, too. Some delightful low-budget films have been made wholly in Ireland in recent years, such as *Eat the Peach*, set in Longford.

Top: John Wayne and Maureen O'Hara starred in The Quiet Man, *roughly a cross between* The Taming of the Shrew *and* Much Ado about Nothing, *set in rural Ireland*

204

Richard Harris in pensive mood in the immensely successful The Field. *Critics, however, could never quite decide whether the plot lived up to the dramatic scenery*

Ireland stars In many films, Ireland itself is the star of the big screen. Directors of many nationalities have used Irish locations for movies—even ones not set specifically in Ireland—the soft beauty of its landscapes overcoming the vagaries of its climate. Earliest films included *Life on the Great Southern and Western Railway* (1904) and *In the Days of St. Patrick* (1919). Better remembered is Robert Flaherty's *Man of Aran,* made in 1934. This documentary of the harsh lifestyle endured on the Aran Islands has now become a classic, though it was not accurate in all respects—shark-fishing, for example, had not been customary on the Aran Islands for over 60 years. It is regularly shown in Kilronan, the largest community on Inishmore, during the summer tourist season. *The Dawn,* set in Killarney, was made in 1937 by Tom Cooper, a story of the War of Independence using highly effective location sequences. In 1947 a British film was made about the story of Captain Boycott (see panel on page 189), villain of the struggle for tenants' land rights during the 19th century, starring Cecil Parker and Stewart Granger.

A stunning backdrop Several films of the 1950s used Irish backdrops, too. Most notable of these was probably *The Quiet Man,* a John Ford film of 1952 with John Wayne and Maureen O'Hara. Much of the filming was done around Cong, in County Galway, and some of the stars stayed at the local posh hotel, Ashford Castle. It's a Beatrice and Benedick love story of an American who returns to Innisfree to find a bride, and good-naturedly perpetuates many Hollywood myths about the Irish. Yet another version of *Moby Dick* appeared in 1956, and the director, John Huston, chose the picturesque Cork town of Youghal for his harbor scenes. Rock Hudson is said to have sampled all the bars of Trim, County Meath, in 1955 during the filming of *Captain Lightfoot,* where the old Norman bridge played a leading role.

The National Film Studios were established at Ardmore in 1975, although lack of capital made this indigenous enterprise still largely dependent on foreign investment.

Films set in Ireland

Only John Boorman's production *Excalibur* (both produced and financed in Ireland) could be descibed as an "Irish film" of the thirty or so films made there between 1975 and 1980. Stanley Kubrick used Caher Castle, Tipperary, and Huntington Castle, in County Carlow, for *Barry Lyndon,* a gorgeously photographed, if rather static, version of Thackeray's tale about an Irish adventurer.

1980s and 1990s Many more recent films have featured Irish locations. *Cal*, by Pat O'Connor, dealt sensitively with I.R.A. conflicts, *Far and Away* used the Temple Bar district of Dublin to represent 19th-century Boston, and *Educating Rita* found Trinity College a more suitable icon for an English university than either Oxford or Cambridge. *The Commitments* and *My Left Foot* (the moving story of a severely handicapped writer played in Oscar-winning style by Daniel Day-Lewis) were also set in Dublin. So was *The Lonely Passion of Judith Hearne* (though Brian Moore's novel was set in Belfast), a poignant tale of a genteel spinster music teacher, played by Maggie Smith, who falls disastrously in love with a gold-digging ne'er-do-well—Bob Hoskins. *The Miracle*, directed by Neil Jordan (recently more famous for *The Crying Game*, which also has Irish connections) is set in Bray and Dublin, and is one of his more "Irish" films.

In sharp contrast, the lush location photography of *The Field*, filmed in the Connemara village of Leenane, sears itself on the viewer's retina; that sort of Irish green almost hurts your eyes. Leenane was a natural choice for this grim tale written by John B. Keane, full of tiny fields and looming hills. John Hurt and Richard Harris starred, and once again, the film created a local legend, with many residents earning bit parts as extras. Many of the buildings and pubs in the village proudly commemorate their appearance in the film. *December Bride*, a spare tale of nonconformist passion, is one of the few non-terrorist films to be set north of the border.

Ryan's Daughter

The blockbuster in 1970 was unquestionably David Lean's emotive love story, *Ryan's Daughter*. For this an entire village was built on the beautiful far western tip of the Dingle peninsula, at Dunquin. Few vestiges of this remain today, but the film still lives on in the imaginations of local people, many of whom were used as extras, and for a while had a taste of Hollywood glamor. The story, by Robert Bolt, is set at the time of the Easter Rising and tells of an Irish woman who falls for a British officer, to the horror of all. The film had a star cast (John Mills, Sarah Miles, Robert Mitchum) and had great box-office success, if dismissed as over-romanticized by the critics. Certainly Lean picked his set with care—Dunquin is a magical place.

Local extras stare down the street of the purpose-built village in Ryan's Daughter. *One critic, Pauline Kael, wrote of the film, "Gush made respectable by millions of dollars tastefully wasted"*

Fort Dunree

A short way north of Buncrana is Fort Dunree Military Museum, an example of a coastal defense battery. The building was originally constructed in 1880 to guard the entrance to Lough Swilly. Martello towers augmented a series of heavy guns. At the beginning of World War I a British fleet of 40 warships assembled at Dunree Head to protect the convoys that gathered here for the North Atlantic run. In 1917 a U.S. base was established there, but 21 years later it was handed over to the Irish Republic and was last manned in 1952.

Some believe that the Grianán of Aileach was designed for sun-worshipping rituals, with hundreds watching the goings-on from the terraces

►► Grianán of Aileach 195D4

This remarkable circular fortress lies about 8 miles south of Buncrana, perched on a hilltop and reached by a small winding lane. Aerial photographs of it, such as the one below, show the stone ring-fort in an emerald pool of grassland amid scrubby tufts of brownish heather and gorse. The name means "stone palace of the sun." Similar *cashel* forts can be seen elsewhere in Ireland, such as Staigue Fort in County Kerry. Its precise age is disputed, some authorities dating it well before the Christian era (about 1700 BC), others rather later. Its suspiciously neat appearance is due to enthusiastic restoration during the 1870s by Dr. Walter Bernard, a Derry historian. The round enclosure measures about 75 feet across, with walls 17 feet high and 13 feet thick. A single gate allows access to the interior, which contains four tiers of steps and various passages or storage places. It was recorded by Ptolemy in the 2nd century AD and was used as a stronghold by the O'Neill kings for several centuries before its gradual destruction. If you are lucky enough to visit it on a fine day the views from this hilltop are amazing, stretching for huge distances over Derry, the Fanad and Inishowen peninsulas, and the Swilly estuary.

►► Inishowen peninsula 195E4

Ireland's most northerly point lies in the Republic on this ragged triangular headland, not in Northern Ireland as most people would expect. Lough Foyle and Lough Swilly virtually isolate Inishowen from the rest of the county. The interior is a mix of low white farms and cottages huddling roped against the wind, and grand brown mountains rising toward Slieve Snaght. The scenic 100-mile route around the edge of Inishowen takes in Malin Head, castles, churches, High Crosses and pre-Christian antiquities. None of these is essential viewing, but the tour, which takes a full day, is a dramatic and varied drive.

Buncrana is the main center, a popular holiday resort much favored by inhabitants of Derry. Throughout the

centuries it witnessed many clashes between English and Irish. Ireland's remote extremities were always feared (not without reason) as a potential Achilles' heel in English defenses against invading Catholic forces from Spain or France, and any hints of disaffection were dealt with ruthlessly. In 1602 the O'Dohertys prepared to welcome a second Spanish armada here and a couple of centuries later Wolfe Tone was held in Buncrana Castle after his abortive rebellion in 1798. Buncrana also has a Vintage Car Museum.

Malin▶ is a 17th-century plantation village built around a green, its most striking feature a long bridge of stone arches. Malin Head relays weather reports from the fishing village of Ballyhillin, sheltered from the worst of the storms by the rocky promontory. Several minor historical sights—such as crosses and stone circles—are clustered around Carndonagh.

Inch Level
Inch Level, on Lough Swilly, at the base of the Inishowen peninsula, is the most important wetland habitat in the Northwest and has international status as a bird reserve. Mute and whooper swans live here or visit it for part of the year. Brent and barnacle geese and other wildfowl migrate to Trawbreaga Bay in winter.

▶ **Letterkenny** *195D3*

Donegal's county town is now the main commercial center of the Republic's Northwest region and, as such, has several bustling shopping centers. It guards the lowest bridging point on the River Swilly, just before it widens into the scenic fjord known as Lough Swilly. There are few especially attractive views of this from the town itself, however, which is on the whole not all that interesting. Its main claims to fame are the longest main street in Ireland and the lofty spire of the Victorian neo-Gothic St. Eunan's Cathedral, which has a handsome altar of Carrara marble and rich stained glass. Look for the Four Masters carved on the pulpit. The Irish patriot Wolfe Tone was captured in Letterkenny in 1798 after his foiled invasion with French allies, and taken to Dublin under heavy guard. The county museum is housed in the old workhouse and the regional tourist office just out of town on the N56. Letterkenny makes a useful base for exploring inland Donegal, including the Blue Stack Mountains and the Glenveagh National Park.

St. Eunan's Cathedral, Letterkenny, was built by Donegal masons using Donegal sandstone

207

▶ Lough Gartan   195D3

Donegal's local saint, Columba (or Colmcille/Columbcille in Irish), was born by the beautiful shores of Lough Gartan in AD 521. A modern building on the eastern shore houses the **Colmcille Heritage Centre▶**, which outlines the saint's life (see page 114) and the rise of Christianity in Ireland. An interesting feature is an exhibition on the preparation of illuminated manuscripts, using parchment and natural pigments. At the saint's alleged birthplace are two sacred stones around which various superstitions have spread. Pregnant women pray at the Natal Stone to ensure a safe delivery, while the Stone of Loneliness warded off the anguish of homesickness and was a popular place of pilgrimage for those about to emigrate.

▶▶ Parke's Castle   194B2

A fortified manor house with an interestingly checkered history stands by the calm waters of Lough Gill. Built in 1609 by an Ulster settler, Captain Robert Parke, it occupies the site of a much earlier tower house belonging to the O'Rourke clan, rulers of the kingdom of Breffni. The last unfortunate O'Rourke lord sheltered a shipwrecked Spanish Armada officer and was executed in London, for treason. Features of the medieval structure can be seen in the later house. Recently it has been sensitively restored using original materials and local craftsmanship, and now represents a fascinating piece of research and reconstruction. Its witch-hat turrets face the mirror-like lake, and there are splendid views from its ramparts. Beyond the outer defenses near the water's edge lies a little beehive hut of stone. This is a sweatbox, or early Irish sauna, used to alleviate various ailments. Exhibitions and an audio-visual show about the castle and many local places of interest, including Sligo's impressive range of antiquities, can be seen inside; free guided tours are available. From the jetty you can take a boat around Lough Gill, calling at the Yeatsian island of Innisfree (see panel).

Parke's Castle stands on the shores of Lough Gill, considered one of Ireland's most picturesque loughs. About 5 miles long, Lough Gill resembles a smaller version of the Lakes of Killarney

The eerie light of dawn on Lough Gill

▶ **Rathmelton**   195D3

This dignified plantation town is all stately warehouses and seemly Georgian buildings on a salmon river. It was built by Sir William Stewart for settlers during the early 17th century. The River Leannan was once an important waterway and in earlier times Rathmelton was a significant port exporting grain, salmon, butter and linen (a more unusual product was iodine, made from local seaweed). A new heritage center in the former Presbyterian meeting house displays information both on the town's history and on the founding of American Presbyterianism.

An exhibit from the Flight of the Earls Heritage Centre, Rathmullan

▶ **Rathmullan**   195D3

The eastern side of the Fanad peninsula, overlooking the fjord-like scenery of Lough Swilly, is the most appealing drive, and this fortified harbor village is one of the most interesting places to visit. Before the battery was constructed by the English to ward off Napoleonic attacks, Rathmullan figured twice in Irish history. First, it was the place where "Red Hugh" O'Donnell, the Ulster chieftain, was treacherously lured on board a disguised merchant ship for a convivial drink, only to find himself in chains on his way to Dublin Castle, where he languished for six years. Twenty years later, the Earls of Tyrone and of Tyrconnell finally left Ireland from Rathmullan in the incident known as the Flight of the Earls (see pages 34–5). Initially they had hopes of raising support against the English from Spanish allies, but their plans came to nothing and they died in exile, leaving their great estates and castles to be occupied by Ulster settlers. A heritage center in the old fort recounts the history of this period. Another of Rathmullan's attractions is a country house hotel, Rathmullan House (see Hotels and Restaurants, page 276), one of Donegal's most comfortable bases, with a good restaurant.

209

The Dominican Friary, more usually known as Sligo Abbey

The Battle of the Books
A tragic storm in a teacup —but an important principle of copyright—lies at the heart of this curious incident, which took place at Cooldrumman, north of Sligo. In AD 561 St. Columba borrowed a psalter from St. Finian and surreptitiously copied it. When St. Finian found out he angrily demanded the copy. St. Columba refused and the pair went to arbitration at the court of the High King, Diarmuid. He decided in favor of St. Finian, with the famous judgment, "To every cow its calf; to every book its copy." St. Columba refused to accept the ruling and raised an army against St. Finian; more than 3,000 men were killed. St. Columba was the victor, but, stricken with remorse, he went to live in exile in Iona off the Scottish coast, where he died in 597.

The eye-catching monument to W. B. Yeats, winner of the Nobel Prize for Literature in 1923, in Sligo Town

► **Sligo** 194B2

Sligo is one of the largest towns in the Northwest, a lively market town and center for music pubs and eating places, designed more for its own 18,000 inhabitants than for tourists. Colorful houses stand alongside the River Garavogue, which runs through the center, and the town still has many old quarters and shops of great character. Its literary associations give it a cultural cachet and it now receives a great annual influx of scholars and students on the Yeats trail, especially during August when a Yeats summer school is held.

Sligo was sacked by the Vikings in 807 and, situated as it is on the fringes of Connaught and Ulster, later became a key location for warring clans. The Anglo-Norman Fitzgeralds held sway in the 13th century when the castle (now vanished) and abbey were built. Later the O'Conors and O'Donnells fought for supremacy, and in Cromwellian times the town was one of the last Jacobite strongholds. During the Famine the population fell drastically and massive emigration occurred.

Sligo's main sights are its 13th-century Dominican abbey, sacked in 1641, and its **museum and art gallery►** which houses many documents relating to W. B. Yeats, together with paintings by his brother, Jack. The town has two cathedrals, the Church of Ireland St. John's, designed by Richard Castle in 1730, and the 19th-century Catholic cathedral. Hargadon's pub is a local institution. It recently deigned to allow women inside, but otherwise firmly retains its old-world character and décor, with tiny dark booths and swiveling windows around which drinks could be passed with ease.

Outside the town loom the great hulks of Benbulben (1,722 feet) and Knocknarea (1,083 feet), like upturned ships. Both hills can be climbed, but can be treacherous in the mist because of the deep fissures in the rain-eroded limestone. Benbulben is the legendary death site of Diarmuid, who eloped with Gráinne. Knocknarea, to the southwest, is supposed to be the burial place of the warrior Queen Maeve (though she died elsewhere), and is surmounted by a massive cairn of 40,000 tons of rock.

YEATS COUNTRY

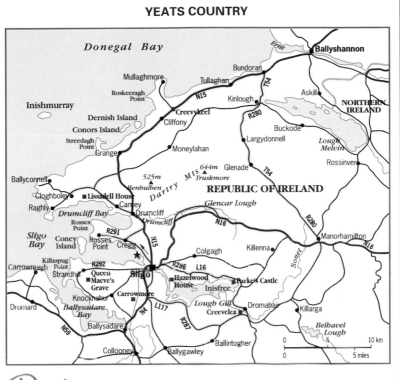

𝒟rive Yeats Country and Benbulben

You're never far from **Benbulben** on this tour, the mountain that so inspired Yeats. The coast is quiet and much broken; inland are lakes and pastures.

This area is called "Yeats Country" as the poet passed much of his childhood and was eventually buried here, though his adult life was largely spent in Dublin, and in Galway at Thoor Ballylee or at Coole Park. Above Sligo Town the curious hulk of Benbulben looms like a capsized ship, its flat limestone top scored by erosion. Off N15 north of Sligo is **Drumcliff** churchyard, where Yeats's tomb lies. Minor roads from N15 lead past the headland of **Rosses Point▶**. Farther up, follow the coastal turning to **Lissadell House▶** (open June–mid-September), 19th-century home of the Gore-Booth family. Sisters Eva Gore-Booth and Constance Markiewicz (see page 66), friends of Yeats,

took part in the Easter Rising. The house, in need of restoration, is surrounded by rampant vegetation. On the promontory of **Mullaghmore** is Classie Bawn (private), former home of Lord Mountbatten, who was killed on his boat by the I.R.A. in 1979.

From the resort of **Bundoran▶**, a well-marked drive to Manorhamilton takes you past typical limestone ridge scenery. From there, go west around the north shore of **Glencar Lough,** where a waterfall drops 33 feet through ferny rocks to a pool (in Yeats's poem *The Stolen Child*). Return to Sligo, then strike east for a drive around of **Lough Gill▶▶**, famous for the lake-isle, Innisfree. Summer cruises are available from Sligo, Dromahair or Parke's Castle (see page 208). Other sites on the lough are the ruined Creevelea Friary, and the Deerpark Monument, a series of stone burial chambers dating from about 3500 BC.

Victorian homage to the art of drinking: the Crown Liquor Saloon in Belfast

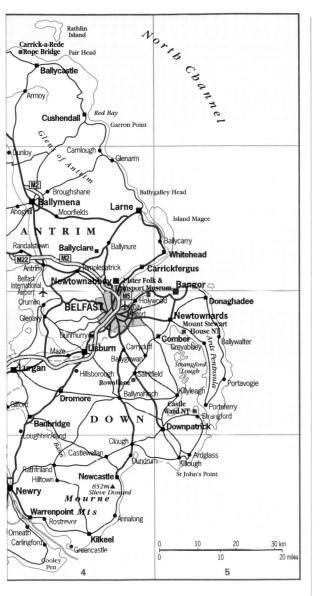

Northern Ireland For many years, the Troubles have been a significant factor in any decision to visit Northern Ireland. The ghastly incidents that have periodically hit the headlines in the past may suggest that sectarian violence and random slaughter are constant. This isn't so. Northern Ireland is, most of the time, in most places, as tranquil as anywhere in the South—and that makes it pretty quiet. Statistically, tourists are much less likely to suffer misadventure than in many other resort locations; street crime rates are low, personal violence rare. This doesn't mean you shouldn't keep your wits about you, particularly in sensitive zones such as Derry, Armagh, or Newry.

The relief of Derry,
see panel on page 224

Crossing the border
Don't pick up hitchhikers near the border. Before driving in Northern Ireland, check your insurance. If you have rented a car in the Republic you must inform the company when you pick up the car that you intend traveling in the North (and vice versa). Major rental companies are fully covered for all Ireland and make no extra charge.

In most places the transition from the Republic to the North is barely noticeable. An unmanned or sleepy checkpoint, a wave of a hand and you're through. Nonetheless, always be ready to stop, state your destination and produce a passport or driver's license. Security forces on both sides are courteous to bona fide travelers and traffic is rarely delayed for long.

Cars are best parked in official parking lots or in pay-and-display areas (where you buy a sticker allowing you to park for a certain length of time). Some towns and cities have signed control zones where vehicles must not be left unattended, and illegal parking may cause a security alert. Outside the trouble spots, Northern Ireland feels, and is, entirely peaceful. Wherever they come from, visitors receive a warm welcome. Local people, whether Catholic or Protestant, are extraordinarily hospitable. Most of them are on perfectly good terms with their neighbors of whatever creed and it is often baffling to imagine where the tension lies. The vast majority of people are simply interested in getting on with their lives in peace.

Scottish connections The closeness of Scotland to Ulster (a mere 13 miles at its narrowest point) has always influenced the province strongly, even before the plantation years (see pages 34–5). Waves of invaders made the short sea crossing, most notably Edward Bruce, brother of the famous Scottish leader, Robert, who first arrived at Carrickfergus with his "gallowglasses" (mercenaries) in 1315. Settlement hasn't always been one-way: during the 4th and 5th centuries AD, Irish Celts made their way to various westerly parts of Britain. But the people who returned during the reign of James I were mostly Scottish Presbyterians—tough, industrious, and determined to the point of intransigence. Northern Ireland has been supported since the plantation years by massive financial support from Britain, but its economic success could not have been achieved without the settlers' Protestant work ethic and resourcefulness. These characteristics show in the many pioneers who left Ulster to seek their fortune in the New World. The "Scotch-Irish" who emigrated to the United States have had an influence out of all proportion to their numbers. Presidents Kennedy and Reagan were of Irish Catholic stock, but about a dozen former presidents were of Ulster Scottish descent. Theodore Roosevelt was one of these and his mother described her Antrim forebears in these telling terms: "grim, stern people... relentless, revengeful, suspicious... also upright, resolute and fearless, loyal to their friends and devoted to their country."

Town and country The scenery of Northern Ireland is its primary attraction and most of the tourism is concentrated in a few clearly defined rural areas: the Mountains of Mourne; the Glens of Antrim; the Causeway Coast; and the Lakes of Fermanagh. Other less well-known areas such as Lough Neagh and the wild Sperrin Mountains are now becoming more popular destinations for walking, fishing, etc., and several forest parks have been created. The Ulster Way is one of Ireland's best long-distance footpaths, leading through the province's most scenic and beautiful landscapes in all six counties. But it is the cities of the North, especially Belfast and Derry, that give a complete picture of the province and these cannot be ignored if you want to see more than the surface prettiness.

The North is particularly strong on museums and boasts a fine collection of stately homes and gardens (its Georgian houses are generally better preserved than in the Republic). In many ways Northern Ireland's landscapes are similar to the Republic's, however the North is more intensively industrialized (in parts) and the towns and villages seem generally more prosperous and tidy.

Checkpoints aside, it's easy to get around. Roads are generally good and the traffic regulations, like the telephone and postal systems, are the same as in the rest of the U.K. Irish *punts* are accepted in some places but most take only sterling.

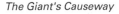

The Giant's Causeway

BELFAST

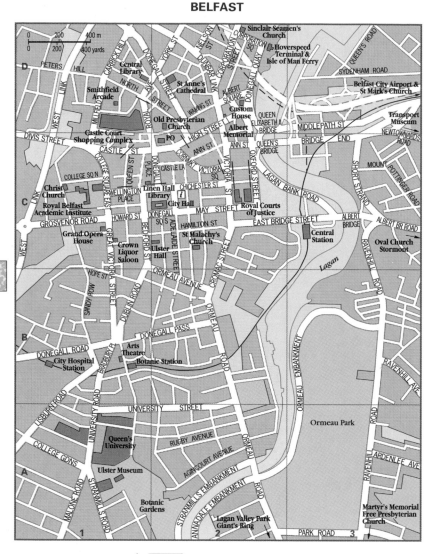

► **Belfast** *213B4*

Since Partition, Belfast has been the official capital of Northern Ireland. It is not the seat of government, however; Northern Ireland has been ruled directly from Westminster since 1972 and the grandiose and ornate Stormont, the former Northern Ireland Parliament building, is now administrative offices. With a population of around 400,000, Belfast is much smaller than Dublin and a large exodus of the younger middle classes during the past two decades to dormitory suburbs has unbalanced the city center's demography, although it is still a transient home for over 8,000 university students. Apart from its two best museums, none of its sights is hugely compelling, but there is certainly plenty to do for a day or two, and the city has a highly distinctive atmosphere.

Few people unfamiliar with the city will immediately warm to the prospect of a stay there. Religious bigotry, sectarian violence, and deliberately high-profile security measures have in the past given the impression to outsiders that Northern Ireland's capital is a war zone. Like many things in Ireland, however, the reality is a surprise. If anything, Belfast is less of a risk for the average visitor than Dublin. Security checks and searches (much less stringent since the 1994 ceasefire) are endured with the stoicism that prevailed during World War II, when Belfast's dockyard targets caused many civilian casualties. Despite security alerts, the show goes on. Indeed, Belfast hosts one of the U.K.'s liveliest and most acclaimed arts festivals at Queen's University each November, as well as an impressive year-round series of concerts, exhibitions, opera and drama. Restaurants along its Golden Mile bustle; sports events flourish.

The great engineering works that once made Belfast so prosperous are in sad decline and unemployment figures in the province are among the highest in the U.K. Its earliest industries included rope and linen making, cotton spinning, and printing. In 1859 the U.K.'s largest shipyards were established here by the Yorkshire engineer Edward Harland and a marine draftsman from Hamburg, Gustav Wilhelm Wolff. Two vast yellow cranes

Like Dublin, Belfast lies close to hills, in this instance Cave Hill, north of the city

217

The welcome at Larry's Bar is warmer than the ghostly images might imply

with the initials "H & W" painted on them still dominate the dockland skyline as powerfully as any cathedral and are affectionately known as Samson and Goliath. The recent cutback in these mighty shipyards was a great psychological blow to the city, as well as an economic one. Other firms closely associated with Belfast are Shorts, the aircraft manufacturers, and Gallahers, the tobacco giant.

Belfast's setting is often praised more than the city itself. The name derives from the Gaelic *beal feirste*, meaning "mouth of the sandy ford," and Belfast stands at the head of a deep seawater lake surrounded by unspoiled hills, the River Lagan cutting through its heart. Belfast has abundant parks and open spaces, all documented by the tourist authorities (pick up leaflets in their office on North Street). Within minutes fast roads can take you beyond the city to scenic areas such as the Ards Peninsula or Strangford Lough; it is a slightly longer trip to the Mountains of Mourne or the Glens of Antrim.

The city's commercial center and university area lie close to the river on its western side; prosperous residential districts are to the east and south. On the far west of town, beyond the dividing pale of the Westlink motorway, are the notorious sectarian ghettos that have given the city its

Belfast's City Hall was designed by Crumwell Thomas in 1906; the staircase in the Entrance Hall is lit by seven stained-glass windows depicting scenes from the city's history

worst reputation. The overcrowded, rundown areas of Ballymurphy, Falls, and Shankill are depressing and can easily be avoided. To some, however, they are oddly fascinating, and intrepid visitors venture there to see their vivid and sometimes highly artistic displays of street mural propaganda (both Catholic and Protestant varieties, incidentally, may be carried out by the same artist!). There are slight risks; in 1992 a tourist visiting her family was killed by a stray sniper's bullet. If you want to visit these areas, you can take one of the black cabs that assemble in lines at the edge of the city center, plying strictly within either Catholic or Protestant territory. To see the Catholic Falls

The City Hall, in the background, is built around a central quadrangle

The *Girona*
Legend has it that one of the strange formations along the Causeway Coast confused the sailors of the Spanish Armada, fleeing after their defeat, who believed it to be Dunluce Castle (2 miles west). The galleass *Girona* was wrecked in 1588 at Port-na-Spaniagh with all but five hands—a loss of about 1,300 lives. Artifacts salvaged from the ship in 1967 are now on display at Belfast's excellent Ulster Museum, including cannon, rings, coins, and a quaint, gold salamander ornament set with rubies.

The Palm House at Belfast's Botanic Gardens is one of the oldest examples of a structure made of cast iron and curved glass, dating from 1839–1852

area (Andersonstown), pick up a cab at Castle Street; to visit Shankill, go to North Street. Bear in mind that your fare could possibly be a donation toward some terrorist organization, to which the driver may (or may not) belong. On the Falls route you will pass the notorious Divis Flats, some of the saddest housing in Europe, and St. Peter's Catholic Cathedral in 19th-century Gothic. The Peace Line is a barricade of iron dividing Protestant and Catholic areas. On the Protestant side, murals can be seen all along the Shankill and Donegall roads, the most famous image being King William on a white steed, rearing from the waters of the Boyne.

Main sights

Belfast is essentially a Victorian city, modeled on those robust mercantile centers such as Liverpool and Manchester across the water. The poet John Betjeman found much to admire in the city's civic architecture, notably its **Custom House**▶ near the docks (not open to the public), several palatial bank buildings near the High Street, and the **City Hall**▶▶ on Donegall Square, a flamboyant structure of white Portland limestone. Inside, the City Hall contains many interesting features and rich decorations of marble and glass—guided tours are available on Wednesday mornings. Donegall Square contains gardens, statues and several other noteworthy buildings, such as the **Linen Hall Library**▶, with a fine collection of volumes in its old-fashioned interior. The Albert Memorial Clock, on Victoria Street, was built in 1865 by William Barre, and depicts Prince Albert in the robes of the Order of the Garter. The tower now leans slightly from the vertical.

Also in the city center (large parts of which are pedestrianized) is **St. Anne's Cathedral**▶, on Donegall Street.

The Grand Opera House had fallen into such disrepair that it closed in 1971, eventually reopening in 1980 after five years of restoration. Since then it has sadly fallen victim to terrorist bombs, being badly damaged in both 1991 and 1993

Belfast's Anglican cathedral is austere neo-Romanesque, enlivened inside by mosaics and a floor made of stone from all parts of Ireland. Sir Edward Carson, architect of Partition, is buried there. **St. Malachy's►►**, in Alfred Street, was built in 1844, the plain red-brick exterior of this Roman Catholic church disguising a glorious inner riot of plasterwork in Strawberry Hill Gothic style. **Sinclair Seamen's Church►** in dockland is another of Belfast's most striking churches, with a jaunty nautical theme. The oval **First Presbyterian Church►**, opened in 1783, has an unusual interior designed by Roger Mulholland. For a truly unforgettable flavor of Belfast, head for the Martyrs' Memorial Free Presbyterian Church, also east of the river, where the Reverend Ian Paisley presides each Sunday, denouncing the Church of Rome and all its works.

Belfast has some extremely florid architecture, particularly at the start of its Golden Mile, stretching along Great Victoria Street towards the university. The **Crown Liquor Saloon►** is a splendidly ornate, gaslit Victorian pub now in the care of the National Trust, all colored marbles, tiles, mirrors, and paneled booths. Good Irish food is served, but lunchtimes can be busy. The **Grand Opera House►►** is a beautiful Victorian theater, badly damaged in bomb attacks in 1991 and 1993. It contains a typically lavish auditorium and presents performances of many kinds. Of the same era, but in a different style, is **Queen's University►** on University Road. The main building boasts an impressive façade of Tudor Gothic red brick and stone mullions. Close by are the **Botanic Gardens►** in Stranmillis Road, an oasis of lawns and gardens sloping to the river. Its two main structures are the **Palm House►** and the **Tropical Ravine House►**.

On the grounds of the Botanic Gardens is a modern building housing what is certainly one of Ireland's best museums. The **Ulster Museum►►►** has a varied and extensive collection, though anything but wearisome.

Queen's University, with its Tudor style building, was founded in 1849

Belfast's tropical jungle is to be found at the Botanic Gardens, south of the city

Belfast Castle (completed in 1870) was built in the style of Balmoral, the Queen's Scottish residence, and designed by W.H. Lynn

Flamingos cope with unfamiliar weather at Belfast Zoo

Schoolchildren delight in its dinosaurs; others may prefer its sparkling minerals or exquisite ceramics. The sections devoted to Belfast's industrial heritage are excellent, as is its clear and unpartisan summary of Ulster's history. One of its most popular sections contains treasures and artifacts from the Spanish Armada ship, *Girona*, wrecked on the Causeway Coast. It has a fine collection of paintings, too, including some interesting 18th-century representations of the Giant's Causeway by Susanna Drury.

Outside the city center lie several other sights. **Belfast Castle►**, some way north on the lower slopes of Cave Hill, is a Victorian Scottish baronial house, with attractive gardens and fine views of the harbor area. Belfast's **zoo►** is pleasantly set in former gardens near the castle and is just one of many parks and open spaces in and near the city boundaries. **Lagan Valley Park►** is one of the largest of these, with 10 miles of towpaths and locks; nearby is a prehistoric earthwork called **The Giant's Ring►**. On A20, 4 miles east, is **Stormont►**, a grand, classical building, once housing the Northern Ireland Parliament and now serving as administrative offices. It stands proudly at the top of a sweeping drive through neat parkland. The Scottish baronial Stormont Castle nearby contains the office of the Northern Ireland Secretary of State, the British Cabinet Minister responsible for the province. Both can be viewed only from outside for obvious reasons. See page 235 for details of Ulster's Folk and Transport Museum in Cultra, on the Bangor road.

If you want to stay in Belfast, the best area to head for is the university area to the south of the city center. In the seemly residential streets of Stranmillis, Malone, and Botanic are a number of moderately priced guesthouses—safe, clean, and respectable (see Hotels and Restaurants, pages 269–83). Several well-known hotels in the central areas have been terrorist targets in recent years.

▶▶ Armagh 212B3

Armagh has often been the scene of battle, and today, this close to the border, security precautions are in force. County Armagh is predominantly Catholic, especially in the South, but the city itself is a Protestant stronghold. The two rival cathedrals, both dedicated to St. Patrick, scowl at each other from two of Armagh's seven small hills. The Protestant one has to be kept locked for security reasons, but instructions for obtaining the key are posted on the door. Solid, squat, and square, it is mostly 19th century in perpendicular Gothic style, with a fringe of grotesque heads around its otherwise plain exterior. It is the burial place of Brian Ború, the warlike king who finally drove the Vikings out of Ireland. The Roman Catholic cathedral, completed in 1873, stands proudly twin-spired at the top of a long flight of steps. The interior is astonishingly ornate—walls and roof covered with rich mosaics of saints and angels. The Mall, a broad, tree-lined square, is surrounded by some of Armagh's finest Georgian buildings, including the courthouse and the Royal Irish Fusiliers and County Museums. Armagh's most unusual sights are the 18th-century **Observatory▶** and neighboring **Planetarium▶▶**, where computer displays and models track down heavenly bodies. **Navan Fort**, now just a huge mound to the west, was the ancient palace of Queen Macha, a site which rivaled Tara, and the court of Ulster's chivalrous Red Branch Knights.

▶ Carrickfergus 213C4

The main landmark of this small seaside town is its vast Norman **castle▶▶**, still mostly intact, on a basalt ledge by the shore. Displays of its history are housed inside and today the castle plays amiably to the gallery by hosting medieval banquets and a Lughnasa festival in August. William of Orange entered Ireland via these shores in 1690 and a Williamite trail can be followed around the town. Just to the east is the **Andrew Jackson Centre**—an 18th-century cottage with re-created period interiors and displays relating to the seventh U.S. president, whose parents lived nearby.

Peatlands Park
This nature reserve in County Armagh, near the southern shore of Lough Neagh, was set up by the Irish Peat Development Company and covers about 600 acres of lakes, orchards, woodland, and virgin bogland. A visitor center explains the fragile bogland ecosystem, and various sections of the reserve can by visited on foot using carefully marked pathways or by means of a narrow-gauge railway. Turf-cutting demonstrations are always interesting. Further information is available from the park (tel: 0762 851102).

223

There are few remaining signs of Eamhain (or palace of) Macha, at Navan Fort, County Armagh. The site is thought to be 4,000–5,000 years old, and is associated with Cuchulainn, the Ulster hero (see page 28 for more details of his exploits)

Bullets, or road bowls
This ancient game is played along the local roads near Armagh (a version of it can also be seen in Schull, County Cork). A heavy iron ball, about the size of a baseball, is hurled along the lanes and the aim is to reach the end of the winding 2½-mile course in the fewest number of throws. Betting is fierce. Ask for details in local pubs if you want to see a game—most take place on Sunday afternoons. The first Sunday in August is championship day.

The fine, underrated city of Derry

The siege of Derry
Catholic James II expected a welcome from Derry's governor when his troops arrived in 1688, but 13 Protestant apprentices, fearing reprisals, stole the city's keys and locked the gates against the Jacobite forces. Supporters of William III, who had deposed James II as King of England, joined the apprentices' cause and flocked into the city. They remained under siege for 105 days, the longest siege in British history, during which time the population was reduced to eating a grisly diet of rotting horse-meat, dogs, and rats. More than 7,000 of the 30,000 crammed within Derry's walls died from starvation and disease. Yet when offered the chance to capitulate, the defenders merely raised a crimson standard signifying "No Surrender"—which has since become the rallying cry of the Protestant Unionist cause. The courage of the apprentice boys is still celebrated in Loyalist marches. Eventually William's soldiers raised the siege and James's troops retreated.

►► **Derry (Londonderry)**   *212D2*

Londonderry (an allusion to James I's gift of the city to the livery companies of London) is widely known by its original name of Derry, especially by its mostly Catholic population. Derry's notorious Bogside district has seen much unrest, for it is there that Catholic/Protestant tribalism is most sharply polarized. Catholics, unwillingly stranded right on the Republic's border, have suffered much discrimination under gerrymandered Protestant control, while Loyalists find it impossible to cast off their atavistic siege mentality. On a free-standing gable-end near the Bogside (once an I.R.A. no-go area and the scene of "Bloody Sunday," when 13 Catholic civilians were killed in 1972 during a civil rights march) are the giant words "You are now entering Free Derry." Protestants reply a few streets away with the defiant slogan "No Surrender."

For all its political ill-feelings, Derry is a fascinating city, retaining intact the **17th-century walls►►** that have played such a significant role in its history. These sturdy ramparts, 25 feet high and up to 30 feet thick, have never been breached. Five of the cannons that defended the city during its long siege stand above Shipgate Quay. Walkways lead along parts of the city walls, giving excellent views of both the inner city and the lower city with its great modern bridge spanning the River Foyle. Within the walls are an extraordinary little enclave of old-fashioned shops and bars, the Protestant cathedral of St. Columb in "Planters' Gothic" style and a typical Ulster central square known as the **Diamond►**. A hopeful sign of constructive community spirit is the Derry Craft Village, where modern artisanry burgeons in a village-like complex, and a pleasant coffee shop called The Boston Tea Party provides an excuse to sit down.

►   **Downpatrick**   *213B5*

In contrast to Derry, the market town of Down has lengthened its name, in honor of its most distinguished visitor, St. Patrick (see page 226). Down Cathedral stands in the highest part of the town amid seemly Georgian buildings. It is small, mostly 18th century and, perhaps surprisingly, is Anglican, not Catholic. Inside, the original Regency box pews have been preserved.

Not far down the hill is Downpatrick's other major sight, the **Down County Museum►►**, set in the local jail. The **St. Patrick Heritage Center►►** is well worth seeing for a coherent version of what is known of the saint's life and times (film and exhibition) and there are good local history and wildlife sections. The old prison cells can also be visited. These grim, dark, cramped rooms once housed the leader of the United Irishmen, Thomas Russell, who was convicted and executed here in 1803 for his part in Robert Emmet's rebellion (see pages 38–9).

From Downpatrick the land-locked sea-inlet called **Strangford Lough►►** and the **Ards peninsula►►** can be explored. Both of these shore roads are attractive, especially the easterly one, but to reach this, it is necessary to take the car ferry across the straits between Strangford and Portaferry, where the tides rush with great force. The lake is an important wildlife habitat supporting many unusual species. To find out more details about this remarkable ecosystem, simply stop at Portaferry's **aquarium►**, Exploris, near the quayside, which is devoted to local marine life. At Strangford, on the western side of the straits, is Castle **Ward►►**, built in a jarring mixture of styles (see page 230).

The gruesome figure of Death makes an appearance at the Derry Festival, held in February/March

St. Patrick is remembered in this stained-glass window (1937) at Down Cathedral

St. Patrick is not only Ireland's patron saint, but one of the best-known saints in Catholic hagiography. His importance to the island is evident from the huge number of places associated with him and from the number of Patricks, Pats, or Paddys (including a whiskey) named after him.

The shamrock
This plant, *trifolium minus*, is a trifoliate, or clover-like plant, thought to have been used by St. Patrick to illustrate the doctrine of the Trinity. It is one of Ireland's national emblems, traditionally worn on St. Patrick's Day (March 17).

226

The summit of Croagh Patrick—St. Patrick's mountain— appears to be perfectly conical from some angles

The saint is reputed to be buried in Downpatrick's cathedral graveyard, though the evidence for this is shaky. The rough granite slab that marks his "tomb" dates from about 1900 and was placed over the site of a large pit excavated by relic-hunters eager to find his bones. Downpatrick is, nevertheless, the best place to learn about St. Patrick (visit the heritage center in the Down County Museum).

St. Patrick, son of a minor Roman official, was born in western Britain at the turn of the 5th century. He was captured by Irish raiders at the age of 16 and spent six years in Ireland in slavery, working as a shepherd on Slemish Mountain, County Antrim. Eventually he escaped to France, where he trained as a cleric. Haunted by a vocation to convert the Irish to Christianity, he returned in about AD 432 and spent an energetic 30 years preaching and founding churches, mostly in Ulster, Leinster, and Connaught. In AD 433, he challenged Laoghaire, High King of Tara, by lighting the paschal (Easter) fires on top of the Hill of Slane against the pagan king's express command. Laoghaire was so impressed by Patrick's fiery sense of purpose that he let him continue his mission unhindered.

In County Mayo, the mountain Croagh Patrick is sacred to his memory. Legend has it that here the saint rang his bell and the snakes of Ireland fled. Of course there never were any snakes, but the mountain remains shrouded in mystery (and often mist) and is visited annually by countless devout pilgrims. The jeweled shrine said to contain St. Patrick's bell is held in the National Museum, Dublin.

► **Enniskillen**   *212B1*

This appealing little town owes much of its attractiveness to its setting on an island where the two sections of Lough Erne constrict to their narrowest point. Several routes converge on Enniskillen's strategic location and at busy times it can be a traffic bottleneck. Nevertheless, it makes a good base for exploring Fermanagh's lakeland, where boat trips, fishing and several islands offer many diversions. In the town the main places of interest are the quaintly turreted Watergate and the castle, which contains two museums. One is a heritage center devoted to Fermanagh life and customs, the other the Regimental Museum of the Royal Inniskilling Fusiliers. The town's military associations with famous regiments (the other is the Inniskilling Dragoons) have made it a terrorist target. In 1987 Enniskillen suffered one of the I.R.A.'s most heinous outrages, when a Remembrance Day ceremony was bombed; 11 people were killed, 61 injured. Parking control zones are enforced within the town center.

Many boat trips operate from various points on Lower Lough Erne (the northern lake), where several islands can be visited. **Boa Island►**, **White Island►**, and **Devenish Island►** all have interesting Celtic or early Christian antiquities. Reached via the pretty lakeshore roads, Castle Archdale Country Park and Castle Caldwell Forest Park have good woodland walks and picnic sites. Near Enniskillen are the grand houses, Castle Coole and Florence Court (see page 230).

At the far western tip of the lake, straddling the border with the Republic, **Belleek►** is famous for its pottery. Guided tours around the factory can be arranged and a museum and visitor center display some of its wares. Belleek pottery is extraordinarily elaborate and delicate; clay is extruded in thin strands which are then laid over each other in complex lattice patterns to form the classic "basketware" style. The results command high prices.

The Belleek Pottery

Marble Arch Caves
These caverns, 9 miles southwest of Enniskillen, are among the best in Ireland. The 90-minute tour takes place partly on foot, partly by boat. The impressive formations are given the usual fanciful names. Near the exit is a nature reserve where the River Cladagh emerges through a gorge into a bluebell wood.

Marble Arch Caves

Carrick-a-rede Rope Bridge
If you arrive on the Causeway coast between April and September, be sure to visit this curiosity linking the mainland with the salmon fisheries on Rathlin Island. The bridge is put up each spring and provides an exhilarating 60-foot walk along planks with wire handrails, swaying alarmingly 80 feet above a rocky cleft. You cross at your own risk (inadvisable in high winds), but the trip looks a lot more terrifying and perilous than it actually is, and it's great fun.

The Giant's Causeway; the other end of Finn MacCool's construction is on the Scottish island of Staffa, where there is a similar (but smaller) causeway

Old Bushmills Distillery
In 1608 Sir Thomas Phillips was granted a license to distil whiskey in the village of Bushmills, south of the Causeway coast. Continuing the tradition today, Old Bushmills is the oldest continuously run (legal) distillery in the world. Now it is also a tourist attraction, offering tours (Monday–Thursday, morning and afternoon, Friday, morning only), with tastings of course (hot toddies in winter). Two blends and one malt are made. Reserve a place in high season (tel: 012657 31521)

▶▶▶ Giant's Causeway   212D3

This extraordinary phenomenon is Northern Ireland's most famous landmark, studied by the Royal Geographical Society as long ago as 1693. Visitors have flocked here from far and wide ever since. The Causeway is set on a cliff-lined coast of outstanding natural beauty and is now in the care of the National Trust. In April 1987 it was declared Ireland's only World Heritage Site.

The Causeway is a complex series of promontories, but the most spectacular section consists of about 37,000 polygonal columns of dark basalt, many tawny with lichen, packed so neatly together that it is easy to imagine them as building blocks of some supernatural hand. Most columns are hexagonal, forming a honeycomb pattern, but some have five, seven or as many as ten sides. They measure about a foot across and may reach a height of 40 feet. Besides classic "threepenny-bit" stacks are other extraordinary formations, some like bulbous eyes, others like ramparts. All were formed about 55 million years ago, after a volcanic eruption poured molten basalt out above the chalky bedrock, crystallizing into these regular structures as it cooled. Legends have arisen about the origins of the Causeway; the main one tells how the Ulster giant, Finn MacCool, built it to walk across to Scotland.

At the top of the cliffs, a large modern visitor center contains an interesting exhibition about the Causeway and the local history and wildlife. During high season a minibus shuttles tourists down the steep path to the Causeway, but this rather spoils the magic of the place; the best way to enjoy it is to walk along the North Antrim Cliff Path. Off-season, when no other visitors are around and the waves crash on these bleak, dark rocks, the Causeway is memorable.

THE GLENS OF ANTRIM

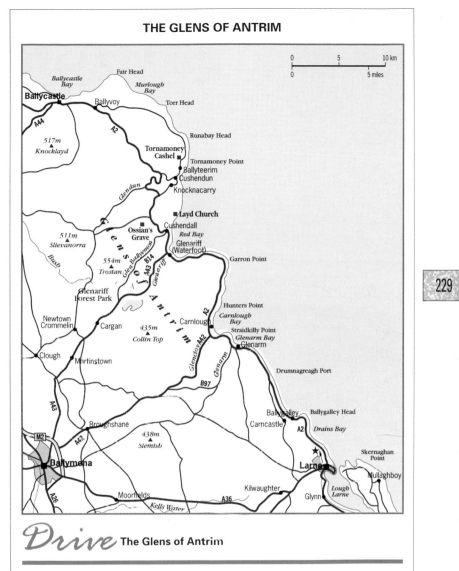

𝒟rive The Glens of Antrim

Road access to the glens is from A2 from Ballycastle to Larne. The area is good for walking, with the Ulster Way running along the coast past all the glens. From Larne, **Glenarm**, heavily wooded with forest trails and picnic sites, and **Glencoy**, near Carnlough, are the first glens you reach. Further north is the most popular of the glens, **Glenariff▶▶**, described by William Thackeray as a "mini-Switzerland," with waterfalls and a forest park. **Cushendall▶▶**, the "capital of the glens," has a number of minor sights, including a sandstone tower (the Curfew, or Garrison Tower), once used as a lock-up for "riotous - persons," the ruined 13th-century Layde Old Church, and Ossian's Grave, a Stone Age burial mound dating from 3000 BC. The pretty conservation village of **Cushendun▶▶** sits at the foot of Glendun, wildest of the glens. North of Ballyteerim is the Tornamoney Cashel, a stone fort dating from AD 500–AD 1000.

The properties and landscape owned by the Northern Ireland branch of the National Trust (N.T.) are an impressive collection. Ireland's grand houses temper classical orthodoxy with a lively dash of idiosyncrasy, even eccentricity. Besides the well-known set pieces such as Castle Coole or the Giant's Causeway, the National Trust also protects many minor and surprising sights— a lively Victorian pub in Belfast, a printing press and a beetling mill (used in the old linen industry) in County Tyrone, the curious rope bridge at Carrick-a-rede in County Antrim, and several follies and castles.

Joining and membership

For an annual fee members of the National Trust (or National Trust for Scotland) gain free admission to almost all the properties managed by the Trust throughout the U.K. Membership is open to all, but don't forget to take your card with you.
Contact the National Trust, P.O. Box 39, Bromley, Kent BR1 1NH, U.K.

Wellbrook Beetling Mill

The last stage of manufacturing linen is known as beetling, a process in which the flax fibers are hammered to produce a smooth surface. The cultivation of flax was Northern Ireland's largest industry and many deserted mills can be seen. West of Cookstown, in County Tyrone, is Wellbrook Beetling Mill (above) where the machinery is still in working order. It last operated commercially in 1961.

Country Houses The grand Palladian mansion of **Castle Coole▶▶▶**, home of the Earls of Belmore, is the most impressive house of its age in Ireland. Its original cost was enormous (furnishing it was even more expensive than its construction) and it has recently been faithfully restored, at vast expense, by the N.T. A masterpiece by James Wyatt, completed in 1798, the house contains magnificent plasterwork and curved doors of ancient mahogany. Entrance to the landscaped parkland is free.

Ardress House▶, in parkland near Portadown, dates from the 17th century. The interior contains paintings and good plasterwork. Livestock and farm implements are on show outside; visitors may explore the gardens and woodlands.

Not far away from Ardress House is **The Argory▶▶**, very little changed since its construction in the 1820s. It has many original contents and a pretty, early-Victorian sundial garden. The interior is still lit by a rare acetylene gas plant surviving in the laundry yard. The surrounding wooded countryside offers many fine walks.

On the shores of Strangford Lough is **Castle Ward▶▶**, a mansion which clearly displays the diverse tastes of its 18th-century owners, Lord and Lady Bangor. He liked Classical style; she favored Gothic. Architecture was not all they disagreed on and eventually they separated. Despite its disparity of styles, the house and contents are of great interest, giving a vivid impression of Victorian life (see the laundry and the playroom). Within the 670-acre estate are a 17th-century tower house, a wildfowl collection, and an exhibition about Strangford Lough.

Florence Court▶▶▶ is a particularly fine mid-18th-century Palladian (classical) house. The seat of the Earls of Enniskillen, it was superbly restored after a disastrous fire in 1956. Splendid plasterwork is the main feature, best preserved on the staircase and dining-room ceiling, which quick-thinking workmen saved from collapse by drilling holes to drain flooded water. The grounds contain a water-powered sawmill and a 220-year-old Irish yew tree, said to be the parent of all Irish-type yews. The 3rd Earl's fossil collection is exhibited in one of the side pavilions.

A thatched "long-house" dating from about 1691, **Hezlett House►** in County Londonderry was probably first used as a parsonage. Its most unusual feature is the crucktruss (curved timber) roof. Inside, it is simply furnished in 18th-century style and contains a display of early building and joinery methods. Further south is **Springhill►**, former home of the Conynghams, a military family of Ayrshire origins. The edifice dates from the 17th century (with later additions). Outbuildings house a costume museum of 18th-, 19th- and 20th-century clothes. The gunroom contains weapons from Vinegar Hill and the siege of Derry.

Gardens There are two fine gardens in County Down. **Mount Stewart Gardens►►** were created by the wife of the 7th Marquis of Londonderry in the 1920s. The mild microclimate created by neighboring Strangford Lough enables many rare and tender plants to flourish. The house is richly furnished and contains political memorabilia. One forebear was Viscount Castlereagh, the 19th-century politician who signed the Act of Union. James Stuart's Temple of the Winds in the grounds echoes a similar building in Athens. The county's other horticultural attraction is at **Rowallane►►**. This plantsman's garden was created over the first half of the 20th century on a drumlin (smooth glacial hills) site of 50 acres and contains specimens from all over the world. Its pride and joy are the azaleas and rhododendrons in May and early June, but the gardens are worth seeing throughout the opening season from April to October.

Gray's printing press
Strabane, in County Tyrone, was an important center of the Irish printing industry in the 18th and 19th centuries. The National Trust now preserves the only surviving printers, Gray's, on Strabane's Main Street. John Dunlap, printer of the American Declaration of Independence and publisher of America's first daily newspaper, *The Pennsylvania Packet*, is said to have learned his trade here, as is James Wilson, grandfather of President Woodrow Wilson. Visitors may inspect an impressive array of decorative printing presses, all kept in working order, and other antique printing equipment. Gray's Printer's is open in season, afternoons only (not Thursdays and Sundays).

231

Mount Stewart House and Gardens, County Down

With only one road leading through the Mountains of Mourne, they can only be properly appreciated on foot

►►► The Mountains of Mourne   213A4

These wild, steep-sided granite hills present an unforgettable aspect when seen across Carlingford Lough from the Republic. They reach to an average height of about 2,000 feet and are largely inaccessible except on foot, though the range is ringed by roads. Greencastle is a notable landmark near the entrance to Carlingford Lough. It changed hands many times and now stands gaunt and ruined near the rocky shore. Other places of interest along the coastal route are the marine park and restored 19th-century corn mill at Annalong, and the Murlough National Nature Reserve, a stretch of sand dunes by Dundrum Bay providing an important habitat for many birds.

There is not much to recommend the town of Newry as a base to stay. If you want to explore the Mourne area, choose one of the eastern coastal resorts or stay in the delightful village of Carlingford over the border in the Republic. **Newcastle** is the main tourist center for the Mourne Mountains. The resort, though pleasantly set, is of no great interest, but it has a good sandy beach and a wide range of accommodations. There are many walks in the nearby forest parks of Tollymore and Castlewellan.

Slieve Donard is the highest Mourne peak (2,796 feet) and it is said that on rare, clear days you can see all the countries of the British Isles from its summit (a relatively safe and easy climb), where there is also a hermit cell. At one time the mountains were a remote and ungovernable area inhabited by smugglers. A maze of ancient tracks lead through open moorland and upland pasture which make excellent walking country. For good maps and information, make for Newcastle's tourist office or the Mourne Countryside Center at 91 Central Promenade. Rock climbing is popular on the steeper cliff faces. The most accessible section is a well-marked tourist route called the Silent Valley which leads up to two reservoirs

Bessbrook
This neat little town northwest of Newry was built during the 19th century by a Quaker linen manufacturer, John Grubb Richardson. It was designed to house his flax-mill workers, whose living conditions must have been much better than many of their colleagues at other mills. They may have regretted the absence of a pub, however. The tidy, slate-roofed houses are grouped around two village greens.

serving the Greater Belfast region. A visitor center stands there and shuttle buses take tourists from the parking lot to Ben Crom Reservoir (other traffic is banned). The upper sections of the Mourne hills are characterized by tiny fields and dry-stone walls. The Mourne Wall is the largest of these, 22 miles long and more than 6 feet high, enclosing the water catchment area around the Silent Valley. Many semiprecious stones have been mined in the mountains around Hare's Gap.

The Ulster Way Northern Ireland is excellent for walking and its interconnected paths form a magnificent 435 mile long-distance footpath through all six counties. For most of the way it hugs the perimeter of the province fairly closely, ducking inland across the Sperrin Mountains and briefly touching the shores of Lough Neagh. Obviously some sections are more scenic and easier to follow than others. The paths running through the Mountains of Mourne, the Glens of Antrim, the Causeway coast, and the Lakes of Fermanagh are the most popular and most clearly marked, and it is in these well-known tourist areas that you can most easily find accommodations. At various points the Ulster Way links with other routes leading through the Republic. Near the border areas it is advisable not to stray from the marked paths. For the most part walking in Northern Ireland is safe and straightforward; no special equipment is needed apart from a good map and sensible footwear and clothing. Route guides and detailed maps are both available from various sources, notably the Sports Council for Northern Ireland, House of Sport, Upper Malone Road, Belfast BT9 5LA (tel: 01232 381222). The Youth Hostel Association of Northern Ireland (22 Donegall Road, Belfast BT12 5JN, tel: 01232 315435) also organizes rambling and hiking vacations throughout the year.

Newcastle nestles under the shadow of the Mountains of Mourne

NORTHERN IRELAND

Ulster-American Presidents

A dozen Americans of Ulster stock have made it to the White House, 11 as presidents, including three first-generation emigrants. Some of the more memorable include: Andrew Jackson, whose family came from Boneybefore outside Carrickfergus; Ulysses S. Grant, the Civil War hero, with roots in Aughnacloy in County Tyrone; Woodrow Wilson, whose thatched ancestral home is at Dergalt near Strabane; and Theodore Roosevelt, whose maternal family hailed from Antrim. The twelfth man was Major General Robert Ross, fighting for the English, who burned down the White House in 1814. Ulster émigrés also produced two prime ministers of New Zealand and a South Australian governor.

Past centuries are imaginatively re-created at the Ulster-American Folk Park

▶▶▶ **Ulster-American Folk Park** *212C2*

This theme park near Omagh, County Tyrone, has been set up with a generous endowment by the Mellon banking magnates who founded Pittsburgh, Pennsylvania. Thomas Mellon left Ulster in 1818 with his family and became vastly prosperous. The park has been re-created in the peaty bogs around his birthplace at Camphill, a modest whitewashed cottage, and traces the progress of those early Ulster émigrés from the Old World to the New. A guided walk takes visitors from a large reception and exhibition center through birch groves. In the first section, reconstructed buildings create the atmosphere of a typical 18th-century Ulster village—a blacksmith's forge, a weaver's cottage, a dour Presbyterian meeting house where interminable sermons were preached. Costumed staff cook up griddle cakes over open peat fires, spin wool and organize "lessons" in the village school (quill pens are used). School parties visit regularly. One of the more imposing buildings is Hugh Campbell's house, where extracts from the journal of 1818, written during his emigration voyage, can be read: "During the night every moveable in the ship was put in motion by the great heaving,... buckets full of all kinds of filth were hurled in the greatest confusion through the steerage to the great offence of our smelling organs!" On July 12 he wrote, "This day the anniversary of the Battle of the Boyne was commemorated by a certain part of our passengers to the no small annoyance of another part," which suggests that not much has changed in the intervening years. Visitors then pass through the Emigration Gallery, a replica emigration ship (complete with sound effects of creaking timbers and roaring seas) and on to the New World, where typical log barns, wagons and farmsteads of the early settlers can be seen. Of its type (and there are many similar projects throughout Ireland) this theme park is highly successful without sacrificing historical authenticity. A café, craft shop, and genealogy library are also on site.

▶▶▶ Ulster Folk and Transport Museum   213B4

This museum is located about 5 miles east of Belfast in the extensive grounds of Cultra Manor on the Bangor road. Typical Ulster buildings have been re-erected or reconstructed here and furnished in turn-of-the-century style. The exhibits include urban terraces, shops and cottages, farmhouses, a flax mill, forge, and school. Inside, demonstrations of local crafts such as spinning and weaving take place. An entertaining exhibition of domestic, social, and agricultural life in Ulster can be seen in the gallery which functions as an introduction to the park. Exhibits change from time to time. The transportation galleries on the opposite side of the main road house the entire Belfast Transport Museum and include many exhibits from horse-drawn carts to the ill-fated De Lorean sports car (see panel). The Irish Railway collection is one of the best sections. Local engineering heroes, such as Harry Ferguson, receive due attention, as do the great Belfast transport firms such as Shorts, the aircraft manufacturers, and Harland & Wolff, the shipbuilders (one of their commissions was the *Titanic*). Make sure that you allow plenty of time to see everything; you could spend the best part of a day here.

▶ Ulster History Park   212C2

This attraction near the Gortin Glen Forest Park traces the history of settlement in Ireland, starting with prehistoric societies dating back to about 8000 BC (life-size replicas of *crannógs* and neolithic huts) through early Christian architecture (Round Towers and churches), Norman castles, ring-forts, and planters' houses of the 17th century.

A number of drives, parks and beauty spots can be visited in the nearby Sperrin Mountains, a range of ancient and desolate hills in which minute traces of gold have been found. The rare hen harrier flies high above the remoter uplands.

The Ulster Folk and Transport Museum

The pioneering spirit lives on at the Folk Park

De Lorean
The famous gull-winged sportscar venture funded by public money to create employment in Belfast caused a major crisis in the Thatcher years when the enterprise crashed spectacularly, amid accusations of business malpractice and fraud. Investors and employees suffered greatly, and confidence in Northern Irish manufacturing projects took a sharp nosedive.

The Children of Lir
According to Irish myth, the second wife of King Lir (not to be confused with Shakespeare's Lear) became inordinately jealous of her four step-children and turned them into swans, condemning them to roam for 900 years over the waters of Ireland—300 on Lough Derravaragh (Westmeath), 300 on the Sea of Moyle (the waters between Ireland and Scotland) and 300 on the Bay of Erris (Mayo). After their long enchantment the swans assumed human forms, but as ancient, wizened creatures who expired almost immediately.

Waiting for the racing results at Birr, County Offaly

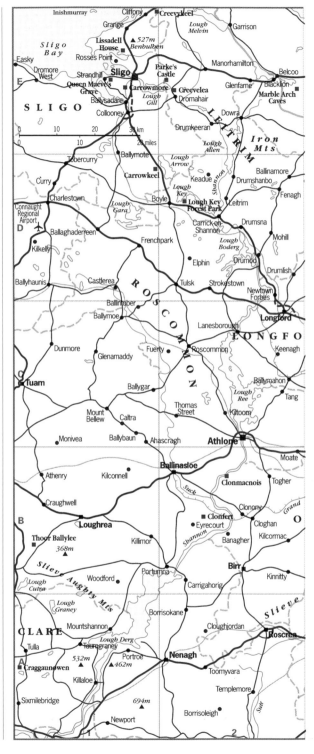

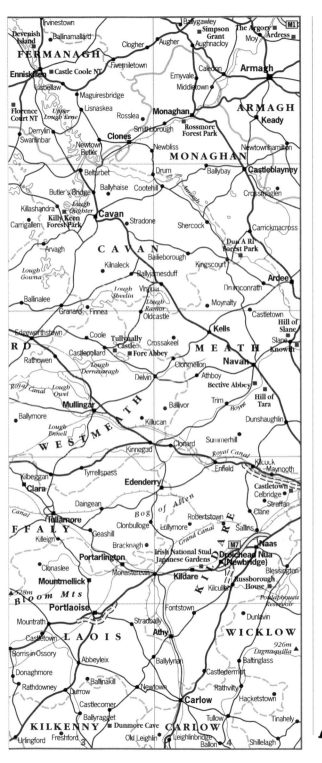

THE OFFICE OF
PUBLIC WORKS

CLONMACNOIS

NATIONAL MONUMENT

ADULT

081045

LAKELAND COUNTIES

Castle Island on Lough Key (County Roscommon) is named after a 19th-century folly

Sionna and the Salmon of Knowledge
This legend echoes the story of Adam and Eve. Sionna, granddaughter of the great King Lir (see page 236), desired the gift of knowledge, which was granted to men alone. She went to Connla's Well to search for the Salmon of Knowledge. Whoever ate the salmon would acquire its wisdom. As Sionna tried to trap the fish, it lashed its tail and the well overflowed. Sionna was swept away and drowned in the Shannon Pot (the source of the Shannon in Cavan).

Grand Canal
Until the early 19th century the Grand Canal, running from Dublin through these lakeland counties to the River Shannon at Ballinasloe, was a most important transport route, and it carried freight until 1959. The heyday of the Royal and Grand Canals, however, occurred before the Act of Union in 1801, which effectively destroyed Ireland's ability to compete with the Industrial Revolution in Britain. Horses would gallop along the towpaths, hauling barges at speeds of up to 10m.p.h. In recent years many canals have enjoyed something of a renaissance, thanks to their recreational use.

Lakeland counties These small, watery counties—Cavan and Monaghan near the Northern Ireland border, and Westmeath, Laois, Offaly, Roscommon, and Longford—form the geographical heart of Ireland, yet are usually portrayed as places to get *through* on the way to somewhere more interesting. Initially they are not prepossessing. Dreary main roads blast through on radial routes from the capital, often slow with heavy traffic. Closer exploration of these unsung plains is surprisingly rewarding, however. There are historic towns, abbey ruins, and grand houses to visit, and masses of outdoor activities. Highlights include Strokestown House, Birr Castle Gardens, and the monastic ruins of Clonmacnois.

Facilities for visitors are limited compared with parts of the more popular western or southeastern counties. Budget accommodations, especially campsites or hostels, are scarce, but the area has some highly distinctive country house hotels, offering good value. These central counties also offer a less stereotyped picture of the Emerald Isle. Visitors are welcomed with true Irish hospitality, with no pressure to buy sweaters or shamrock table linen.

Waterlands The landscape seems at first monotonous—a shallow saucer of endless unremarkable arable and pasture land, broken up by a maze of lakes and river systems. Few grand vistas can be seen; the eyeline generally stops at the first broken hedge. The small-scale, piecemeal landscape appears intimate and domesticated, although its most significant geographical feature, the River Shannon, is the longest in the British Isles, carving its ponderous course through the brimming flood plains and water meadows of several counties. It provides many things—scenic interest, wildlife habitats, an important navigable waterway, and a profitable playground for fishermen and boat-lovers. As if more water were needed, long canals slice through the bogs—the Grand Canal in the heart of Offaly and the Royal Canal linking Dublin with the Shannon. These waterways and the massive lakes of the Shannon and its major tributaries are extensively exploited for recreational use. Myriad smaller pools dot the wavering horizons of Monaghan and Cavan. A practiced topographical eye will quickly identify this borderland area as drumlin country, where glacial deposits have been left in distinctive ridges, or eskers (the only geological term to be derived from the Irish language) and pear-shaped hills (drumlins) forming a classic "basket of eggs" landscape.

Laois has the highest hills, the Slieve Blooms, which rise to a modest maximum of 1,729 feet. Amid these low-lying plains, however, they seem grand indeed and the long-distance footpath called the Slieve Bloom Way attracts many walkers.

Settlers, invaders, and bandits Patterns of settlement are complex. Invaders and adventurers throughout the centuries tramped across these mournful boglands to find out what lay beyond, and the fierce clans who established themselves here posed a constant threat to the Anglo-Normans walled up in the Pale around Dublin. The area is full of castles, dour planters' churches, and the estates of great families. In Elizabeth I's time many estates were confiscated from their original Gaelic owners and parceled out to Scottish and English landlords.

The wild border counties of Monaghan and Cavan harbor further resentment. Once part of the old kingdom of Ulster, they were torn from their ancient allegiances by Partition. Complex geography makes a national frontier virtually impossible to police, and parts well deserve the sobriquet "bandit country." Political activists and smugglers crisscross the uncertain border on unofficial, potholed tracks. The bizarre course of the boundary between North and South seems to epitomize, by its perverse loops and twists, the irrationality of the present dividing line. There is not much reason to linger on this section of the border and, while there, it is prudent to adopt the local habit of remaining tight-lipped on political opinions.

Bog butter
Butter has always been eaten in Ireland in great quantities. In medieval times it was sometimes flavored with garlic or onions. Before the days of refrigeration, it was discovered that Irish peat-bogs conserved food remarkably well, and caches were often buried in wooden barrels where they were safe from plunderers. It developed a distinctive cheesy flavor but would last for hundreds of years. Bog butter from long ago is still occasionally unearthed during turf cutting.

239

14th-century Cloughouter Castle stands in Lough Outer (Cavan)

▶ **Athlone** *236C2*

The "capital of the Midlands" stands at one of Ireland's most central points, midway along the Shannon and an important rail, road, and river junction on the border between Leinster and Connaught. The town was besieged and badly damaged by Williamite forces after the Battle of the Boyne, when the defeated Jacobites retreated here and were finally routed at nearby Aughrim. Unsurprisingly, its strategic location necessitated a stronghold, and one of its most significant historic buildings is a 13th-century castle▶ in the market square, whose curtain walls, towers, and keep are still intact. The castle has been put to good modern use as the setting for a museum of local history; its most interesting section is an exhibition on the famous tenor, John McCormack, who was born in the town. Recordings of McCormack's voice can be heard on his own 78r.p.m. gramophone. Elsewhere in the town is his birthplace, in a narrow street called The Bawn. Apart from the castle, a handful of abbey ruins and a fine Jacobean house (Court Devenish) dating from 1620, there is no very pressing reason to visit Athlone, but it makes a good base for boat excursions on Lough Ree and its various islands. Of these, Inchclearaun and Inchbofin both have churches and Early Christian graveslabs; Inchclearaun is also associated with the legendary warrior Queen Maeve, who met her death here bizarrely, struck by a missile of cheese!

John McCormack
A legend in his own lifetime, John McCormack (1884–1945) is still regarded as one of the greatest lyrical tenors in recorded history and, fortunately, he lived in an era when his voice could be captured on early gramophone disks. He quickly achieved fame and was internationally recognized in Italy, England, and the United States. He spent his fortune from his repertoire of popular music on his other two oddly varied passions: horse-racing and the Catholic Church. For his charitable services he was awarded the unusual honor of being made a Papal Count.

The Anglo-Norman fortress of Athlone Castle

▶ **Birr** *236B2*

This pleasant, quiet Georgian town was formerly known as Parsonstown, after the family name of the Earls of Rosse, whose seat is **Birr Castle▶▶**. The building is 17th-century Gothic and not generally open to the public, but the 100 acres of gardens are open all year and heartily reward a visit. They contain many rare specimen trees and shrubs, and the tallest box hedges in the world (33 feet high). The gardens are memorable in spring and autumn, when flowering trees, bulbs, and colorful foliage

240

are at their best. Walks lead beside the lake and rivers, around which the grounds are landscaped. The most fascinating feature of Birr Castle, however, is the remains of a remarkable early telescope. Built by the 3rd Earl of Rosse in the 1840s, it was then the largest and most powerful in the world, its 72-inch lens enabling the aristocratic astronomer and his son, the 4th Earl, to study the spiral nebulas and measure the heat of the moon. The supporting walls that held this massive instrument can still be seen; taped information provides background history. Birr Castle's Dower House, Tullanisk, is an exceptionally attractive place to stay (see Hotels and Restaurants, page 278). Several fine Georgian houses and streets survive in the town.

► **Boyle** *236D2*

The main reason to visit Boyle is to see the ruined **Cistercian abbey►** dating from 1161, founded by the same group of monks who built Mellifont. Although central and near one of the town's main streets, the abbey seems tranquil beside its rushing stream, and a good proportion of it is still intact, despite innumerable attacks by warring Irish clans. The restored 16th–17th-century gateway contains an exhibition. The 12th-century church within the compound shows Gothic and Romanesque arches and interesting carvings. For a couple of centuries from Elizabethan times the abbey housed a military garrison. A short distance east of Boyle is the **Lough Key Forest Park►►**, part of the Rockingham estate, an enormous estate which once belonged to the King family (Edward King, drowned in the Irish Sea in 1636, was the subject of Milton's elegiac poem *Lycidas*). Rockingham originally belonged to the MacDermots, the local chieftains and Lords of Moylurg, but was handed to the King family in 1617. The big house in what is now the forest park was burned down in 1957, but King House, the family's town mansion in the main street, can be visited. There is little else to see in this quiet town, but with the Curlew Mountains close by and its excellent opportunities for walking and fishing, Boyle is an increasingly popular touring base.

The grounds of Birr Castle straddle the boundary between Counties Offaly and Tipperary

An Irish Romeo and Juliet
Castle Island in Lough Key, near Boyle, is traditionally taken to be the burial place of two young lovers, Una MacDermot and Thomas Costello, the subject of a famous traditional Irish poem (*Úna Bhán—White Una*). Her parents would not allow the match and Thomas departed grief-stricken from his home, promising to return only if he were recalled before he crossed a nearby river. He tarried at the ford, but finally crossed—too late to learn that Una had died of a broken heart. She was buried on Castle Island, where Thomas used to swim his horse each night to lament his lost love until he collapsed lifeless over her grave. Two ash trees grew above the tomb and entwined over this Irish Romeo and Juliet, united at last in death.

241

Ireland is one of the most hospitable countries in the world. Tourist accommodations are big business and there is a vast range of places to stay at all price levels, from modest cottages to great castles. A genuinely warm welcome, a homelike atmosphere, and an excellent breakfast are features of many of them.

Distinctive houses

Cheaper options include Blanchville in County Kilkenny, Bruckless House in County Donegal, Ballycormac House in Tipperary, and several Glebe Houses (once providing accommodations for Church of Ireland clergy)—those in Dowth, County Louth, and Ballinadee, County Cork are highly recommended. More modest but excellent value are Fergus View, convenient for the Burren, Church Villa or Dunmore Lodge (both in Dunmore East, County Waterford), Kille House in County Galway, Hanora's Cottage in County Waterford, Larchwood House in Cork, or Rosturk Woods in County Mayo.

The dining room at Tullanisk, near Birr, in County Offaly

Useful publications Anonymous business hotels or luxury castles will give you reliable hot water and T.V., but little of the real Ireland of conversation and idiosyncrasy that you will find in more personally run places. To meet the increasing demand for places with something special, several useful listings have been made. Pick up the booklets in any tourist office. *The Blue Book* lists a fine range of country-house hotels and restaurants, often with some historic interest or culinary distinction. Staying in most of these places is a memorable, but generally expensive, experience.

The Hidden Ireland provides an even more interesting selection of *homes* offering hospitality (as opposed to commercially operated hotels). In many of these you may dine *en famille*, join a country-house-party atmosphere, get to know the owners or join in locally available sports such as hunting or fishing. All the places are rural and of some architectural distinction, many are fascinating and distinguished old houses filled with family mementos and antiques. *Friendly Homes of Ireland* is a personal choice (by John Colclough, a well-known journalist) of generally less expensive places offering family hospitality in interesting settings. (There is some overlap between these listings.) Many visitors base their whole vacation on these selected houses, and although not every establishment may be to your taste, they all have merit, and if you have little idea of where to start looking, are of great help. Here

The elegance of Clohamon House, Bunclody, County Wexford

are just a few places offering exceptional and typically Irish hospitality—informal, effortless, unsnobby, and warm. (For details see pages 269–83.)

Luxurious mansions At the more expensive end of the price range, **Hilton Park** in Clones, County Monaghan, overlooking extensive parkland which includes a golf course and three lakes, offers a splendid Anglo-Irish country-house stay. Four-poster beds, elegant furnishings, and many memorabilia add to the interest of the house, home of the Madden family for some 250 years. Organic produce from the gardens appears on its excellent dinner menus. **Bantry House** in Cork is a magnificent stately home still owned by descendants of the White family, who lived there in 1739 and helped to foil Wolfe Tone's invasion. Accommodations are provided in a separate wing of newly refurbished rooms, all very comfortable, overlooking the lovely Italianate gardens. Concerts are a specialty. The state rooms are open to the public, so don't expect complete seclusion: Slightly less expensive are **Ballyvolane House** (also in County Cork), dating from 1728, elegantly remodeled in early Victorian times. It has lovely peaceful grounds, private fishing, and excellent Irish country cooking. **Clohamon House** in Wexford is an 18th-century house in the Slaney Valley surrounded by beechwoods and gardens of rare trees. The estate land contains a Connemara pony stud. Antiques and family portraits lend a gracious air, although the atmosphere is entirely unstuffy. **Newbay House**, closer to the Wexford coast, is another cheerful, relaxing Georgian home in sweeping parkland. **Ballinkeele House** was designed by Daniel Robertson (of Powerscourt fame) in 1840, and is the ancestral home of the Maher family, who dispense effortless hospitality and excellent cooking amid 340 acres of farmland. **Roundwood House** in Laois is one of the best of all Irish country houses for character and idiosyncratic charm. It is also one of Ireland's finest Georgian homes, in the Palladian style. **Tullanisk**, also in Lakeland (County Offaly) is the former Dower House of the Earls of Rosse, who own Birr Castle. **Gurthalougha House,** on the shores of Lough Derg, Tipperary, dates from the early 19th century and stands in a private forest.

Ballymaloe House
This rambling, Georgian mansion with a Norman keep is in farming country east of Cork. Owned by the Allen family, produce from the 395-acre farm is used to good effect, for Myrtle Allen is one of Ireland's most celebrated chefs, happy to pass on her skills in books, television broadcasts, and through the Ballymaloe cookery school, run by her son and daughter-in-law, Timothy and Darina Allen. The hotel has many facilities and is lavishly furnished, but retains the feel of a family home and is utterly relaxing.

Tullanisk, in the Birr Castle Estate; guests are given free admission to the Castle gardens

243

Clonalis House (1878), seat of the O'Conors

Goldsmith country
The poet and playwright, Oliver Goldsmith (1728–1774) was born at Pallas, County Longford, and spent much of his childhood in Lissoy parsonage, near Auburn crossroads. Villages most associated with Goldsmith's writings (particularly his long poem, *The Deserted Village*) include Tang, where he went to school, and Ballymahon, his widowed mother's home. Most of his adult life was spent in London, but he recalled his Irish childhood and the gentle, humdrum lifestyle of this rural area in idyllic terms. The Three Jolly Pigeons pub, immortalized in *She Stoops to Conquer*, can be seen on the Ballymahon road near Athlone.

■■■■■ **Castlerea**   236D1

The town itself is not in the least riveting, but **Clonalis House►**, on the southwestern outskirts, is worth a look. Guided tours are conducted by the family owners, and you can even enjoy an unusual, if expensive, brand of aristocratic B.&B. in its palatial bedrooms, or you can rent one of the nearby cottages. Clonalis House is a late-Victorian mansion in fine parkland whose main interest consists in its contents and its inhabitants. It is a rare example of a clan house, the seat of an ancient Gaelic family which can, it claims, trace its line back through 60 generations to the Kings of Connaught and the last High Kings of Ireland. The O'Conors have owned the local land for the best part of two millennia and many castles and abbeys in the region are associated with the clan. The house is sumptuously furnished with antiques, and full of archive material and family memorabilia, including silver, porcelain, costumes and manuscripts. One of its most prized items is a harp belonging to the great 18th-century bard Turlough O'Carolan.

►►► **Clonmacnois**   236B2

These extensive and impressive monastic remains stand in velvety, emerald water meadows by a rushy bend in the River Shannon, a place of almost tangible stillness, especially at dawn or dusk when the few visitors who venture here are absent. In earlier centuries it was even more isolated by the river and surrounding bogland, and was accessible only by boat, or along the esker (see caption) ridge known as the Pilgrims' Causeway. Founded by St. Ciarán (or Kieran) in about AD 548, this Celtic site became the most important religious establishment of its time in Ireland and was renowned as a place of art and learning throughout Europe. St. Ciarán himself died of plague at the age of only 33, just seven months after the monastery site had been established, but news of his good works eventually spread beyond Irish shores. Several ecclesiastical treasures produced here are now on display at the National Museum in Dublin. The gold and silver Crozier of Clonmacnois, decorated with strapwork and animal patterns, is one of these. The *Book of the Dun Cow*, one of the earliest and most famous manuscripts in the Irish language, was also produced here.

Clonmacnois was once a royal city and the burial place of the High Kings of Tara and Connaught, including the last High King, Rory O'Conor (see Castlerea). Like most settlements of its type, it suffered constant depredations at the hands of Vikings and Normans and was devastated by English forces in 1552. Still visible within its enclosing walls are the remains of a cathedral, eight churches, two Round Towers, many carved gravestones and several High Crosses. The most interesting antiquities are displayed in the visitor cener. The splendid Cross of the Scriptures, erected in the 9th or 10th century, depicts, among the usual biblical scenes, King Dermot helping St. Ciarán erect the first cornerpost of the monastery at Clonmacnois.

The Nuns' Church stands beside a quiet lane outside the main enclosure and is reached via a path through the modern cemetery and out into the road beyond. It is worth making the short excursion to this pleasant spot; the tiny church with its finely carved arches is sheltered by tall trees in a peaceful little meadow. It was built by Dervorgilla, Ireland's equivalent of Helen of Troy, whose abduction by Dermot MacMurrough provided the excuse for Strongbow's Anglo-Norman invasion (see pages 32–3). On the other side of the monastic buildings, not far from the parking lot, vestiges of a Norman castle are on the slopes beside the river. Little of the castle survives except for its courtyard and a crazily leaning tower.

The Dead at Clonmacnois
In a quiet water'd land, a
  land of roses,
Stands Saint Ciarán's city
  fair;
And the warriors of Erin in
  their famous generations
Slumber there.

T.W. Rolleston (1857–1920);
from the medieval Irish
poem by Enóg Ó Gilláin.

Clonmacnois, strategically sited on an esker beside the Shannon. (An esker is a winding ridge of gravel deposited by a meltwater stream running beneath a glacier)

245

Many of the sporting activities of this central region are based upon its rivers, lakes, and forests. Several forest parks have been created, partly for environmental conservation, but also to allow for recreation and to increase the region's tourism potential. Some of these designated parks have become rather overdeveloped, with plentiful picnic tables and similar amenities. If you prefer a slightly wilder scene, head for the Slieve Bloom Mountains.

Lacemaking

County Monaghan is famous for its lace industry. Carrickmacross and Clones are the two main centers and, in both cases, the craft was introduced during the 19th century by local rectors' wives, partly as a means of relieving the area's chronic poverty. The fortunes of the industry waxed and waned as a result of changing fashions and periodic overproduction. Lace is still made by hand in these centers, although the genuine article is extremely labor-intensive and correspondingly expensive. Carrickmacross lace incorporates hundreds of intricate fine loops. Clones lace is crocheted and often features small raised knots known as Clones dots.

Lacemaking, County Monaghan

Forest parks Lying just outside Boyle, in the grounds of the former Rockingham estate, the **Lough Key Forest Park►►** extends over about 840 acres along a lakeshore and includes a cypress grove, deerpark, ice-house, temple, bog garden full of peat-loving plants such as azaleas, and many marked paths. Boats tour the lake from Rockingham Harbour, and row boats can be hired. There are ring-forts and islands to explore, and a vantage point called the Moylurg Tower can be climbed for views of the surrounding scenery. The gateway and lodge of the old estate still exist, though the main house, designed by Nash, was burned down in 1957.

Northwest of Cavan on N3, the 593-acre **Killykeen Forest Park►** is set amid the complex Chinese puzzle of water and islets that forms Lough Oughter. Marked walks, nature trails, etc., enable visitors to enjoy fishing, birdwatching, and exploring early fortifications.

Rossmore Forest Park lies near Monaghan Town on the Newbliss road and consists of 692 acres of gentle hills and lakes interconnected by forest walks through rhododendron plantations. Just beyond Newbliss is the Victorian Annaghmakerrig House, former home of theater director, Sir Tyrone Guthrie, and now left to the nation as a center for writers and artists. Visitors can picnic and walk in its beautiful surroundings.

Haunted by Red Squirrels, **Dún A Rí Forest Park►** provides 568 acres of wooded walks southwest of Carrickmacross. From the hilltop parking lot are views of the Mourne Mountains and a ruined Elizabethan fortress. A wishing-well called Tobar na Splinnc is set into a rocky ledge above the River Cabra, and Sarah's Bridge supposedly commemorates a lady who was so startled by a belated proposal of marriage from a man she had been meeting for 30 years that she fell off and drowned!

Lough Muckno Forest Park is a former Georgian estate near Castleblayney. Situated beside Monaghan's largest lake, it offers signposted walks through beautiful grounds of mixed woodland and gently undulating drumlins. Caravans and campers can be accommodated nearby.

The Slieve Bloom Mountains Though not particularly high, the Slieve Blooms►► rise quite dramatically from the low-lying boggy plains that surround them, their looming purple shoulders a backdrop to many a view in this area. It is said that they are named after Bladhma, an

Killykeen Forest Park lies on the shores of Lough Outer in County Cavan

ancient hero, who once took refuge from his enemies in these hills Later, in Cromwellian times, the Slieve Blooms again became a place of hiding for men whose lands had been confiscated by the Parliamentary forces.

The slopes are rounded rather than steep, many covered in conifer plantations, and the high density of well-marked paths and tracks (so unusual in Ireland) make them ideal for walking. A long-distance footpath called the Slieve Bloom Way runs for about 20 miles around these hills, on a route past waterfalls and glens, through bog and moorland, conifer woods, and an ancient (pre-Ice Age) river valley. Though the hills are mostly too gentle for really dramatic views, the slopes do in some places drop away sufficiently to reveal the great plains below stretching mistily into the distance. Look for the rare pine marten, which haunts the mountains, together with Irish hares, fallow deer, and mountain goats. Good starting points for the walk are Glen Barrow or the standing stone at Forelacka. Despite their unthreatening altitude (maximum 1,729 feet), these hills can be treacherously misty and waterlogged, so adequate footwear, clothing, and equipment are essential.

Boating
An excellent way to enjoy the peaceful Midland scenery is from the deck of a boat, and you can charter boats in many centers on the 300 miles of navigable lakes, rivers, or canals in the region. Tullamore, on the Grand Canal linking Dublin and the Shannon, is one of the most popular starting points for narrow boats, and the scenery spans flower-filled banks, gentle pasture and open bogland (Celtic Canal Cruisers, tel: 0506 21861). Other good centers include Athlone (Athlone Cruisers Ltd, tel: 0902 72892, for boat trips round Lough Ree), Banagher, or Glasson.

Lough Key, a perfect place to enjoy some of Ireland's finest fishing

LAKELAND COUNTIES

The seven wonders
Fore is famous for its seven wonders:
1. The monastery on a quaking scraw.
2. A mill without a mill-race.
3. Water that flows uphill.
4. An ash tree that won't burn.
5. Water that never boils.
6. The great stone above the old church door.
7. The Holy man in a stone (an anchorite's cell).
Many stories are told to explain the origin of these, but the grains of truth in some should be mixed with pinches of salt in others.

St. Brigid's Chapel in Mullingar Cathedral

▶ **Monaghan**   *237E4*

This garrison town shows a strong Scots Presbyterian influence, with solid mercantile buildings and a central square known as the Diamond, similar to those in Derry and Donegal. Its location close to the Northern Irish border is not fortunate and, although it prospered from the linen industry introduced mainly by Ulster settlers in the 18th century, it has been a hotbed of unrest from time to time. Charles Gavan Duffy, one of its most famous inhabitants who eventually became Prime Minister of Victoria, Australia, characterized the town's political awareness by founding the Irish Tenant League and a nationalist newspaper called *The Nation*. The flamboyant 19th-century Gothic spire of **St. Macartan's Catholic Cathedral** lords it over the more sedate classical and Regency buildings of the town center. In the Diamond, the elegant 1792 Market House, with its fine, carved decorations, is now the tourist office. The Rossmore Memorial, a huge Victorian drinking fountain, with eight gray marble columns and a sandstone canopy, also in the Diamond, necessitated the removal from here of the old 17th-century market cross, once a sundial, to another square in the town (Old Cross Square). The town's most interesting sight is its **County Museum▶** on Hill Street near the tourist office, an award-winning collection of local history and art. One of its prize exhibits is the processional Cross of Clogher, beautifully embossed with figures and ornaments, and dating from about 1400.

■ **Mullingar**   *237C3*

This busy county town is the center of a prosperous commercial and cattle-raising area. The main reason to visit the town, otherwise, is to see its museums and its modern Catholic cathedral. Best of the museums is the **Military Museum▶**, with a section devoted to the old I.R.A., a more idealistic and honorable organization than it is today. The **Cathedral of Christ the King▶**, not in itself a remarkable building, contains two famous mosaics by a Russian artist, Boris Anrep, and an ecclesiastical museum

Adolphus Cooke
Not far from Mullingar on the road to Delvin is the small village of Reynella, where the graveyard contains a strange tomb in the shape of a beehive. This is the grave of a celebrated local eccentric, Adolphus Cooke, who believed that one of his flock of turkeys was his reincarnated father. He also tried his favorite dog, Gusty, for the crime of repeatedly straying and cavorting with the common dogs of Mullingar. The setter was eventually reprieved when the hangman claimed that the dog addressed him in a foreign tongue, thereby proving Cooke's theory of reincarnation. Market Hall Museum in Mullingar contains a few relics relating to this extraordinary person.

housing the vestments of St. Oliver Plunkett (see page 114). North of Mullingar and near the underrated Lough Derravaragh is **Tullynally Castle►**, seat of the Earls of Longford, a castellated stone building much remodeled in the 19th century, with fine gardens. Inside is an interesting collection of domestic utensils and a celebrated private library, indicating the literary bent of the Pakenham family, whose scions include the present Lord Longford's gifted daughters, Antonia Fraser and Rachel Billington. The castle is open only from mid-July to mid-August, the grounds from June to September. Nearby is **Fore Abbey►**, founded in the 7th century by St. Fechin. This large religious community was destroyed many times during the Dark Ages, but a church dating from the 10th century survives, along with a 13th-century Benedictine priory built by the de Lacy family.

► Roscommon 236C2

The huge **Norman castle►**, standing in fields on the edge of Roscommon, seems out of proportion to anything else in this little county town. It dates from the 13th century, though was altered much in later years, with refined Tudor mullions added in the 16th century. The quarrelsome O'Kelly and O'Conor clans seized it periodically, but its last definitive remodeling took place at the hands of Cromwellian troops and its drum towers now stand lopped and hollow around a rectangle of neatly mown turf. In the town are the **Dominican priory ruins**, last resting place of the priory's 13th-century founder Félim O'Conor, a king of Connaught, whose tomb is decorated with effigies of gallowglasses (Irish or Scots mercenaries). The main street, with attractively restored Georgian and Victorian shops, bifurcates around a copper-domed Georgian courthouse (now a Bank of Ireland branch). Nearby is the castellated county jail, where Roscommon's redoubtable lady hangman carried out her civic duty (see panel). Another curiosity is James J. Harlow's Funeral Requisites and Furniture Stores, a beautifully restored hardware shop and bar crammed with household gadgets and nostalgic examples of advertising.

Lady Betty
Roscommon's condemned prisoners faced a female executioner during the 18th century. Condemned to death herself, allegedly for the unwitting murder of her only son, she volunteered to step into the breach when the hangman was ill, on condition that her life be spared. She was subsequently appointed as the town's "hangwoman" with a salary and accommodations at the prison, and there she remained for about 30 years, performing her grisly duty with apparent efficiency and detachment. She drew charcoal portraits on her walls of some of her clients, whom she dispatched from a hinged board outside her third-floor window.

Richard Cassels or Castle
This architect (1690–1751) was one of the formative influences on Anglo-Irish architecture during Georgian times. Among his great works are Powerscourt and Russborough in County Wicklow, Westport in Mayo, Newbridge in Dublin, and Strokestown House in Roscommon. He came from a Huguenot family settled in Hesse-Kassel in Germany. He first arrived in Ireland in 1728 to work on a project in County Fermanagh and soon became known to Lord Burlington and his circle. Before long he was the most sought-after architect in Ireland. His style was Palladian, with heavy moldings and muscular sculpted stonework. His name appears most often in its anglicized form—Castle.

▶▶ **Strokestown**   *236D2*

Many Irish towns and villages reveal their Georgian origins in wide streets, but Strokestown's is certainly exceptional—originally modeled on Vienna's Ringstrasse, which had greatly impressed one of the local landowners, it is said to be the widest provincial main street in Ireland. The village is little more than an adjunct to the enormous **Strokestown House**▶▶ which lies beyond the Gothic triple arch on this main street. Home of the Pakenham Mahon family, their 17th-century farmhouse was reconstructed by Richard Castle (see panel) in the 1730s in Palladian style for the Anglo-Irish M.P., Thomas Mahon. Its most famous (and infamous) proprietor was Major Denis Mahon, who presided over the Strokestown estate during the unproductive Famine years, and found himself so short of cash that he pressed his tenants to emigrate to the New World. Rumors spread that he was chartering the dreaded "coffin ships" in which so many Irish emigrants perished, and Mahon was shot dead near Strokestown in 1847. In 1979 the dilapidated house was sold to an enterprising local garage firm, who gallantly resisted the mood of the times to let all traces of "British imperialism" (including its superb Georgian heritage) lapse into ruin. The company energetically restored the premises, replanted the parkland and established the Famine Museum in the house commemorating the tragic events of the 1840s.

Strokestown House is one of Ireland's finest and most authentic Palladian buildings and gives a real flavor of the life and times of the Anglo-Irish families and their tenants. One of its most fascinating features is the galleried kitchen in the south wing from which the lady of the house could drop menus and instructions to the kitchen staff without troubling herself by any closer proximity. Tunnels allowing tradesmen and staff to perform their duties unseen link the main house to the kitchen and stables located in the wings.

At the far end of Strokestown, the County Heritage and Genealogical Center (open only from May to September) offers regional displays and an audiovisual show about County Roscommon.

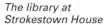

The library at Strokestown House

TRAVEL FACTS

Arriving

U.S. citizens need a passport to enter both Ireland and Northern Ireland. First-time applicants should apply at least five weeks before their departure to one of the 13 U.S. Passport Agency Offices. Also, local county courthouses, many state and probate courts, and some post offices accept passport applications. Necessary documents include (1) a completed passport application (Form DSP-11); (2) proof of citizenship (certified birth certificate, issued by the Hall of Records of your state of birth, or naturalization papers); (3) proof of identity (valid driver's license or state, military, or student ID card with your photograph and signature); (4) two recent, identical, two-inch-square photographs (black-and-white or color), with a white or off-white background; (5) $65 application fee for 10-year passport (those under 18 pay $40 for a five-year passport). Check, cash (exact change), or money order are accepted. Passports are sent in 10 to 15 business days.

You may renew in person or by mail. Send a complete Form DSP-82; two recent, identical passport photographs; a passport less than 12 years old from the issue date; and a check or money order for $35.

A visa is not required for tourists staying in Ireland for up to 90 days, or in the North for up to 180 days. Tourists may be asked to show onward/return tickets. For further information, cantact the **Embassy of Ireland** (2234 Massachusetts Ave., NW, Washington, DC 20008, tel: 202/462 3939), the **Embassy of Great Britain** (3100 Massachusetts Ave., NW, Washington, DC 20008, tel: 202/462 1340), or the nearest Consulate General.

By Air Ireland's international airports are Dublin, Shannon, Cork, Belfast International (well linked by public transport to the city centers), and Knock. Until 1994, all transatlantic flights to the Republic were required to land at Shannon, near Limerick, as part of a scheme to bring tourism and employment to the western regions. This is no longer mandatory, but if you are visiting the West anyway, Shannon makes a convenient landing point. Most European flights land in Dublin or Belfast, but other airports are served from the U.K. Flying time from London is an hour to Dublin or Belfast (90 minutes to Shannon, Cork or Knock). You can fly to Ireland from many regional U.K. airports. Both Shannon and Dublin have well-stocked duty-free outlets with many Irish products on sale.

The major airlines offer a range of tickets that can increase or decrease the price of any given seat by more than 300 percent, depending on the day of purchase. As a rule, the further in advance you buy the ticket, the less expensive it is but the greater the penalty (up to 100 percent) for canceling. Check with airlines for details.

The best buy is not necessarily an A.P.EX. (advance purchase) ticket on one of the major airlines. These tickets carry certain restrictions: They must be bought in advance (usually 21 days); they restrict your travel, usually with a minimum stay of seven days and a maximum of 90; and they also penalize you for changes—voluntary or not—in your travel plans. But if you can work around these drawbacks (and most travelers can), they are among the best-value fares available.

Charter flights offer the lowest fares but often depart only on certain days, and they are seldom on time. You may be able to arrive at one city and return from another; however, you may lose all or most of your money if you cancel your trip. Don't sign up for a charter flight unless you've checked with a travel agency about the reputation of the packager. It's particularly important to know the packager's policy concerning refunds in the event of a canceled flight; some agents recommend that travelers purchase trip-cancellation insurance if they plan to book charter flights. One of the most popular charter operators to Europe is **Council Charter** (205 E. 42nd St., New York, NY 10017, tel: 212/661 0311 or

800/800 8222), a division of the **Council on International Educational Exchange** (C.I.E.E.). Other companies advertise in Sunday travel sections of news-papers.

From North America, it is probably a cheaper option to fly to London and reroute from there, although this will add time to your already long journey. In the United States and Canada there are many discount fares available. Aer Lingus and Delta operate scheduled services to Dublin, America Trans Air to Belfast; there are charter flights to both Dublin and Belfast. Boston–Shannon flying time is around five and a half hours. Direct flights are also available from many European cities.

Aer Lingus offices can be found at the following addresses:
● Republic of Ireland: Dawson Street, Dublin 2 (tel: 01 6772089)
● U.K.: Aer Lingus House, 83 Staines Road, Hounslow, Middlesex (tel: 0181-569 5555), and 223 Regent Street, London W1
● U.S.: 122 East 42nd Street, New York 10168 (tel: 212/557 1090)
● Northern Ireland: 46 Castle Street, Belfast (tel: 01232 245151)

Dun Laoghaire harbor, the port of entry for many visitors from Britain

Camping and caravanning
Lists of caravan (trailer) parks and campsites are available from both national tourist boards; those in Bord Fáilte's brochure are regularly inspected and graded. All these sites have facilities, including water faucets and electricity, showers, toilets, and sometimes restaurants and play areas. Unofficial camping is widespread in Ireland, however, and as long as you have the land-owner's permission and cause no disturbance you may camp in any field. You may be asked to pay a *punt* or two in tourist areas. Many hostels will allow cheap camping on nearby land with use of showers and kitchens. State run forest parks in the Republic do not permit camping, whereas many in the North do.

Caravans can be hired, sometimes in conjunction with ferry deals. These vary from luxuriously furnished mobile homes to the picturesque, horse-drawn Romany caravans of the Irish brochures (see below for more information).

Horse-drawn caravans If you want to rent a horse-drawn caravan, it is best to arrange third party liability insurance. Expect to cover no more than 10 miles per day, and stick to the quiet, flatter lanes of rural Ireland. Most caravans are four-

253

berth. Don't expect luxury facilities aboard (bed linen and simple cooking utensils are provided, but no toilets, for example; take your own towels and matches for lighting gas burners). Before you set off, rental companies give you full instructions on routes, and handling and looking after the horse. Prices are seasonal; a deposit is required, and you should allow IRÆ8 for each overnight stop. Riding horses can be rented to accompany the caravan. Two of the best-known companies are Slattery's Horse-Drawn Caravans, 1 Russell Street, Tralee, County Kerry (tel: 066 26277, fax: 066 25981) or Clissman's Horse-Drawn Caravans, Carrigmore Farm, Wicklow (tel: 0404 48188, fax: 0404 48288). C.I.E. Tours International, based near London, can also arrange rentals (tel: 0181-667 0011).

Car breakdown

If the car is rented, contact the rental company (their nearest contact number should be on your contract or other rental documents). Automobile Association (A.A.) members, or members of affiliated motoring organizations belonging to

The road between Glengarriff in County Cork and Kenmare in Kerry

the A.I.T. (*Alliance International de Tourisme*), may call on the A.A. rescue services (provided in the Republic by the Automobile Association of Ireland). Both the A.A. and the R.A.C. operate a breakdown service for their members in Northern Ireland.

Car rental

Renting a car in the Republic is expensive—rates are among the highest in Europe, although they are cheaper in the North. Tariffs vary and, as elsewhere, small local firms will often give you a cheaper deal than the major international companies. To offset this, the vehicle may in some cases be less roadworthy, pick-up points less convenient, and service less efficient. You may also have to return the car to the pick-up point rather than dropping it off in another town (check drop-off charges in advance). The large companies are geared to a nationwide operation, so if you rent in Dublin and break down in Donegal you won't have a problem. Just phone the nearest office. Major companies also insure you automatically to drive on either side of the border, though you should always specify this when you accept the car; check the booking conditions and insurance cover carefully. Most multinational companies have offices at the main airports and ferry terminals, as well as in large cities. Rental charges at Northern Ireland airports, however, may be higher than renting with the same firm in the city. The tourist offices or the Automobile Association will be able to offer advice on approved companies.

Avis/Johnson & Perrott (based in Cork but with offices in most airports and cities) are the largest operators in the Republic, supplying cars for several major travel firms, airlines, etc. They provide clean, reliable cars and a good back-up service. Other large firms include Hertz, Murray's/Europcar and Budget. Rates are very seasonal. The cheapest way to book a rental car is to arrange an inclusive package-deal in advance with a tour operator, airline and ferry company (fly-drive or rail/ferry-drive) rather than waiting until you arrrive in Ireland.

To rent a car you must have a valid driver's license (an international license with an English translation if you are a non-E.U. resident). Some companies specify age limits for drivers (usually a minimum of 21 or 23 and a maximum of 70 or 75). Make sure you take out collision damage waiver (C.D.W.) as well as the standard third-party insurance. Manual transmission vehicles are usually supplied unless automatics are specifically requested. Almost all rental cars use unleaded fuel. The best-value deals include unlimited mileage.

Climate

No one goes to Ireland for a tan. It has a fine climate (mild, free from extremes, good for plants), but perhaps too much weather. As the pressure systems sweep in from the Atlantic, Ireland gets it all—and rain follows sunshine with immense rapidity. Ireland's "soft days" of fine drizzle and low cloud are unavoidable, but it is unfortunate if you should happen to be touring the Ring of Kerry on one. Be prepared for the four seasons in a single day. The Southeast is appreciably sunnier and drier than the west coast. July and August are the warmest months (average temperatures 50°F at night, 64°F during the day), but May, June or September may well be drier. Ireland has the added advantage of being less crowded in late spring and early autumn. It is impossible to predict fine days at any time of year. If the sun comes out, enjoy it while you can. If it rains, cover up or head for the pub. It probably won't last long.

Crime

In general, rural areas of both the Republic and Northern Ireland are extremely safe. Unpleasant sectarian incidents or terrorist attacks hit the headlines at regular intervals, and very occasionally visiting tourists have been caught up, but this is extremely rare. The

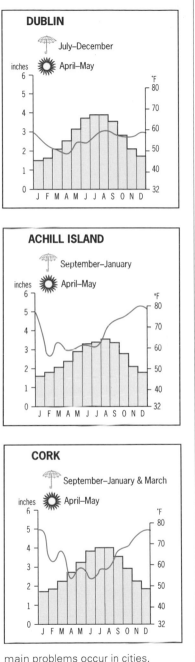

main problems occur in cities, particularly in the deprived areas of Dublin, where car theft is pervasive. Limerick also has a significant problem of violent crime and theft.

255

Large gatherings (festivals, markets, horse-sales, etc.) attract a criminal element, as anywhere, and it is sensible to take precautions with your belongings. In particular, don't leave tempting valuables visible in a car. Personal violence or sexual assaults on strangers are fortunately rare, although women traveling alone should not take unnecessary risks (for example, by hitchhiking).

Customs regulations

Since 1993, E.U. travelers have been able to import the following quantities of *duty-paid* goods for personal use only: up to 50 liters of beer; 25 liters of wine; and 800 cigarettes. *Duty-free* allowances (not available when traveling between Britain and Northern Ireland) are lower: 200 cigarettes; 1 liter of spirits; 2 liters of wine, 50g of perfume and 250ml of toilet water, plus other dutiable goods to the value of IR£34 (IR£17 if under 15 years of age). However there are some restrictions on importing certain food items into both the Republic of Ireland and Northern Ireland (the latter if traveling from outside the U.K.). To obtain further information, get in contact with the Custom House either in Dublin (tel: 01 873 4555) or in Belfast (tel: 01232 234466).

The Irish are enthusiastic cyclists

Cycling

Cycling is without doubt one of the best ways to get around in Ireland, especially granted decent weather. The secondary roads are mostly empty, built-up areas limited, and open countryside all around. Most airlines will carry bikes for free as long as you don't exceed your weight allowance. If you bring your own bike it's advisable to bring a spare tube and tire with you, as Irish sizes are unusual. It is very easy to rent a bike when you arrive in Ireland. Raleigh is the biggest operator, with a nationwide organization of pick-up and drop-off points, but local dealers, hotels, and hostels can provide them too. It is advisable to rent cycle helmets, available in some places but not everywhere. Check brakes and tires and get a pump and repair kit. Bikes can be carried on long-distance buses and trains, but there is a charge. Collect leaflets on cycling from Bord Fáilte or the Northern Ireland Tourist Board (N.I.T.B.). Several companies in Britain and Ireland arrange cycling holidays, with accommodations, transport of luggage, lunches, and guides, including: Celtic Cycling, Bagenalstown, County Carlow (tel: 0503 75282), Bike Tours (in Avon, England, tel: 0225 480130) and the Irish Travel Bureau, Manchester (tel: 061-976 3887).

People with disabilities

Associations for people with disabilities can give advice on travel and mobility problems. Registered drivers with disabilities may park free of charge with an orange badge. The national tourist boards both produce useful literature (Bord Fáilte's *Accommodation Guide for Disabled Persons* is available free). Increasing numbers of hotels and guesthouses cater to people in wheelchairs, and access to many sights, museums, etc., is being adapted. Addresses you may find useful include:

● National Rehabilitation Board, 25 Clyde Road, Dublin 4 (tel: 01 668 4181)

● Irish Wheelchair Association, Blackheath Drive, Clontarf, Dublin 3 (tel: 01 8338241, fax: 01 8333873)

● Disability Action, 2 Annadale Avenue, Belfast BT7 3JR (tel: 01232 491011).

Driving

Motorists drive on the left in Ireland, although driving habits are erratic, particularly in rural areas. Hazards for the motorist include slow-moving farm vehicles, often without lights, that lurch suddenly into the roadway from field gates—or equally suddenly, turn into farm entrances without signaling. Herds of cows, flocks of sheep, seemingly endless loose gravel, and unexpected roadworks are all part of Irish driving. Farm dogs enjoy chasing cars. There is no need to swerve or brake for them; they know exactly how far to go. Poor public transportation networks and the importance of the pub in Ireland result in a high incidence of drivers on the roads with alcohol on board, though penalties for drinking and driving are severe. In short, a considerable amount of care is required at all times if you are driving on Irish roads.

Documents required A valid driver's license is required (with an English-language translation if you wish to rent a car). Non-E.U. residents should obtain an international driver's license from their country of origin. If you do bring your own vehicle to Ireland, take the registration document with you, and also a letter of authorization from the owner if he or she is not traveling with the vehicle. Both the car and any trailer or caravan should carry an appropriately sized nationality sticker. Insurance is compulsory; a Green Card is a well-recognized international proof of cover.

Regulations Irish residents are not insured to drive non-Irish visitors' cars, other than a garage hand with written permission. A red warning triangle or hazard lights should be used if you break down. Use low-beam headlights in poor visibility. Front seat belts should be worn at all times in the Republic; rear seat belts (if fitted) in the North. Children under 12 must travel in the back. Offenses such as speeding may attract an on-the-spot fine. Motorcyclists and passengers must wear helmets.

Speed limits Despite most signposts in the Republic being in kilometers, speed limits are defined on both sides of the border in miles per hour. In the Republic:

● 30m.p.h. (48k.p.h.) in built-up areas

● 60m.p.h. (96k.p.h.) in country areas unless otherwise indicated

● 70m.p.h. (113k.p.h.) on expressways.

In Northern Ireland:

● 30m.p.h. (48k.p.h.) in built-up areas

● 40–60m.p.h. (64–96k.p.h.) in country areas

● 7m.p.h. (113k.p.h.) on divided highways and expressways

In both the limit for vehicles with trailers is 40m.p.h. (64k.p.h.).

Roads In the Republic there are very few stretches of expressway, although roads are being rapidly improved with the aid of E.U. grants. There are three road classifications: National Primary (labeled N, plus a number of between 1 and 50); National Secondary (N plus a number over 50) and Regional (R). These categories give little indication of how good the road actually is. Roads near large cities (Dublin, Cork, Waterford, and Limerick) may suffer from congestion in rush hours. Elsewhere roadworks may cause delays, but generally speaking roads are empty and driving in Ireland is a relaxing affair. Roads in Northern Ireland are much better, whether A-roads, expressways, or B-roads.

Road signs In the Republic a single signpost may be cluttered with up to a dozen signs, some broken or turned the wrong way, in a mix of English and Gaelic. Distances are in kilometers on green Euro signs, but in miles on older black-and-white signs—even in Irish miles (equal to 2.05km or 1.3 miles) on some milestones—so the distance from your destination wavers as you travel! Part of the entertainment of driving in Ireland is finding your way in these circumstances, helped by local directions, often of the "I wouldn't be starting from here" variety.

Fuel Unleaded fuel is now widely used on both sides of the border. Gas stations usually stay open till around 8PM (later in built-up areas) in the Republic and some are open on Sundays. In the North gas stations stay open longer, some 24 hours.

Parking Several larger cities in the Republic have a disk parking system. Buy a disk from local shops or garages to allow you to park for a

An unavoidable hazard on Irish lanes

specified time. Elsewhere, multi-story or pay-and-display parking lots are the norm. In Belfast or Northern Irish towns, park only in authorized places. Many towns have control zones where you may not leave a vehicle unattended. If you do, you may cause a security alert.

Crossing the border (See panel on page 214 for more details.) You should use only approved roads for border crossings, and be prepared to stop at checkpoints, state your destination and show identification. A passport is useful, especially if you have rented a car with Irish Republic plates. Make sure that your insurance covers you across the border.

Automobile Association Offices
The main A.A. offices in Ireland are at:
● 23 Rockhill, Blackrock, Dublin South (tel: 01 283 3555)
● 23 Suffolk Street, Dublin 2 (tel: 01 677 9950)
● 12 Emmet Place, Cork (tel: 021 276922)
● Fanum House, 108–10 Great Victoria Street, Belfast BT2 7AT (tel: 01232 328924).

Electricity
The standard supply is 230 (240 in Northern Ireland) volts AC (50Hz), with mostly flat 3-prong sockets as in Britain (occasionally older round 2- or 3-prong ones may be found). North American appliances require both a transformer and an adapter—bring them with you.

Embassies and Consulates
Embassies in the Republic:
● Australia: Fitzwilton House, Wilton Terrace, Dublin 2 (tel: 01 676 1517)
● Canada: 65 St. Stephen's Green, Dublin 2 (tel: 01 478 1988)
● U.K.: 31 Merrion Road, Dublin 4 (tel: 01 269 5211)
● United States: 42 Elgin Road, Dublin 4 (tel: 01 668 8777).

Consular offices for Northern Ireland:
● Australian High Commission: Australia House, The Strand, London WC2B 4LA (tel: 0171-379 4334)

- Canadian High Commission: Macdonald House, 1 Grosvenor Square, London W1X 0AB (tel: 0171-258 6600)
- New Zealand High Commission: New Zealand House, 80 Haymarket, London SW1Y 4TQ (tel: 0171-930 8422)
- United States: Queens House, 14 Queen Street, Belfast BT1 6WEQ (tel: 01232 328239).

Irish consulates abroad:
- Britain: 17 Grosvenor Place, London SW1X 7HR (tel: 0171-235 2171)
- Australia: 20 Arkana Street, Yarralumla, Canberra 2600, ACT (tel: 062 733 022).
- Canada: 170 Metcalfe Street, Ottawa K2P 1P3, Ontario (tel: 613/233 6281)
- United States: 2234 Massachusetts Avenue NW, Washington DC 20008 (tel: 202/462 3939/40/41/42) Also in Chicago, Boston, New York, and San Francisco.

Emergency telephone numbers
Dial 999 throughout Ireland for police, fire or ambulance, or rescue services (coastal, mountain, cave).

Health
There are no special health requirements or recommended inoculations for visitors to the Republic or to Northern Ireland, and no particular hazards or diseases.

It is advisable for any visitor to take out adequate medical insurance. A good travel policy will cover loss and theft of property, cover you for any legal emergency, and get you home if you're stuck. If you have to have medical treatment, keep all bills and medical receipts for any subsequent claim. Take some convincing identification with you when you ask for treatment, and proof of insurance.

The International Association for Medical Assistance to Travelers (I.A.M.A.T.) offers a list of approved, English-speaking doctors whose training meets British and U.S. standards. In the United States contact: 417 Center St., Lewiston, NY 14092 (tel: 716/754 4883). In Canada: 40 Regal Rd., Guelph, Ontario N1K 1B5 (tel: 519/836 0102). In Europe: 57 Voirets, 1212 Grandlancy, Geneva, Switzerland. Membership is free.

In Washington, the Department of State Citizens Emergency Center (tel: 202/647 5225) provides information about health conditions in other nations; what U.S. citizens can do in the event of an emergency overseas; whether any notices, cautions, or warning exist in the area to which you're traveling; and how to obtain passports and visas.

Language
Everyone in Ireland speaks English, but officially the Republic is bilingual, and Gaelic (Irish) is the first language in areas of Cork, Waterford and parts

A detail from a mural at the Irish Life Center in Dublin

of the West (especially Dingle and Connemara). Irish citizens can be heard in Irish if summoned to court, and it is an entry requirement for university (except T.C.D.). Radio, television, and newspapers have features in Gaelic.

In practice you don't need to speak Gaelic as a visitor, but you may find a warmer welcome if you show an interest. Pronunciation is difficult, bearing scant relation to spelling, and it is hard for a non-native to attempt a rendering of some place-names without hearing an Irish speaker first. There are several dialects of Gaelic and pronunciation varies from place to place.

Lost property

Serious losses should be reported to the police, who should give you a copy of your statement if you wish to make an insurance claim. Inform your embassy if you have lost a passport; a bank displaying the Eurocard symbol if you have lost credit cards or traveler's checks (keep a note of the numbers and your purchase receipt *separate* from the checks in order to obtain replacements rapidly).

❏ Here are a few of the words and phrases you are most likely to come across:

Bord Fáilte (Irish Tourist Board, literally "board of welcomes")—pronounced "bord fawlcha"
Céad míle fáilte (literally, "a hundred thousand welcomes")—"kay-d mille fawlcha"
céilí (Irish dance night)—"kaylee"
Gaeltacht (Irish-speaking region)—"gale-tackt"
Garda Síochána (police)—"gawr-da sheekawnah"
poteen (alcohol distilled from potatoes, illegal and often dangerous)—"potcheen"
sláinte (good health)—"slawn-cha"
slán (goodbye) –"slawn"
Taoiseach (Prime Minister)—"teeshock"
uisce beatha (whiskey, literally "water of life")—"ishka baha"
Most importantly, on toilets, *Mná* means women and *Fir* means men.

And a few words that appear in place-names:
ard height (Ardmore, Ardglass)
ath ford (Athlone, Athlumney)
bal, baile, bally town (Ballymena, Ballinrobe)
carrick rock (Carrickfergus, Carrickmacross)
drom, drum ridge (Dromahair, Drumcondra)
dún fort (Donegal, Dungannon)
ennis, inis island (Enniskillen, Innisfree)
glen vale, glen (Glendalough, Glengarriff)
kil, cille church (Killarney, Kilkenny)
lios, liss mound, ring-fort (Lismore, Lisdoonvarna)
rath fortified homestead, ring-fort (Rathmullen, Rathkeale). ❏

The Irish seem very keen to get as much use as possible from their signposts, overloading them with countless signs—as seen here at Dromahair, County Leitrim

Media

Republic of Ireland television broad-casting is operated by a state-sponsored body called R.T.E. (Radio Telefís Éireann). It has three radio and two television channels (R.T.E.1 and R.T.E.2). You can receive them all over Ireland, including the North. In much of the Republic, you can pick up B.B.C. (radio and television) and Ulster Television. Local radio, including many independent stations, offers blasts of Irish music, chat, and lilting Gaelic (also useful for traffic and weather reports, and events). British visitors will hear a new slant to Irish or world affairs—or the problems of the North—on Irish news broadcasts.

The main newspapers available in the Republic are the *Irish Times*, the *Irish Press*, and the *Irish Independent*—all slim publications which are expensive by U.S. standards, but a great insight into Irish life and politics. Another respected newspaper is the *Cork Examiner*, which comments on world affairs with *gravitas*. Sunday papers include the *Sunday Tribune* (good arts reviews and listings), the *Sunday Press*, *Sunday Independent*, and *Sunday Business Post*. The *International Herald Tribune* and the *Wall Street Journal* are available in Dublin and major cities. The most widespread local paper in the north is the evening *Belfast Telegraph*. In the mornings you have a choice of the nationalist *Irish News*, or the loyalist *News Letter*.

Money matters

Currency In the North the currency used is the pound sterling (as in the rest of the U.K.). In the Republic it is the *punt* or Irish pound (written IR£), divided into 100 pence. When the U.K. was forced out of the European Monetary System and devalued sterling sharply in late 1992, the *punt* was left badly exposed to every economic chill wind, though many in the Republic found it hard to restrain their glee at the sight of an Irish pound worth considerably more than a British one for almost the first time in history. Eventually the *punt* has settled down to its customary level

CONVERSION CHARTS

FROM	TO	MULTIPLY BY
Inches	Centimeters	2.54
Centimeters	Inches	0.3937
Feet	Meters	0.3048
Meters	Feet	3.2810
Yards	Meters	0.9144
Meters	Yards	1.0940
Miles	Kilometers	1.6090
Kilometers	Miles	0.6214
Acres	Hectares	0.4047
Hectares	Acres	2.4710
U.S. Gallons	Liters	3.7854
Liters	U.S. Gallons	0.2642
Ounces	Grams	28.35
Grams	Ounces	0.0353
Pounds	Grams	453.6
Grams	Pounds	0.0022
Pounds	Kilograms	0.4536
Kilograms	Pounds	2.205
U.S. Tons	Tonnes	0.9072
Tonnes	U.S. Tons	1.1023

MEN'S SUITS

U.K.	36	38	40	42	44	46	48
Rest of Europe	46	48	50	52	54	56	58
U.S.	36	38	40	42	44	46	48

DRESS SIZES

U.K.	8	10	12	14	16	18
France	36	38	40	42	44	46
Italy	38	40	42	44	46	48
Rest of Europe	34	36	38	40	42	44
U.S.	6	8	10	12	14	16

MEN'S SHIRTS

U.K.	14	14.5	15	15.5	16	16.5	17
Rest of Europe	36	37	38	39/40	41	42	43
U.S.	14	14.5	15	15.5	16	16.5	17

MEN'S SHOES

U.K.	7	7.5	8.5	9.5	10.5	11
Rest of Europe	41	42	43	44	45	46
U.S.	8	8.5	9.5	10.5	11.5	12

WOMEN'S SHOES

U.K.	4.5	5	5.5	6	6.5	7
Rest of Europe	38	38	39	39	40	41
U.S.	6	6.5	7	7.5	8	8.5

261

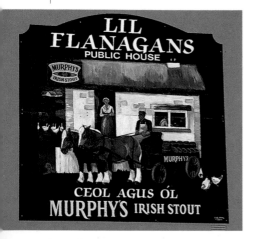

A Kilkenny pub sign

(within 5 percent of sterling). Increasingly, you can use either currency at parity in both the Republic and the North, whatever the exchange rate, but in general it is best to use the appropriate currency or you may lose out in the conversion process. Have a supply of both currencies ready if you are crossing the border. Traveler's checks or a Eurocheque book and card are the safest way to carry your cash. There is no limit to the amount of currency you may take into Ireland.

Changing money This is best carried out at a bank; see below for opening hours. Exchange facilities are also available at international airports, travel agencies, hotels and some tourist offices, although the rates may not be as favorable at these places.

Credit cards Major credit cards (those bearing the Mastercard and Visa symbols), are widely accepted all over Ireland, particularly in shops catering to tourists. Charge cards, such as American Express and Diners Club, are also acceptable in some outlets (less so in the North). You can use Visa to withdraw cash from banks displaying the card's symbol. Smaller retailers or restaurateurs and bed-and-breakfast owners prefer cash.

National holidays
New Year's Day, St. Patrick's Day (March 17), Easter Monday, Christmas Day and St. Stephen's Day (December 26: known as Boxing Day in the North) are public holidays in both the North and the Republic. The Republic has the following public holidays:
● first Monday in May
● first Monday in June
● first Monday in August
● last Monday in October.

Northern Ireland also takes these days as holidays:
● first Monday in May
● last Monday in May
● Orange Day (July 12)
● last Monday in August
Good Friday is not a statutory holiday, but is observed as a holiday in most parts of Ireland.

Opening hours
Times given below are general and subject to local variations. In the Republic—particularly in rural areas—shop hours may be erratic, but shopkeepers are also flexible and may be willing to open up specially. In Dublin and Belfast, hours may be longer, with late-night shopping on Thursday or Friday. Museums and other tourist sights vary greatly: the largest stay open all year; others close from mid-September or October until Easter. Summer opening hours are usually longer than in winter. Some museums close on Monday; *always* check with the tourist office before making a long journey. Published times may be unreliable, or sights closed for renovation, etc. The following opening hours apply in the Republic:
● shops: 9–5:30, Monday–Saturday, with earlier closing on Monday, Wednesday, or Thursday
● banks: 10–12:30; 1:30–3, Monday–Friday (closed national holidays). Many banks stay open until 5 on Thursday in Dublin, some now open at lunchtime
● post offices: 9–5:30 or 6, Monday–Friday; 9–1 Saturday (usually closed at lunchtime). Village post offices close early one day a week
● pubs: 10:30AM–11:30PM, Monday–Saturday; 12:30–2, 4–11:30,

Sunday (during the summer months). Pubs tend to close at 11 in winter. Opening hours in the North are slightly different:

● shops: 9–5:30, Monday–Saturday, with one midweek early closing day (Wednesday or Thursday). Some close for lunch, while many Belfast stores open late (until 9) on Thursday

● banks: 9:30–4:30, Monday–Friday. Some banks close 12:30–1:30

● post offices: 9–5:30, Monday–Friday; 9–1, Saturday. Some close for lunch, or, alternatively, all day Wednesday

● pubs: 11:30AM–11PM, Monday–Saturday (some pubs in Belfast have a late license until 1AM on Friday and Saturday nights); 12:30–2:30, 7–10, Sunday (at the landlord's discretion).

Pharmacies (chemists)
Besides medicines, these places also stock cosmetics and photographic products. When closed, they should display a notice outside giving the list of chemists that stay open late. In an emergency, contact the local hospital. Contraceptives (condoms) are much more widely available in the Republic than they were a few years ago (when they were illegal!) but you may still find them hard

The view from the Rock of Dunamase, County Laois

to obtain in some rural areas, and they are still products to be kept under the counter, not out on general display.

Places of worship
Ireland naturally has many churches, though it may surprise visitors to see how many are Church of Ireland (Protestant), not Roman Catholic. Some churches open only for services and are otherwise locked. You can usually obtain the key by asking someone nearby where it is kept. If you cause no disturbance it is acceptable to slip in and out of a church during mass for a quick look around (don't barge about during the service, of course). There are few non-Christian places of worship, but Belfast and Dublin have synagogues, Dublin a mosque (check with tourist boards for details). Marian shrines, such as the one at Knock, or grottoes like Ballinspittle, attract many pious Catholics, the majority of whom are women.

Police
In the Republic, the police are called the Gardaí ("gardee"), wear blue-and-black uniforms, and are unarmed. In the North the police force is the Royal Ulster Constabulary, and they wear green uniforms. They carry arms, and police stations all over the North have very tight security.

Post offices

Easily identifiable, even in the Republic, by the word "Post" in green. The postal services are notoriously unreliable in the Republic, and postage is expensive (postcards are cheaper than letters). In the North postal rates are the same as in the rest of the U.K. (a two-tier system is used: first and second class, the former purportedly buying speed). Mail boxes are red in the north, green in the south. The correct stamps must be used either side of the border. The G.P.O. in O'Connell Street, Dublin, is open longer hours than elsewhere, including Sundays and bank holidays. See also the opening hours section, above.

Public transportation

In general, local public transportation in the Republic is very limited, which is why you see so many young people hitchhiking. Things are better in the North, though it is still immeasurably more convenient to have your own transport.

Air Regular air services connect Dublin with the West (Shannon and Cork) and if money is no object, it is a very quick trip (30–40 minutes). Regular flights also connect Galway and the Aran Islands (15–25 minutes), operated by Aer Arann, weather permitting. Business travel and tourism have opened up a number of provincial airports with regular internal services and flights to the U.K. run by Aer Lingus and Ryanair.

Train The rail network in the Republic is controlled by the state-owned Irish Rail (Iarnrod Éireann), the rail division of C.I.E. (Coras Iompair Éireann). Trains are fairly slow and infrequent, but generally reliable and comfortable. Most routes radiate from Dublin. The only service connecting the Republic and the North is the Dublin–Belfast Express (about six trains each way a day). Large parts of the country are not covered by the rail network at all, such as Donegal and the border counties, Clare, Connemara, and southwest Cork. Fares are complex and not especially cheap—consider a discount pass if you plan to do much rail travel (see Passes, below). The Dublin area has its own transport system, D.A.R.T. (Dublin Area Rapid Transit), a suburban electric train service operating between Howth and Bray. In Northern Ireland there are three routes run by Northern Ireland Rail. You can take a bike on mainline trains if there is room, but there is a charge.

Bus Bus Éireann and Ulsterbus respectively provide the Republic's and Northern Ireland's national express bus systems, supplemented by Dublin Bus in the Dublin area, and by many private bus lines (sometimes cheaper and faster than the national buses, though insurance cover may be dubious). Various bus operators offer sightseeing tours (such as Gray Line). Bus travel in the Republic is often very slow, but fares are much cheaper than train fares. Off-season services may be very infrequent, but conversely weekend services may be oversubscribed. Small villages are sometimes served by only a couple of buses a week. Many bus indicators are in Irish, so check your destination carefully. Midweek "single" (one-way) tickets can be used for a free return trip and remain valid for a month. Bikes can be carried (for a charge) at the driver's discretion—if there is room. Bus travel in the North is generally reliable and serves most areas not reached by train.

Post boxes are green south of the border, and red to the north

The D.A.R.T. at Dun Laoghaire station

Ferry or boat Three useful car ferries across estuaries cut down long detours inland. One is at Waterford (between Ballyhack and Passage East), linking Counties Waterford and Wexford. The second is across the Shannon estuary between Killimer and Tarbert, linking Kerry and Clare and cutting out the bottleneck journey through Limerick. The third is between Strangford and Portaferry in County Down.

Most of Ireland's islands can be reached by ferry, too. There are regular services to the Aran Islands from Galway City, Rossaveal (farther west along the south Galway coast) and Doolin in County Clare. The islands off Donegal (Inishbofin, Aran Island) and those off Cork (Bear, Sherkin and Clear Island) are also linked with regular ferries. Others can be reached by private charter services (such as the Blaskets, Skelligs, and Tory Island), usually in the summer only. Get the tourist office leaflet *Island Boat/Air Services* (No. IS50C) for further details. Rathlin is reached from Ballycastle.

Passes Many different discount schemes operate, but you need to assess your probable usage carefully before investing in a pass. Ask the tourist office which would be most appropriate for you. Emerald Cards cover unlimited bus and rail travel throughout Ireland for eight or fifteen days. Rambler or Rover Tickets buy you unlimited travel on Bus Éireann or Irish Rail for so many days within a given period. Runaround tickets are valid on Northern Irish trains. Check at tourist offices for up-to-date information.

More information Irish Rail (Iarnrod Éireann) (tel: 01 8366222); Bus Éireann (tel: 01 8366111);Ulsterbus (tel: 01232 333000); Northern Ireland Railways (tel: 01232 89941). For guided tour information, contact CIE Tours International, 35 Lower Abbey Street Dublin (tel: 01 873 1100) or, in Northern Ireland, the Ulsterbus Travel Centre, Glengall Street, Belfast (tel: 01232 333000).

Security
Most of Ireland is extremely relaxed; even in the tension zones of the North security measures are less stringent than before. Nonetheless, be vigilant. Leave no baggage unattended and always park in authorized places (some central areas are controlled zones where unattended vehicles will be removed or possibly detonated by security forces). If there is an alert, you may have to move very fast. Be prepared to show identification (a passport or driver's license). Always stop at road checks. There are no public places to store

luggage in the North, but lockers are usually available at bus and train stations in the Republic. It is generally illegal to take photographs of police or military barracks in the North and if you are noticed you may be suspected of terrorism. Security forces on both sides of the border are usually extremely polite to bona fide travelers, and if you have nothing to hide, you have nothing to fear.

Student and youth travel
Discounts are available for young people and students. Check fares through specialist agencies such as British-based S.T.A. Travel or Campus Travel, or ask ferry and airline companies direct. Tickets may be subject to availability (only bookable the day before you travel for example) so you need to be more flexible than you might like during busy periods. Check youth fares against other types of discount tickets—there are many cheap fares available. You may need an international student identity card (I.S.I.C.), Youthcard or Travelsave Stamp to obtain these low fares; in some cases a passport or driving license will do. Eurail passes (for under-26-year-olds) are valid in Ireland.

Cheap travel concessions (such as combined accommodations and rail or bus tickets) are also available from The Irish Youth Hostel Association, **An Óige**, based at 61 Mountjoy Street, Dublin 7 (tel: 01 830 4555). It has about 50 hostels all over the Republic, some in attractive old buildings and beautiful settings. The Youth Hostel Association of Northern Ireland runs six hostels (Y.H.A.N.I., 22 Donegall Road, Belfast BT12 5JN, tel: 01232 315435). The 93 hostels of the Independent Hostel Owners group (I.H.O. Information Office, tel: 073 30130) are run along rather more relaxed lines, with private double, single and family rooms as well as traditional dormitory accommodations. Bord Fáilte runs an inspection scheme for independent hostels. Budget accommodations can become overcrowded during peak season.

Telephones
You can find public payphones in street booths and bars or shops (some with a sign saying "you can phone from here"). Older-style call boxes in the Republic are blue and cream and marked in Gaelic "*Telefón.*" Some are antique; follow the instructions carefully. Northern Irish phone booths are red. Newer automatic glass and metal boxes are replacing both types. International calls must be made from newer machines, or from some post offices. Calls connected by the operator—dial 10 (100 in the North)—are much more expensive than direct-dial calls (no cheap rate in the Republic, after 6PM and on weekends in Northern Ireland); so are those made from hotels. Calls to Britain and parts of Europe (including E.U. countries) *are* cheaper after 6PM; to the U.S. or Canada after 10PM; both are cheaper at weekends. Lower rates operate between the Republic and Britain than elsewhere (cheapest of all between midnight and 8AM—direct-dial from an ordinary phone only). Other countries have no reduced-rate call times. Cardphones are a

The older style of Irish phone box

convenient way of making long-distance calls (buy cards at newsdealers or post offices). Many Dublin and Galway numbers have changed, often by adding an extra digit at the beginning. A useful booklet summarizing telephone information and listing international codes can be picked up at airports, post or tourist offices.

Time
Ireland is on Greenwich Mean Time (G.M.T.) in winter; G.M.T. plus one hour in summer (British Summer Time or

---

❏ International Dialing
Omit the initial zero of the local code when dialing internationally.
Access codes to Ireland from:
● United States 011
● Canada 011
● Britain 00
● Australia 0011
● New Zealand 00
followed by 353 for the Republic or 44 for Northern Ireland.

Access codes from the Republic:
● United States 001
● Canada 001
● Britain 0044
● Australia 0061
● New Zealand 0064.

● To dial the North from the Republic, dial 08, followed by the local code (in full, including the initial S.T.D. zero). Check in the phonebook or dial 1190 for local codes.
● To dial the Republic from the North dial 00, followed by 353, then the local code, omitting the initial zero. ❏

Central European Time). "Summer" runs from March to October.
When G.M.T. is in effect, it is five hours later in Ireland than in New York, eight hours later than in California.

Tipping
If service is not included (it often is, at 12 percent or 15 percent), leave a 10 percent–15 percent tip on restaurant

The greener form of transport

bills. Taxi drivers, hotel porters, lounge bar waiters, and so forth like receiving tips as much as anyone, but in general help and advice to strangers is proffered as a natural courtesy in Ireland, without expectation of reward. Tipping is not customary in pubs.

Toilets
Public conveniences (rest rooms) are generally available in towns and tourist sites throughout Ireland. You may see the Gaelic signs *Mná* (women) or *Fir* (men) on some, but ideograms usually leave you in no doubt which is which. Rest rooms in traditional spit-and-sawdust bars may not be particularly well kept.

Tourist information
A list of all Ireland's tourist information offices can be picked up in any tourist office, North or South. All these centers can supply maps, town plans, timetables, brochures, and information on all local sights, events, sports facilities, etc., though for many items a charge is made. Bord Fáilte's green information sheets give useful summaries on many topics (such as fishing, car rental, horse-drawn caravans, Irish folklore). Maps of Ireland are often out of date and inaccurate, fine for general motoring, but not ideal for exploring in detail. Local maps,

such as those produced by Tim Robinson to Connemara, the Aran Islands and the Burren, are the best bet for walking.

Northern Ireland has useful (free) information. Most tourist offices will book accommodation for you, though you have to pay a fee for the telephone calls—it is often better to get the lists and do your own phoning. A 10 percent deposit is taken at the time of booking, later deducted from your final bill. Accommodations unlisted by Bord Fáilte are not necessarily substandard.

Bord Fáilte (Irish Tourist Board)
● Britain: 150 New Bond Street London W1Y 0AQ (tel: 0171-493 3201); also at All-Ireland Tourism, 12 Regent Street, London SW1Y 4PQ (personal callers only)
● Australia: 5th Level, 36 Carrington Street, Sydney, NSW 2000 (tel: 02 299 6177)
● Canada: 160 Bloor Street East, Suite 1150, Toronto, Ontario, M4W 1B9 (tel: 416/929 2777)
● United States: 345 Park Avenue, New York NY 10154 (tel: 212/418 0800)
● Northern Ireland: 53 Castle Street, Belfast BT1 1GH (tel: 01232 32788)

Northern Ireland Tourist Board
● Britain: Northern Ireland Business Center, 11 Berkeley Street, London W1X 5AD (tel: 0171-355 5040 or 0800/282662); also at All-Ireland Tourism, 12 Regent Street, London SW1Y 4PQ (personal callers only)
● Canada: 111 Avenue Road, Suite 450, Toronto, Ontario M5R 3J8 (tel: 416/925 6368)
● Republic of Ireland: 16 Nassau Street, Dublin 2 (tel: 01 679 1977)
● United States: Suite 701, 551 Fifth Avenue, New York NY 10176 (tel: 212/922 0101 or 800/326 0036)

Within the Republic there are about 100 tourist offices marked with the information symbol "i" on a green background. Those in major towns usually stay open all year, Monday to Saturday. Dublin's main tourist office is at 14 Upper O'Connell Street (personal callers only). The Irish Tourist Board is at Baggott Street

A Kinsale character

Bridge, Dublin 2 (tel: 01 676 5871). Northern Ireland has about 30 tourist information centers; N.I.T.B. head office is at 59 North Street, Belfast (tel: 01232 246609).

Useful things to bring
Warm clothes, comfortable footwear, and rain gear are essential. Bring rubber or Gore-tex boots if you are planning to explore the boglands, sensible walking shoes and a compass if you are planning to do any serious walking. A flashlight can be handy for dark churches, caves, or castle ruins, or simply for finding your way home from the pub late at night. Take a sleeping bag for staying in hostels. A good flower or bird identification guide and binoculars are musts for keen naturalists. Camera film is quite expensive in the Republic. Bring any prescribed medicines or contraceptives you need; they may not be available locally. Non-British visitors with electrical appliances will need an adaptor and possibly a transformer. Take your driver's license if you want to rent a car. A passport provides useful identification, even if you don't need to bring it (see entry formalities above). Leave room in your suitcase, though, for an Irish sweater or some tweed clothing. You will certainly want to take home something from the Emerald Isle.

ACCOMMODATIONS

Accommodations registered with the Irish Tourist Board (in the Republic) have a shamrock sign outside. All accommodations in the North are inspected and graded by the N.I.T.B. This isn't always a guarantee of excellence, but it does indicate that some basic standards have been met. Standards of accommodations have risen dramatically recently. Many establishments have been totally renovated in the last few years, with modern bathrooms and all conveniences. Some may feel the old-style charm and period interest has consequently been lost.

There are many splendid country-house hotels in Ireland, and lots of good-value, friendly B. & B.s Middle-range accommodations offering character and value are harder to find— there are many dull and shabby commercial hotels and seedy guesthouses with few attractions for the tourist. In high season all available accommodations can be very busy and it is advisable to book ahead, especially if some popular event or festival is taking place (the Kinsale Food Festival or the Cork Jazz Festival, for example). All the Bord Fáilte and Northern Ireland Tourist Board offices will call around to book a room for you for a small fee.

Three leaflets are well worth looking out for: *The Blue Book*, *The Hidden Ireland*, and *Friendly Homes of Ireland*. The Tourist Office publications *Town and Country Homes, Farm Holidays in Ireland* and *Be Our Guest* also have useful if less discriminating selections. In addition it may be worth getting hold of a copy of *Where to Stay in Northern Ireland*, published by the N.I.T.B., and listing all the recommended accommodations in the province. If you want to stay really cheaply, look for the leaflet *Irish Hostel Guide*, a list of approved independent hostels, or contact An Óige, the Irish Youth Hostel Association (61 Mountjoy Street, Dublin 7, tel: 01 830 4555 in the Republic, and the Youth Hostel Association of Northern Ireland (22 Donegall Road, Belfast BT12 5JN, tel: 01232 315435) in the North. You need an international youth hostel membership card to stay in these hostels. *Self-catering,* listing cottage rentals, is also available. Irish Rent a Cottage plc (85 O'Connell Street, Limerick, tel: 061 411109) is one of the largest specialist companies.

The list of accommodations that follows has been divided into three price categories, based on rates in high season (including tax):

● budget (£): you are likely to find a double bedroom for less than IR£50, including breakfast for two;

● moderate (££): you are likely to find a double bedroom for between IR£50 and IR£80, including breakfast for two;

● expensive (£££): you are likely to pay more than IR£90 for a double bedroom, including breakfast for two.

DUBLIN
(the code for Dublin is 01)

Ariel House (££) 52 Lansdowne Road, Ballsbridge, 4 (tel: 6685512). Well-run Victorian guesthouse, with garden.

Avalon House (£) 55 Aungier Street, 2 (tel: 4750001). Cheerful modern budget accommodations, bright, neat, practical. Self-service café. Rooms sleep 2–6.

Avondale House (££) Scribblestown, Castleknock (tel: 8386545). Elegant 18th-century house near Phoenix Park. Country-house atmosphere (former estate hunting lodge). Trains to center. Good home-cooking.

Buswells (£££) 23/27 Molesworth Street, 2 (tel: 6764013). Gracious town houses in heart of Georgian Dublin. Family-run, formal but relaxing, popular with journalists and politicians.

The Georgian House (£££) 20–21 Lower Baggot Street, 2 (tel: 6618832). Stylishly converted town house near St. Stephen's Green. Elegant lounge, cozy brasserie and seafood (see also restaurant section).

Gray Door (£££) 22–23 Upper Pembroke Street, 2 (tel: 6763286). Restaurant-with rooms in Georgian setting. Accommodations are good, if somewhat impersonal (see also restaurant section).

ISAAC'S (£) 2–5 Frenchman's Lane, 1 (tel: 8749321). Pleasant hostel in converted 18th-century warehouse. Accommodations simple but adequate. Good self-service restaurant. Friendly and well run.

Kinlay House (£) 2–12 Lord Edward Street, 2 (tel: 6796644). Simple, friendly U.S.I.T. (Union of Students in Ireland Travel) hostel for young travelers near Dublin Castle.

Leeson Court (££) 26–27 Lower Leeson Street, 2 (tel: 6763380). Intimate, cheerfully furnished Georgian houses. Patio/beer garden at rear; night-club in basement; evening bar music (well insulated).

Longfield's (££) 9–10 Lower Fitzwilliam Street, 2 (tel: 6761367). Attractively furnished Georgian town-house with intimate basement restaurant (see also restaurant section).

Merrion Hall (£) 54–56 Merrion Road, Ballsbridge, 4 (tel: 6681426). Clean, tastefully furnished Victorian guesthouse. Breakfast served in conservatory.

No 31 (££) 31 Leeson Close, 2 (tel: 6765011). Unusual and stylish house, secluded off smart Georgian street. Architect-designed interior. Lavish bathrooms. Friendly, unassuming owners. Excellent breakfasts. Roof garden.

Raglan Lodge (££) 10 Raglan Road, Ballsbridge, 4 (tel: 6606697). Attractive

Victorian guesthouse in quiet residential area. Antiques. All bedrooms have private bathrooms. **Shelbourne (£££)** 27 St. Stephen's Green, 2 (tel: 6766471). Dublin's grandest hotel in a prime location, immortalized in *Ulysses*. The interior is smartly comfortable, but not daunting (see restaurants). Good for morning coffee and pre-dinner drinks.

Simmonstown House (££) 2 Sydenham Road, Ballsbridge, 4 (tel: 6607260). One of Dublin's least-known but most elegant guesthouses, preserving its civilized Edwardian atmosphere. Bedrooms individually designed.

Stephen's Hall (£££) 14–17 Lower Leeson Street, 2 (tel: 6610585). Georgian exterior; bland modern furnishings within. All suite accommodations with good facilities for business visitors.

EASTERN COUNTIES

County Kildare

Barberstown Castle (£££) Straffan (tel: 01 6288157). Newly renovated restaurant-with-rooms in a mix of medieval, Elizabethan and Victorian surroundings. Expensive reproductions and heavy fabrics; large, sumptuous bedrooms (see also restaurant section).

Moyglare Manor (£££) Moyglare, Maynooth (tel: 01 6286351). Sybaritically furnished Georgian house in extensive parkland, an easy run from Dublin (see also restaurant section).

Silken Thomas (£) The Square, Kildare (tel: 045 22232). Well-kept central inn with ornate conservatory reception rooms and lavish Victoriana. A rear annex, the Lord Edward Guest House, contains practical modern accommodations. Some may find the décor overdone. Decent bar food.

County Louth

Boyne Valley Hotel (££) Drogheda (tel: 041 37737).

Rambling terra-cotta Victorian mansion in waterside grounds. Traditionally comfortable interior. Conservatory bar and Swiss restaurant.

Carlingford House (£) Carlingford (tel: 042 73118). Welcoming family home quietly set in village center. Attractively decorated bedrooms with easy chairs, some with original fireplaces.

The Gables (£) Ardee (tel: 041 53789). The main focus of attention is on the food here. Accommodations in this suburban roadside house are plain and unfrilly, but the welcome is warm (see also restaurant section).

McKevitt's Village Hotel (££) Market Square, Carlingford (tel: 042 73116). Cozy inn, the social heart of this charming village. Firelit bars where snacks are served. Well-equipped, sensibly planned bedrooms in cottagey style with modern pine.

Red House (££) Ardee (tel: 041 53523). Georgian house in parkland, once the home of Lord Carlingford.

Viewpoint (£) Omeath Road, Carlingford (tel: 042 73149). High-quality, split-level, motel-style accommodations with restaurant; superlative views of Carlingford Lough and the Mountains of Mourne. Friendly welcome.

County Meath

Annesbrook (££) Duleek (tel: 041 23293). Imposing Georgian house offering relaxed family hospitality.

Conyngham Arms (££) Slane (tel: 041 24155). Unpretentious but comfortable stone-built village hotel, newly renovated in Edwardian style with modern facilities. Good bar snacks and cakes.

The Glebe House (£) Dowth, Drogheda (tel: 041 36101). A splendidly hospitable, beautifully furnished country house right next to the great passage grave at Dowth (Newgrange is just down the road). Peaceful,

tasteful, and comfortable, with excellent views and good home-cooking.

Station House (££) Kilmessan (tel: 046 25239). This rambling, white Victorian house was indeed once a station linking lines from Dublin with County Meath. Now it is attractive and comfortable, decorated in restful floral prints, overlooking peaceful grounds. The Hill of Tara is just up the road (see also restaurant section).

County Wicklow

Ballyknocken House (£) Glenealy (tel: 0404 44627). Simple 200-acre working farm with peaceful gardens, transformed by its welcoming hostess into a charming guesthouse.

Corner House (£) Enniskerry (tel: 01 2860149). Small guesthouse over the village shop offering good-value B. & B. with showers in each room. A cheap base for Powerscourt or the Wicklow Mountains.

Derrybawn House (£) Glendalough, Laragh (tel: 0404 45134). Attractive and peaceful guesthouse a little way from the tourist traps of Glendalough. Modest facilities, but good value. Log fires and a full-size snooker table. Dinner by arrangement.

Enniscree Lodge Hotel (££) Glencree Road, Enniskerry (tel: 01 2863542). Homey if unremarkable interior redeemed by a spectacular location and views. Popular for Sunday lunch.

Hunter's Hotel (££) Newrath Bridge, Rathnew (tel: 0404 40106). Splendid, old-fashioned coaching inn of unspoiled character and with a long history. Still family-run and idiosyncratic, with luscious gardens, cozy fires and relaxing charm (see also restaurant section). Close to Mount Usher Gardens.

Lissadell House (£) Ashtown Lane, Wicklow (tel: 0404 67458). White detached house on working farm. Modest interior but a warm family welcome.

271

HOTELS AND RESTAURANTS

Old Rectory (£££) Wicklow (tel: 0404 67048). Smartly furnished Regency-style house with good facilities and a secluded atmosphere, on the edge of town (see restaurants).

Rathsallagh House (£££) Dunlavin (tel: 045 53112). Rambling country-house hotel in parkland. Converted from a Queen Anne stable-block when the original house was burned down, this is now a supremely comfortable and appealing place. Tastefully and imaginatively furnished throughout, with gorgeous gardens. Apartment annex, tennis and indoor pool (see also restaurant section).

Tinakilly (£££) Rathnew (tel: 0404 69274). Once the house of Captain Halpin, that Victorian seafarer who commanded the *Great Eastern*. Though now somewhat businesslike in style, the house retains the imposing dimensions specified by its creator, and overlooks lovely gardens to the sea (see also restaurant section).

SOUTHEASTERN COUNTIES

County Carlow
Lorum Old Rectory (£) Kilgreaney, Bagenalstown (tel: 0503 75282). Comfortably furnished house in scenic Barrow Valley.

County Kilkenny
Abbey House (£) Jerpoint Abbey, Thomastown (tel: 056 24166). Strikingly modernized guesthouse very close to the abbey.

Blanchville House (£) Dunbell, Maddoxtown (tel: 056 27197). Elegant Georgian country house with spacious and tasteful rooms. Welcoming atmosphere.

Butler House (££) 16 Patrick Street, Kilkenny (tel: 056 22828). Interesting Civic Trust restoration of the former Dower House of Kilkenny Castle, this now combines stylish modern conveniences with gracious 1770 proportions. Walled

garden. Small conferences sometimes held.

Cullintra House (£) Inistioge (tel: 051 23614). Idiosyncratic but thoroughly interesting creeper-covered farmhouse in wooded valley. Candlelit dinners and open fires. Lovely walks and views.

Garranavabby House (£) The Rower (tel: 051 23613). Simple but appealingly quaint farmhouse dating from 17th century, in glorious scenery. Fresh home cooking.

Lacken House (££) Dublin Road, Kilkenny (tel: 056 61085). Comfortable modern bedrooms with good facilities in this Victorian roadside restaurant-with-rooms (see also restaurant section).

County Tipperary
Aherlow House (££) Glen of Aherlow, Bansha (tel: 062 56153). Chintzy interpretation of old hunting lodge in lovely forest scenery. Antiques and modern furnishings.

Ballycormac House (££) Aglish, near Borrisokane (tel: 067 21129). Charming country house run on informal but decidedly upscale lines. Equestrian holidays a specialty. Excellent food.

Bansha Castle (£) Bansha (tel: 062 54187). Imposing early 19th-century house, a former residence of the Butler family. Now run as a friendly and informal guesthouse.

Bansha House (£) Bansha (tel: 062 54194). Pleasant Georgian guesthouse in 100 acres of farmland where brood mares and foals roam. Modest modern furnishings.

Cappamura House (£) Dundrum (tel: 062 71127). Agreeable pink-washed farmhouse in quiet Golden Vale surroundings, comfortably furnished in a mix of traditional styles.

Cashel Palace (£££) Cashel (tel: 062 61411). Architecturally imposing bishop's residence in quiet setting below the Rock,

somewhat staid inside (see also restaurant section).

Clonmel Arms (££) Clonmel (tel: 052 21233). Reliable if unremarkable town-center hotel.

Gurthalougha House (££) Ballinderry, Terryglass (tel: 067 22080). Delightful Regency farmhouse in forest by Lough Derg. Very peaceful and relaxing. Tastefully furnished and home-like. Good cooking. Outdoor pursuits.

Inch House (£) Bouladuff, Thurles (tel: 0504 51348). Distinguished 300-year-old manor in 330-acre estate. Furnished carefully in period style with antiques and log fires.

Riverrun House (£) Terryglass (tel: 067 22125). Quality new B. & B. venture in peaceful village setting. Light, spacious bedrooms furnished in tasteful modern styles. Log fires. Good breakfast.

County Waterford
Church Villa (£) Dunmore East (tel: 051 383390). Friendly and comfortable B. & B. opposite church. Very good value.

Clonea Strand (££) Clonea Strand, Dungarvan (tel: 058 42416). Recently modernized resort hotel on lovely beach. Leisure and fitness center; no antique charm but lots for families.

Diamond Hill (£) Slieverue, Waterford (tel: 051 32855). Very competently run modern guesthouse just outside town center—somewhat impersonal accommodations but an Irish welcome with award-winning gardens.

Dunmore Lodge (£) Dunmore East (tel: 051 83454). Well-furnished and civilized accommodations in welcoming guesthouse overlooking the bay. Good breakfasts.

Foxmount Farm (£) Halfway House, Waterford (tel: 051 383454). Pleasant 17th-century house in mature gardens. Comfortable furnishings. Good value and convenient for exploring Waterford City or the attractive harbor scenery.

Hanora's Cottage Guesthouse (£) Ballymacarbry, Nire Valley, via Clonmel (tel: 052 36141). Unusual formula offering glorious peaceful valley scenery, modest but pleasant accommodations, afternoon teas, and a short, careful dinner menu. Lots of activities nearby (fishing, riding, golf, etc.). Friendly family atmosphere. Riverside gardens.

Hillfield House (£) Ballymabin, Dunmore East (tel: 051 383565). Enterprising modern B. & B. venture in quiet open farmland. Attractive, well-equipped bedrooms. Spacious and light.

Richmond House (££) Cappoquin (tel: 058 54278). Civilized and interesting Georgian house, once part of the Earl of Cork's estate. Antiques and individual furnishings.

Waterford Castle (£££) The Island, Ballinakill, Waterford (tel: 051 78203). Deluxe hotel on private island (reached by ferry). Lavish Tudor reproduction supplements genuine antiques and tapestries. Many sports facilities (see also restaurant section).

County Wexford

Ballinkeele House (££) Ballymurn, Enniscorthy (tel: 053 38105). Delightful, welcoming house built (imposingly) in 1840. Early Victorian-period feel and many interesting features. Excellent country-house cooking. The owners farm local land and take a great interest in the Wexford Opera Festival.

Clohamon House (££) Bunclody (tel: 054 77253). Charming 18th-century house in 170 acres of land; aristocratic ownership. Dairy farm and pony stud. Private fishing rights and local country activities. Furnished with antiques, family portraits and romantic four-posters. Irish home cooking.

Clonard House (£) Clonard Great, Wexford (tel: 053 43141). Peaceful location

just outside Wexford. Above-average country-house B. & B. in elegant Georgian building (dairy farm). Unassuming hospitality. Informal dinners. Good value.

Kelly's Strand (££) Rosslare (tel: 053 32114). This rambling hotel looks brashly modern, but has a surprisingly long family pedigree. Today it houses predictable modern furnishings and good leisure facilities. Many awards for service and food.

Marlfield House (£££) Gorey (tel: 055 21124). Opulently furnished with flair. Both bedrooms and public areas of this aristocratic country house are a memorable experience (see also restaurant section).

Newbay Country House (££) Newbay, Wexford (tel: 053 42779). Civilized but relaxing country-house hospitality in tastefully furnished Georgian house. Parkland and woods around. Excellent food.

Whites Hotel (££) George Street, Wexford (tel: 053 22311). Solid, comfortable hotel with good facilities, right in the middle of town. Modern boxlike additions spoil the original 19th-century core.

SOUTHWESTERN COUNTIES

County Cork

Arbutus Lodge (££) Montenotte, Cork (tel: 021 501237). Victorian villa in hilly suburbs. Fine city views. Some antiques and interesting plasterwork; other sections are practical and modern. Solid comfort in the bedrooms and renowned food (see also restaurant section).

Assolas Country House (£££) Kanturk (tel: 029 50015). One of Ireland's most charming country houses—and one of the oldest (17th-century in parts). Serene surroundings, period features and antiques throughout. Welcoming atmosphere and lovely gardens. Excellent food (see also restaurant section).

Bailick Cottage (£) Midleton (tel: 021 631244). Charming B. & B. in a creeper-clad house overlooking the estuary. Tasteful and attractive throughout. Excellent breakfasts and a welcoming hostess. Simple meals by arrangement.

Ballylickey Manor House (£££) Ballylickey, Bantry Bay (tel: 027 50071). Peaceful 17th-century manor, now luxuriously furnished in country-house style. Lovely gardens and bay views.

Ballymakeigh House (£) Killeagh, Youghal (tel: 024 95184). Excellent value guesthouse with superb views down to the sea. Very comfortable and well furnished throughout. Welcoming atmosphere and good cooking.

Ballymaloe House (£££) Shanagarry, Midleton (tel: 021 652531). A well-loved hotel, offering peace and some of the best food in Ireland (see also restaurant section). The keep of an old castle stands by the mellow creeper-covered farmhouse. Several outbuildings now house extra accommodations. Modern paintings add to the hotel's imaginative and tasteful décor, including many works by Jack Yeats. Superbly relaxing bedrooms. Family-run with enthusiasm and enterprise.

Ballyvolane House (££) Castlelyons, Fermoy (tel: 025 36349). Georgian mansion offering classy but completely unpretentious hospitality in a fine Italianate setting. Beautiful park and gardens and country-house cooking. House-party style dining at one table.

Bantry House (£££) Bantry (tel: 027 50047). Classy B. & B. offered in a stately home. Recently refurbished bedrooms are spacious and well equipped in light modern colors. Incomparable views of the bay.

Blue Haven (££) Kinsale (tel: 021 772209). Very central small hotel, ever-popular for its excellent, reasonably

273

HOTELS AND RESTAURANTS

priced food (see also restaurant section) and attractive accommodations. Bedrooms may be small but are well equipped. Lively and welcoming.

Conna House (£) Ballynoe, Conna, Tallow (tel: 058 59419). Exceptional B. & B. in Victorian house set in 10 acres of woods and lawns. Beautiful furnishings, including Asian and Middle-Eastern rugs and curios.

Dunauley (£) Seskin, Bantry (tel: 027 50290). Delightful B. & B. in a pleasantly designed modern house overlooking Bantry Bay.

Glebe House (£) Ballinadee, Kinsale (tel: 021 778294). Attractive Georgian rectory, beautifully furnished, very welcoming hosts. Accommodations are simple, but civilized and very good value.

Innishannon House (£££) Innishannon (tel: 021 775121). White-painted house in peaceful riverside setting. Bright, attractive, tasteful furnishings and some interestingly shaped bedrooms. Undaunting, straightforward hospitality.

ISAAC'S (£) 48 MacCurtain Street, Cork (tel: 021 500011). One of the best budget options in the city center. A pleasant, sensibly run hostel in a converted warehouse, with basic, but attractive facilities in dormitory, family, double and single rooms. Good self-service restaurant (open to visitors, see also restaurant section).

Larchwood House (£) Pearsons Bridge, Ballylickey, Bantry (tel: 027 66181). Attractive modern house with light, well -coordinated color schemes. The main attractions of this apparently modest guesthouse, however, are its welcoming owners, beautifully landscaped gardens and exceptional food (see also restaurant section). Very peaceful.

Longueville House (£££) Mallow (tel: 022 47156). One of Ireland's most renowned country manors, a grand building overlooking many

acres of parkland. Inside it is predictably elegant, but has a warm, welcoming feel. Conservatory extension, formal dining room where oil portraits watch you eat superb food, and many period features (see also restaurant section).

Marine (££) Glandore (tel: 028 33366). Simple village hotel in idyllic location overlooking cove.

The Moorings (££) Scilly, Kinsale (tel: 021 772376). Large modern bungalow, somewhat suburban in style but with magnificent glazed extensions giving unparalleled views over Kinsale Harbour. Comfortable and welcoming.

Morrisons Island (£££) Morrisons Quay, Cork (tel: 021 275858). Suite accommodations in a warehouse-styled building overlooking the harbor. If you prefer the unrestricted aspects of a self-contained apartment, this could be the answer. Restaurant and all modern conveniences. Business facilities.

O'Donovan's (£) Clonakilty (tel: 023 33250). Time-warp hotel, emphatically family-run. Furnishings are old-fashioned and basic, but the hotel has many interesting features, including a museum of historical associations. The Republican hero Michael Collins was born just up the road.

Old Bank House (££) Pearse Street, Kinsale (tel: 021 774075). Well-run and tastefully furnished Georgian building near the quayside, offering discreetly upscale B. & B.. The owners run one of Kinsale's best restaurants (the Vintage, see also restaurant section).

Old Presbytery (£) Cork Street, Kinsale (tel: 021 772027). Personally and interestingly furnished, welcoming and homelike B. & B. in quiet (but central) location. Warmly recommended, and with excellent breakfasts. Good evening meals occasionally available.

Scilly House (££) Scilly, Kinsale (tel: 021 772413). Charming and beautifully

located guesthouse with romantically opulent bedrooms.

Sea View House (££) Ballylickey, Bantry (tel: 027 50462). Large white house in lovely gardens, well furnished in traditional style with some more modern additions. Bedrooms are large and light, some overlooking the sea. Genteel and welcoming air.

Seven North Mall (££) 7 North Mall, Cork (tel: 021 397191). Classy B. & B. in a listed Georgian building. Accommodations are practical enough for business people, with all modern conveniences. Breakfasts are excellent. A good location for exploring Cork City, overlooking the river.

County Kerry

Benner's Hotel (££) Main Street, Dingle (tel: 066 51638). Solid, well-furnished town hotel in distinguished Georgian building.

Captain's House (£) The Mall, Dingle (tel: 066 51531). Charming B. & B. in town center, tastefully furnished.

Cleevaun Country Guest House (£) Lady's Cross, Dingle (tel: 066 51108). Simple but welcoming B. & B. in modern bungalow. Rural setting.

Doyle's Seafood Bar and Townhouse (££) John Street, Dingle (tel: 066 51174). This sophisticated establishment is well known in the West for its excellent, tastefully furnished accommodations and brilliant food (see also restaurant section). Unstuffy and informal.

Kathleen's Country House (££) Madam's Height, Tralee Road, Killarney (tel: 064 32810). Modern building, comfortably furnished. What makes it special is Kathleen's brand of effortless hospitality which engulfs you as soon as you set foot inside.

Muxnaw Lodge (£) Castletownbere Road, Kenmare (tel: 064 41252). Atmospheric and welcoming B. & B. just outside town.

Park Hotel (£££) Kenmare (tel: 064 41200). All the trimmings of this fine hotel in lovely grounds make it expensive, but its particular brand of luxury is more than merely professional. It is also remarkably friendly. Excellent food (see also restaurant section).

Royal Hotel (££) College Street, Killarney (tel: 064 31853). If you have to stay in the center of Killarney this is a safe bet, a well-run, traditional town hotel, recently refurbished.

Sheen Falls Lodge (£££) Kenmare (tel: 064 41600). Newly opened and very large luxury hotel hogging the views of these spectacular waterfalls.

Smugglers Inn (£) Cliff Road, Waterville (tel: 066 74330). Simple, inexpensive option on the Ring of Kerry. Enjoy the sea, or a game of golf. Seafood available.

Tahilla Cove (££) Tahilla (tel: 064 45204). Charming guesthouse overlooking bay. Pretty gardens.

Towers Hotel (££) Glenbeigh (tel: 066 68212). Modest, homey hotel in popular resort village. Many local activities.

County Limerick

Adare Manor (£££) Adare (tel: 061 396566). Elaborately Victorian Gothic, former seat of the Earls of Dunraven, now a luxury hotel under American ownership. All modern conveniences and baronial flourishes. Palatial bedrooms.

Dunraven Arms (£££) Adare (tel: 061 396209). A well-known village inn, unspoiled by its hordes from bus tours. Tasteful décor, some antiques and cozy public rooms. Refurbished bedrooms. Good food, formal and informal (see also restaurant section).

WESTERN COUNTIES
County Clare

Carnelly House (£££) Clarecastle (tel: 065 28442). Beautifully proportioned Queen Anne style building in 100 acres of farmland, designed by Francis Bindon. As elegant inside

as out, it now has stylish guesthouse accommodations and classy dinners. Bedrooms are spacious and very tasteful.

Dromoland Castle (£££) Newmarket-on-Fergus (tel: 061 368144). Luxuriously appointed castle hotel in large estate, mostly favored by the wealthy. Private golf course.

Fergus View (£) Kilnaboy, Corofin (tel: 065 37606). Reasonably priced guesthouse quietly set above lakes. Exceptionally wholesome cooking. Pleasant, simple décor.

Gregan's Castle (£££) Ballyvaughan (tel: 065 77005). The most stylish country house hotel on the Burren, overlooking a classic scene of gray limestone. Comfortable, cottage-look décor with all modern conveniences. Attractive, well-kept gardens.

Hyland's Hotel (££) Ballyvaughan (tel: 065 77037). Simple (but homey) village inn with comfortable bedrooms and good public areas. Music sessions in bar.

Lahardan House (f) Crusheen (tel: 065 27128). Modern farmhouse in peaceful countryside, offering slightly bleak accommodations but a family atmosphere.

Rusheen Lodge (£) Knocknagrough, Ballyvaughan (tel: 065 77092). Highly thought of guesthouse in white bungalow on edge of village. Inexpensive base for exploring the north of the Burren. Modern furnishings.

Sheedy's Spa View (££) Lisdoonvarna (tel: 065 74026). Large complex offering unexceptional accommodations but renowned for its food (see also restaurant section).

Smyth's Village (£) Feakle (tel: 061 924002). Modern complex of cottage-like buildings in lovely countryside. This unusual enterprise offers simple accommodations and restaurant facilities for a

moderate price. Private functions may take over at times. Activities can be arranged. Evening music in summer.

Thomond House (£££) Dromoland (tel: 061 368304). The former laird of Dromoland, Lord Inchiquin, now lives in this modest Georgian pastiche on the estate grounds and will share it with you for a nominal fee. It is very comfortable, though lacks the authenticity of Ireland's many genuine Georgian country houses.

County Galway

Ardagh (££) Clifden, Connemara (tel: 095 21384). Modern, stylish Dutch-owned hotel overlooking a splendid chunk of Connemara's coastal scenery from the upper restaurant windows. Pleasing décor (lots of plants) and extensive public rooms. Bedrooms are comfortable, spacious and well equipped.

Ardilaun House (££) Taylors Hill, Galway (tel: 091 21433). Smartly furnished mid-market hotel near the resort of Salthill. Considerable business trade.

Ballynahinch Castle (££) Recess, Connemara (tel: 095 31006). Somewhat on the bus tour circuit at lunch or tea-time, but this large estate house (once bought by a Maharajah) in beautiful scenery is very comfortable indeed for residents (see also restaurant section).

Cashel House (£££) Cashel Bay, Connemara (tel: 095 31001). Luxuriously furnished small hotel in white-painted Victorian house by coast. Lush, sheltered subtropical gardens. Many antiques and excellent food and wines. Peaceful, upscale atmosphere.

Crocnaraw (££) Moyard, Connemara (tel: 095 41068). Attractively furnished and very quiet country house in splendid Connemara countryside. Stylish throughout, with lovely gardens.

275

Currarevagh House (££) Oughterard, Connemara (tel: 091 82312). This secluded country house offers utter lakeshore peace —it may even be too quiet for some. A slightly staid air prevails, and some furnishings are a little dowdy. However, it is comfortable and the views from spacious bedrooms are splendid.

Delphi Lodge (££) Leenane (tel: 095 42211). Welcoming atmosphere in relaxingly informal family home. Seven guestrooms all have bathrooms and lovely views. Extremely peaceful, with good country cooking. Good for fishing and walking. Some rooms with kitchens.

Erriseask House (££) Ballyconneely, Connemara (tel: 095 23553). Attractively decorated modern farmhouse in lovely coastal scenery. Light, airy bedrooms. Stylish but informal public areas.

Johnston Hernon's Kilmurvey House (£) Inishmore, Aran Islands (tel: 099 61218). Comfortable eight-bedroomed stone farmhouse near Dun Aengus fort. Good fresh fish, and minibus transport to harbor and airport.

Kille House (£) Kingstown, Clifden, Connemara (tel: 095 21849). Pleasantly furnished guesthouse in distinguished early Victorian house in isolated location off the beautiful Sky Road northwest of Clifden. Very peaceful. Good cooking by arrangement.

Moycullen House (££) Moycullen, Connemara (tel: 091 85566). Secluded white-painted house in lush grounds. Interestingly furnished inside, each bedroom is different. Welcoming atmosphere. Good home-cooking by arrangement.

Rock Glen Manor House (££) Clifden, Connemara (tel: 095 21035). This traditional hotel occupies a lovely setting above the bay. Inside it is solidly comfortable, springing no decorative surprises, but

has a relaxing and friendly air.

Rosleague Manor (£££) Letterfrack, Connemara (tel: 095 41101). Imposing Georgian house overlooking Ballinakill Bay, now converted into a peaceful and comfortable country-house hotel with a fine reputation for good food (see also restaurant section).

County Mayo

Ashford Castle (£££) Cong (tel: 092 46003). Sister hotel of Dromoland, it offers substantially the same package of Gothic-revival grandeur and a splendid parkland and lakeshore setting.

Enniscoe House (££) Castlehill, near Crossmolina, Ballina (tel: 096 31112). One of Ireland's finest Georgian mansions—"the last great house of North Mayo." Many period features remain intact, and the house is furnished and decorated throughout with great taste, though it feels informal too. Good cooking. Heritage center and small museum on estate.

Healy's (££) Pontoon (tel: 094 56443). Low-slung old stone building in scenic lakeshore setting. Simple bar food and hearty Irish cooking in the restaurant. Clean, comfortable bedrooms. Good site for birdwatching.

Newport House (££) Newport (tel: 098 41222). Elegantly furnished country-house hotel, formerly the seat of a branch of the O'Donnell family, Earls of Tyrconnell who were dispatched west of the Shannon by Cromwell. The house is full of history and interesting objects. A good fishing base.

Olde Railway Hotel (££) The Mall, Westport (tel: 098 25605). Old-fashioned town hotel, now comfortably refurbished in traditional style.

Rosturk Woods (£) Mulrany (tel: 098 36264). Exceptionally pleasant guesthouse in quiet location, furnished with taste and flair throughout.

NORTHWESTERN COUNTIES
County Donegal

Bruckless House (£) Bruckless (tel: 073 37071). Attractive 18th-century farmhouse in large grounds of well-kept gardens and woodland. Sea views from some windows. Good home cooking.

Castle Murray House (£) St. John's Point, Dunkineely (tel: 073 37022). Acclaimed restaurant-with-rooms in splendid location (see also restaurant section).

Gortfad (£) Castlefinn (tel: 074 46135). Family home in Victorian/Edwardian house. Peaceful touring base.

Harvey's Point Country Hotel (££) Lough Eske, Donegal Town (tel: 073 22208). Modern luxurious Swiss restaurant with rooms on shores of lough. Many sports facilities (see also restaurant section).

Kee's Hotel (££) Main Street, Stranorlar, Ballybofey (tel: 074 31018). Family-run hotel in village near the Bluestack Mountains. 19th-century coaching inn, recently refurbished. Leisure center.

Rathmullan House (££) Rathmullan (tel: 074 58188). One of Donegal's few country-house hotels, dating from the 18th century. Lovely gardens stretch towards the beach. Rooms overlook Lough Swilly, a fjord. Saltwater pool. Good food (see also restaurant section).

St. Ernan's (£££) St. Ernan's Island, Donegal Town (tel: 073 21065). Beautifully situated on a wooded island linked to the mainland by a causeway, this 19th-century pinkish-cream house is a haven of peace. Furnishings echo the Regency theme of the house. Good food (see also restaurant section).

Sand House (££) Rossnowlagh (tel: 072 51777). Long-established and family-run resort hotel on one of Donegal's best beaches. Castle-like architecture. Inside it is lively but relaxing, with roaring fires and bright furnishings.

276

Smuggler's Creek (£) Rossnowlagh (tel: 072 52366). Cheerful and popular bistro-style bar overlooking the bay. Bedrooms are fresh and clean with floral wallpapers and modern pine. Breakfast served in conservatory extension with lovely views (see also restaurant section).

County Leitrim
Glebe House (£) Mohill (tel: 078 31086). Attractive rectory guesthouse in 38 acres of farmland and woods. Many local activities.
Stanford's Village Inn (£) Dromahair (tel: 071 64140). Simple village pub with accommodations in the heart of Yeats country. Bedrooms are small and modest but have showers. Period interest in the museum-like old-fashioned bar next door.

County Sligo
Coopershill (££) Riverstown (tel: 071 65108). One of Ireland's best-loved and most hospitable country-house hotels, peacefully set in extensive wooded grounds. The handsome Georgian house retains many period features, including splendidly antique bathroom fittings. House-party atmosphere and notable food. Family-run for several generations.
Cromleach Lodge Country House (£££) Castlebaldwin, near Boyle (tel: 071 65155). Modern restaurant-with-rooms taking advantage of beautiful hilltop views. Bedrooms are very spacious and comfortable with stylish new furnishings (see also restaurant section).
Markree Castle (£££) Collooney (tel: 071 67800). Impressively castellated in the 19th century, this house, seat of the Cooper family, is nonetheless genuinely old. Inside it is in parts drafty and cavernous, but mostly comfortable and relaxing, with lovely views of gardens and parklands (see also restaurant section).

Ross House (££) Riverstown (tel: 071 65140). Friendly farm B&B offering simple, reasonably priced accommodations with character.
Temple House (££) Ballymote (tel: 071 83329). Unusual Georgian mansion revamped to contain 100 rooms in Victorian times, overlooking a lakeside Templar castle. Good local produce served.
Urlar House (£) Drumcliffe (tel: 071 63110). Simple but civilized farmhouse accommodations in the shadow of Benbulben. Peaceful.

NORTHERN IRELAND
County Antrim
Ash-Rowan Guest House (££) 12 Windsor Avenue, Belfast (tel: 01232 661758). Above-average B. & B. in quiet, roomy Victorian house. Each bedroom individually decorated with private facilities. Good breakfasts. No-smoking house.
Auberge de Seneirl (££) 28 Ballyclough Road, Bushmills (tel: 012657 41536). Stylishly furnished restaurant-with-rooms converted from an old country schoolhouse. Indoor pool, sauna, solarium (see also restaurant section).
Ballygally Castle (££) 274 Coast Road, Ballygally (tel: 01574 583212). A Scottish planter castle, complete with ghost, converted to a comfortable modern hotel: Sea views from some windows.
Camera House (££) 44 Wellington Park, Belfast (tel: 01232 660026). Charming B. & B., a bright spark amid streets of unremarkable guesthouses in the university area. Clean, personal and friendly.
Dobbins Inn (££) 6 High Street, Carrickfergus (tel: 019603 51905). Ancient family-run inn in town center, offering plain accommodations with private baths. Popular, lively bar—good snacks and morning coffee.
Dukes (£££) 65 University Street, Belfast (tel: 01232 236666). Stylish new hotel

in university area with good facilities and plenty of greenery in public areas.
Dunadry Inn (£££) 2 Islandreagh Drive, Dunadry (tel: 018494 32474). Whitewashed building incorporating country-club facilities. Large gardens. Handy for airport.
Londonderry Arms (££) Harbour Road, Carnlough (tel: 01574 885255). Creeper-covered coaching inn with seaside garden, and antique furnishings in Georgian style. Some rooms are modern and functional. Hearty Irish food served, with traditional music in summer.
Malone Guest House (£) 79 Malone Road, Belfast (tel: 01232 669565). Simple but clean and practical accommodations offered in a residential district near the university.
Stranmillis Lodge (££) 14 Chlorine Gardens, Belfast (tel: 01232 682009). Quiet suburban location near university and botanic gardens. Inside, furnished to a high and practical standard with modern, inoffensive furnishings. Evening menu available.
Whitepark House (£) Whitepark Bay, Ballintoy (tel: 012657 31482). Certainly one of the more imaginatively furnished country guesthouses within striking distance of the Giant's Causeway. Secluded setting and attractive gardens.

County Down
Culloden (£££) 142 Bangor Road, Holywood (tel: 012327 425223). Grand baronial mansion in palatial woods and parkland. Luxurious facilities and décor. High-profile security. Close to Ulster Folk Museum.
Glassdrumman Lodge (££) 85 Mill Road, Annalong (tel: 013967 68451). Stylishly furnished modern house at the foot of the Mountains of Mourne. Very comfortable light bedrooms with all modern conveniences. Relaxing and secluded. Acclaimed food (see also restaurant section).

277

Portaferry Inn (££) The Strand, Portaferry (tel: 012477 28231). Whitewashed inn overlooking Strangford Lough, a stone's throw from the ferry. Well-kept modern rooms with predictable but enjoyable seafood.

County Fermanagh
Jamestown House (££) Magheracross, Ballinamallard (tel: 0136581 209). Fine Georgian house near Lough Erne. Spacious well-furnished bedrooms. Private fishing. Good food.
Killyreagh (££) Tamlaght, Enniskillen (tel: 01365 387221). Lord Hamilton's elegant 19th-century house in parkland.

County Londonderry
Beech Hill Country House (££) 32 Ardmore Road, Derry (tel: 01504 49279). Grand Victorian house comfortably furnished and in lovely gardens. Serious food (see also restaurant section).
Blackheath House (££) 112 Killeague Road, Blackhill, Coleraine (tel: 01265 868433). Listed 18th-century rectory amid extensive landscaped gardens. Furnished in traditional styles with some antiques. Good food (see also restaurant section).
Camus House (£) 27 Curragh Road, Coleraine (tel: 01265 42982). Charming stone farmhouse overlooking River Bann near salmon leap, dating back to 1685. Bedrooms are decorated in light colors.
Coolbeg (£) 2e Grange Road, Coleraine (tel: 01265 44961). Modern bungalow in suburban setting, quiet and well equipped. Suitable for visitors with disabilities.
Greenhill House (£) 24 Greenhill Road, Aghadowey, Coleraine (tel: 01265 868241). Georgian country house in secluded countryside. Homey and welcoming atmosphere with substantial country cooking.

LAKELAND COUNTIES
County Laois
Roundwood House (££) Mountrath (tel: 0502 32120). Delightful Georgian house, intriguing both for its Palladian villa architecture (splendidly intact thanks to its owners' keen support for the Georgian Society) and its food (see also restaurant section). The atmosphere is always cheerful, hospitable, informal and very, very Irish. The preservation of its period character takes precedence over 20th-century superfluities such as television. Try good conversation or a book instead.
Tullamoy House (£) Stradbally (tel: 0507 27111). Sympathetically furnished 19th-century stone house in quiet countryside. Good home-cooking and plenty of leisure pursuits nearby: golf, fishing, and the Curragh. Dogs and children welcome.

County Longford
Carrigglas Manor (£££) Longford (tel: 043 45165). Gothic-revival house near the Shannon, grandly furnished within. Excellent trout fishing and many other outdoor pursuits. Good traditional cooking. Some rooms with kitchens. Non-residents visit the house to look around. Tearooms, costume museum, guided tours.

County Monaghan
Hilton Park (£££) Clones (tel: 047 56007). Palatial mansion set in fine parkland, home of the present occupants for many generations. Run very much as a family home; furnishings are full of character and the food is excellent. Country-house atmosphere.

County Offaly
Tullanisk (££) Birr (tel: 0509 20572). The former adjunct to Birr Castle estate has a reputation far and wide as one of the most charming and hospitable country houses in the Midlands. Many sporting opportunities. Beautifully furnished, excellent cooking.

County Roscommon
Clonalis House (££) Castlerea (tel: 0907 20014). Ancestral home of the O'Conors of Connaught (last High Kings of Ireland). The house, though not especially old, is full of interest. Bedrooms are palatially sized and have good park views. Some with kitchens.

County Westmeath
Mornington (£) Multyfarnham (tel: 044 72191). Delightful late Victorian house (with Georgian core) offering most comfortable accommodations and excellent cooking, using fresh local produce. Dinner is by candlelight. Fine views across Lough Derravaragh to Knock Ion. Sporting opportunities, including croquet, fox hunting, and fishing.

RESTAURANTS

The following restaurants have also been divided into three price categories: budget (£); moderate (££) and expensive (£££).

DUBLIN
(the code for Dublin is 01)
Aisling (£££) (the restaurant of the Shelbourne Hotel, see accommodations). Distinguished, expensive menu worth dressing up for.
Ante Room Seafood Restaurant (££) (the restaurant of the Georgian House, see accommodations). Intimate setting, sophisticated atmosphere. Music some nights.
Bad Ass Café (£) Crown Alley, Temple Bar, 2 (tel: 6712596). Lively pizza place in converted warehouse where Sinéad O'Connor was once a waitress. Popular with all age groups.
Beshoff's (£) 14 Westmoreland Street, 2 (tel: 6778026). One contender for Dublin's fish-and-chip crown. Edwardian bistro décor.
Bewley's Oriental Café (£) Four central locations: South Great George Street, Mary

Street, Westmoreland Street, and the main one in Grafton Street (tel: 6776761). Coffee shop *par excellence*, embellished with mahogany and stained glass. Sticky buns or full meals. Upstairs (in Grafton Street) it's less crowded, with a museum. All walks of life end up here.

Burdock's (£) 2 Werburgh Street, 2 (tel: 5403606). A legend in fish and chips. Closed Sunday.

The Commons (£££) Newman House, 85–86 St. Stephen's Green, 2 (tel: 4752597). Urbane, classic French cooking served amid a fine collection of commissioned modern art and startling furnishings.

Le Coq Hardi (£££) 35 Pembroke Road, 4 (tel: 6689070). Gentleman's club surroundings and ultra-serious gourmet food and wine. Popular with business fraternity.

Eastern Tandoori (££) 34 South William Street, 2 (tel: 6710428). Popular authentic Indian cuisine, décor, and music. Extensive vegetarian choice.

Elephant and Castle (££) 18 Temple Bar, 2 (tel: 6793121). Bustling, chic venue for drinks or dinner. Eclectic, Californian-style cuisine—burgers, guacamole and tortilla chips, pasta, omelettes. Good for people-watching.

Fitzers, National Gallery Restaurant (£) Merrion Square, 2 (tel: 6614496). Good self-service restaurant to stave off hunger brought on by cultural overdose. Reasonably priced wine. Daytime only.

Gallagher's Boxty House (£) 20 Temple Bar, 2 (tel: 6772762). A formula based on griddled Irish potato cakes (boxties) wrapping up all kinds of savoury fillings. Bacon and cabbage, champ, smoked fish, and other Irish fare. Always popular. Homey (modern) country décor of pine and pottery.

Imperial (££) 12a Wicklow Street, 2 (tel: 6772580). Superior Chinese, specializing in dim sum. Popular at

Sunday lunchtime. Good value if you stick to tea rather than wine.

Kapriol (££) 45 Lower Camden Street, 2 (tel: 4751235). Vibrant North Italian cooking amid Dolomite décor.

Kilkenny Kitchen (£) Nassau Street, 2. (tel: 6777066). On first floor of Kilkenny Design Center. Excellent self-service coffee shop and restaurant, capitalizing on the success of the stylish original in Kilkenny. Always busy at lunchtime.

La Stampa (££) 35 Dawson Street, 2 (tel: 6778611). Elegant mirrored surroundings reflect a serious but unstuffy interest in food. Despite the name, the style is French, the clientele young and cool.

Les Frères Jacques (££) 74 Dame Street, 2 (tel: 6794555). Ambitious food—mostly French with Irish farmhouse cheeses.

Mitchell's Cellars (££) 21 Kildare Street, 2 (tel: 6680367). Bistro-style wine bar and restaurant. Pâtés, quiches, casseroles. Lunchtime only. Closed Sunday.

No 10 (£££) (the restaurant of Longfield's, see accommodations). Intimate basement dining room with stylish white linen and crystal. Elegant atmosphere. Successful blend of French and Irish cooking.

Pasta Fresca (£) 3–4 Chatham Street, 2 (tel: 6792402). Stylish Italian cuisine, including good versions of well-known favorites and more unusual things. The pasta, of course, is *fresca*.

Patrick Guilbaud (£££) 46 James Place, Lower Baggot Street, 2 (tel: 6764192). Hushed, reverential atmosphere indicates that this is *cuisine serieuse*, and the only place in Dublin with a Michelin rosette. Business clients dine in discretion here. Mostly classic French, with an occasional pig's trotter thrown in for regional interest.

Periwinkle Seafood Bar (£) Powerscourt Center, South

William Street, 2 (tel: 6794203). Bar-counter restaurant popular with grazing shoppers. Good chowder.

Pigalle (££) 14 Temple Bar, 2 (tel: 6719262). Good French *paysanne* food like gratins, tarts, mousses, and soups in cramped bistro setting.

Pizzeria Italia (£) 23 Temple Bar, 2 (tel: 6778528). Cheerful, lively restaurant where Italianate décor provides a suitable backdrop for good-value pizzas, pastas and plenty more, all served with good humor and efficiency.

Rajdoot (££) 26–28 Clarendon Street, Westbury Center, 2 (tel: 6794274). High-quality Moghul specialties here, in elegant, discreetly formal setting.

Royal Hospital (£) Kilmainham (tel: 6718666). The coffee shop restaurant is good here, especially at Sunday lunchtimes, when whole families appear. Simple home cooking.

Shalimar (££) 17 South Great George's Street, 2 (tel: 6710738). Yet another of Dublin's surprising ethnic winners. North Indian and Pakistani cooking.

Sichuan (£££) 4 Lower Kilmacud Road, Stillorgan (tel: 2884817). State-owned Chinese restaurant (owned by the People's Republic of China, that is). Authentic ingredients and real Chinese chefs.

EASTERN COUNTIES
County Dublin
Abbey Tavern (££) Abbey Street, Howth (tel: 01 390282). Olde-worlde tavern specializing in fish. Traditional Irish music most nights (separate annex).

Ayumi-Ya (£££) Newpark Center, Newtownpark Avenue, Blackrock (tel: 01 283 1767). Acclaimed Japanese food.

Guinea Pig (££) 17 Railway Road, Dalkey (tel: 2859055). Accomplished seafood specialties are served up by a former local mayor. Good-value early bird dinner menu.

HOTELS AND RESTAURANTS

King Sitric (££) East Pier, Howth (tel: 01 8325235). Celebrated seafood in delightful harborside setting.

Na Mara (££) Railway Station, Harbour Road, Dun Laoghaire (tel: 01 2806767). Meat and fresh seafood in one of Ireland's earliest railway stations.

Red Bank (££) 7 Church Street, Skerries (tel: 01 8491005). Relaxing family-run seafood restaurant in converted bank. Dinner only.

County Kildare
Barberstown Castle (££) Straffan (tel: 01 6288157). Imaginative dishes served in the 16th-century stone banqueting hall (see also accommodations section).

Doyle's Schoolhouse (££) Castledermot (tel: 0503 44282). Modern country cooking in 1930s school.

Lawlor's Restaurant (££) Poplar Square, Naas (tel: 045 97085). Hearty steaks and fish for the racing crowd. Lighter meals in the bar.

Moyglare Manor (£££) Moyglare, Maynooth (tel: 01 6286351, see also accommodations section). Elaborate French menu complements the sumptuous décor.

County Louth
Buttergate (££) Millmount, Drogheda (tel: 041 34759). Spirited French cuisine on the upper floors of the converted barracks buildings by the museum.

Forge Gallery (££) Collon (tel: 041 26272). Well-established restaurant, decorated with the work of local artists. Generous portions of French provincial and traditional Irish cooking.

The Gables (££) Ardee (tel: 041 53789, see also accommodations section). French country cooking served with a generous spirit in traditional surroundings of velvet, linen, lace, and silver.

Jordans (££) Carlingford (tel: 042 73223). Village center pub bistro. Good fish and some exotic surprises.

County Meath
Station House (££) Kilmessan (tel: 046 25239, see also accommodations section). Local fresh produce served in calm, unflashy setting.

County Wicklow
Hunter's (££) Newrath Bridge, Rathnew (tel: 0404 40106, see also accommodations section). Traditional country-house cuisine using local produce, such as Wicklow lamb. Afternoon teas in the garden.

Old Rectory (£££) Wicklow (tel: 0404 67048, see also accommodations section). Talented and imaginative fare served in intimate surroundings. Interesting Spanish wines. Local organic produce.

Rathsallagh House (£££) Dunlavin (tel: 045 53112, see also accommodations section). Small but classy dining-room serving hearty but utterly interesting country cooking.

Tinakilly (£££) Rathnew (tel: 0404 69274, see also accommodations section). Elegant Irish/French cooking in rather formal surroundings.

Tree of Idleness (££) Seafront, Bray (tel: 01 2863498). Unusually excellent Greek-Cypriot cooking in Victorian house. Dinner only.

SOUTHEASTERN COUNTIES
County Carlow
Lord Bagenal Inn (£) Leighlinbridge (tel: 0503 21668). Famous old inn now serving a good range of undemanding food in the bar with more sophisticated French cuisine in the restaurant. Open fires and rustic décor.

County Kilkenny
Kilkenny Design Center (£) Castle Yard, Kilkenny (tel: 056 22118). Sparkling self-service restaurant in attractive upper floors of the castle stable building, housing a fine selection of Irish craft products.

Lacken House (££) Dublin Road, Kilkenny (tel: 056 61085, see also accommodations section). Traditionally furnished cellar dining-rooms, serving imaginative international cuisine.

County Tipperary
Bee's Knees Bistro (£) Clonmel (tel: 052 21457). Good organic café for daytime snacks.

Cashel Palace (££) Cashel (tel: 062 61411, see also accommodations section). The Buttery restaurant downstairs is one of the coziest places in Cashel for a snack, full meal or drink. Open fires in winter.

Chez Hans (££) Cashel (tel: 062 61177). Parisian bistro-style in the setting of an old Baptist church. Generous portions. Cashel blue cheese figures on the menu.

County Waterford
Dwyers (££) Mary Street, Waterford (tel: 051 77478). Pleasantly intimate restaurant a block or two back from the waterside. Small, interesting menu. Evenings only.

Ship Inn (££) Dunmore East (tel: 051 83141). Nautically decorated pub with interesting fishy dishes.

Waterford Castle (£££) The Island, Ballinakill, Waterford (tel: 051 78203, see also accommodations section). Classily presented gourmet food (lobster, asparagus, poached salmon) and home-made classics like bread-and-butter pudding.

County Wexford
Cellar Restaurant (££) Horetown House, Foulksmills (tel: 051 63771). Fine country cooking in the splendid setting of a 300-year-old Georgian manor.

The Galley (££) New Ross (tel: 051 21723). Mobile, cruising restaurants operate between Waterford and New Ross during the summer, offering fresh local produce.

Marlfield House (£££) Gorey (tel: 055 21124, see also accommodations section). The style of the food matches the rest of the house—rich, opulent, complicated.

Neptune (££) Ballyhack (tel: 051 89284). Near the castle and the car ferry that plies to Passage East, this agreeable little seafood restaurant is worth crossing the water for. Harp recitals.

Oyster Restaurant (££) Rosslare Strand (tel: 053 32439). Wine bar and seafood restaurant in the heart of the resort.

SOUTHWESTERN COUNTIES
County Cork
Aherne's (££) Youghal (tel: 024 92424). Excellent range of seafood produced in various levels of elaboration in this thriving enterprise. Modern, well-equipped accommodations also available.

Arbutus Lodge (££) Montenotte, Cork (tel: 021 501237, see also accommodations section). Classic Cork favorites are the things they do best here, though ambitious chefs strive for perfection in many directions.

Assolas House (£££) Kanturk (tel: 029 50015, see also accommodations section). Skillful use of the best available local produce ensures the success of this country-house restaurant.

Ballymaloe House (£££) Shanagarry (tel: 021 652531, see also accommodations section). An Irish legend which now dispenses the talent and experience of the Allen dynasty through its cookery school. Superbly accomplished and reasonably priced food, using local produce to full advantage.

Blairs Cove House (££) Durrus (tel: 027 61127). Buffet-style seafood starters, local fish and meat, and splendid desserts served on the grand piano. A lovely Georgian house overlooking the sea.

Blue Haven (££) Kinsale (tel: 021 772209, see also accommodations section). Excellent range of undemanding, filling seafood, snacks, and meat.

Chez Youen (££) Baltimore (tel: 028 20136). Popular

seafood restaurant near harbor.

Cliffords (£££) 18 Dyke Parade, Cork (tel: 021 275333). Smart, formal, French-style restaurant in town center.

Crawford Gallery Café (££) Emmet Place, Cork (tel: 021 274415). A scion of the Allen family of Ballymaloe House (see above) masterminds this attractive gallery restaurant. Whether you call in for a cake or a full meal, excellence is assured. Now open several evenings a week too (Wednesday—Friday).

Dunworley Cottage Restaurant (££) Dunworley, Butlerstown, Clonakilty (tel: 023 40314). News of this isolated restaurant has steadily filtered through to the "foodies" of West Cork. Dynamic food served in modest surroundings.

Finins (££) 75 Main Street, Midleton (tel: 021 631878). Simple meat and seafood dishes, filling soups, etc. unpretentiously served.

ISAAC'S (£) 48 MacCurtain Street, Cork (tel: 021 500011, see also accommodations section). Good-value hostel self-service restaurant. Mostly organic foods.

Larchwood House (££) Pearsons Bridge, Bantry (tel: 027 66181, see also accommodations section). Imaginative and satisfying Irish country cooking in a modest guesthouse.

Longueville House (£££) Mallow (tel: 022 47156, see also accommodations section). August and formal food for serious eaters.

Quay Coop (£) 24 Sullivans Quay, Cork (tel: 021 317660). Thoroughly imaginative wholefood and vegetarian specialties.

Shiro (£££) Ahakista, near Bantry (tel: 027 67030). Remarkably situated restaurant serving exquisitely presented authentic Japanese food. Attentive service. Advance booking always essential.

The Vintage (££) 50 Main Street, Kinsale (tel: 021 772502). Cozy and

romantic setting for a Hamburg chef to conjure up some of Kinsale's best cuisine.

County Kerry
Doyle's Seafood Bar (££) John Street, Dingle (tel: 066 51174, see also accommodations section). Excellent and highly praised seafood dishes (and other things) served with minimal ceremony.

Lime Tree (££) Kenmare (tel: 064 41225). Intimate setting for uncomplicated fish and meat dishes.

Nick's (££) Killorglin (tel: 066 61219). Relaxed beamed dining room where excellent fish dishes are prepared.

Park (£££) Kenmare (tel: 064 41200, see also accommodations section). Gourmet food in serene surroundings.

Strawberry Tree (££) 24 Plunkett Street, Killarney (tel: 064 32688). Lively and generous meals served with plenty of calories; friendly staff.

County Limerick
Dunraven Arms (££) Adare (tel: 061 396209, see also accommodations section). Reliable Irish cooking, whether a sandwich in the bar or a full meal in the restaurant.

Mustard Seed (£££) Adare (tel: 061 396451). Inventive food in charming cottage setting.

WESTERN COUNTIES
County Clare
Bunratty Castle (££) Bunratty (tel: 061 360788) Classic medieval banquets in castle setting with full program of entertainment. Two sittings; book at any tourist office.

Claire's Restaurant (££) Ballyvaughan (tel: 065 77029). Simple dining room at the back of a craft shop dispenses attractive combinations of Burren goat's cheese, Ballyvaughan crab, or plain Galway Bay oysters.

The Cloister (££) Abbey Street, Ennis (tel: 065

281

29521). Simple seafood and snacks are available in the bar from lunchtime onwards; more complex fish dishes in the dining-room. Treacle bread and Inagh goat's cheese salad are specialties.

Knappogue Castle (££) near Quin (tel: 061 360788) Medieval feasting in well-restored castle accompanied by entertainers recounting stories of Celtic Ireland; book at any tourist office.

MacCloskey's (£££) Bunratty House Mews, Bunratty (tel: 061 364082). In the middle of Bunratty's shamrock-and-leprechaun version of Ireland, this hard-headed and competent restaurant is a breath of fresh air. Classical and *nouvelle cuisine* combine local ingredients with skill and flair in intimate, romantic surroundings.

Manuel's Seafood (££) Corbally, Kilkee (tel: 065 56211). If you find yourself exploring the south Clare coast you might try this place at dinnertime for local seafood or vegetarian specials in a small modern hilltop restaurant.

Sheedy's Spa View (££) Lisdoonvarna (tel: 065 74026, see also accommodations section). The Orchid Room restaurant is often praised for its outstanding five-course set dinner—French/Irish cuisine prepared by the family owners. Friendly atmosphere and hearty servings.

County Galway
Aran Islands Hostel Restaurant (£) Kilronan Harbour, Inishmore, Aran Islands (tel: 099 61255). A good place for inexpensive daytime snacks and vegetarian evening meals.

Ballynahinch Castle (££) Recess, Connemara (tel: 095 31006, see also accommodations section). The dining room produces formal and correct food here, a serene and relaxing setting. If you want something simpler, there is an excellent range

of bar food available in the Fisherman's pub.

Drimcong House (££) Moycullen (tel: 091 85115). A fine 17th-century house provides the setting for this attractive restaurant which produces carefully thought out concoctions of local products in imaginative combinations of sweet and savory flavors. One of the West's foremost restaurants, and acclaimed throughout Ireland.

Dunguaire Castle (££) Kinvara (tel: 091 37108). Banquet fare accompanied by literary gleanings from Synge, Shaw, and O'Casey; book at any tourist office.

Fat Freddy's (£) Quay Street, Galway (tel: 091 67279). One of the best places for pizza, cheerful, youthful, informal.

McDonagh's Seafood Bar (£) 22 Quay Street, Galway (tel: 091 65001). A great place for seafood, relaxed and informal, with long opening hours.

Moran's Oyster Cottage (££) The Weir, Kilcolgan, Clarinbridge (tel: 091 961113). Oysters are what they do best here, as the name suggests, from their own beds just outside. But you can get a great chowder, and lots of other seafood besides, accompanied by delicious soda bread and chilled white wine—or decent Guinness.

O'Grady's Seafood (££) Clifden (tel: 095 21450). Reasonably priced seafood in unpretentious surroundings.

Paddy Burke's (££) Clarinbridge (tel: 091 96226). Another great location for oyster-sampling, but you can find plenty of other seafood and hearty Irish cooking here. Always popular and bustling.

Rosleague Manor (£££) Letterfrack, Connemara (tel: 095 41101, see also accommodations section). Award-winning restaurant featuring seafood and home-grown vegetables.

County Mayo
Asgard (££) The Quay, Westport (tel: 098 25319). A smart candlelit dining room

above a pub provides an intimate setting for seafood specialties. Nautical décor and brass ceiling fans. Efficient and trendy service.

Chalet Seafood (£) Keel, Achill Island (tel: 098 43157). Simple versions of fresh local seafood (such as home-smoked salmon).

Continental Café (£) Westport (tel: 098 26679). Simple homemade fare, including soups and cakes.

Quay Cottage (££) The Quay, Westport (near entrance to Westport House) (tel: 098 26412). Atmospheric high-ceilinged wine bar and shellfish restaurant converted from a waterside cottage. Open fires and nautical knick-knacks on the rafters.

NORTHWESTERN COUNTIES
County Donegal
Castle Murray House (££) St John's Point, Dunkineely (tel: 073 37022, see also accommodations section). Thierry Delcros's smart French cooking is served amid distracting views.

Harvey's Point (££) Lough Eske, Donegal (tel: 073 22208, see also accommodations section). French cuisine in *nouvelle* style. Fairly formal atmosphere.

Le Chateaubrienne (££) Sligo Road, Bundoran (tel: 072 42160). This professional but welcoming family-run place has had a dynamic impact on Donegal's food scene. The emphasis is on quality without pomposity. Imaginative use of local ingredients.

Rathmullan House (££) Rathmullan (tel: 074 58188, see also accommodations section). Table d'hôte menus available in the evenings. Hearty Irish home cooking. Seafood and farmhouse cheeses.

Restaurant St. John's (££) Fahan (tel: 077 60289). Simple, traditional food with well-priced wine in a strangely suburban outpost of wildest Donegal.

St. Ernan's House (£££) St. Ernan's Island, Donegal (tel: 073 21065, see also accom-

282

modations section). Attractively presented five-course dinners served in Irish country-house style. Stylish, traditional décor of crisp linen and Regency stripes.
Smuggler's Creek (£) Rossnowlagh (tel: 072 52366, see also accommodations section). Imaginative range of bistro fare in simple stone-built inn. Fresh seafood and organically-grown vegetables.
Water's Edge (££) Rathmullan (tel: 074 58182). Glorious views over Lough Swilly enhance the local ingredients here—mostly fresh fish.

Country Sligo
Cromleach Lodge (£££) Castlebaldwin, near Boyle (tel: 071 65155, see also accommodations section). Accomplished if expensive food served with lovely views.
Markree Castle (££) Collooney (tel: 071 67800, see also accommodations section). Knockmuldowney Restaurant has moved (with its owner) from its former address to the medieval-looking setting of this castle. The food is just as assured.
The Moorings (££) Rosses Point (tel: 071 77112). A cozy seafood restaurant serving fresh-cooked, popular dishes at reasonable prices. Close to the waterfront. Good for Sunday lunch.
Truffles (££) 11 The Mall, Sligo (tel: 071 44226). New Age pizzas of distinction.

NORTHERN IRELAND
County Antrim
Auberge de Seneirl (££) 28 Ballyclough Road, Bushmills (see also accommodations section). Accomplished French cuisine in decidedly generous portions.
Crown Liquor Saloon (£) 46 Great Victoria Street, Belfast (tel: 01232 249476). The National Trust's superbly restored Victorian pub is a must for any visitor; good lunchtime food, including oysters throughout the year. Irish dishes also available.

Front Page (£) 106 Donegall Street, Belfast (tel: 01232 324269). Good seafood, to the accompaniment of live music.
Nick's Warehouse (£) 35–39 Hill Street, Belfast (tel: 01232 439690). Morning coffee, lunchtime or evening snacks, or full meals are all available here either in wine bar or formal restaurant settings. Terrines a popular specialty.
Ramore (£££) The Harbour, Portrush (tel: 01265 824313). Streamlined décor accompanies some sophisticated food. There is a good-value wine list.
Restaurant 44 (£££) 44 Bedford Street, Belfast (tel: 01232 244844). Stylish colonial décor and accomplished French food. Good selection of vegetarian dishes.
Roscoff (£££) Shaftesbury Square, Belfast (tel: 01232 331532). Chic and renowned, one of the best in the province. Vaguely marine décor, befitting the fishy specialties. Wide range of ingredients. Good value.

County Down
Bistro Iona (££) 27 Church Road, Holywood (tel: 01232 425655). Informal, comfortable place to bring your own wine and enjoy a range of healthy dishes from the menus chalked up on a blackboard.
The Gaslamp (££) 47 Court Street, Newtownards (tel: 01247 811225). Popular, especially with business people. Generous portions of French cuisine, mostly with claret.
Glassdrumman House (£–£££) 242 Glassdrumman Road, Annalong (tel: 01396 768451, see also Glassdrumman Lodge in accommodations section). There are no less than three restaurants in this establishment: the Gallery serves light snacks, coffee, and teas; the Kitchen Garden is fully licensed and à la carte; Memories serves gourmet French blowouts on Saturdays.

County Fermanagh
Blake's of the Hollow (£) Enniskillen (tel: 01365 322143). Good sandwiches in Victorian pub.
The Cedars (££) Castle Archdale, Drumall, Lisnarick (tel: 013656 21493). Home-cooking and classic favorites, including really blue steak (if you want it that way).
Florence Court House (£) Florence Court (tel: 01365 348249). National Trust tearooms; wholesome lunches and snacks.
The Sheelin (££) Bellanaleck (tel: 01365 348232). Thatched-cottage bakery serving teas and snacks, and gourmet dinner.

County Londonderry
Beech Hill Country House (£££) Ardmore Road, Derry (tel: 01504 49279, see also accommodations section). Carefully prepared food using mostly organic produce.
Blackheath House (££) 112 Killeague Road, Blackhill (tel: 01265 868433, see also accommodations section). MacDuff's Cellar Restaurant is open to non-residents, offering well-prepared concoctions of local meat, game and seafood.
Linenhall Bar (£) Derry City (tel: 01504 371665). Good for lunchtime pub food.

LAKELAND COUNTIES
County Laois
Roundwood House (££) Mountrath (tel: 0502 32120, see also accommodations section). Accomplished cooking by a natural hostess in magnificent Palladian surroundings.
The Stables (££) Oxmantown Mall, (tel: 0509 20263). Simple but comfortable surroundings of plain white walls and oakwood chairs make a perfect foil for competently prepared local produce.

County Westmeath
Crookedwood House (££) Crookedwood, Mullingar (tel: 044 72165). Copious and good, interesting food served in relaxing fireside setting.

283

Index

INDEX

INDEX

288

Picture credits

The Automobile Association would like to thank the following photographers, libraries and associations for their assistance in the preparation of this book.
MIKE BANKS 8b Joss Lynam. BORD FÁILTE 22a horse-racing, 22b hurling, 23 football, 30a Muiredach's Cross, 102–3 Punchestown races, 105 Malahide Castle, 112b Slane Abbey, 122 Ardmore Round Tower, 127b Rock of Cashel Museum, 141 cannon, Rosslare, 142 Georges St, Waterford, 164b Ashford Castle Hotel, 165 Adare Manor Hotel, 175 banquet, Knappogue Castle, 179a flora, 190a Thoor Ballylee, 202a Glebe House, 202b Glencolumbcille standing stone, 207 St. Eunan's, 249 Old Gaol. H CHEVALLIER 177b Aran Island gate. G GOSSIP 164a Bantry House, 242a Hilton Park Hotel, 243a Clohamon House, 242b, 243b Tullanisk. CHRISTOPHER HILL PHOTOGRAPHIC 3 Glencolumbcille, 5c Roundstone, 7a lobster fishing, 10b Dunluce Castle, 15 Irish dancing, 16a W B Yeats, 18a Irish fry, 18–19 seafood, 20b farming, 24b Roundstone Bog, 32a Boa Island Figure, 79a seafood, 155b Rowallane Gardens, 182–3 Clifden, 186 Oyster Festival, 190b Westport, 199 Donegal, 200–1 Atlantic Drive, 206 Grianán of Aileach, 208 Parke's Castle, 209a Lough Gill, 210a Sligo Abbey, 210b W B Yeats, 212 Crown Liquor Saloon, 214 Relief of Derry, 217a Belfast, 217b Larry's Bar, 218, 219a City Hall, 219b Palm House, 220 Opera House, 221a Queen's University, 222a Belfast Castle, 222b Belfast Zoo, 223 Navan Fort, 224 Derry, 225b St. Patrick's window, 226a Stone, 230b Wellbrook Mill, 232 Mourne Mountains, 235b Transport Museum, 238 Lough Key, 247b Lough Key, 251 Giant's Causeway, 256 cycles. KOBAL COLLECTION 204a The Quiet Man, 204b The Field, 205 Ryan's Daughter. MARY EVANS PICTURE LIBRARY 17a Samuel Beckett, 17b G B Shaw, 26a creatures, 27 Cuchulainn, 36b William III, 37 James II, 39 Lord Kilwarden, 40b de Valera and Lloyd George, 42b Sir Edward Carson, 63a G B Shaw, 63b W B Yeats, 114 St. Columba, 138 James Joyce. NATIONAL MUSEUM OF IRELAND 66 Tara Brooch. NATURE PHOTOGRAPHERS LTD 180a mountain avens (R Bush), 180b fly orchid (P Sterry), 181a pine marten (W S Paton), 181b corncrake (P Sterry). NORTHERN IRELAND TOURIST BOARD 227b Marble Arch Caves. OFFICE OF PUBLIC WORKS, DUBLIN 34a Silken Thomas. REX FEATURES 12b Mary Robinson. ROYAL GEOGRAPHICAL SOCIETY 28a map. STROKESTOWN PARK 250 Strokestown Park. THE SLIDE FILE 4 cottages near Moate, 8a Lord Killanin, 10a children, 24–5 turf cutting, 126 Cashel Rock, 179b Burren, 194 currach, 198 weaving, 239 Lough Oughter Castle, 245 Clonmacnois, 247a Killykeen Forest Park. THE MANSELL COLLECTION 34b Richard II campaign, 35 Oliver Cromwell, 36–7 Siege of Londonderry, 38b Emmett, 40a Sackville St, 41 signing treaty, 43a Parnell, 43b Liberation of O'Connell, 54a Easter Rising, 54b GPO 1916, 55a Easter Rising, 62 Oscar Wilde. WATERFORD CRYSTAL 143a Copper Wheel Engraver, 143b Master Cutter. ZEFA PICTURE LIBRARY (U.K.) LTD (Cover) shopfront, 12a U.K. flag, 13a Irish flag.

All remaining pictures are held in the Association's own library (A.A. PHOTO LIBRARY) with contributions from: L BLAKE 11, 110, 115a, 145, 184, 185, 187, 188, 191, 226b, 240a, 241, 244, 246a, 260. J BLAND-FORD 9b, 21, 25, 121, 136, 146, 148, 149b, 152, 154, 155a, 159, 161, 163a, 163b. D FORSS 33, 51, 149a, 152–3, 162. S HILL 5a, 5b, 14b, 30b, 150a, 150b, 151, 156, 157, 158, 167a, 167b, 168, 169, 170, 171, 172, 174, 176, 177a, 189, 192a, 193a, 266, 268. J JENNINGS 19b, 38a, 192b, 193b, 196, 225a, 235a, 246b. T KING 46, 55b, 83a, 98. G MUNDAY 6, 26b, 29, 49a, 52, 53, 57a, 57b, 61a, 68a, 68b, 69a, 69b, 70a, 70b, 72b, 76, 96, 104, 112a, 116, 213, 219b, 215, 221b, 227a, 228, 230a, 231, 233, 234, 269. M SHORT 7b, 9a, 13b, 16b, 20a, 28b, 32b, 44–5, 48a, 48b, 49b, 50, 56, 58b, 59, 60, 65b, 67, 71, 72a, 74a, 74b, 75, 78, 79b, 80, 81a, 81b, 82, 83b, 84a, 84b, 85, 87, 88, 89a, 89b, 91b, 92, 94, 95, 97a, 97b, 99a, 99b, 100b, 101, 102a, 103, 106a, 109, 111, 113, 115b, 117, 123a, 124a, 124b, 128, 130a, 130b, 131, 132, 133, 135, 137, 139a, 140, 236, 248, 253, 258, 259, 262, 263, 264, 265. W VOYSEY 42a, 58a, 61b, 65a, 77a, 77b. P ZOELLER 91a, 107, 108a, 108b, 118, 120, 123b,125, 127a, 129, 144, 166, 267.

Acknowledgments

The author would like to thank the following for their help in the production of this book: Bord Fáilte; Aer Lingus; Avis/Johnson & Perrott; and British Midland Airways Ltd.

Contributors

Series advisor: Ingrid Morgan   **Designer:** Tony Truscott
Joint series editor: Susi Bailey   **Indexer:** Marie Lorimer
Copy editor: Hugh Chevallier   **Verifiers:** Ian Hill, Letitia Pollard